Spain and the American Revolution

The Revolutionary Age

Francis D. Cogliano and Patrick Griffin, Editors

Spain and the American Revolution
New Approaches and Perspectives

**Edited by
Gabriel Paquette and
Gonzalo M. Quintero Saravia**

University of Virginia Press
Charlottesville and London

This book was published with the assistance of the National Society of the Sons of the American Revolution and Joseph W. Dooley.

University of Virginia Press
Originally published in 2020 by Routledge
Published by arrangement with Routledge, a member of the Taylor & Francis Group, an Informa business
© 2020 selection and editorial matter, Gabriel Paquette and Gonzalo M. Quintero Saravia; individual chapters, the contributors
All rights reserved
Printed in the United States of America on acid-free paper

First University of Virginia edition published 2022

ISBN 978-0-8139-4763-1 (paper)

9 8 7 6 5 4 3 2 1

Library of Congress Cataloging-in-Publication Data is available for this title.

Frontispiece: "Bandera Tomada en América por Bernardo de Gálvez en sus Campañas Americanas (1779–1783)." (Reproduced courtesy of the Museo del Ejército, Toledo, Spain)

Cover art: *Conquest of the Stronghold of Panzacola* [sic] *with the Surrender of West Florida to the Arms of King Carlos the Third in the Year 1781 (Toma de la plaza de Panzacola y rendición de la Florida Occidental a las armas de Carlos III).* (Ministerio de Defensa de España, AMN 6-A-20)

To Joe Dooley—patriot, patron, friend

Contents

List of illustrations xi
Acknowledgements xii

1 Introduction: Spain and the American Revolution 1
  GABRIEL PAQUETTE AND GONZALO M. QUINTERO SARAVIA

2 The American Revolution and Spanish America, 1776–1814 37
  ANTHONY MCFARLANE

3 The rise and fall of the Spanish–French Bourbon armada, from Toulon to Pensacola to Trafalgar 62
  LARRIE D. FERREIRO

4 José's secrets: Minister Gálvez's master plan for Spain's participation in the American Revolution 77
  MARÍA BÁRBARA ZEPEDA CORTÉS

5 "Foreseeing what great occasions might come": American independence and Spanish naval reformers 91
  MANUEL LUCENA-GIRALDO

6 The Spanish slave trade during the American Revolutionary War 100
  EMILY BERQUIST SOULE

7 Spain's bid for the American interior? The imperial contest over the revolutionary Great Lakes 122
  JOHN WILLIAM NELSON

8 Spain and the American Revolution: A Pacific perspective 135
  EMMANUELLE PEREZ TISSERANT

9 Law in early modern diplomacy: The Jay–Floridablanca negotiations of 1780 147
  BENJAMIN C. LYONS

10 Sarah Livingston Jay (1756–1802): A republican lady in Spain 159
MARY-JO KLINE

11 Securing the borderlands/seas in the American Revolution: Spanish–American cooperation and regional security against the British Empire 171
ROSS MICHAEL NEDERVELT

12 Spain and the birth of the American Republic: Establishing lasting bonds of kinship in the Revolutionary Era 184
GREGG FRENCH

13 A new guardian: The values of the American Revolution in post-Revolutionary Spanish Louisiana settlements 197
ERIC BECERRA

14 Spanish America and US constitutionalism in the Age of Revolution 210
EDUARDO POSADA-CARBÓ

Bibliography 224
Index 254
Notes on contributors 261

Illustrations

Table

1.1 Cost of the war with Britain (1779–1783)   13

Maps

1.1 The Americas c. 1775   3
6.1 The West African Coast in the Era of the Slave Trade   101

Acknowledgements

The essays published in this book were first presented as papers at the 2018 Sons of the American Revolution Annual Conference on the American Revolution held at The Johns Hopkins University in Baltimore, Maryland, in June 2018. The conference theme was "Spain and the American Revolution" and it was inspired by the work of two scholars whose contributions to the international history of the American Revolution are immense and to whom the conference was dedicated: Professor Sylvia Hilton of the Universidad Complutense in Madrid, Spain, and Professor David Armitage of Harvard University in Cambridge, Massachusetts. It was a special thrill to have Professors Hilton and Armitage in attendance; all participants benefited from the thoughtful, incisive feedback these two eminent historians offered on the original, pre-circulated papers.

The conference was made possible through the enormous generosity of the National Society of the Sons of the American Revolution, a non-profit, patriotic, and educational organization with a worldwide membership of 37,000. It is increasingly rare to encounter a non-academic benefactor eager to support historical scholarship. The SAR, in keeping with its mission, generously supports scholarship shedding fresh light on the Revolution. The SAR Annual Conference on the American Revolution is a major undertaking. The 2018 SAR Annual Conference was made possible by the generous support of the following: The Mount Vernon Ladies' Association; Museum of the American Revolution; George Washington Endowment Fund of the National Society SAR; Knight-Patty Memorial Trust Fund of the Virginia Society SAR; California Society SAR Ladies Auxiliary; Missouri Society SAR Ladies Auxiliary; Powell Enterprises; Samuel C. Powell, Ph.D.; WinSet Group LLC; Joseph R. Godfrey, Ph.D.; David N. Appleby; Lanny and Ann Patten; Ward Family Fund; Edward W. Ward; Timothy E. Ward; Rt. Rev. and Mrs. Louis V. Carlson, Jr.; Mr. & Mrs. John H. Franklin, Jr.; Warren and Nancy Alter; Ernest B. Coggins, Jr.; Peter M. Davenport; and the George Washington Chapter and the George Mason Chapter, both of the Virginia Society SAR.

Beyond fostering scholarship, the SAR has long drawn public attention to Spain's role in the American Revolution. In fact, the SAR has highlighted Spain's role in numerous ways over several decades, among which the following are examples: the California Society of the SAR has placed plaques in Santa Barbara, San Diego, and Monterey that recognize the considerable financial contribution (*donativos*) Spain (including Spanish subjects) made to the insurgent cause. The New Mexico and Arizona Societies of the SAR placed similar plaques to recognize Spain's financial contribution to the American Revolution at the Governor's Palace in Santa Fe, and at the Presidio in Tucson. The Arizona Society of the SAR also placed a marker on the grave of Juan Manuel Ortega (1757–1817), a Spanish soldier at the Tubac Presidio, who paid a *donativo* in support of the Revolution. The Gulf Coast is another region where the SAR has strenuously drawn attention to Spain's contribution to the Revolution. In 1996, the Florida Society of the SAR placed a plaque on the site of Fort George in Pensacola, which had been captured by Bernardo de Gálvez in 1781. In 2009, the General Gálvez Chapter of the SAR placed a monument to its namesake in Bicentennial Park in Baldwin County, Alabama. The SAR is behind another plaque in Avoyelles Parish, Louisiana, honoring soldiers of French ancestry who served under Gálvez. There are SAR chapters named after Gálvez in Alabama, Texas, and Louisiana, and another SAR chapter named after Fernando de Leyba in Saint Louis, Missouri. In 2014, the SAR unveiled a monument commemorating the Battle of San Carlos, also known as the Battle of Saint Louis, very close to Busch Stadium.

This book is dedicated to Joseph W. Dooley. Joe is the past President General of the SAR (2013–2014) and founded the SAR Annual Conference. He has been a tireless advocate of a more inclusive (and thus more accurate) understanding of the American Revolution and the various personages of all provenances who contributed significantly to its outcome and legacy. Not only did Joe embrace the idea of a conference on Spain's role, but he found the resources to bring the entire project to fruition and organized almost every aspect of the conference himself. We are proud to dedicate this book to Joe.

Spain and the American Revolution

1 Introduction

Spain and the American Revolution

Gabriel Paquette and Gonzalo M. Quintero Saravia

At the Palace of Aranjuez, outside of Madrid, in the summer of 1780, war was in the air. Spain, together with its ally France, had in the previous year launched a failed armada to invade Britain, which, had it achieved even its most modest aims, would have brought the war to an end. In the middle of this escalating conflict between Western European powers, a relatively minor—if extremely well-connected—playwright and man of letters, Richard Cumberland, arrived, with his burgeoning family, as an official emissary of the British government. Cumberland, whose inexperience, temperament and talent proved ill-suited for the delicate diplomacy with which he was entrusted,[1] had been forbidden to enter into negotiations with Count Floridablanca, Spain's chief Minister, unless he received explicit word that Spain did not intend to broach the subject of cession or exchange of either Gibraltar or Minorca.[2] He had not received such an assurance, but engaged with the Spanish minister anyway.

Also in residence at Aranjuez that sweltering summer was an emissary from the rebellious 13 seaboard North American colonies, John Jay. Those rebels had entered into an alliance with France, Spain's arch ally. One might expect Jay to have been warmly received and Cumberland treated coolly, but the reception was the inverse of this expectation. As Cumberland informs us in his *Memoirs*, the Prince of Asturias, the heir to the Spanish throne, entertained his family, and the King himself "gave orders for any pictures to be taken down [from his various Madrid and Escorial palace galleries] and placed at an easel, which I might wish to have a nearer view of; he also gave directions for a catalogue to be made at my request, which I have published and attached to my account of the Spanish painters."[3]

Contrast this lavish hospitality and convivial, languorous summer interlude with Jay's treatment. By any measure, Jay was by far the more impressive of the two men: he had served as President of the Continental Congress, and he would go on, following American independence, to hold the offices of Secretary of State, Governor of New York, and Chief Justice of the Supreme Court. Yet he was rarely (and, even then, furtively,) invited to dine and socialize with the Spanish aristocratic families who summered with the royal family in Aranjuez. He was the emissary of recalcitrant colonies Spain did not recognize, even if its chief ally, France, did. Jay's audiences with Floridablanca at this time were infrequent, informal, and unsatisfying. Jay was dejected, for the purpose of his mission was to convince Spain to enter the war formally on the American side, to provide material and monetary aid directly, and to begin the task of delineating the border demarcating what he was certain would soon be an independent polity, carved from the British empire, and the Spanish empire.

He had made, by the summer of 1780, little headway on any of these three fronts. Jay was perplexed by Spanish obduracy. As he wrote to John Adams, future President of the US and then emissary to the French Court, "Spain will be our Neighbor. We both have territory enough to prevent our coveting each others' and I should be happy to see that perfect amity and cordial affection established between us, which would ensure perpetual peace and harmony to both."[4] To his chagrin, Spain did not view matters the same way. While engaged in his fruitless mission, Jay received messages of encouragement from two of the great figures of the American Revolution, imploring him to continue his courtship of Spain and not to despair when his entreaties were rebuffed or ignored altogether. Adams tried to revive Jay's spirits:

> [Floridablanca] is agreed to be a man of abilities, but some how or other, there is something in the European understanding different from those we have been more used to. Men of the greatest abilities, and the most experience, are with great difficulty brought to see what appears to us as clear as day. It is habit, it is education, prejudice, what you will, but so it is.[5]

Adopting a somewhat different approach to shake Jay from his despondency, polymath patriot Benjamin Franklin reminded Jay that,

> Spain owes us nothing therefore whatever friendship she shows us in lending money or furnishing cloathing & Ca., tho' not equal to our wants and wishes, is however *tant de gagné*; those who have begun to assist us are more likely to continue than to decline, and we are still so much obliged as their Aids amount to.[6]

This introductory chapter will assess what aid Spain provided to the American cause and what that aid amounted to in the outcome of the American Revolution.

The historiography of Spain's involvement in the American Revolution

On both sides of the Atlantic, the study of the role of the Spanish Monarchy in the War of American Independence has been heavily influenced by the

Map 1.1 The Americas c. 1775

perceptions of Spain and the United States in each other's eyes. On the United States' side, interest in Spain and its history began during the first half of the nineteenth century with the works of Washington Irving (1828, 1829, 1831, 1832), Henry Wadsworth Longfellow (1863a, 1863b, 1863c, 1863d, 1843), George Ticknor (1823, 1849), and, especially, William Hickling Prescott (1838, 1843, 1847, 1858–1859). From this milieu emerged what Richard L. Kagan called Prescott's Paradigm, "created by a Protestant intellectual and social elite centered in Boston and New York" (Brown, 2002, ix), in which Spain was "everything that the United States was not" (Kagan, 2002b, 9, 2002c). The Spanish American War, which began in 1898, reinforced this disparaging depiction while adding strong negative undertones rooted in the anti-Catholic "Black Legend" of Spain's alleged nefarious conduct in the colonization of the Americas.[7] It was not a coincidence that precisely in that year a re-edition of a seventeenth-century English book was published, this time with the telling title *Horrible Atrocities of Spaniards in Cuba. An Historical and True Account of the cruel massacre and slaughter of 20,000,000 of people in the West Indies by the Spaniards* (Powell 1971, 160; Hanke 1963).[8]

The twentieth century would witness a slow shift in Spain's image in America. An important factor contributing to the reappraisal was the undoubtedly romantic, positive vision of Archer Milton Huntington, who in 1904 founded New York's Hispanic Society and, in 1927, donated his massive collection to the Library of Congress in Washington D.C., the seed of this institution's prestigious Hispanic Division. Another crucial contributor in this period was historian Herbert Eugene Bolton (1920, 1930, 1933, 1939), whose work on borderlands would summon the attention of American historians to the Spanish imprint in the history of the United States. The 1930s witnessed a renewed interest in Spain, as a newly founded Spanish Republic strove toward the ideals of democracy and liberty that the United States considered as genuinely American. A new image of Spain emerged, tinged with romanticism as well, which, according to Gabriel Jackson (2001), crystallized into a new paradigm, shaped indelibly by Ernest Hemingway (Noya, Rodríguez and Ruiz 2008), from which emerged the works of Samuel Flagg Bemis (1926 [1960], 1931, 1957) and John Walton Caughey (1934 [1998]).

The Spanish Civil War of the 1930s would polarize the image of Spain in the US. While some would support the Spanish Republic, even with the blood of the volunteers of the Lincoln Brigade, others, especially the Catholic community, would support the Nationalist forces under General Francisco Franco (Tierney 2007). US President Franklin D. Roosevelt's administration would declare the US's neutrality in the conflict in line with the policy of non-intervention adopted by the United Kingdom and France, which was followed by 27 European countries under the Non-Intervention Agreement. The close alignment of Franco with the Axis Powers during the Civil War and first years of the Second World War accounted for Spain's international isolation after 1945, which produced not only a lack of interest in Spain within academic circles and from the American public, but also denied impoverished Spain the beneficence of the Marshall Plan.

The Cold War, however, would provide Franco with the opportunity to polish his anti-communist credentials, allowing Spain to become a second-class ally through the three US–Spanish Agreements, signed in 1953, that granted several military bases on Spanish territory to the United States. It was during this decade that both governments tried to improve their respective images in the other. While the United States included Spain in the Fulbright Scholarships Program in 1959, Spain could do little more than sponsor some publications about the historical relations between the two countries (Morales Padrón 1952a, 1952b, 1955a, 1955b; Hayes 1952; Gil 1952a, 1952b; Sanz y Díaz 1953; Manfredi 1955). In the late 1970s, Spain's transition towards a full democracy, its economic development, and the positive image projected by a young king contributed to the normalization of the image of Spain in the United States, in the sense of stripping it of most of its old romantic connotations. Bilateral relations became more balanced with Spain's membership of NATO (1982) and the European Economic Community (1986), and the signature in 1998 of the Mutual Defense Assistance Agreement and the Agreement on Defense Cooperation between Spain and the United States (revised by two protocols in 2012, and a third one in 2015).

The final factor to take into account when considering Spain's image in the United States is its double status both as a European and a Latin American country. That Spain is a European country derives from a simple geographical fact, though it must not be forgotten that parts of Spain are also geographically in the eastern Atlantic and Africa (the Canary Islands, Ceuta, and Melilla). Spain's Latin American dimension requires some explanation. When the US Census Office classifies US citizens and residents by country of origin, it includes the category of Hispanics, also known as Latinos, and in the list of countries included under this heading is Spain. Therefore, the descendants of Spaniards living in the US and Spanish immigrants who have become citizens or residents of the United States are officially members of the Hispanic community. This demographic classification has had implications beyond the realm of bureaucracy, extending to the perception of Spanish history in the United States.

In Spain, the study of the Spanish Monarchy's role in the American War of Independence would emerge from a combination of political interests and the effects of a certain Spanish inferiority complex vis-à-vis the United States. In the 1920s, books by Valentín Urtasún (1920–1924), Manuel Conrotte (1920), and Juan F. Yela Utrilla (1925) shared the aim of nationalistic historical vindication. For some of these writers, Spain's crucial role was insufficiently recognized by the Americans because they were either ungrateful or could not fathom the notion of owing anything to Spain.[9] It would take more than three decades and the Cold War, when the Franco regime needed to portray itself as a viable partner of the United States, for the next, more conciliatory wave of histories to appear.[10] In the late 1970s, the same motivation, but this time under the newly established Spanish constitutional monarchy that emerged after Franco, accounted for renewed interest in the subject. Taking advantage of the bicentenary of American Independence, a plethora of studies would appear, most of them published through official patronage. In particular, the Ministry of Foreign Affairs, besides publishing a collection of historical studies by renowned Spanish historians, undertook the monumental task of collating and printing a *Collection of Documents Related to the Independence of North America in Spanish Archives*, which took more than a decade (1977 to 1986) to compile and ultimately filled 14 volumes.[11] A new generation of Spanish historians would build a new historiographical approach to the subject thanks to this documentary collection, as demonstrated by the annual bibliographies published by Sylvia L. Hilton between 1983 and 1996 (Hilton 1983, 1984, 1985, 1986, 1987, 1988, 1989, 1994a, 1994b; Hilton and Labandeira 1990, 1991, 1993; Hilton and Paredes 1996).

Parallel to the evolution of Spain's and the US's respective images, the increasing attention given to the role of Spain in the American Revolutionary War is also a product of the evolution in historiography towards the study of subjects and geographical areas beyond the traditional Eurocentric approach. Before this evolution, much of the attention to the subject was only given by historians working on the international aspects and diplomatic history of the American Revolution such as Ramón E. Abarca (1970), Samuel Flagg Bemis (1926 [1960], 1931, 1957), Samuel Gwynn Coe (1928), Jonathan R. Dull (1975, 1985), Ronald Hoffman and Peter J. Albert (1981), Richard B. Morris (1965), and J. Horace Nunemaker (1943). When the study of Native American communities looked beyond their relations with the British, contacts with the French and Spanish empires in the region became an object of study. The groundbreaking working works by Richard White (1991) and Daniel H. Usner (1992) on the French–Indian relations have been complemented by the study of Spanish–Indian contacts by David J. Weber (1992, 2005) and Ramón Gutiérrez (1991), which have been followed by the important contributions of Steven W. Hackel (2005), Kathleen DuVal (2006, 2015), Juliana Barr (2007), and Pekka Hämäläinen (2008), among others. Something similar happened with the study of slavery with comparative analysis between the British and Spanish slavery, both slaves of African origin and indigenous slaves, from the classic and much-revised work of Frank Tannenbaum (1946) to the contributions of Jane Landers (1984, 1990, 1999, 2010), James F. Brooks (2002), and James H. Sweet (1997).[12] In the process of enlarging the geographical scope of Early American History, several previously ignored regions would be incorporated. The American West was opened by Bolton's studies of the Spanish Borderlands (1930, 1933, 1939), a concept that has been re-considered and updated by John Francis Bannon (1970) and other scholars. The Caribbean also has received increasing attention with the work of Andrew O'Shaughnessy (2000). A comprehensive continental approach to United States' early history has been advanced by historians as Silvio Zavala (1961), Paul W. Mapp (2009), Jeremy Adelman and Stephen Aron (Adelman and Aron 2009), and Daniel H. Usner Jr. (2006). Comparative history has also widened the scope of the study of imperial institutions and practices, as exemplified by the works of John H. Elliott (2006, 2009) and Jorge Cañizares-Esguerra (2001). Atlantic History, as practiced by Bernard Baylin (2005), Philip D. Morgan (2009), Jack P. Greene (Morgan and Greene 2009), David Armitage (2009), and Cécile Vidal (2012), offers an even broader vision of an interconnected space in which Atlantic empires interacted.

The notion of "Entangled History" has reinforced the importance of the interconnections between Atlantic empires, highlighting the asymmetry of the exchanges by turning upside-down the traditional mental map of the region. In this framework, Eliga H. Gould (2007) has proposed that the English-speaking Atlantic should be considered as a "Spanish Periphery."[13] Nor is this suggestion mere hyperbole. Whether assessed in terms of the size of territory and population, the number and complexity of its cities and its culture, the number and prestige of its universities, and the wealth of core vice-royalties, Spain's massive empire was superior to that of Britain in the Americas. Havana, Lima, and Mexico City far outstripped Boston, New York and Philadelphia in terms of sheer size, per capita GDP, and other measures. Philadelphia, the largest city in the 13 seaborne colonies, had a population one-fifth the size of Mexico City. Average GDP per capita, admittedly an imperfect measure, in Latin America in 1700 was 128 percent that of the Anglo-North American level in 1700. Even in 1800, Cuba's GDP was 112 percent of that of the US (Coatsworth 1998, 26). In 1700, there were 17 thriving universities in the Spanish Atlantic World compared to a mere three in British North America, for example. If not quite a backwater, the North American seaboard colonies that eventually rebelled were certainly far from the center of the action in the eighteenth-century Atlantic World.

Spanish global interests in the American Revolution

On the specific subject of the role of Spain in the American Revolutionary War, the few book-length treatments have been complemented by other studies on certain aspects, including those related to the history of Louisiana and Florida during the American Revolution, military campaigns, and the figure of general Bernardo de Gálvez, Spanish Louisiana's Governor and supreme commander of the Spanish forces during the war.[14] The war that is known as the American Revolutionary War or the War of American Independence was much more than what those names suggest, for North America was merely one theater in a global war. It was a world-spanning conflict among rival empires, one of the results of which was the independence of the US. Britain found itself at war with France, Spain, and the Dutch Republic in three continents. In the Americas, Britain fought France on land and sea; the Dutch lost their Caribbean posts of St. Eustatius, Saba, and Saint Martin to Britain; and Spain's far-flung involvement saw engagement along the Mississippi, in Louisiana, Alabama, and Florida, but also in Central America and the Caribbean. In Europe, Spain laid a long, amphibious siege of British-held Gibraltar, conquered the island of Minorca, and even plotted with France to invade the British Isles. In Asia, the siege of Pondicherry, and the naval battle of Cuddalore, saw the French and British as adversaries, while the Dutch fought the British in the Bay of Bengal. America thus was merely one theater. In 1780, of the 100,000 troops under British command, only 30,000 were deployed in North America due to the geographical scope of the war (Colley 2002, 209).

The American Revolution therefore must be studied in global perspective. King George III's intransigence in the face of America's declaration of Independence, for example, is well known if often exaggerated to the verge of caricature. But the reasons for his refusal to countenance independence deserve attention. He feared that the loss of America would result in Britain's loss of prestige within Europe. Prosecution of the war was not about preservation of the North American colonies in the narrow sense, whether for economic advantage or national self-worth, but rather because the prospective forfeiture of international prestige was an outsized factor in his calculus. Were independence granted, George III informed Lord North in early 1780, "I shall despair of this country being ever preserved from a state of inferiority and, consequently, falling to a very low class among the European states; if we do not feel our own consequence other nations will not treat us above what we esteem ourselves."[15] This position was consistently held, not fleeting despair, for a year later he told North that "we are contending for our whole consequence whether we are to rank among the Great Powers of Europe or be reduced to one of the least considerable."[16] This aim (or aspiration) was a crucial dimension of the American Revolution, particularly in its latter phases. The American Revolution was lost neither in America nor in Britain itself, but rather in the breakdown of British diplomacy that preceded imperial dismemberment. As historian Brendan Simms noted, "No amount of domestic mobilization, moral purity, insular virtue and naval prowess could replace the continental system of alliances on which British security, prosperity and imperial expansion had rested" (Simms 2007, 678).

It is also relevant to recall that while the American Revolutionary War could be considered a result of the failure of the British imperial reform program of the 1760s, the Spanish empire also experienced a period of system-wide changes and reforms that reinforced connections between the Peninsula and Spanish America. The older view of the impact of the Bourbon reforms of the second half of the eighteenth century was that they precipitated the Spanish American independence movements of the early nineteenth century. The main argument behind this interpretation was that the reforms strengthened royal authority and metropolitan control over the American territories at the expense of the power and autonomy of the local American societies, especially the creole elites. However, recent contributions have undermined this interpretation.[17] Now the Spanish monarchy of the late eighteenth and early nineteenth centuries is no longer viewed as an empire verging on collapse, but rather as an integrated ensemble with a high degree of administrative unity. The origins of Spanish American independence are found not in the Bourbon imperial reforms, but in the French invasion of the Iberian Peninsula in 1808 (Guerra, 1992; Breña, 2006, 2015; Echeverri, 2016). The involvement of Spain in the American Revolution must be understood within the context of imperial reforms that prompted a reassessment of Spain's foreign policy (Abol-Brasón, 2009; Hernández Sánchez-Barba, 1991; Lynch, 2009; Rodríguez Casado, 1941). The chief precipitant of Spain's entry into the American Revolution was the Seven Years' War (1756–1763). Initially, Spain had clung to its neutrality. But its fateful alliance with France led Spain to enter the war belatedly, and without proper preparation, in 1762. Word of Spain's belligerent turn was leaked to Britain before Spain had informed its own colonists and readied its own defenses. Britain sacked and occupied Havana and Manila, in the Philippines, which suggests the global threat Britain posed to Spain's empire. Britain returned Havana and Manila to Spain in the Peace of Paris (1763), but still gained much from the resulting treaty, including a new colony, West Florida, with Pensacola as its capital, as well as the restitution of East Florida. Although it is doubtful that Britain had the intention or possessed the resources to make a broader assault on the Spanish empire in North America or the Caribbean, even in the aftermath of the effective siege and capture of Havana in 1762, British military planners were cognizant that permanent occupation was imperiled by the disease environment of the Caribbean.[18] Nevertheless, the British presence in the Floridas threatened the maritime route followed by Spanish convoys carrying New World silver, which then represented 20 percent of the total revenues of the Spanish Treasury.

Facing potential cataclysm, Spain embarked on a major program of reform to fortify its empire, beginning with naval reconstruction and the modernization of defenses to be sure, but also efforts to reinvigorate the transatlantic economy. Steps in this direction included experimentation with new forms of "free" (deregulated) trade as well as administrative reorganization. By the early 1770s, the reforms were bearing fruit. Spain capitalized on almost 15 years of peace after 1763, realizing that the competition for empire in the Americas, as well as for primacy in Europe itself, made conflict with Britain inevitable. Many administrative changes had been undertaken by the mid-1770s. Mention should be made of the creation of the viceroyalty of Río de la Plata; a half dozen smaller provinces on northern coast of South America were consolidated into the Intendencia of Venezuela (1776), with Caracas as its capital; Chile was governed as a Capitanía General from 1778. The 1770s were also a decade of remarkable expansion northward: garrisons were established in San Diego and Monterey, in California, in the early 1770s; San Francisco's was established in 1776. Nor were the core viceroyalties—the vital mitochondria of empire—of New Spain (Mexico) and Peru neglected. As David Brading has written, by 1776, "a small army of official, clerks and guards, stationed in all of the chief towns of New Spain, administered taxes, new and old, with unparalleled vigor and efficiency" (Brading 1971, 29). On the other side of the Atlantic, a new generation of civil servants, mainly drawn from the middle classes and strongly committed to the enlightened reform project, the so-called "watchmakers of the Spanish Monarchy" (López-Cordón 1996), worked "like dogs."[19] According to Guillermo Céspedes del Castillo (1985, 324), those were intense years in which the Spanish reformers worked in concert, "creative, optimistic, and bold times, albeit tinged with a premature triumphalism."

From a foreign policy chiefly built around the concept of military defense, a new approach based on a much broader notion of security would be adopted after 1763. And whereas defense was understood mostly in military terms, the new policy encompassed economic and strategic concerns (Hernández Sánchez-Barba 1977). The revision of Spain's foreign policy included evaluating the usefulness of the military alliance with France built upon the three Family Compacts (*Pactos de familia*), which had made conflict with Britain the norm, at least until 1777, when José Moñino y Redondo, Count of Floridablanca, was appointed Secretary of State. He articulated a new vision of international relations based more on diplomacy and trade than on the projection of sheer military power. Ironically, precisely at this juncture, a gathering storm of circumstances was preparing the ground for war with Britain. Two years earlier, at the outbreak of the conflict between England and its colonies in North America, Carlos III had asked for the opinion of his ministers, who provided all manner of advice (Hilton 2007, 35). Several historians argue that Spain incorrectly assessed the new situation, in which its own national interests demanded a change of alliance—namely, leaving the French to support British efforts to suppress the revolt in its North American colonies (Becker 1906; Marfil García 1907, 130; Yela Utrilla 1925, v. 1, 484). José Luis Villacañas argued that Spain was not strong enough either to separate from France or to confront Britain (Villacañas Berlanga 2009, 12).

In any case, in the mid-1770s, the main policy objective was "to keep the peace at all costs in order to develop our trade and industry" (Rodríguez Casado 1944, 233), so that Spain would benefit from prolonging the war as much as possible in order to wear down both opponents, which would not only strengthen its relative power but hopefully resolve once and for all Spain's grievances against Britain concerning Gibraltar, Minorca, the coast of Campeche (Mexico), and Honduras (Ruigómez 1978, 225; Hernández Franco 1984, 334). This delaying tactic was summed up by Floridablanca himself, who declared that Spain should "prepare for the war, as it is inevitable, but do everything to prevent it" (Batista González 1985, 81; Avilés Fernández 1982, 73). To achieve this aim, Spain offered to mediate between Britain and the Thirteen Colonies, an offer that was ambiguously received by the former, partially welcomed by the latter, and strongly opposed by the French, who at that time believed they would profit more from a military victory that from a diplomatic settlement (Voltes 1967). The American revolutionaries' support for mediation was conditional on Spain's recognition of their independence, a request that was impossible for the government in Madrid to grant.[20] Furthermore, Floridablanca's mediation proposal included an armistice that would have permitted Britain to maintain possession of the American territories then held by its armies while peace talks occurred. There was no guarantee that the United States' independence could be secured by such an arrangement.

The first phase of Spanish involvement: weakening the British by supporting the American rebels

During the three years between the start of the Revolutionary War and Spain's declaration of war on Britain, Spain would officially proclaim its neutrality while doing everything it could to help the rebels' cause (Alonso Baquer 1970, 82), a support that was mainly aimed at weakening the British more than strengthening the Americans. In order to prolong the war for as long as possible, the Thirteen Colonies could not be crushed by the might of the British empire. The first aid offered by Spain was one million French *livres* sent to the rebels in late 1775, which was followed by shipments of arms and materiel through Spanish Louisiana, a territory that had been ceded by the French in 1763, assistance that was recognized by the US Congress on several occasions.[21]

As important as the aid channeled through Louisiana was, it was only part of the total Spanish contribution, both in cash and supplies, to the American Revolution. Between 1776 and 1778, Spain supplied the American revolutionaries with between 5 and 8 million *reales de vellón*.[22] To these figures, one must add the contributions made after the official declaration of war. Taking all calculations into account, the total Spanish economic aid to the American revolutionaries would be closer to 13 million *reales de vellón*—to be exact, 12,906,560 *reales de vellón*, including 4,961,960 *reales de vellón* in loans and 7,944,600 in non-repayable grants (Bemis 1926 [1960], 334; Armillas Vicente 1978; Ribes-Iborra 2008, 165). According to American sources, the total was even slightly higher, but this discrepancy can be attributed to the difficulty of converting Spanish *reales de vellón* to French *livres tournoises*.[23] French financial aid to the Americans would be about 46 million *livres tournoises* (34 million *livres tournoises* in loans and 12 million in non-repayable grants), equivalent to nearly 167 million *reales de vellón* (Aulard 1925, 331–332).[24]

According to these figures, the total Spanish financial contribution to the American Revolution was less than 10 percent of France's outlay. But other non-financial contributions by Spain must also be taken into account, such as the vital opening of Spanish Caribbean ports to US trade, which was essential to sustain its military effort (Armillas Vicente 2008, 188–192). This access was also important for the small US Navy, which benefited from safe docking places where crews could rest and ships could be repaired and provisioned—sometimes even at the expense of the Spanish Royal Treasury.[25]

An important instrument in the Spanish support to the American rebels was the Spanish commercial firm Gardoqui & Sons, based in Bilbao, which since the 1760s had been a fixture of the cod industry in Boston and Salem. Gardoqui & Sons would become a sort of American agent, selling their cod in Spain and France, and buying supplies, and also transporting in their ships arms, ammunition, cloth for uniforms, and other military equipment that was secretly paid by the Spanish Royal Treasury (Calderón Cuadrado 2008, 214). Most of the shipments went from the Iberian Peninsula to Havana and then to New Orleans. In January 1777, a courier ship from Havana arrived in the port of New Orleans with uniforms, medicine, and 300 muskets, in theory destined for the Spanish Louisiana Fixed Infantry Regiment. British spies in the city sent notice to the British Governor of Pensacola, who officially complained to the Spanish authorities about its real final destination. Bernardo de Gálvez, Louisiana's Governor, staged a public auction of the textiles and medicine, while the muskets and ammunition were conveniently misplaced while in the Royal Treasury's warehouse. From there they eventually ended up in the hands of Oliver Pollock, the United States' unofficial representative in New Orleans, who successfully smuggled them into American-controlled territory (Armillas Vicente 2008, 185). Not only supplies but also funds were transmitted from Louisiana through Pollock, who procured a Spanish loan to finance George Rogers Clark's campaign into the Illinois country in June 1778 (James 1937, 174–176; McDermott 1974, 329–331). Between 1776 and 1777, more than 1.5 million *reales de vellón* were transferred to support the American cause, chiefly via New Orleans and Havana.[26]

Spain was underwriting the American Revolution with cash and supplies while remaining legally neutral in the conflict between the Thirteen Colonies and Britain. A neutrality that, as Bernardo de Gálvez stated in March 1778, "would not compromise [Spanish] hospitality" to the Americans.[27] Through this hospitality policy, Spain would grant asylum to those who fled to its territories from the war in the Thirteen Colonies,[28] but also used it to carry out all sorts of covert actions in support of the rebels. Besides the direct aid provided to the American revolutionaries, Spain also funded an important part of costs incurred by its French allies. For example, French vessels were repaired and supplied at no cost in the port of Havana and, during the second half of 1781 only, the French forces deployed in the Caribbean received 3–3.5 million *pesos* from the Spanish Treasury.[29]

The aid in cash and materiel supplied to the American revolutionaries was only part of Spain's total financial contribution to the American Revolution. To complete the picture, the cost of the war itself must be considered. Since there is no separate record of the amounts effectively spent by Spain on its war with Britain, we have taken an indirect approach, comparing the amounts spent in the defense of Spanish possessions before and after the war with the outlay during the war. The difference between these can provide a rough estimate of the cost of the war itself. Although an important portion of expenses before the war should also be considered as part of the total cost of the war, as they include preparations for what followed, we have been unable to include this since the available data does not provide enough detail to do so. With all these caveats in mind, the estimate of the total cost for Spain of its war with Britain was approximately 431 million *reales de*

Table 1.1 Cost of the war with Britain (1779–1783)[31]

Year	Amount[32]	Average defense expenditures during peace time[33]	Difference in expenditures during the war over average during peace time
1775	323,031,000	336,425,400	
1776	351,082,000		
1777	325,280,000		
1778	337,515,000		
1779	336,489,000		63,600
1780	462,678,000		126,252,600
1781	410,506,000		74,080,600
1782	502,240,000		165,814,600
1783	401,496,000		65,070,600
1784	345,219,000	336,425,400	
Total expenditures during war over the average during peace time			431,282,000

vellón,[30] a significant sum, since it is equivalent to the total annual revenue of the Spanish Royal Treasury during this period.

From June 1779, the *Junta de Medios* (Treasury Council) started to put in place several mechanisms for raising the funds to cover the cost of the war. Due to the varied fiscal structure throughout the Spanish empire, different measures were applied to each of its territories. Taxes were raised; in Castile and in the Crown of Aragon, some tax rates increased up to a third and the tax on salt was raised to four *reales* per bushel.[34] In the Americas, viceroys were authorized to "establish the contributions they deemed necessary according to the local circumstances."[35]

Other sources of revenue were the *donativos*, donations from private individuals and institutions that either could be voluntary or compulsory, depending on the circumstances. During the first stages of the war, a great number of loyal subjects from both sides of the Atlantic volunteered cash and other resources, as the many and long lists of donors published in the *Gazeta de Madrid* testify. Although much research has been done on the *donativos* raised in the Americas (Marichal 1990; Valle Pavón 2012; Guillén 2018; Kraselsky 2018), Rafael Torres Sánchez has argued that "it does not make sense to separate those from the others coming from other parts of the Spanish empire since the intended use of all these resources was the Spanish armed forces that operated at an imperial scale" (Torres Sánchez 2013, 97). When voluntary contributions decreased, compulsory donations were decreed, such as the contributions of one *peso* from "all freemen and indians," and two *pesos* from every "Spaniard and nobleman," established by the royal decree of August 17, 1780.[36] In addition, cash held by local councils and the Church was seized with the promise of the payment of a 4 percent annual interest through the rents of the tobacco monopoly.[37] In addition, the Church was "asked" for a donation and a loan totaling 16.5 million *pesos*.[38] Among other measures specifically designed for Spanish America were lotteries in the main cities and the sale of titles of nobility and posts in the colonial administration to American-born Spaniards.[39]

Soon it became evident that, in a war in which the two main operational theaters were as far apart as America and the Mediterranean, ordinary fiscal mechanisms were inadequate and new ones had to be found. In the meetings of the *Junta de Medios* of June 29, 1779 and July 22, 1781, it was agreed that the Royal Treasury would issue *vales reales*, a form of government bond. These *vales reales* were the first banknotes in the history of Spain (Teijeiro de la Rosa 2007, 102). Even though it was not the first time that the Royal Treasury resorted to debt financing, on this occasion it was decided that to make the *vales reales* more attractive to investors they would yield 4 percent interest rather than the traditional 3 percent, and that the notes must be accepted at their face value in certain transactions, such as the payment of taxes (Tedde de Lorca 2008, 228). During the war with Britain, there were three issues of public debt certificates: August 1780, for 149 million *reales de vellón*; March 1781, for 79 million; and May 1782, for almost 222 million, a total of 450 million *reales de vellón* (Tedde de Lorca 2008, 228–233). Not counting the banker's fee (10 percent in the first issue and 6 percent in the other two), a total of 417 million *reales de vellón* was raised for the Royal Treasury—a figure very close to the 431 million *reales de vellón* that we have previously estimated as the total cost of the war.[40]

Spain joins the war against Britain

Despite Spain's reluctance to enter into another war against Britain, a confluence of circumstances eventually instigated conflict. The American victories in the battles of Saratoga (September 19 and October 7, 1777) proved both the resolution and the capacity of the rebels to wage war to gain independence. The signature of the Treaty of Alliance between the United States and France on February 6, 1778, followed by the British declaration of war against France a month later signaled the final countdown for the full involvement of Spain in the war. On April 12, 1779, France and Spain signed the Treaty of Aranjuez, which sealed its alliance against Britain and, on June 21, 1779, Spain officially declared war on Britain. Spain's objectives in the war were clearly stated in Article 7 of the Treaty of Aranjuez,

> The Catholic king has the intention to acquire by war and the future peace treaty the following advantages: 1st, the restitution of Gibraltar; 2nd, the possession of the river and the fort on Mobile; 3rd, the restitution of Pensacola with all the coast of Florida near the Bahama Channel, expelling from it all foreign domination; 4th, the expulsion of the British from the Bay of

Honduras and the fulfillment by them of the prohibition stated in the 1763 Treaty of Paris to establish neither there nor in any other Spanish territory any kind of settlement; 5th, the revocation of the privilege granted to the British of cutting logwood [*palo de tinte*] on the coast of Campeche; and 6th, the restitution of the island of Minorca.[41]

Distilled to its essence, by the Treaty of Aranjuez, France pledged not to make peace without Spain's consent and to continue the war until Gibraltar and Minorca (and sundry other territories) were recaptured and restored to Spain. As historian Richard Morris observed, "France had in effect modified her alliance with America, and changed and enlarged the purposes of the war without America's consent and even without her knowledge" (Morris 1965, 15–16). The Treaty of Aranjuez was the closest Spain came to an alliance with the US itself, Jay's indefatigable efforts notwithstanding. In effect, Spain committed itself to a treaty with France in support of its alliance with the US rebels against England, but not to an alliance with the rebels themselves.

The official entry of Spain into the war not only tipped the balance of the conflict, giving France and Spain numerical superiority both at land and sea, but also profoundly changed the general strategy of the war.[42] The combined Bourbon navy in 1779 had 121 ships of the line compared to 90 for Britain, 117 compared to 95 in 1780, and 124 compared to 94 in 1781 (French 1990, 76). This clear superiority opened up new theaters in the global war, spreading British resources thin. It compelled Britain to fight on multiple fronts. Britain would be forced to abandon a purely American perspective of the conflict and to adopt a more global view of the war in which she had to relinquish her freedom to choose when and where to strike and instead to assume a defensive position, which prevented concentration of its forces against the North American rebels (Scott 1990, 277). Not only was Britain compelled to change its strategy but also the French had to modify their own strategy since the Spanish government succeeded in imposing its own priorities for the use of the combined forces in the Americas (Reeve 2010, 86; Dull 1975, 111).

As previously noted, Spain entered the war against Britain as an ally of France, but not of the US. This important distinction was clearly explained by Diego José Navarro, Governor and Captain General of Cuba between 1777 and 1781, in a memorandum sent to several Spanish officials in America on June 12, 1779.

> There is no positive order or political basis for the United States of America to be seen or considered under any other concept but that of neutrality, since, not acting as subjects of Great Britain, they do not deserve our hostility; and not openly being friends of the Spanish nation, they should not benefit from our war efforts. Thus you will observe with

them, their ships, and [their] vassals the orders issued last November 6, limiting aid to them to what is demanded by the right of hospitality.[43]

This statement had profound implications. For example, even though both Spain and the United States shared a common enemy, it would not be possible to plan or execute joint military operations. This particular issue arose when Diego José Navarro received an American suggestion to plan, or at least discuss, this kind of initiative. Aware of the general policy, Navarro gave a formal and cold answer to the American rebels, telling them that since the matter exceeded his own authority he had to consult with his superiors.[44] Three months later, he received a letter from Madrid informing him that he had behaved properly by responding that he "had no orders to participate in such actions and that the naval and land forces in Cuba were busy with other objectives of the utmost importance."[45] In November 1781, the Minister of the Indies wrote to Bernardo de Gálvez, supreme commander of the Spanish and French forces in the Caribbean and his nephew, that after the conquest of British Jamaica, which was being planned at the time, no more help should be given to the Americans in their war against Britain.[46]

Before considering the military actions of Spain in the Americas, it is important to mention those in Europe which involved the largest number of men, ships, and resources of the war. Gibraltar and Menorca had been ceded to Britain by the Treaty of Utrecht signed in 1713. Since Spain's principal war aim was to recover Gibraltar, it is unsurprising that its siege proved to be the costliest, largest, and longest operation of the conflict. Spain mobilized its army and navy for the siege immediately following its declaration of war, but preparations were slow and the British navy was able to supply Gibraltar's garrison in January 1780 and then in April of the following year. By early 1782, Spain had deployed around 28,000 soldiers in its Gibraltar campaign, about a third of its metropolitan army. With the arrival of the French contingent, the total land forces would increase to 35,000 while the British garrison at that time hovered around 3,500 men.

Despite their massive numerical superiority and the appointment of the experienced Duke de Crillon as supreme commander of the joint Franco-Spanish forces, the British withstood the siege (Adkins and Adkins 2017; Panero 2008; Terrón Ponce 2000). Prince William, Duke of Clarence, who had traveled on a ship accompanying and protecting a British merchant fleet bound for the Mediterranean in January 1780, confidently told George III that Spain's prospects were not promising: "The idea of the Spaniard was to take Gibraltar by famine, but, as long as we keep a superiority at sea it is impossible. To take it by storm would be hardly practicable, for it is too strongly fortified, both by nature and art."[47] His prediction proved accurate. Though 39 ships of the line were involved, and an innovative tactic of using floating batteries was employed, Franco-Spanish forces failed in their amphibious siege and the naval Battle of Cape Spartel was largely inconclusive, too. Britain's defense of Minorca did not meet with similar success: its garrison would surrender to the joint French-Spanish forces in early 1782, after a seven-month campaign, a victory that restored Spain's position in the western Mediterranean (Alcaide Yebra 2004; Terrón Ponce 1981).

Tallying victories and defeats, however, may shroud the benefits Spain derived from its more aggressive policy. Viewed from Madrid, once the conflict had commenced, Spain clearly profited from its continuation. The stalemate in North America helped its Mediterranean policy, for example. In August 1780, a Franco-Spanish fleet came upon a convoy of English merchant ships bound for the Caribbean and Indian Ocean off Cape St. Vincent and managed to capture 59 of the 63 vessels and brought them triumphantly to Cádiz. The loss of cargo was estimated at 1.5 million pounds, plus 1,350 seamen and 1,255 troops (Bemis 1931, 85–88). In mainland North America, too, the inconclusive, protracted nature of the war created a large buffer zone separating New Spain from the nascent United States. Madrid's ambitions were compatible with, and even assisted by, strong allied, non-European nations, whether Anglophone creoles or Chicksaws, Creeks and Choctaw Amerindians. Spain entertained a vision of the Gulf Coast region filled with French and English-speaking landowners who remained or became Spanish subjects (DuVal 2015, 223, 227, 258). Spain also gained the flexibility to enact new commercial policies. Spanish involvement in war actually boosted free trade within the empire, decreed in 1778. In 1779, for example, Charles III gave Philippine merchants the freedom to bring ships laden with Asian goods to Latin America (Ardash Bonialian 2012, 436–427).

Yet, in spite of the advantages accrued, nothing was inevitable about Spain's involvement in the conflict. Many leading British statesmen were certain that Spain did not wish to remain a belligerent. In a sense, they were right. Spain sought certain objectives, but humiliation of Britain was not a principal one. Spain would have exited the war in exchange for Gibraltar, even without recovering Minorca. George III easily grasped this, and (by 1781) was willing to contemplate this cession, as were many of his key parliamentary allies. In late 1782, Lord Shelburne reported on conversations with de Rayneval, the French envoy, on what Vergennes, France's Foreign Minister, was prepared to countenance. Various swaps were proposed: for example, Minorca for Oran, in North Africa, was broached. But, in 1782, Britain held out for Puerto Rico in exchange for Gibraltar. As George III stated explicitly to Shelburne, "Puerto Rico is the object we must get for that fortress [Gibraltar]."[48] What emerges from this correspondence is that Gibraltar was deemed expendable, but that King and Shelburne were reluctant to offer it explicitly or to make the proposal themselves, hoping that Spain, either directly or via France, would suggest it. The King explicitly approved of this negotiating strategy: "The holding of Gibraltar very high is quite judicious and if not taken I should hope Porto Rico may be got for it."[49] Two months later, George III remained disposed to cede Gibraltar, but his asking price had risen. He now demanded "the compleat restitution of every possession Spain has taken during the war" in addition to Puerto Rico (or the dyads of

Martinique and St. Lucia OR Guadalupe and Dominica), calling such a hypothetical exchange "highly advantageous to this kingdom." A few weeks later, however, he was prepared to accept considerably less, averring that "peace is so desirable, that as far as relates to myself, I should not be for another year's war."[50]

The Cabinet, however, was animated by different ideas. In December 1782, Lord Grantham was tasked with informing the King that the Guadeloupe–Gibraltar swap had generated little enthusiasm. Other permutations were considered more desirable: for example, if the Bahamas were returned, Minorca restored, and the rights of logwood cutters in Honduras guaranteed, then a Guadeloupe for Gibraltar swap was palatable. Trinidad also was raised and appraised, though there was uncertainty concerning which other colonial possession could be ranked as its equivalent for the purposes of exchange. The failed Spanish siege of Gibraltar changed the equation in some respects, but George III still believed that Gibraltar was expendable if its cession could bring the war to a close and secure a lasting peace. "I am ready to avow," he told Grantham, "that peace is not compleat unless Gibraltar be exchanged with Spain."[51] He justified this stance in a letter to Shelburne: "I would wish if possible to be rid of Gibraltar, and to have as much possession in the West Indies as possible; for it has been my purpose ever since peace has been on the carpet to get rid of ideal advantages for those that by a good administration may prove solid ones to this country."[52] Spain entered the war against Britain for purely strategic imperial motives. Its alliance with France not only made their combined military and naval forces superior to the British, but also forced the latter to assume a defensive position and made it impossible to concentrate her forces against the American revolutionaries.

War in the Americas

Long before Spain declared war on Britain, a new Governor had been sent to Louisiana with specific instructions to gather all possible information about the conflict between the Thirteen Colonies and Britain and to prepare for Spain's eventual entry into the war. In December 1776, Bernardo de Gálvez, a young colonel of 30, arrived in New Orleans as head of the Louisiana Fixed Infantry Regiment and acting Governor of the province. His first priority would be to ensure the fidelity of the inhabitants to Spain, not an easy task since the formerly French population of Louisiana had rebelled against their new Spanish rulers a mere eight years earlier. With a savvy combination of economic concessions to the wealthy planters and merchants, gifts and expanded trade with the Amerindians, a reinforcement of the military garrison, and the new Governor's deft personal touch, in just two years the Spanish new administration succeeded in winning the support of the vast majority of the population of Louisiana (Quintero Saravia 2018, 79–136).

On May 18, 1779, Spanish officials in America were secretly informed about the imminent war against Britain. Governor Gálvez immediately started preparations for an attack against the British settlements along the Mississippi River. However, the campaign was delayed due to a strong hurricane that hit New Orleans on August 18, so the heterogeneous force assembled (170 veterans, 330 raw recruits, 20 carabineers, 60 militiamen, 80 free blacks and *mulatos*, and 2 American officers and 7 American volunteers) would not be able to leave the city until later that month. Along the march, around 600 men from the Acadian and German settlements, and 160 Amerindians from different groups joined the Spanish forces.[53] The objective was Fort Manchac, also known as Fort Bute, on the left bank of the Mississippi south of Baton Rouge, a British fortified post with a small garrison. On September 6, the Spanish forces arrived before Fort Manchac but instead of demanding the surrender of the garrison, which most probably would have been easily granted, Gálvez ordered his troops to attack. The Spanish forces needed a quick victory to build the morale of their inexperienced recruits and to provide them with their baptism by fire. After a short battle, Fort Manchac was captured.

From Manchac, they marched towards Baton Rouge, a better-defended British stronghold with a larger garrison, which was also rapidly conquered through the clever use of the artillery brought from New Orleans. Two days after the surrender of Baton Rouge, reinforcements arrived from Cuba, a force used to guard the 557 British prisoners of war. Their arrival permitted Gálvez to send a detachment of 50 men, under the command of Captain Juan Delavillebeuvre, to take possession of Fort Panmure in Natchez, almost 125 miles up the Mississippi, which controlled a great part of the river's left bank.

From the strategic point of view, the Spanish operations along the left bank of the Mississippi seized control of territory regarded by the crown as vital to "the protection of the vast empire of New Spain,"[54] and succeeded in dispersing British forces that otherwise could have united against Spain or the American rebels. They also relieved pressure from the British against Georgia and South Carolina and made it impossible for the two British armies operating in the North and South to unite. It additionally ensured that Spanish aid to the revolutionaries would safely reach General Washington's Continental Army. And last, but certainly not least, it removed the menace of a British attack against New Orleans.[55] From Baton Rouge the Spanish troops returned to New Orleans to regroup and plan for the next move against Mobile and Pensacola. Despite his recent victories along the Mississippi, Gálvez, who in the meantime had been promoted to the rank of general, received paltry support from Cuba. Governor Diego José Navarro considered Gálvez too inexperienced to lead the next Spanish thrust against the British. Due to a combination of surprise, daring, and overwhelming force, the first phases of the war in the Americas were completely favorable to Spain, but those that followed would require significantly larger military and naval forces against a much better prepared enemy.

On January 14, 1780, 1,300 men aboard three small warships and several transports left New Orleans, but when they were sailing in open sea a heavy storm destroyed most of the ships (Gálvez 1780). In the words of Gerónimo Girón Moctezuma, colonel of the Príncipe Regiment and Gálvez's second in command during the expedition against Mobile, "the troops found themselves ashore without arms or ammunition, naked and with nothing to eat in a land surrounded by enemies. There they remained for twelve days without tents or food other than the rice brought from Havana."[56] On February 27, all of the troops and supplies were on shore near Mobile and the following day military engineers inspected the placement of the encampment and the batteries as they prepared for the siege of Fort Charlotte at Mobile.

Because of the inferior numbers of the defenders—between 120 and 300 British troops to 1,300 Spanish attackers—their only hope was to receive reinforcements from Pensacola.[57] Although Pensacola's British military commander, General John Campbell, had been informed as early as February 12 of a strong Spanish military presence near Mobile, he was slow in coming to their aid.[58] At sunrise on March 12, the Spanish battery was in place. At ten o'clock, it opened fire. According to Gálvez, the shots hit their targets with great accuracy and "non-stop [fire] from both sides lasted till sunset, when the enemy hoisted the white flag." After a short negotiation, the two commanders signed the articles of capitulation.[59] The British soldiers were taken prisoner, and the Spaniards hurried to take their positions inside Fort Charlotte in case of an attack by Campbell's forces, which were less than a day's march from Mobile. At the end, General Campbell decided against attacking and returned to Pensacola.

John Adams, who was about to leave Paris, wrote to Vergennes that "the advantages which Spain has gained in West Florida, and particularly of late at Mobile, and the probability that they will succeed in acquiring both the Floridas, show that the English are on the losing hand in this quarter."[60] According to Representative William C. Houston, the news of the conquest represented that "the bitter Cup of ill Tidings is dashed with a little mixture of a different Quality."[61] Gálvez spent the days following the British surrender reconstructing Fort Charlotte, which he renamed Fort Carlota in honor of King Carlos III. In Mobile, Gálvez left 800 men under the command of José de Ezpeleta, who had to face not only the hostility of the local population, both of European origin and Native Americans, but also the prospect of a British counterattack which would become a reality in early 1781 and that would be repelled by a combination of blunders on the side of the attackers and fierce resistance from the Spanish defenders.[62]

After recovering from their initial surprise, the British responded by trying to regain control of the Mississippi with an attack against San Luis de Ilinueses, modern St. Louis, Missouri. In May 1780, they attacked the Spanish garrison under the command of Captain Fernando de Leyva. Leyva's 29 soldiers and 281 armed civilians were confronted by more than 300 British soldiers and 900 Indian warriors. The February 16, 1781 issue of the Spanish official newspaper, the *Gazeta de Madrid*, published an account of the defense emphasizing Captain Leyva's gallant defense and the cruelties committed by the enemy while retreating from San Luis de Ilinueses.[63]

From Mobile, Gálvez planned to go directly to Pensacola where he expected to catch the British garrison by surprise before any reinforcements could arrive. He needed the reinforcements promised from Havana, but these were nowhere to be seen, so he was forced to return to New Orleans victorious, embittered that the conquest of Pensacola had slipped from his hands. In a long report to José de Gálvez, Minister of the Indies in November 1780, he openly complained about Admiral Bonet, the supreme commander of the Spanish fleet in the Caribbean, who,

> under the pretense that the conquest of Pensacola was not now in the king's interests ... only demanded for me to fortify and satisfy myself with Mobile; adding that the greatest service I could render to the king was that, and nothing would make me a better servant than to sacrifice the glory and promotions that could be awarded to me for the conquest of Pensacola ... It seems to me that the admiral was doing nothing but finding ways to deprive me of ships by using them for other pursuits and leaving us abandoned.[64]

As Gálvez became exasperated with the delays, he decided to leave New Orleans for Havana, where he arrived on August 2, 1780. The following day, a fleet under the command of Admiral José Solano arrived from Cádiz in southern Spain. Gálvez's hopes for a prompt departure for Pensacola soon dissipated when the parlous condition of the disembarking troops became apparent.[65] The tensions that Gálvez had experienced earlier with Admiral Bonet were soon duplicated with his replacement, Victorio de Navia,[66] but at least the arrival of José Solano improved Gálvez's relationship with the navy. Solano played a key role in expediting preparations for the departure of the expedition against Pensacola. On October 16, 1780, 3,822 soldiers and 169 officers, on board a fleet commanded by José Solano, set sail from the port of Havana for Pensacola.[67] Just two days later, a nearly weeklong hurricane sank several ships, damaged the rest, and knocked the remaining ships off-course. Despite repeated efforts, it was impossible to regroup, as the hurricane had thrown ships to such far-flung places as Havana, Campeche, Mobile, and New Orleans.[68] When Gálvez returned to Havana, the senior military officers there awaited the downfall of the ambitious young general, but with the support of his uncle, the Minister for the Indies, he was able to maintain his position. Nevertheless, since Gálvez needed the assistance of the military and naval authorities in Havana, he avoided direct confrontation by presenting them with a new plan that instead of directly attacking Pensacola focused on reinforcing Mobile in order to prevent the British from retaking the recently conquered town (Medina Rojas 1980, 651–669).[69]

On February 28, 1781, 5 warships, 27 transports, and more than 1,500 soldiers set sail from Havana,[70] but General Gálvez did not even pretend to go to Mobile or New Orleans but instead headed directly for Pensacola. The Spanish forces were clearly insufficient for a successful attack on Pensacola, but Gálvez was betting that once the siege started the military commanders in Cuba would have no option other than to send reinforcements. To that end, he counted on the support of Francisco de Saavedra, the special envoy of the Minister of the Indies, who had arrived in Havana and who played a crucial role in the campaign.

The voyage was uneventful, and, on March 9, the Spanish ships sighted the island of Santa Rosa, at the entrance of Pensacola Bay, where it was believed that the British had erected a fort to defend the entrance to the bay. To the attackers' surprise, a handful few soldiers were posted there and it was easily occupied. The main challenge was the shallow water over a sandbank that connected Santa Rosa island to the mainland. It was especially worrying for the *San Ramón*, a ship of the line with a deeper draft than the rest of the ships of the fleet. On March 11, its commander, naval captain José Calvo, gave the order to enter the bay, but the *San Ramón* ran aground. Gálvez insisted that the rest of the ships could easily enter the bay, but the naval officers refused to follow. Although Gálvez was the commander of the Spanish military expedition, his powers did not extend to the navy squadron, which was only responsible to Admiral de Navia in Havana. Tension escalated between Gálvez and the navy commander, verging on open rebellion. Unable to give a direct order, Gálvez resorted to challenging the navy. He went aboard the *Galveston*, a brig that had been seized to the British and that was under Gálvez's direct authority as Governor of Louisiana, hoisted the banner of chief of squadron, delivered a rousing speech where he stated that he alone would sail into Pensacola harbor to prove to the navy that it could be safely done, and gave orders to proceed. When the *Galveston* crossed unharmed inside the bay, the navy had no choice but to follow.

At this point the siege of Pensacola began, but for it to be a success, more reinforcements were desperately needed. Pensacola was strongly defended by a series of fortifications and by a garrison with between 1,800 and 1,900 men (Coker 1981, 118–119; Gálvez 1781 [1959]). The Spanish only had 1,500 soldiers. On March 22, reinforcements arrived from Mobile under the command of his trusted friend José de Ezpeleta; the following day a flotilla entered the bay carrying 1,378 more men, this time from New Orleans; and a couple of days later additional troops arrived by land, also from Louisiana's capital.[71] With these additions, Gálvez now commanded just over 4,000 men, still insufficient to lay a siege, which, according to the military theorists of the time, required between 6,000 and 8,000 troops (Noizet de Saint-Paul 1792, 178, n. 2).

In order to have that number of men, reinforcements from Cuba were needed. In Havana, Francisco de Saavedra, who was in charge of coordinating the Spanish and French forces to prepare for a joint attack of Jamaica, succeeded in convincing the French and Spanish commanders that while waiting for everything to be ready they should reinforce the siege of Pensacola in case of British reinforcements were sent there. Saavedra forced the situation and a joint Franco-Spanish fleet departed from Cuba and arrived in Pensacola Bay on April 19, with more than 5,500 soldiers, 1,505 officers and sailors of the Spanish navy, and 725 French troops, who volunteered "so they could share in the glory of this conquest."[72] The total number of men of the Franco-Spanish force was almost 7,500. But men were not matched with sufficient supplies and the Spanish artillery was running dangerously low on large caliber cannon balls, to the point that soldiers were paid two *reales* for each British cannon ball which could be re-fired against Penacola's defenses. The situation was far from promising for the Spaniards, but at daybreak on May 8, construction was finished on the Spanish battery closest to the Queen's Redoubt, and the exchange of fire began. All signs pointed to another long and uneventful day, with the siege continuing at its exasperatingly slow pace, but at half-past nine in the morning, a shot from the Spanish battery directly hit the British magazine producing a great explosion that destroyed most of the Redoubt. Spanish troops were quickly assembled for the assault, but before the order was given a white flag was hoisted in Fort George. After several hours of negotiations, the British garrison in Pensacola surrendered not only the city but the whole of British Florida.[73]

The news of the Spanish-French victory at Pensacola went uncelebrated by the American revolutionaries for several reasons. First, because the terms of the British capitulation stated that its soldiers were to be returned to British territory only on the condition of not bearing arms against Spain or France in the present war, which left them free to fight against the American rebels. Second, as Spain's national interest had been to prolong the war in order to weaken the British position in the continent, now the Americans would have preferred that Spain continue the war in Florida in order that the British could not concentrate their forces there. Furthermore, with the conquest of Pensacola, Spain had acquired West Florida from the British, thereby blocking the Americans' access to the Caribbean. The American rebels were not fighting the British only for their enemy's territories to be seized by another European colonial power.[74]

The conquest of Pensacola had another important consequence for the cause of American independence. After the successful cooperation between the French and the Spanish navies, Spain assumed responsibility for the defense of the entire Caribbean, including all French possessions there, thus allowing the French fleet, commanded by the Count de Grasse, to confront the British fleet under the command of Rear Admiral Sir Thomas Graves at the Battle of the Chesapeake (September 5, 1781) which would facilitate General George Washington's victory at Yorktown. Pensacola was a precondition for the larger Franco-Spanish design in the Caribbean. Jamaica had not only remained loyal to the British crown and was the source of crucial revenue to the Royal Treasury, but the wealthy planters of the island had succeeded in building a powerful lobby both in Parliament and in court. In this way, the defense of the island would become a major, if not the main, British priority (O'Shaughnessy 2000,

234–237). From this moment, Britain would be on the defensive, incapable of concentrating sufficient forces against the American rebels to secure victory.

The complex preparations for the expedition against Jamaica delayed the attack. In the interim, the Spaniards decided to mount a smaller operation against the island of New Providence, in the Bahamas. In mid-April 1782, 2,000 soldiers aboard 57 ships sailed from Havana. The small garrison in Nassau (170 men, mostly ill or unfit for service) surrendered immediately after the arrival of the Spanish force in early May, but not before a serious confrontation between the Spanish military and naval commanders and Commodore Alexander Gillon, captain of the USS frigate *South Carolina*. At the bay of Nassau, Gillon demanded the immediate payment in cash of his services. The incident with Gillon had consequences, since both Havana and Madrid would seriously question "Anglo-American" participation in any Spanish military operation.[75] The problem had deeper implications than just an obstreperous American captain. If any operation were to be considered a joint one, it would contravene orders that stated specifically that Spain was only allied with France in the war against Britain, and while Spain shared a common enemy with the United States, the latter should not be considered an ally. In an *oficio reservadísimo* (secret instruction—the equivalent of a top secret order today) dated April 6, 1782, from José de Gálvez to Bernardo de Gálvez, the former interpreted and elaborated upon a November 16, 1781 royal order by stating clearly that neither Bernardo de Gálvez nor José Solano—the latter on specific instructions from the Minister of the Navy—should "ever agree to use the army or the navy of His Majesty to help the war of the American colonists against their motherland ... [but] if in the course of the operation against Jamaica this is demanded by the French, such a request should not prevent them from working closely with the French generals."[76]

Just when the Spanish troops were sailing towards New Providence, the joint Franco-Spanish attack against Jamaica received a serious blow when the British fleet under the command of Admiral Sir George Rodney defeated the French navy at the Battle of the Saintes (April 9–12, 1782). Without the participation of the French Navy, the plans for the invasion of Jamaica were postponed and ultimately cancelled. The Battle of the Saintes and the conquest of New Providence would be the last military actions of the American Independence War since peace negotiations started shortly afterwards. Britain was exhausted both financially and militarily. France teetered on the brink of bankruptcy. The revolutionary government struggled through the labor pains of giving birth to a new polity amid the tensions between the central authority of the Continental Congress and the real power that remained in hands of the Thirteen States. By contrast, Spain was in a far better position than its rivals and confident that it could achieve its objectives in the war either through military means or in diplomatic negotiations.

From the start of Spain's participation in the American Revolutionary War, Central America became an important theater of operations in the struggle with Britain (Floyd 1967). Just a few months after the declaration of war, the Captain General of Guatemala, Matías de Gálvez, father of Bernardo de Gálvez and brother of José de Gálvez, was ordered to attack the British settlements in Belize. Yet before an expedition could be mounted, the British commodore, John Luttrell, sailed from Jamaica with three frigates to reinforce Belize. Then Luttrell changed his destination and decided to attack San Fernando de Omoa, in modern Honduras. The Spanish garrison in Omoa resisted the British attacks for almost a month but finally capitulated on October 20, 1779. The British occupation of the place would be short-lived, since less than a week later a Spanish relief force arrived in Omoa and recovered the fort for Spain.

Andrew O'Shaughnessy has described British military operations in Central America as "a ludicrously ambitious series of campaigns" (O'Shaughnessy 2000, 189). The intention was to seize the San Juan River and its source, Lake Nicaragua, and to thus divide the north and south dominions of Spanish America. On March 1780, 400 British soldiers and 600 Miskito Indians entered the San Juan River. With the support of the guns of the frigate *Hinchinbrook*, under the command of 22-year-old Horatio Nelson, and the expert Miskitu boatmen the British attacked the Inmaculada fort which fell after a month's siege (Dziennik 2018, 171–172). The extremely insalubrious conditions of the place determined that its British garrison had to abandon it by the end of July and shortly afterwards it was re-occupied by Spanish forces.[77] By December 1781, Matías de Gálvez left the capital of Guatemala for the port of Trujillo in the coast of Honduras, where he concentrated most of his troops for an attack against the British garrison in the island of Roatán, which surrendered on March 17, 1782 after a short battle. Returning to the mainland, the Spanish forces captured the British forts of Criba and Quepriva in Honduras. The defeat of the French fleet under admiral de Grasse at the Battle of the Saintes in April 1782 allowed Archibald Campbell, Governor of Jamaica, to send an expedition with 400 men under the command of Colonel Edward Marcus Despard that reconquered both forts in August.

Though the Central American and Caribbean campaigns were far from resounding successes, Spain was able to realize dreams it had long harbored. Britain was removed from what is now the Southeast of the US. Both Floridas—West and East—were recovered. Britain retained its Caribbean colonies, of course, but without mainland ports, Spanish shipping was safer than it had been for well over a hundred years and the treasure fleet more secure than it had been for nearly two centuries. A British invasion and occupation of Spanish America was now implausible. If anything, Spain now appeared poised to expand in North America, to make good its legal claims in the American Southwest. Where Spain and Britain clashed in North America thereafter was in the distant north, far from the most prosperous viceroyalties, in the Nootka Sound in British Columbia.

The 1780s were, perhaps, the apogee of the Spanish empire. It was a decade of revival, marked by tremendous economic growth, demographic expansion, and sustained peace. The picture was not entirely rosy, of course. The conflict drove home to Spain's ministerial elite that colonies might rise up against the mother country and seek to separate themselves from it. In the early 1780s, numerous rebellions roiled the Spanish empire, notably in what is now Peru-Bolivia and Colombia, over just the same sorts of things—taxes (too many of them) and representation (not enough)—that had proved harbingers of Revolution in Anglo-North America. As Spanish officials had feared, the nascent US fascinated Spanish Americans. One writer in Bogotá (now Colombia) in 1793 said (disapprovingly):

> Since the establishment of the Anglo-American provinces as a free republic, the peoples of America have taken on a character which is entirely different from that which they had ... the common coin of erudite discussion groups (in Spanish America) is to discuss and even form plans around the means of enjoying the same independence that they enjoy.[78]

Aftermath of revolution: The 1783 peace and beyond

The war ended with four separate peace treaties: between the United States and Britain signed in Paris; France and Britain at Versailles; Spain and Britain, also at Versailles (all three signed on September 3, 1783); and Britain and the Netherlands on May 20, 1784. This complex diplomatic patchwork was designed to end the war but left open several questions that would negatively impact the diplomatic relations between Spain and the United States for decades to come. First, there was the Mississippi River question. For the United States, it was vital to have full access to the river which was their border with the Spanish empire but whose estuary South of the 31st parallel was inside Spanish territory. During the war itself, the Continental Congress initially had offered Spain exclusive navigation of the Mississippi River in return for substantive contributions toward the war effort. In the Continental Congress's "Resolution Approving Jay's Conduct in Spain" (1782), that body made clear that "the surrender of the Mississippi was meant as the price of the advantages promised by an early and intimate alliance with the Spanish monarchy; and if that alliance is to be procrastinated till the conclusion of the war, the reason of the sacrifice will no longer exist."[79] In the Paris Treaty of 1783, Britain transferred her navigation rights along the Mississippi to the United States, but the separate treaty between Spain and Britain made no mention at all of the issue, and therefore Spain did not recognize it. While Spain tried to impose taxes on all US commerce on the river, it had little military power to enforce them, so incidents between Spanish authorities in Louisiana and American ships were common. The issue would not be finally resolved until Pinckney's Treaty, also called the Treaty of San Lorenzo, on October 27, 1795, article 4 of which granted the United States free navigation of the Mississippi.

The second unresolved issue was the border with the Floridas. The United States wanted the border as far south as possible, while Spain wanted the opposite. The issue would also be settled by Pinckney's Treaty, which determined that the border would be drawn at the 31st parallel, thus accommodating the Unites States' wishes. In order to properly evaluate the Spanish concessions in this treaty, it is crucial to bear in mind that while these questions were somewhat relevant to the Spanish empire, they were vital for the United States. Similarly, the presence of the Spanish administration, both civil and military, was extremely weak in the region, which meant that the Spanish positions could not be backed by either the use or the threat of the use of force. Nevertheless, by 1784, Spain was treating the US as a hostile power, closing the port of New Orleans and the lower Mississippi to American navigation. It required Americans in borderland regions to swear an oath of loyalty to Charles III. Spain extended its own territorial claims eastward, into western parts of Georgia, Kentucky and Tennessee. As historian Eliga Gould (2012, 122–123) argued, "the result was a veritable war of all against all, in which Spain and the US engaged in low-grade hostilities against each other ... while vying for the allegiance of Indians, loyalists and Americans."

The third outstanding issue after 1783 was the regulation of commerce between the United States and the Spanish empire, both in Old World and the New. During the Revolutionary War, Spain opened its ports to all American vessels. This policy was conceived from the start as a temporary measure. When the peace was signed, this access was revoked, something greatly resented by American merchants.[80] Pinckney's Treaty did not re-open Spanish ports to American commerce, but it allowed ships from both nations to seek refuge in each other's ports when in distress or when harassed by pirates. This clause would be much abused by merchants from both countries and de facto established a flourishing although non-official trade relation between the United States and Spain (Narrett 2015, 72, 285).

The fourth issue placing stress on US–Spanish relations was the status of several Amerindian polities. Although neither Spain nor the United States had attracted them to their side during the war, Spain was in a better position to gain their trust than the nascent United States. Spain's ambitions in North America were compatible with, and even bolstered by, strong allied, non-European nations, whether Anglophone creoles or Chicksaws, Creeks and Choctaw Amerindians. Spanish statesmen envisaged a Gulf Coast populated by French and English-speaking landowners who remained or became Spanish subjects (DuVal 2015, 223, 227, 258). The United States's situation stood in sharp contrast to that of Spain. It was bound to confront Amerindians, whose lands were coveted to ensure the expansion of European-origin settlers. Pinckney's Treaty tried to consolidate the status quo, but the fact is that the Amerindian policy carried out by Spanish authorities in North America tipped the scales in Spain's favor. The policy designed by Bernardo de Gálvez, when he became Viceroy of New Spain, would also have "several intriguing parallels" with subsequent policies carried out by the United Sates, especially during Thomas Jefferson's presidency (Babcock 2016, 8). Although Bernardo de Gálvez and Thomas Jefferson had very different personalities, backgrounds, and careers, both were steeped in the Enlightenment, and in addition to embracing the myth of the noble savage, they shared the idea of a demographic imperialism, that considered that hunting and gathering were to be replaced in favor of husbandry as the most productive use of land. For both, semi-nomadic Native Americans had to become sedentary farmers in order to be "civilized," and they preferred to trade with them because it was a cheaper alternative to war, but nonetheless they were willing to wage war simultaneously if needed.

The fifth and final source of tensions between Spain and the United States during the late eighteenth and early nineteenth centuries was slavery. Spanish Louisiana and, especially, Spanish Florida were perceived as a constant threat by the politically powerful slave owners of Georgia. From the late seventeenth-century Spanish authorities in Florida had granted sanctuary to runaway slaves from the British colonies in an attempt to populate its borders and prevent foreign encroachment, in this context was born the settlement of Gracia Real de Santa Teresa de Mose, a few miles North to St. Augustine, where a free-black community became a beacon luring British and later United States' slaves into Spanish territory. However, the fluid situation in the Floridas between its surrender to Bernardo de Gálvez in 1781 and the implementation of the peace treaties of 1783 forced the new Spanish Governor, Vicente Manuel de Zéspedes, to issue an order on July 26, 1784 to clarify the legal situation of the black inhabitants of the province, which required their registration before the Spanish authorities. The order had a deep impact since it changed the traditional Spanish policy of considering all blacks in Northern Florida as free-people unless proven otherwise by legal documents. During the following years, "a newly emerging sense that the slave trade and African slavery were essential to the wealth of nations" (Schneider 2015, 3) and growing pressure from the United States government, especially from Thomas Jefferson as Secretary of State, would succeed in reversing the traditional policy of granting sanctuary to fugitive slaves in Spanish Florida. Although runaway slaves already settled in Spanish territory would not lose their free status, further fugitives would no longer be welcomed and, at least in theory Spanish authorities would cooperate with United States' agents in their capture and return to their American owners (Landers 1984, 1990; TePaske 1975).

Not all Americans believed that the uneasy jostling for primacy along the western frontier and other conflicts portended permanent enmity. In 1787, Thomas Jefferson observed: "Our connection with Spain is already important and will become daily more so ... Besides, this antient part of American history is chiefly written in Spanish."[81] The Spanish American independence movements, though, shifted the US stance toward Spain. After 1815, popular opinion embraced the revolutionaries who sought to establish republics in place of an empire governed by a distant king. US merchants sold arms and ammunition, thousands of Americans sailed as mercenaries and privateers to fight against Spain. Some imagined an entire hemisphere composed of "sister republics." By

1830, over 200 American babies had been named for the South American liberator, Simón Bolívar, along with numerous towns and hamlets.[82]

The US government displayed more caution than its zealous citizenry. It did not want to embroil the US in another war so soon after the War of 1812. Congress passed the 1817 Neutrality Act to stanch the flow of arms. The government sought to keep commerce flowing between Cuba and also involved in delicate negotiations with Spanish government to acquire Florida, which occurred several years later. Much of the nineteenth century would see rising tensions between Spain and the US over Cuba, in particular, but also over Puerto Rico. Spain gradually became demonized, far from Jefferson's appreciation of Spanish culture and his anticipation of Hispano-Anglo-American relations. Spain became the US's foil. It was, in the words of historian Ivan Jaksic, "the antithesis of democratic, enterprising America. The country was corrupt beyond measure, its former glories but a distant memory."[83] And in 1898, of course, such prejudice was whipped into a frenzy by the war between Spain and the US, which resulted in the annexation of Puerto Rico, the Philippines and, for a time, Cuba itself.

What of Britain and Spain? Was the damage caused by Spain's intervention in Britain's war of colonial counterinsurgency irreparable? There were undoubtedly lingering resentments after 1783. Spain remained fixated on Gibraltar. The Falklands/Malvinas were a source of further conflict. But these disputes must not distract attention from the main story, which was the normalization of relations after 1783. In the 1780s, Britain remained Spain's largest customer while Spain was Britain's fifth largest continental trading partner.[84] The French Revolutionary Wars once again saw Britain and Spain as adversaries. But the Napoleonic invasion and occupation of Spain from 1808 to 1813 touched off a wholesale revaluation of Britain's relations with the Peninsula. British support for the Spanish patriots and its military intervention, decisive in driving French troops from the Peninsula, brought many young Britons into contact with Spain's culture and landscape. It is estimated that at least 200,000 British soldiers served in Iberia during the Peninsular War, of whom 40,000 perished during the conflict.[85]

British solidarity with the Spanish patriots assumed non-martial forms, from the moral and material sustenance furnished by Lord and Lady Holland to the provocative articles in support of Spain published in the *Edinburgh Review*.[86] Even Coleridge asserted that "it was not until the Spanish insurrection that Englishmen of all parties recurred, in toto, to the Old English principles, and spoke of their Hampdens, Sidneys, and Miltons, with the old enthusiasm."[87] The debates at the Cortes of Cádiz, culminating in the 1812 Constitution, one of the great documents of early nineteenth-century liberalism, also aroused keen interest in Spain in Britain, and there is some evidence the nineteenth-century usage of the word "liberal" owed much to the ideas and projects pursued by the Spanish *liberales*.[88] In the early 1820s, Jeremy Bentham seemed to concur with these sentiments when he wrote,

Magnanimous Spaniards! For years to come, not to say ages, in you is our best, if not our only hope! To you, who have been the most oppressed of slaves, to you it belongs to give liberty to Europe ... As to our liberties—our so much vaunted liberties—inadequate as they always were, they are gone: corruption has completely rotted them.[89]

Beyond the political and ideological impact of the independence of the United States (Armitage 2007), which sparked "the Age of Revolutions" (Armitage and Subrahmanyam 2010), the American Revolutionary War had a crucial impact on the three major European empires that fought it. For France, the cost of the war left the Royal Treasury almost empty. To stave off bankruptcy, King Louis XVI had no other option but to convene the Estates-General in January 1789, the death knell of the Ancien Régime in France. For Britain, the American Revolution was the denouement of its "first" empire. Since the American Revolution began when the colonists clamored for recognition of their rights as Englishmen, Britain's subsequent imperial forays were marked by hierarchy, difference, and executive fiat. For Spain, the decade of the 1780s would be the zenith of its empire, a revival and efflorescence often obscured by its vertiginous fall, sparked by war in Europe, in the early nineteenth century.

Notes

1 Cumberland, chiefly known as a playwright and poet, had served as Secretary of the Board of Trade from 1775, but he was, as Samuel Flagg Bemis observed, "a man whose political experience had been limited to the art of pleasing patrons and impressing little people, a man without political imagination or real knowledge of the world," Bemis, *Hussey-Cumberland Mission*, 48.
2 Bemis, *Hussey-Cumberland Mission*, 49.
3 *Memoirs of Richard Cumberland* [London, 1806] Ed. Henry Flanders (London, 1856; and re-issued in 1969 [New York: Benjamin Blom]), 255–257; the work to which Cumberland referred was "Anecdotes of the Eminent Painters of Spain during the 16th and 17th century", published in 1782.
4 Jay to Adams, June 4, 1780, in Jay 1975, 766.
5 John Adams to John Jay, May 13, 1780, in Nuxoll 2010, v. 2: 115.
6 Ben Franklin to John Jay, October 2, 1780, in Nuxoll 2010, v. 2: 280.
7 The classic study and the origin of the term "Black Legend" is by Julián Juderías (1914). The subject has been much studied in Spain with mixed results since several of the works tend to approach the subject trying to vindicate Spanish colonialism. The most recent, best-selling and highly controversial book on the Spanish black legend is by María Elvira Roca Barea (2016). In English, the subject was first historically approached by Charles Gibson, William S. Maltby, and Philip W. Powell with books all published in 1971. The most recent English study is by Irene Silverblatt (2007).
8 The book was based on two seventeenth-century editions: Casas 1699, and Casaus [*sic* Casas] 1656. Interestingly, in the twenty years between the two English editions, the number of people massacred by the Spaniards doubled.
9 The accusation of being ungrateful was made by Manuel Conrotte (1920, 5–6) and Juan F. Yela Utrilla (1925, v. 1, 485). Vicente Blasco Ibañez in his novel *Queen*

Calafia (1925) stated that the reason why the figure of Bernardo de Gálvez was completely unknown to the American public was because he was a Spaniard.
10 An indication of the official interest in the subject is that Morales Padrón's book was published both in Spanish and in English in 1952 by *Publicaciones Españolas*, the official publishing arm of Franco's regime.
11 In order to commemorate the United States' bicentennial, the Spanish Ministry of Foreign Affairs embarked on a large-scale editorial enterprise by publishing a series of studies by Spanish historians, including those by Antonio Acosta Rodríguez, Pablo Tornero Tinajero, Luis Ángel García Melero, Elena Sánchez-Fabrés Mirat, and María Pilar Ruigómez de Hernández. The Ministry of Foreign Affairs also published between 1977 and 1986 fourteen volumes of the collection of documents related to the American Independence in Spanish Archives (*Documentos relativos a la independencia de Norteamérica existentes en archivos españoles*, 14 vols., Madrid, MAE, 1977–1986) including those preserved in the Archivo General de Indias (hereafter AGI) in Seville, the Archivo Histórico Nacional (hereafter AHN) in Madrid, and the Archivo General de Simancas (hereafter AGS) in Simancas, Valladolid.
12 For a revision of Tannenbaum's work, see Alejandro de la Fuente 2004.
13 Besides Eliga Gould's thesis, for the methodological questions and tools provided by Entangled Histories, see the works by Michael Werner and Bénédicte Zimmermann (Werner and Zimmermann 2006) and by Natacha Gally (2012).
14 Books on the Spanish role in the American Revolutionary War include those by Thomas E. Chávez (2002), Eric Beerman (1992), Martha Gutiérrez-Steinkamp (2013), and Larrie D. Ferreiro (2016). Studies on Spanish Louisiana include those by Gilbert C. Din (1996) and David E. Narrett (2015). For Florida, see the work of Joseph Barton Starr (1976). For military campaigns, see William S. Coker and Robert R. Rea (1982), William S. Coker (1981), Jack D. L. Holmes (1965), and N. Orwin Rush (1966). For the life and career of Bernardo de Gálvez, the studies by John Walton Caughey (1934 [1998]), Jack D. L. Holmes (1978), Eric Beerman (1994), Carmen de Reparaz (1993), and Gonzalo M. Quintero Saravia (2018).
15 King to Lord North, March 7, 1780, in Fortescue, v. V, 30 (no. 2963).
16 King to Lord North, June 13, 1781, in Fortescue, v. V, 247 (no. 3357).
17 On the evolution of the historiography on this subject see: Paquette 2009; Varela 1994; Wasserman 2009; Herzog 2004; Donézar 2004.
18 In 1762, the Earl of Albemarle (George Keppel), who led the campaign, concluded that military planners should anticipate that one-third of their force would be unfit for service at any one time. During the siege of Havana itself, Albemarle had 11,000 men under his command, but only just over 5,000 were fit for duty (Charters 2014, 66, 72).
19 Queen María Amalia de Sajonia (King Carlos III's wife) to Bernardo Tanucci, February 13, 1760 (quoted in Guasti 2006, 55).
20 See: Delegates of Rhode Island to William Greene, Philadelphia, December 8, 1778, in Smith 1976–2000, v. 11: 304–305; Gouverneur Morris to the Journal Pensylvania Packet, s.l., February 27, 1779, in idem v. 12: 115–121; Committee of Commerce to Bernardo de Gálvez, Philadelphia, July 19, 1779, in idem. v. 25: 658.
21 In June 1777, the Congress' Secret Committee wrote to the Spanish Governor of Louisiana that "we are informed by means of Mr. Oliver Pollock of the favorable disposition you have been pleased to manifest towards the Subjects, interest and cause of the United, Free and Independent states of America upon every occasion that has presented since your Excellency's accession to the Government of New Orleans & Louisiana" (Secret Committee to Bernardo de Gálvez, Philadelphia, June 12, 1777. In Smith 1976–2000, v. 25, 624–625). The Congress' Committee of Commerce also expressed its gratitude several times to Governor Bernardo de Gálvez (Committee of Commerce to Bernardo de Gálvez, Pennsylvania, October 24, 1777, in Smith 1976–2000, v. 25, 636–638; Committee of Commerce to

Bernardo de Gálvez, Pennsylvania, November 21, 1777. In Smith 1976–2000, v. 25, 638–639). The Congress itself, on October 31, 1778, declared that "Governor Gálvez be requested to accept the thanks of Congress for his spirited and disinterested conduct towards these States, and be assured that Congress will take every opportunity of evincing the favorable and friendly sentiments they entertain of Governor Gálvez, and all the faithful subjects of his Catholic Majesty inhabiting the country under his government" (Continental Congress, Minutes of the October 31, 1778 session, in Ford 1904–37, v. 12: 1083–108).

22 Of all the Spanish contemporary testimonies, the two most important are those of Diego María de Gardoqui and the Count of Aranda. In 1794 Gardoqui, who would become the first ambassador of Spain to the United States, stated that between 1776 and 1778 Spain contributed a total of "7,944,906 *reales* and 16 *maravedíes de vellón*" in cash and supplies. Diego María Gardoqui to the Duke de Alcudia, dispatch, October 26, 1794. AHN, Estado, 3884. In settling the account so as to submit a claim to the new United States, the Count of Aranda, Spain's ambassador to France at the time, offered the figure of 5.5 million *reales de vellón* for the same period (the exact amount rendered by the count of Aranda was 5,634,910 *reales de vellón*. Socorros dados a los Estados Unidos de América por medio del sr. Conde de Aranda, Embajador de España en aquel tiempo. AHN, Estado 3889 bis, ex15. In Armillas Vicente, 2008, 187).

23 In his 1926 article, Samuel Flagg Bemis determined the amount of the Spanish financial aid to the United Sates in 13,551,888 dollars (397,230 non-refundable, and 248,098 in loans), which converted in French *livres* would be 3,387,972, and 13,551,888 Spanish reales de vellón (Bemis 1926, 93; Perkins 1986, 195–199; Dull 1985). For the conversion of the French currency to the Spanish one, see Bails, 1790, 286, 305, 372.

24 The exact amount of the French financial assistance to the American Revolution in Spanish currency was 166,980,000 *reales de vellón* (Armillas Vicente 1977).

25 Diego José Navarro to José de Gálvez, letter n. 365, Havana, October 23, 1778. AGI, Santo Domingo 1598 A and B.

26 The exact amount is 1,507,670 *reales de vellón*. "Razón de los préstamos o socorros en dinero que en la Nueva Orleans y en La Habana se han dado a los colonos americanos por disposición de sus respectivos gobernadores, deducida de la correspondencia de éstos desde fin de diciembre de 1776 hasta junio de 1779, New Orleans, 13 September 1780". AHN, Estado 3884, ex. 4, n. 74. In Armillas Vicente, 2008, 187, 194.

27 Bernardo de Gálvez to the inhabitants of the colony of Louisiana, order draft copy, New Orleans, March 3, 1778. AGI, Cuba 112. Bernardo de Gálvez to Baltasar de Villiers, official letter n. 43, New Orleans, January 2, 1779. AGI, Cuba 112.

28 Bernardo de Gálvez to John Ferguson, certified copy of the letter, New Orleans, May 15, 1778. AGI, Cuba, 1232. Bernardo de Gálvez to the commanders of the Mississippi River, Punta Colorada, and Manchac, letter draft copy, s.l., July 14, 1778. AGI, Cuba 112.

29 Saavedra 2004, entries of July 21, 1781, 204; July 25, 1781, 204; August 1–16, 1781, 206–8; and September 12, 1781, 214. Juan Ignacio de Urriza to José de Gálvez, letter no. 861, Havana, October 26, 1781, AGI, Santo Domingo, 1657; 2,000,000 *pesos* for the French, in Juan Ignacio de Urriza to José de Gálvez, official letter no. 1038, Havana, December 20, 1782, AGI, Indiferente General, 1583.

30 The exact figure is 431,282,000 *reales de vellón*.

31 Sources: Merino 1987; Tedde de Lorca 2008, 221–224.

32 All the figures in *reales de vellón*.

33 This figure is the result of adding the defence expenditures of the years 1775, 1776, 1777, 1778, and 1784 and divided the result by 5 (the number of years). Spain

declared war to Britain on June 22, 1779, so this year has been considered as a war year despite that the defence expenditure during it was little increased, probably because the war expenses for 1779 were registered in the accounts for 1780. The peace was signed in January 1783, but following the previous argument we have considered it as a war year.
34 *Real Decreto*, November 17, 1779. In Gallardo Fernández 1808, v. 7: 49–52.
35 Resolution by the *Junta de Medios* in 1779, in Canga Argüelles 1827, v. 4, 43–44.
36 Real Cédula, San Ildefonso, August 17, 1780 (first of this date), Real Academia de la Historia, Colección Mata Linares, CIX, ff. 120–122.
37 Real Cédula, August 17, 1780 (second of this date).
38 Marichal 1990, 887.
39 Resolution by the *Junta de Medios* in 1779, in Canga Argüelles 1827, v. 4, 43–44.
40 On the role played by the Bank of San Carlos, see Calderón Quijano, 1962, 43; Torres Sánchez, 2006, 145.
41 Treaty of Defensive and Offensive Alliance Between the Crowns of Spain and France Against that of England (Tratado de alianza defensiva y ofensiva celebrado entre las coronas de España y Francia contra la de Inglaterra), Aranjuez, April 12, 1779.
42 For general considerations on the Spanish strategy, see Chávez 2010.
43 Diego José Navarro, memorandum included in an official letter copy, Havana, June 27, 1779, AGI, Santo Domingo 2082.
44 Diego José Navarro to José de Gálvez, confidential official letter n. 105, Havana, February 26, 1780, AGI, Santo Domingo 2082.
45 José de Gálvez to Diego José Navarro, Aranjuez, May 21, 1780, AGI, Santo Domingo 2082.
46 José de Gálvez to Bernardo de Gálvez, most confidential official letter draft copy, San Lorenzo, November 16, 1781, (3rd of this date), AGI, Indiferente General 1578.
47 WC, RA, GEO/MAIN/44612, Prince William to George III, January 26, 1780.
48 Lord Shelburne to the King, September 13, 1782, in Fortescue 1927–1928, vol. VI, p. 123 (no. 3918); King to Shelburne, September 14, 1782, in ibid., p. 126 (no. 3919).
49 King to Shelburne, September 16, 1782, in Fortescue 1927–1928, vol. VI, p. 128 (no. 3923).
50 King to Shelburne, November 21, 1782, in Fortescue 1927–1928, vol. VI, p. 159 (no. 3987); King to Shelburne, December 2, 1782, in ibid., vol. VI, p. 168 (no. 4002).
51 Grantham to King, December 3, 1782, in Fortescue 1927–1928, vol. VI, p. 169 (no. 4005); King to Grantham, December 11, 1782, in ibid., p. 183 (no. 4020).
52 King to Shelburne, December 11, 1782, in Fortescue 1927–1928, vol. VI, p. 183 (no. 4021); on this December 1782 diplomatic moment, see Conn 1942, 220–221.
53 Bernardo de Gálvez to José de Gálvez, dispatch, New Orleans, October 16, 1779 (second of this date), AGS, SGU, leg. 6912, 1. *Gazeta de Madrid*, December 12, 1778.
54 José de Gálvez to Diego José Navarro, confidential letter, San Ildefonso, August 29, 1779, AGI, Cuba, 1290.
55 *Extracto de lo acaecido en la expedición hecha por el brigadier d. Bernardo de Gálvez, gobernador de la provincial de Luisiana, contra los establecimientos y fuertes que tenían los ingleses sobre el río Mississippi, que consiguió tomarles desalojándolos enteramente*, in Diego José Navarro to José de Gálvez, official letter no. 633, Havana, November 11, 1779 (1st of this date), AGI, Santo Domingo, 2082B. José de Gálvez to Diego José Navarro, confidential letter, San Ildefonso, August 29, 1779, AGI, Cuba, 1290. See also: Beerman and Din, 1996, 200; Caughey 1934 [1998], 163; Chávez 2002, 172; Thomas 1981, 41; Ward 2011, 201, 678.
56 Jerónimo Girón Moctezuma to the king, Sevilla, January 24, 1789, AGS, SGU, leg. 6915, 13.
57 Depending on the source, the size of the British garrison varies from 162 (Return of the Killed, Wounded and Prisoners of the Garrison of Forte Charlotte, Mobile,

Surrendered to Spain by Capitulation the 14th day of March 1780, Pensacola, August 26, 1780, PRO, CO 5/597) to around 300 (Hamilton 1897, 252). The Spanish sources mention 126 men: 113 soldiers and 13 officers (Relación de los oficiales, tropas y demás individuos hechos prisioneros de guerra en el sitio de la Mobila, Mobila, March 20, 1780, AGI, Cuba, 2351).

58 General John Campbell to General Sir Henry Clinton, Pensacola, February 12, 1780, PRO, America and West Indies, 137, f. 241.
59 Articles of Capitulation, Mobile (*Artículos de Capitulación propuestos por D. Elías [sic] Durnford, Esq. Teniente de Gobernador de la provincia de la Florida del Oeste, capitán de ingenieros y comandante de las tropas de Su Majestad Británica en el fuerte Charlota de la Mobila, acordados por el Sr. D. Bernardo de Gálvez, caballero pensionado de la Real y Distinguida Orden de Carlos Tercero, Brigadier de los ejércitos de Su Majestad, Inspector, Intendente y Gobernador General de la provincia de la Luisiana y General de la expedición*), Mobile, March 13, 1780, In Gálvez 1780.
60 John Adams to the Count de Vergennes, Paris, July 13, 1780. In Wharton 1889, v. 3, 849.
61 William C. Houston to William Livingston, Philadelphia, June 5, 1780, in Smith 1976–2000, v. 15: 252–53.
62 John Campbell to Lord George Germain, Pensacola, January 5, 1781, PRO, Colonial Office, Series 5/597; John Campbell to Sir Henry Clinton, January 5, 1781, British Headquarters Papers, 9899, reel 27. In Starr 1976, 187. José de Ezpeleta to Bernardo de Gálvez, Mobile, January 19 and 22, 1781, AGS, SGU, leg. 6912, 4.
63 "The king rewards Fernando de Leyva and Francisco Cartabona for their valiant defense of St. Louis (San Luis de Ilionenses)," in *Gazeta de Madrid*, no. 14, February 16, 1781.
64 Representación que ha hecho el mariscal de campo don Bernardo de Gálvez ... AGS, SGU, leg. 6912, EX3.
65 Estado de fuerza del Regimiento Inmemorial del Rey, Havana, August 28, 1780, AGI, Santo Domingo, 2082.
66 Copies of the letter exchanged between Bernardo de Gálvez and Victorio de Navia in Diego José Navarro to José de Gálvez, Havana, October 17, 1780, AGI, Santo Domingo, 2082.
67 *Escuadra del mando del Señor Don José Solano, Jefe de esta clase de la real Armada, y buques de su convoy que transportan la tropa del Ejército a las órdenes del Mariscal de campo el Señor Don Bernardo de Gálvez*, aboard the San Juan Nepomuceno, at sea close to Havana's port, October 16, 1780, AGS, Marina 420.
68 *Estado general que manifiesta los oficiales y tropa que se embarcó en la expedición del mando del mariscal de campo d. Bernardo de Gálvez, que dió vela de este puerto el 16 de octubre de 1780, y parajes a que han arribado hasta hoy día de la fecha a resultas del temporal que experimentó desde el 18 al 23 del mismo mes*, in Diego José Navarro to José de Gálvez, official letter no. 894, Havana, November 20, 1780, AGI, Santo Domingo, 2082; Diego José Navarro to José de Gálvez, official letter no. 898, Havana, November 28, 1780, AGI, Santo Domingo 2082; José de Ezpeleta to Pedro Piernas, official letter, Mobile, November 6, 1780, AGI, Cuba 2.
69 Bernardo de Gálvez to José de Gálvez, official letter, Pensacola, May 12, 1781, AGS, SGU, 6913, Ex3.
70 *Estado que manifiesta los Buques de Guerra y Comboy [sic], del mando del Capitán de Navío, Don José Calvo de Irazábal en el que se conduce el Ejército que, a las órdenes del Sr. Don Bernardo de Gálvez, Mariscal de Campo, se dirige al socorro de la Movila y conquista de Panzacola*, Havana, February 17, 1781, AGS, Marina 421; *Estado que manifiesta los Buques en que se han embarcado las tropas destinadas a las órdenes del mariscal de Campo D. Bernardo de Gálvez, que dieron vela el día de la fecha*, Havana, February 28, 1781, AGI, Santo Domingo, 2083A; *Tropa*

que se ha embarcado a la orden del Mariscal de Campo Don Bernardo de Gálvez en la Habana, Havana, February 28, 1781, AGI, Cuba, 1377.
71 Gálvez *"Diario de las operaciones ..."* (first manuscript), AGS, SGU, 6913, Ex3; *Estado de los oficiales y tropa que, al mando de d. Cayetano de Salla, teniente coronel del Regimiento de Soria, sale de esta Plaza para la Expedición a Panzacola con expresión de presentes y enfermos*, New Orleans, February 28, 1781, AGI, Cuba 563; *Estado que manifiesta los oficiales y tropa que de la Nueva Orleans, salieron el 3 de este mes al mando del teniente coronel d. Cayetano de Salla, con expresión de los que quedan en aquel hospital y buques en que va cada uno, a bordo de la saetía San Francisco de Paula de Escardó*, March 23, 1781, AGI, Cuba 81. They are four versions of Bernardo de Gálvez's journal: two in manuscript form and two in printed form. The first version (manuscript): "Diario de las operaciones de la expedición contra la Plaza de Panzacola concluida por las Armas de S.M. Católica bajo las órdenes del Mariscal de Campo D. Bernardo de Gálvez," Bernardo de Gálvez to José de Gálvez, official letter, Pensacola, May 12, 1781, AGS, SGU, 6913, Ex3. The second version (manuscript): "Diario de las operaciones que ejecuta la expedición del mariscal de campo comandante general de ella del 9 de marzo al desembarco en la isla de Santa Rosa," s.l, s.a., no signature, in AGS, SGU, 6913, Ex12. The third version (printed): August 10, 1781, issue of the *Gazeta de Madrid*. The fourth version (printed) is an offprint from the first printed edition with identical text but no date or place of publication.
72 Gálvez, *Diario de las operaciones de la expedición contra la Plaza de Panzacola concluida por las Armas de S.M. Católica bajo las órdenes del Mariscal de Campo D. Bernardo de Gálvez*, first manuscript version. In Bernardo de Gálvez to José de Gálvez, official letter, Pensacola, May 12, 1781. AGS, SGU, 6913, Exp. 3. Saavedra's Diary, entry of April 22, 1781 (Saavedra 2004,172). *Lista de oficiales franceses que bajaron a tierra de la escuadra del caballero de Monteil. Hace presente en dicha lista se expresan las gracias que los unos esperan de su soberano por la intercesión de nuestro monarca y que los otros se recomienda [sic] a las que SM se sirva dispensarles*, in Bernardo de Gálvez to José de Gálvez, dispatch no. 25, Pensacola, May 26, 1781 (first of this date), AGI, Santo Domingo, 2548, and AGS, SGU, leg. 6913, 4.
73 Articles of Capitulation Between his Excellency Don Bernardo de Gálvez, Knight Pensioner of the Royal and Distinguished order of Charles III, Major-General of the armies of his Catholic Majesty, Inspector, Intendant, and Governor General of the Province of Louisiana, and General of the Expedition &c. &c. &c. and His Excellency Peter Chester Esq; Captain-General, Governor, and Commander in Chief in and over his Majesty's province of West Florida, Chancellor and Vice Admiral of the same, &c. &c. &c. and his Excellency Major-General John Campbell, Commander of His Majesty's forces in the said province of West Florida. In *Scots Magazine*, 43 (1781).
74 George Washington to Francisco Rendón, headquarters in front of York, June 8, 1781, in Fitzpatrick 1931–44, v. 9:345. George Washington to Francisco Rendón, headquarters in front of York, October 12, 1781, in Fitzpatrick 1931–44, v. 9:379. Samuel Huntington to George Washington, Philadelphia, July 3, 1781, in Smith 1976–2000, v. 17: 366–67. Edmund Jennings to John Adams, Brussels, March 4, 1782, in *Adams Papers*. Richard Potts to Samuel Hughes, July 24, 1781, in Smith 1976–2000, v. 17: 440–41.
75 Juan Dabán, acting Governor of Cuba, to José de Gálvez, letter no. 240, Havana, May 27, 1782, AGI, Santo Domingo, 2085 B; Bernardo de Gálvez to José de Gálvez, letter no. 133, Guárico, June 30, 1782, in Juan Ignacio de Urriza to José de Gálvez, letter no. 965, Havana, June 10, 1782, AGI, Santo Domingo, 2084.
76 José de Gálvez to Bernardo de Gálvez, extremely confidential order, Aranjuez, April 6, 1782 (third of this date), AGI, Santo Domingo, 2084.
77 The official account of the campaign in *Gaceta de Madrid*, June 12, 1781: 489–490.

78 Manuel del Socorro Rodríguez, *Copia de la representación dirigida a don Pedro de Acuña y Malbar*, Bogotá, April 19, 1793. AGI, Estado, 53, N. 84-H (1a) folios 1r.–4r. English translation from McFarlane 2006, 44.
79 Continental Congress, "Resolution Approving Jay's Conduct in Spain" (April 30, 1782), in Jay 1980, 164.
80 José de Gálvez to the intendente of Havana, to the Governor of Santo Domingo, to the Governor of Puerto Rico, to the intendente of Caracas, to the Governor of Yucatán, to the Governor of Caracas, and to the Governor of Havana, confidential official letter draft copy, San Ildefonso, August 29, 1782. Archivo General de Indias (Seville), Santo Domingo 2188; Juan Ignacio de Urriza, intendente of Havana, to José de Gálvez, letter n. 670, Havana, April 21, 1780. AGI, Santo Domingo 1657; Martín Navarro to Arturo O'Neill, letter n. 90, New Orleans, June 27, 1782. AGI, Cuba 83; Luis de Unzuaga to Bernardo de Gálvez, official letter n. 134, Havana, May 24, 1783. AGI, Indiferente General 1583.
81 Quotation in Delpar 2008, p. 1.
82 Fitz 2016.
83 Jaksic 2007, 6.
84 Ehrmann 1962, 18.
85 Daly 2013, 2.
86 Moreno Alonso 1997.
87 Howarth 2007, 31; Colley 2014.
88 Hay 2013.
89 Bentham 1821, 16.

2 The American Revolution and Spanish America, 1776–1814

Anthony McFarlane

For historians of the Hispanic world, the American Revolution raises several important issues. Seen from the perspective of Spanish history, the main questions relate to Spain's history as an international power. They focus on why Spain became involved in the Thirteen Colonies' war against Britain; how it intervened and to what effect; and, finally, how participation in the war of American affected Spain's strategic position as a colonial power, particularly in the North American continent.[1] Another related but distinct issue, on which I focus here, concerns the repercussions of the American Revolution on Spain's relations with its own American possessions after 1776.[2]

This has, of course, been a question of enduring interest. Around the time of the American Revolution, some contemporaries – notably Raynal and his fellow *philosophes* – saw it as an historical watershed, a political transformation that foreshadowed an unfolding challenge to European monarchies and their overseas empires. Modern historians have taken similar positions, particularly those who have identified an age of 'Atlantic Revolutions' which, pivoted on the European Enlightenment and the American and French Revolutions, brought ideological and political change across Europe and its colonies, and by the mid-1820s collapsed the French, Portuguese and Spanish empires in the Western Hemisphere.[3] This interpretation has been challenged, however, by historians who have focused on political dynamics and political thinking within the Hispanic world itself. Rather than seeing the Spanish American revolutions as expressions of revolutionary ideas emanating from the American and French Revolutions, the advocates of this position stress their origins in an Hispanic political crisis that was triggered by exogenous forces (Napoleon's invasion of Spain in 1808), and developed along ideological and institutional lines that owed more to Hispanic institutions and traditions of political thinking than to the Atlantic revolutions.[4]

Here, to revisit the question of how Spanish America was affected by the American Revolution and the development of the American Republic, I take up a number of inter-connected themes. First, the impact of the American Revolution on thinking about colonial policy in Spanish government circles; second, the relations and parallels between the American Revolution and the Spanish American rebellions of the early 1780s; third, the external influences on political attitudes and behaviour in Spanish America during the era of the

French Revolution; and, finally, the extent to which such influences impinged on politics during the opening stages of the great crisis of the Spanish monarchy in 1808–1814.

The Spanish monarchy and the American Revolution

Conscious of the need to conserve the stability of Spain's American empire, Charles III and his ministers were reluctant openly to support the rebellion of Britain's colonial subjects when they declared independence in 1776. To aid colonial rebels in armed insurrection against their rightful King not only ran against official political instincts, but required a heavy financial and political investment for an uncertain outcome. However, for Bourbon Spain, war against Britain was a tempting opportunity to avenge the military humiliations and territorial losses of the Seven Years War, to arrest British commercial, territorial and strategic expansion in the Western Hemisphere, and to re-assert Spain's position as a leading imperial power. After France entered the war, these geopolitical considerations prevailed: in 1779, Spain declared war on Britain and, in conjunction with its French ally, embarked on an ambitious military strategy in both Europe and the Americas.

What Spain achieved remains a debatable issue. On the one hand, it seems that, by helping to inflict military defeat on its leading rival, Spain recovered prestige and position among the European powers, and earned a respite from the challenge of British expansion. Spain directly and indirectly strengthened its colonial stance too, in military operations which took territory from the Portuguese in the Río de la Plata, curbed British incursions in Central America, recovered Florida from British hands, and, of course, helped to detach the North American colonies from British rule, thereby easing the pressure of British expansion southwards towards Mexico.

On the other hand, Spain's gains did not match the expectations entertained on entering the conflict. The Franco-Spanish invasion of Britain fizzled out; Spain failed to take Jamaica or force Britain out of North America; Charles III recovered Menorca but not Gibraltar; the costs of the war imposed heavy strains of state finances, and ongoing competition with Britain required the continuation of high levels of military expenditure. Nor did Spain's territorial gains at the Treaty of Versailles (1783) stem British expansion. It soon became clear that Britain's North American losses had not seriously damaged its position and power in the Atlantic, nor reduced its capacity to threaten Spain's colonies. British merchants continued to capture Spanish American resources through illegal trade, and by the 1790s British governments were again entertaining ambitions for territorial expansion in Spanish America, whether by conquest or by encouraging Spanish American Creoles to overturn Spanish rule.

Spain had nonetheless made important short-term strategic gains from its involvement in the War of American Independence without incurring the political damage that affected Bourbon France. Spain's initial engagement with the American rebels was carried out covertly, and when Spain declared war on Britain in 1779, it was as an ally of France rather than a partner of rebellious subjects against their King. The American commissioners who arrived in Spain were carefully sequestered from public view, and, in a setting where censorship of matters moral and political was still powerful, Spain's very limited press did not discuss their business or its outcomes. The Spanish public thus knew little of the Bourbon monarchy's support for the American rebellion, and the images and ideas of the American Revolution did not resonate in domestic politics in the way that they did in neighbouring France.[5]

Spain's engagement in the War of American Independence (with financial aid from 1776 and military intervention from mid-1779) did, however, interact with Bourbon policies and Spanish American politics in important ways. First, the onset of Britain's war with its colonies coincided with a major overhaul of colonial policy. Charles III's appointment of Floridablanca as Minister of State and José de Gálvez as Minister of the Indies in 1776 put in place men who were eager to push ahead with reforms aimed at aggrandising the monarchy.[6] These reforms had been gestating since Charles III's accession in 1759, but acquired a fresh momentum when Bourbon ministers, seeing Britain distracted by fighting with its colonies, seized the chance to assert greater control over Spanish America with measures designed to tighten the grip of government, increase fiscal yields, and change the system that regulated Spain's colonial commerce.[7] This overhaul of policy brought, in turn, a political reaction in regions of Spanish America that was in some ways comparable to the response that Britain's reforms had provoked in Anglo-America. The measures taken by the *visitador* of Peru triggered rebellion in the city of Arequipa in September 1780, shortly followed by the much larger, and largely indigenous, rebellion led by Tupac Amaru in the southern Andes. In mid-1781, the *visitador* of New Granada introduced fiscal and administrative reforms that provoked the rebellion of the Comuneros, another large-scale challenge to government authority.

American Revolution and Spanish American rebellions

Given that these rebellions occurred at the time of the American Revolution, it is not surprising that some contemporary observers saw linkages between them. Francisco Saavedra (a high-ranking official responsible for coordinating Spanish operations in the North American war) was quick to see parallels, pointing out that 'the rebellion of the English colonies had its origins in taxes, that of Lima [sic] had the same beginning, and that of Santa Fe also'.[8] Viceroy Flórez of New Granada saw a more direct connection: he stated that the Comunero rebellion was, if not inspired, certainly strengthened by the North American example, given that 'the form of *independencia* won by the English colonies of the North is now on the lips of everyone … in the rebellion'.[9]

Of these opinions, Saavedra's is certainly plausible, given that the rebellions were all triggered by new taxation. There was, moreover, another feature which, although he did not mention it directly, was shared by the rebellions of

North and South America: namely, the defence of long-standing political conventions against metropolitan policies that were made without regard for the opinion and interests of local elites. In fact, this resemblance had surfaced in the previous decade, when, in 1765–1766, riots against the Stamp Act in Boston had coincided with organised rebellion in the city of Quito. In both instances, protest arose from the combination of plebeian grievances against new taxes with creole dislike of metropolitan encroachments in matters where colonials believed they should be consulted.[10] This belief was strongly restated by the Mexico City *ayuntamiento* in 1771, when, after enduring José de Gálvez's heavy-handed intrusions into New Spain's political life during his 1766–1771 *visita*, it petitioned the crown to recognise that Creoles had the right, as heirs of the conquerors and the patriciate of their lands and peoples, to play a primary part in their government.[11] And, then, a few years later, it resurfaced in the early 1780s, when the rebellions in Peru and New Granada, like the North American rebellion, were powered by the convergence of elite political resistance to metropolitan intrusion with plebeian economic grievances triggered by new taxation.[12]

Viceroy Flórez's view that the American Revolution immediately encouraged ideas of independence is less plausible, as the great majority of Spanish Americans knew little about its ideas and actions. Information about the British American rebellion no doubt reached Spanish America via port cities and government capitals, but it is unlikely that such news spread far. In the absence of newspapers to report events or comment upon them, the realm of public knowledge was very constricted, and, if there was some clandestine importation of North American political texts, their dissemination was inevitably very limited. Moreover, even if Spanish American rebel leaders caught echoes of the Anglo-American struggle for independence, their political ideas and behaviour were shaped by social and cultural contexts that were very different from those of the British colonies. Although the Comunero and Tupamarist leaders shared the North American belief that local elites should participate in their own government, their thinking remained on the particularist level of creole patriotism, without the claims to universal rights implanted by Enlightenment thinkers in North America, nor incorporating radical input of the kind injected into the American Revolution by Paine's *Common Sense* and the Pennsylvania Constitution of 1776. At the time of the rebellions in New Granada and Peru, the radical political ideas of the Enlightenment had scarcely entered Hispanic America, and the rebellions drew on older traditions, both Hispanic and indigenous.

The language and ideas revealed in the few texts which circulated among the Comuneros were rooted in Hispanic political culture, where the authority of the King and the Catholic Church were beyond doubt. Comunero leaders referred to the contractualist idea of an 'unwritten constitution', a pact between the King and his subjects that they believed to derive from the Spanish conquerors' special privileges and to have been enshrined in the practices of Habsburg government. At no point did they challenge the authority of the monarchy; on the contrary, they appealed to the King to defend the 'common good' against the depredations of 'bad ministers'. Their embrace of a monarchy that rested on God, the King, and the *común* (or commonwealth) was reflected in their mobilising slogan, 'Long live the King and down with bad government.' Neither leaders nor followers conceived of overturning the monarchy, still less creating an independent republic; their intention was simply to restore a political relationship which had been disturbed by Bourbon reform of taxes and traditional practices of government.[13]

Tupac Amaru's rebellion in the Cuzco region, and the related rebellions in Upper Peru (at Chayanta, La Paz and Oruro), sprang from similar ways of thinking. Tupac Amaru began his rebellion in the King's name and sought to attract Creole support by appealing to the same idea that animated New Granada's Creoles: that of a pact between King and subjects, which allowed for recognition of local interests and participation in their own government. Cuzco's creole elites had long been jealous of the social and political privileges associated with their descent from the conquerors of Peru, and the indigenous nobles of Cuzco, who had preserved their privileges by collaboration with Spanish rule, shared this sense of entitlement to political privilege in the 'Kingdom of Peru'. Cuzco's sense of a special role was, moreover, reflected in and sharpened by the 'Inca revival' of the eighteenth century. Books and paintings that glorified Inca history and culture reinforced the elites' sense that their historical legacy equipped them to govern in the King's name. Thus, when Tupac Amaru launched his rebellion, he actively sought to build political alliances with Cuzco's Creoles and mestizos on the grounds that they shared a common cause, and he frequently used the term 'peruanos' to suggest that he was acting in the name of all the King's subjects in the Kingdom of Peru. His rebellion was, in short, neither nationalist nor anti-monarchical; it envisaged the preservation of an old order in which creole and Indian nobles exercised local power in the King's name. In fact, Tupac Amaru embraced the idea of kingship, accepted the Spanish monarch as a 'señor natural', and was committed to preserving the social hierarchy.

His rebellion was, nonetheless, quite different from that of the Comuneros in both its social base and the ideas which animated the indigenous peasantry. The tradition of community leadership by caciques allowed Tupac Amaru to mobilise mass support among communities, and the idea of an Inca political revival provided images and a language that helped to bind indigenous leaders to their communities, and to bind community to community in support of a common cause. This mass mobilisation among the indigenous peasantry gave Tupac Amaru's rebellion another special feature too. Massive indigenous insurgency meant that it soon outran Tupac Amaru's plans, and, infused with millenarian ideas, turned a rebellion against Spanish policies into a violent challenge to Hispanic social dominance, with considerable revolutionary potential.[14]

The radicalisation of rebellion among the indigenous peasantry was most obvious among the rebels of Chayanta and La Paz, whose leaders associated themselves with Tupac Amaru, formed loose alliances with his leadership, and continued to extend the rebellion after his death. Their rebellion differed, however, from the Tupamarist movement of the Cuzco region, as they sprang from distinctive social and cultural roots, displayed different forms of behaviour, and pursued different goals. In Chayanta, the rebellion was rooted in the localised protests of indigenous communities during previous years, especially over the question of community rights to choose their own chiefs, in place of those forced upon them. The rebels were less about concerned about Bourbon policies than about local forms of exploitation that weighed heavily on communities, and they appealed to the crown against their local rulers in the hope of re-establishing the old 'pact of reciprocity' practised under Habsburg rule. They looked to the revival of Indian corporate rights, rather than an Inca restoration, and their challenge to the existing order only emerged gradually as community participation widened. The La Paz rebellion, on the other hand, was socially radical and violent from the start. It was not based on traditional community structures like those of Cuzco and Chayanta, and it participants did not attempt to make alliances outside the indigenous world. Instead, they immediately turned against the Creoles and mestizos whom they saw as their exploiters and launched into a race war. These rebels thus embarked on a course that was akin to an anti-colonial movement, in that, by attacking whites, they were also challenging the social hierarchy which upheld Spanish rule. In the end, they did not succeed: driven by local concerns and social hatreds, these uprisings were, like *jacqueries* in Europe, prone to splinter and collapse before they could construct an alternative political order, and were suppressed with considerable violence.[15]

Clearly, then, the differences between Spanish American rebellions of the early 1780s and the American Revolution were greater than their similarities. Although all were influenced by the idea that the descendants of Europeans in the Americas had the same rights as the King's subjects in the European realms of the monarchy, the rebellions in New Granada, Peru and Upper Peru evidently had more in common with each other than with the American Revolution. Formed within a mesh of ideas embedded in the laws and practices of Habsburg monarchy and the Catholic Church, they were shaped by political cultures that were, as yet, impermeable to the modern ideas of the American Revolution. So, when the American Revolution expressed modern ideas about universal rights, learned from the Enlightenment and embraced by political cultures which had a remarkable degree of freedom under colonial rule, such ideas were still largely unknown in Spanish America.

Official reactions to the American Revolution

Although the Comunero and Tupamarist rebellions did not follow the North American example, some Spanish officials saw the American Revolution as a serious threat to the future of Spanish rule. In the first place, the secession of the United States from the British monarchy raised the question of whether Spain could continue to exercise authority over an American empire far larger than the colonies that Britain had lost, despite its great maritime and military power. Bourbon ministers saw the answer in tightening Madrid's control over its American possessions, though they differed about methods. For some, notably José de Gálvez and his allies, the answer lay in more reform, at a faster pace, and over a larger span. Others called for a lighter touch, with fewer restrictions on trade and production, avoidance of new taxes, integration of indigenous peoples as consumers and producers, and fuller recognition of the need to treat Spanish American elites as equal subjects within the monarchy.[16] Both groups understood, however, that the American Revolution had permanently altered the balance of power in the Western Hemisphere, and that its example might inspire Spanish America's Creole elites to see independence as a viable goal.

Some observers were so convinced that the American Revolution was a portent of Spanish America's future that they recommended schemes for reconfiguring the structure of Spanish rule. In November 1781, a month or so after the British defeat at Yorktown, Francisco Saavedra observed that 'the fate of the Indies has been altered greatly with the rebellion of the Anglo-Americans and the independence that they are probably securing', and he advised that Spain 'make many changes in the system that, up to this point, she has observed in her colonies'.[17] José de Ábalos, a prominent official in Venezuela, suggested reform on a grander scale. In September 1781, he wrote to the King to suggest that, in the light of the British American colonial war and the Spanish American rebellions, Spain should make comprehensive changes to the structure of the empire.[18]

Ábalos's proposal was that Spain should retain its most flourishing colonies, while establishing four self-governing kingdoms ruled by Bourbon princes in the Philippines, Peru and Río de la Plata, all regions that he judged to be particularly difficult to govern from Spain. To support his scheme, Ábalos argued from historical example and recent experience. In his view, history showed that empires inevitably declined, sometimes rapidly, and he pointed out that, having lost European territory in the past (in Italy, the Low Countries, and Portugal), it was obvious that Spain would be unable indefinitely to conserve its much larger and more distant dominions overseas. If Britain could not control colonies that were much smaller and closer, Ábalos asked, what hope had Spain to continue ruling territories which were far larger than Britain's, farther from the metropolis, and of much greater diversity of climate and custom? He also pointed to the recent experience of rebellion to show that Spain's colonial subjects were displaying a 'spirit of independence'. The Tupac Amaru rebellion was, he argued, evidence of how deeply corruption and injustice among Spanish officials had alienated the King's American subjects, and he stated his belief that the rebellion would have been impossible to defeat if it had been led by 'a high-ranking white'. As for the Comunero rebellion, it should not be dismissed as just an improvised anti-tax rebellion, but seen for what it was: a premeditated attempt to raise a general insurrection, including the seizure of a Caribbean port and an attempt to seek foreign aid. Moreover, according to Ábalos, the transformation of the empire into a network of associated monarchies, whose kings were related by blood and joined by treaties of friendship and commerce, would benefit both Spain and the new kingdoms. Spain would escape the heavy costs of defending its possessions from frequent foreign attack, and break free from the drag of imperial responsibilities which had made it less prosperous than in the times of the Catholic kings; the new kingdoms would flourish under self-government, and would in time make 'great discoveries in Africa, Asia and the Austral region for the expansion of their crowns, in reward for their religion, and their zeal in propagating true beliefs'.[19]

Ábalos was not alone in suggesting radical surgery to save the Spanish monarchy. On the eve of Spain's entry into war with Britain in 1779, the Conde de Aranda (Spain's ambassador to France in 1773–1787) observed that the American Revolution would change the balance of power to such a degree that Spain should pre-empt colonial rebellion by changing its system of overseas government.[20] At the end of the war, in 1783, he advised King Charles III that, to avert a comparable rupture in Spain's empire, he should establish a dynastic confederation composed of three independent kingdoms (New Spain, Peru and Costa Firme), each ruled by a Spanish *infante*, with the King of Spain as emperor of the whole.[21] Some historians question the authenticity of the *Memorial de Aranda*,[22] but, even if he was not the author of the text, Aranda was certainly aware of the contemporary debate about the future of Europe's empires and convinced that the Spanish monarchy needed serious restructuring. For, in 1786, he suggested to Floridablanca that Spain's interests might best be served by seeking, in some future international negotiation, a radical reorganisation of its territorial holdings. Spain, said Aranda, should consolidate its strength in Europe by exchanging Peru for Portugal, while establishing a Spanish *infante* as a king in Buenos Aires.[23]

These proposals were not necessarily meant to be taken literally; their authors no doubt realised that short-term interests would prevail. They are, rather, best understood by reference to their political and intellectual contexts. In the court of Charles III, emphasis on the subversive potential of the American Revolution was a useful rhetorical device, since, by underscoring the imperative for colonial reform, it matched the reformist agenda of the King and his ministers. Blaming the American Revolution for destabilising Spain's colonies had another function, too: it deflected responsibility for colonial rebellion away from the King and his government, and underlined the need to design reforms that would reconcile Spanish hegemony with a measure of autonomy for Spanish American elites. The idea of devolving authority in an imperial confederation also suggests that Ábalos and Aranda were well aware of the contemporary British and French debate about empire, which tended to represent the traditional European empires as economically and socially wasteful, and doomed to decline.[24]

It is very likely that these men (and other Spaniards interested in contemporary political economy) were familiar with Enlightenment critiques of empire, largely because of the success of Raynal's *Histoire Philosophique*, a work that became increasingly famous as it went through successive editions in the 1770s and early 1780s.[25] Raynal's work was not available in Spanish during these years, for, although the Duque de Almodóvar published Spanish translations under Raynal's title (from 1784 to 1790), they were in fact a heavily modified version of the work, with a different structure and different purposes.[26] We can, nonetheless, be confident that, in these years when ideas about history, society and politics (as well as the natural sciences) were increasingly exchanged across borders, French editions of the works of the *philosophes* circulated among Spanish intellectuals and statesmen, who, like their European peers, scanned foreign political writings for ideas and practices which they might usefully adopt for the advantage of their own states. Certainly Aranda would have been fully aware of the *Histoire* and its critique of empire, for, during his time as Spain's ambassador in Paris, he was well-connected to prominent intellectual and political figures. About Ábalos we know less, but, as a high-ranking official, it is likely that his response to the American Revolution had also been inflected by contemporary debates about the future of European empires.[27]

Spanish American reactions to North American independence

If leading Spanish officials were quick to see how the American Revolution might affect the future of Spain's empire, so too were some Spanish Americans, as the idea of independence took on new meaning. In his work *The Law of Nations* (1758), Vattel had given the concept of independence a positive meaning, as a term that described the autonomy of one political community among others.[28] The success of the American Revolution helped to promote the spread of this new concept in Spanish America, where 'independence' came to mean the secession from rule by an overseas monarchy of the kind carried out by Britain's North American colonies.[29] This concept makes an early appearance in the early 1780s – together with the notion that it might best be secured by British military intervention – in a text by the New Granadan Pedro Fermín de Vargas. In his *Diálogo entre Lord North y un filósofo*, Vargas not only extolled independence as an honourable cause, but called on the British to give up their American colonies and then liberate those of the other nations in Caribbean and South America.[30] The text suggests that, among a small minority at least, the American Revolution had added a new dimension to political discussion, not only because it had established an independent republic but also because it had shown how inter-power rivalry could contribute to that end.

At the time of the American Revolution, the most active proponent of the idea of enlisting foreign aid in support of Spanish American independence was Juan Pablo Viscardo y Guzmán, a Peruvian Jesuit living in Italian exile. Viscardo's call for Spanish American independence was made in 1781, when he wrote to the British consul at Livorno to inform him that Peruvian Creoles would break away from Spain if Britain sent an armed force to aid them. He stated that the current rebellion showed the potential for revolution in Peru, since it reflected the desire among both Creoles and Indians to throw off Spanish tyranny. After centuries of tyrannical rule the Peruvians were incapable of seizing independence by themselves, but could be aroused into action by external military intervention. This was, moreover, in Britain's interest to provide, since it would bring commercial gains that would compensate for its losses in North America.[31]

Vargas's and Viscardo's texts had no public readership at their time of writing, but they show how the coincidence of the American Revolution and the Spanish American rebellions of 1780–1782 allowed creole resentments against Spanish government to be reformulated, moving from the discontents of 'creole patriotism' towards ideas of secession from Spanish rule. At the same time, the American Revolution had demonstrated that independence could be hastened by international intervention. After France and Spain had backed North American independence, Viscardo and Vargas saw that Britain (and perhaps the United States too) might well become allies of Spanish American emancipation, and promoted the idea of using inter-power rivalry as a lever for overturning Spanish rule.

That prospect faded once the American Revolution was over, but it did not disappear. While resident in London, Viscardo dedicated himself to persuading British governments of the benefits of intervention in Spanish American affairs, reinforcing his case for independence by integrating British and French Enlightenment ideas. In his *Projet pour rendre l'Amérique espagnole indépendante* (1790), Viscardo stressed the need for British intervention, but on the grounds that Britain would win moral as well as commercial advantages by liberating Spanish America and helping to create independent states. The *Lettre aux espagnols-americaines* (ca. 1792) went a step further. Viscardo praised the English colonies on their fight for liberty and held up the United States as an example; by now, however, he couched Spanish American independence in the cosmopolitan terms of the Enlightenment. Influenced by Raynal, the *encylopédistes*, and British political economists, he presented the case for independence not as a merely creole concern but as a means to enlarge world trade and thus benefit humanity as a whole.[32]

Viscardo died in obscurity in 1798, but his advocacy for independence, developed in dialogue with the works of Enlightenment anti-colonialists, had growing resonance. At his death, the notion that Spanish America would follow the United States into independence became a commonplace in the public discourses of Britain, France and the United States, where merchants, politicians,and political economists agreed that Spanish American independence was both desirable and feasible. In Spanish America, however, the American Revolution only became a political model three decades later, after 1810, when the creole leaders who displaced Spanish rule adapted elements of American constitutional texts when founding autonomous and independent governments. Until then, innovations in political thinking and changes in attitude towards Spanish rule came, not from direct contacts with the

American Republic, but through cultural changes brought about by the dissemination of 'enlightened' ideas and practices, and by political ideas which, though often inspired by the American Revolution, were refracted through the newer, more far-reaching revolution in France.

Cultural and political change in the later eighteenth century

Some signs of Enlightenment perspectives and ideas are found in Spanish America during the first half of the eighteenth century, but their advance was faster and deeper during the later decades of the century. From around 1760, ideas that challenged traditional science, theology and philosophy became more widespread among the educated elites, together with the enlightened belief that the 'philosophical revolution' had not only transformed ways of understanding Nature, but also opened ways to improve society for the benefit of all its members. In the Hispanic world, Spain was the main source for this shift, which originated in the desire among Spanish intellectuals to overcome Spain's reputation for backwardness, and to connect with European intellectual life. This Spanish variant of Enlightenment had several roots, but its mainstream was bound up with Bourbon regalism.[33]

Reformist ministers who sought to emulate the successes of European rivals encouraged the selective appropriation of ideas that might be tailored to Spanish needs and ambitions, and supported schemes for their propagation. The importation and adaption of Enlightenment ideas flourished under Charles III (1759–1788), when official and cultural elites (including ecclesiastics) propagated reforms of university curricula, schemes for scientific enquiry, and plans for improving agriculture, industry and trade. These elites also established regional associations, such as the famous 'economic societies', which brought noble and bourgeois *ilustrados* together in enquiries into economic and social issues; they also contributed to the development of a periodical press dedicated to discussing and disseminating 'useful knowledge'.[34] The reformist trends of the Peninsula extended to Spanish America, too. Educational reform brought Newtonian physics and Linnaean botany into university curricula; crown-sponsored scientific and mining expeditions stimulated creole interest in the 'useful sciences'; the creation of new periodicals provided forums for circulating official news and projects for economic improvement; new associations (not only 'economic societies' and merchant *consulados* but also the more informal salons or *tertulias*) gave educated elites opportunities to discuss social and political issues.

While Bourbon ministers hoped to tailor Enlightenment ideas to the purposes of the state, they were unable to obviate interest in its political aspects, given that the educated minorities who engaged with modern science and political economy were also interested in the new interpretations of history, society and politics that came from the pens of the *philosophes*. This was not necessarily inimical to Spain's monarchy or empire. Enlightenment in the Hispanic world was, like 'enlightenments' elsewhere, compatible with contending political positions. On the one hand were those who fitted into the mould of the 'Moderate Enlightenment', interested in change controlled by elites who would extend the benefits of scientific advances to society from the top down, without challenging religion or disrupting the existing social and political order. A 'Radical Enlightenment', on the other hand, opposed revelation and religion, denied that human moral values were divinely inspired, and saw freedom of thought and equality as the governing principles of any legitimate political system.[35] Ideas of this kind were adopted by intellectuals who harnessed popular discontents to plans for political and cultural transformation; their political impact was evident in both the American and French Revolutions.[36]

In Spanish America, the balance between Moderate and Radical Enlightenments was heavily weighted in favour of the former. Enlightened officials of State and Church, imbued with regalist ideas, encouraged schemes for bringing modern science and philosophy into universities, and sought to encourage Creoles to take up the practice of scientific methods and their application to the discovery and exploitation of material resources. Thus, for example, after the Comunero rebellion, the Archbishop-Viceroy took steps to co-opt creole intellectuals by patronage of enlightened reform in New Granada. His support for university reform, and for the Expedición Botánica and various other knowledge-gathering projects, reflects official recognition of the need to include Creoles in Bourbon plans to strengthen and unify the Spanish empire.[37] At the same time, official censorship made it difficult for Creoles to obtain prohibited literature (the Index encompassed a very wide range of writings, many devoid of radical political content), as did the high costs of books and infrequency of book sellers. Inventories of books and searches of personal libraries by the authorities in New Granada and Venezuela suggests that the practice of reading was highly eclectic, mixing religious works, the Hispanic literary canon, and contemporary scientific, legal and political texts.[38] The presence of prohibited works was rare, even among bibliophiles such as Antonio Nariño, a creole patrician of Bogotá who mixed the roles of book seller, printer and government official. Although he was keen to acquire and distribute Enlightenment texts among a growing readership, his personal library of some 1,600 books held only 25 that were on the Index. Moreover, interest in such works did not necessarily generate subversive political intentions. Throughout Spanish America, *ilustrados* tended to focus around themes that had political implications, but which remained firmly within the bounds of Bourbon reformism: the comparison of pre-Columbian indigenous societies to Europe's ancient past; the comparability of Old and New World environments and peoples; the analysis of natural resources and their exploitation for social benefit, were key areas for enlighteners, the great majority of whom were, as members of social elites, more interested in reform than revolution.[39]

Enlightened debate could not be entirely confined, however, to the purposes of Church and State. Creole intellectuals sought out Enlightenment texts that were banned for their supposedly heretical and subversive content, and access to such literature provided new, critical perspectives on their experience of

Spanish government. Heterodox political ideas probably entered Spanish America in the 1770s, via Creoles who travelled to Europe, acquired prohibited literature, and circulated critical ideas. José de Baquíjano y Carrillo, a Lima noble who had studied in Spain and returned with a library of European books, is a striking example. He caused a scandal in 1781 when, in a eulogy delivered at the viceroy's inauguration, he condemned the Spanish conquest in terms familiar from Raynal's *Histoire Philosophique*, in an act of defiance that led to the seizure and burning of his books. It was also said that suspect texts circulated in New Granada at the time of the Comunero rebellion: according to the Spanish priest Joaquín Finestrad, the rebels had been led astray by subversive works, while the author of the Comuneros' manifesto was steeped in 'the system of reason' that challenged religion and authority.[40] In fact, at this stage Radical Enlightenment ideas had little intellectual or political weight in Spanish America. For Baquíjano, reference to Raynal was a means of expressing traditional creole resentment at Spanish privilege rather than a justification for rebellion. As for Finestrad's judgement on the Comuneros, he did not distinguish between works of very different kinds (which included Grotius, Raynal and Robertson) nor did he show how they had incited rebellion.[41]

However, during the 1790s, amidst the upheavals caused by the French Revolution, government officials feared that Spanish America was being contaminated with ideas and attitudes that were inimical to empire and monarchy. During the 1780s, the American Revolution and the American Republic were regarded as the principal political toxins. Francisco de Saavedra, the Intendant of Caracas (1783–1788), reported in 1788 that 'there were many indications of emancipation in those countries, that is to say desires for independence', and that the United States 'would serve as the leader, inspiration and model for the rest of that part of the world'.[42] Saavedra also observed that the works of the modern philosophers (including Raynal, Robertson, Rousseau and Voltaire) were widely distributed in Spanish America, bringing about a shift in ways of thinking that was more rapid than in Spain. Although he does not say, the texts of the American constitutions were probably known in Venezuela, possibly through the compilation published in France in 1778 as the *Recueil de Loix Constitutives des États-Unis de l'Amérique*. This was certainly present in Brazil, where in 1789 the conspirators of Minas Gerais plotted to replace Portuguese rule with a republic on the North American model, and in New Granada, where it was later found in Antonio Nariño's library. Indeed, when Manuel del Socorro Rodríguez, the Director of Bogotá's first library and a central figure among the city's Creole intellectuals, warned, in 1793, of the 'dangerous progress which the spirit of sedition and of independence is making on all sides', he observed that the example of the United States was particularly pernicious, since it provided an inspiration for those who espoused enlightened ideas.

Since the establishment of the Anglo-American provinces as a free Republic, the peoples of America have taken on a character which is entirely different from that which they had. All who count themselves as enlightened are enthusiastic panegyrists for the ways of thinking of those (Anglo-American) people: the common coin of erudite discussion groups is to discuss and even to form plans around the means of enjoying the same independence that they enjoy.

What made matters worse was that 'events in France have infused these pernicious reasonings with a new vigour ...' spreading 'the spirit of disloyalty on all sides ...'.[43]

Rodríguez's identification of these dangers arose from the cultural activities of his intellectual acquaintances in Bogotá, who shared readings of the *philosophes*, sought out texts from republican North America and revolutionary France, and discussed the issues of the day in their *tertulias*. Indeed, shortly after Rodríguez reported on these activities, the creole patrician Antonio Nariño (a printer, book dealer and government official in Bogotá) was arrested, along with a group of students, for plotting against the government. The subsequent judicial enquiry revealed a clandestine interest in the 'Constitution of Philadelphia' and the French Assembly's *Déclaration des droits de l'homme et du citoyen*, which Nariño had translated into Spanish and printed for dissemination in and outside Bogotá; he also had a bust of Franklin in his library, accompanied by the motto 'He snatched the lightening from the skies and the sceptre from the tyrant's hand.'[44] Those involved in the supposed plot of 1794 were condemned to harsh punishments and exiled, but, according to Rodríguez, the American Republic continued to be a beacon of subversion. In 1796, he reiterated his denunciation of the United States as a state which promoted revolution and warned that it was 'the meeting place that will strengthen all designs for destroying the good government of our adjacent Spanish dominions'.[45]

During the 1790s, the 'spirit of sedition' which Rodríguez perceived in New Granada appeared in other parts of Spanish America, too. In Quito, Francisco Eugenio de Santa Cruz y Espejo, the secretary of Quito's patriotic society founded in 1792, was arrested for composing subversive pasquinades and imprisoned for sedition in 1795. Minor conspiracies were uncovered in New Spain in 1794, too, one aimed at independence with the aid of the United States, the other with the aid of Britain. In Venezuela, Picornell, a Spanish republican exiled for plotting in Spain, was implicated in a conspiracy at Caracas in 1797, planned by Gual and España, two minor officials inspired by the example of the American Revolution.[46]

These were plots rather than revolts; they did not constitute any serious threat to Spanish rule, nor reveal any underlying swell of rebelliousness among Spanish Americans. They do suggest, however, that the French Revolution had a more direct impact on Spanish American political life than the American Revolution. This was not because the diffusion of revolutionary ideas encouraged the educated elites to seek radical political change in their societies. For, although the enlighteners' commitment to the 'new philosophy' alarmed conservatives, most Creole *ilustrados* limited themselves to the collection and exchange of scientific data, research into material resources, schemes designed to improve the exploitation of local resources, and to bring closer integration into the Spanish commercial system. Indeed, for the *ilustrados*, reform within the monarchy, directed by enlightened elites and patronised by government, was a more acceptable model than the rupture of empire brought about by the French or American revolutions.

That said, the French Revolution had corrosive effects. The Revolution not only disseminated a new and vivid image of 'liberty', but the French Revolutionary and Napoleonic wars imposed considerable strains on Spain's authority over its American territories. In the first place, the revolutions in France and the French Caribbean reinforced the message of the American Revolution: namely, that imperial rule could be overturned and that monarchy was not necessarily the 'natural' order of government. This was especially true in the coastal regions of New Granada and Venezuela, where news of political turmoil in the neighbouring French Caribbean (spread via the movements of traders, soldiers, sailors, prisoners and refugees) and contacts with the republican offshoots of the French Revolution projected an idea of liberty that resonated among blacks and mulattos, while causing fear among whites.[47] Secondly, war between the colonial powers added further elements of instability in regions where the British government – encouraged by British merchants and acting on the intelligence provided by London-based revolutionists such as Francisco de Miranda – tried to provoke Spanish American rebellion by military intervention and insurrectionary propaganda.[48] These were unsuccessful: Miranda's attempt to land a revolutionary expedition in Venezuela in 1806, with ships and men acquired in the United States, was quickly abandoned in the face of superior forces and lack of local support; the unauthorised attack on Buenos Aires, made in the same year by the British naval officer Home Riggs Popham was also repelled by local militias, as were the officially sanctioned attacks that followed in 1807.[49]

Nevertheless, although Spanish American allegiance remained firm in the face of external attack, war with Britain weakened Spanish authority, economically and politically. When Spain was forced to allow neutrals to carry colonial commerce and enter Spanish ports, Spanish Americans not only benefited from freer trade, but encountered citizens from other political systems, particularly from the United States, which became a major neutral carrier. Merchants and sailors from the American Republic not only bore news about their republic and its striking economic progress; some openly preached the virtues of their republic and disseminated copies of its constitutions.[50] The blockage of Spain's commercial system and the concomitant expansion of contraband trade, and the contrast with the rapidly growing United States also reinforced calls for reform modelled on the United States. Valentín de Foronda (Spain's Consul General in Philadelphia in 1801–1807) recommended that Spain follow the example of the United States by divesting itself of its colonies and developing its domestic economy through free trade; Ignacio de Pombo, the Prior of the *consulado de comercio* in Cartagena de Indias wrote a wide-ranging critique of the Spanish colonial system in which he argued that New Granada would prosper only if, like the United States, it had fewer regulations and taxes on production, consumption and commerce.[51] Doubts about Spain's ability to sustain its commercial system were particularly acute in the Caribbean Basin (where the capture of Trinidad in 1797 provided the British with an additional platform for the infiltration of contraband and political propaganda into Venezuela), but also reached the ports of Río de la Plata and the South American Pacific, where illegal trade replaced Spanish commerce.[52]

Turbulence in the international environment, scepticism about Spanish policy, and growing awareness of other forms of government did not, however, generate a movement against Spanish rule in America. Very few Spanish Americans imagined breaking with Spain until the sudden, profound crisis caused by Napoleon's usurpation of the Spanish throne in 1808. Even then, the first response of Spain's subjects throughout the Hispanic world was to rally in defence of the deposed King Fernando VII, in movements shaped more by traditional Spanish political ideas and practices than by the radicalism of the American and French Revolutions. In Spain, urban elites established juntas to govern in the name of Fernando VII, legitimised by the claim that sovereignty reverted to the people in the King's absence.[53] However, following the convocation of a Cortes in 1810, the deputies who acted as representatives for regions in Spain and Spanish America carried through a political revolution. They declared that, as the voice of the people, the Cortes was the repository of national sovereignty, and the representative of a single, united 'Spanish nation' that incorporated the entire Hispanic world. In Spanish America, the elites responded to Spain's political transformation in various ways. Those who defended Spanish authority accepted the authority of the Cortes and its redefinition of the political rules, set out in the 1812 Constitution of Cádiz. Others refused to embrace the new system, and turned to a broader spectrum of constitutional ideas, including those of the United States, as they constructed independent entities of government, outside the orbit of the 'Spanish nation'.

Spanish America, 1810–1814: Hispanic revolutions and Atlantic revolutions

The prominence once given to the connections between the republicanism of the United States and that of the independent states that replaced monarchy in Spanish America during the 1820s has, in recent years, given way to an emphasis on the significance of Hispanic ideas and institutions, notably the assertions of the rights of peoples to retake power in the absence of the King, and ideas of consent based on the principles of natural law.[54] Spain's role in reshaping the political culture of Spanish America has also been underlined by historians who have focused on the effects in Spanish America of the Cortes of Cádiz (1810–1814), where Spanish liberals and deputies who represented Spanish America's regions redesigned the monarchy in a series of debates which led to the Cádiz Constitution of 1812.

The Cádiz Constitution was not, of course, constructed in isolation. It expressed principles drawn from the American and French Revolutions – national sovereignty, individual rights, equality before the law, division of powers, and elections – and was created by liberals who chose between various models of constitutionalism. They disliked the British constitutional monarchy for its aristocratic bias and the power of the executive. They also found the United States Constitution irrelevant to their plans, because of the strength of the executive power and its federalism. Like the Federal Constitution of 1787, the Cádiz Constitution established three separate branches of government, but, unlike the United States Constitution, it accorded them highly unequal powers. For, after the experience of Bourbon absolutism and fear that it might return, liberals aimed to curb the power of the crown and invest it in the Cortes, the parliamentary body where they could introduce and defend their reforms. Thus, in the Cádiz Constitution, the judiciary and executive were both weak, and power was centred in a unicameral legislature. In this, liberals followed the French Constitution of 1791: drawing on ideas learned from the political thought and experience of the French Revolution, they replaced absolutism with constitutional monarchy, but made it a 'republicanised monarchy' where the legislature dominated.[55]

The 1812 Constitution marked a radical break with the past. Subjects became citizens; citizens elected representatives to governing institutions; freedom of expression and a free press amplified the public sphere; the Inquisition was abolished; so too was seigneurial jurisdiction, and in America, indigenous forced labour and payment of tribute. The Cortes did not give citizenship to all Americans; people of African descent were explicitly excluded. It was, however, more inclusive than most contemporary states. A notable difference from the United States was the incorporation of Indians as citizens, which brought large indigenous peasantries into the political community and thus considerably enlarged the social range of political participation. Like the United States, on the other hand, the Spanish Constitution did not abolish slavery. Moreover, the modernity of Cádiz was tempered by tradition in another sense: it not only preserved the principle of a unified monarchy but also enshrined Catholicism as the official religion.[56]

During the decade or so following its promulgation, Spain's 1812 Constitution had considerable influence in Spanish America, mainly because New Spain (Mexico and Central America), Peru, and Quito (modern Ecuador) all remained under Spanish rule, and were therefore incorporated into the framework of government established at Cádiz. Although the Constitution was not fully implemented, it had a lasting impact. By widening political rights and participation, it made Spanish rule more acceptable to elites and populace, stifled interest in political alternatives, and delayed movements towards independence and republicanism until the mid-1820s. The Mexican insurgents looked to the United States as a potential ally and a model for government, but they knew little about its laws and institutions, and made no serious attempt to imitate it.[57] Indeed, New Spain's first independent government was a constitutional monarchy, modelled on Cádiz; the republican alternative, inspired by admiration of the United States, had been suppressed along with the insurgency and had to await Iturbide's overthrow in 1823. Peru remained under Spanish constitutionalist government until 1824, and the United States model did not figure prominently in the debates surrounding its independence.[58] Indeed, during the 1820s, key figures in South American independence (such as San Martín, Belgrano, Camilo Henríquez and Simón Bolívar) were still ready to consider constitutional monarchies for the independent states which they established in Río de la Plata, Peru and New Granada.

Republicanism had considerably more influence outside the regions integrated into the 'Spanish Nation' by the Cortes and the Cádiz Constitution. In New Granada, Venezuela, Río de la Plata and Chile, local elites rejected Spanish authority and established autonomous or independent governments that looked to constitutional models from Britain, France and the United States. In Chile, republicanism was first championed from 1812, under José Miguel Carrera's dictatorship. Carrera brought in a printing press and North American typesetters, and, with the foundation of Chile's first newspapers, republican ideas were more widely publicised. Joel Poinsett, the US agent in Chile, was prominent among advocates for the US model; indeed, he provided Carrera with a draft constitution for Chile. This burst of revolutionary activity was cut short in 1814, when the Viceroy of Peru sent a military force into Chile and restored Spanish rule, but renewed after San Martín liberated the country in 1817. Chile did not immediately become a republic, and, under O'Higgins's leadership, monarchists continued to contend for power. Two political models predominated during the constitutional debates of the 1820s: the British model of parliamentary government and the United States model. The latter was much admired as a successful blend of democracy, political stability and economic progress, and US federalism attracted support in the provinces. However, after years of domestic contention, in which the elites divided between monarchists and different kinds of republican, Chile finally came under an authoritarian leadership and a conservative constitution which, in 1833, repudiated many of the enlightened, liberal reforms previously introduced.[59]

Political leaders who favoured constitutionalism and liberal reform also came to power in the Río de la Plata, but were slow to adopt republicanism. Radicals such as Mariano Moreno wanted to follow the example of republican France, but until 1816 successive governments in Buenos Aires shelved any idea of declaring independence, and, rather than espousing republican ideals, tended to imitate liberal reforms enacted at Cádiz, such as the abolition of the Indian tribute and the inclusion of Indians as citizens. However, in contrast to Spain, where the legislature became dominant, government in Buenos Aires became increasingly centralised, and, using war as a justification for strong government, opposed the provinces' preference for a confederation of city-based governments. When in 1816 the Congress of Tucumán decided to declare independence and drew up a constitution, its members debated a variety of constitutional models. Drawing on British, French and US examples, some favoured constitutional monarchy, while others wanted a republic, with additional differences between those who wanted centralised as opposed to federal government. The Cádiz Constitution exercised an influence, too, although animosity towards Spain prevented it from being openly invoked.[60] When the Constitution of 1819 established a republic – the United Provinces of South America – it decreed that sovereignty resided in the nation, created an executive which might be turned into a constitutional monarchy, and invested considerable power in the central government. It was subsequently voided by provincial rebellion, in 1820, and replaced by a confederation of self-governing states.

In New Granada and Venezuela, on the other hand, admiration for the US republican model was much more noticeable. The juntas established in 1810 were on the same conservative pattern as those in the rest of the Hispanic world, but some moved quickly to outright independence, and between 1811 and 1814 drew up republican and federalist constitutions. This rapid transition suggests that, although the enlightened creole elites were not pressing for independence at the time of the Spanish crisis, they had plenty of ideas about how to construct a new order when the opportunity arose, ideas which they had acquired and discussed covertly in networks which, formed to discuss matters of science and political economy, were from 1808 a medium for the political debate and decision-making that went into the construction of new republics.[61]

North American federalism was a particularly strong influence, since it coincided with Hispanic traditions of local autonomy. Both Venezuela and New Granada's provinces opted for constitutions that drew on the political principles of the American and French Revolutions, defining individual rights to equality before the law and to representation in elected assemblies, and revealing the familiarity with the political ideas of the Enlightenment among the educated elites. They also embraced what they understood as the federalism of the United States, a system congenial to elites who wanted to preserve their local power. When Caracas declared an independent republic (July 1811), it was endowed with a constitution that borrowed heavily from the United States' Federal Constitution of 1787, as the capital tried to pull the provinces of Venezuela together under its leadership. In New Granada, several republics emerged. The United Provinces of New Granada was established under the terms of an Act of Federation that was influenced by both the traditional concept of the pluralist monarchy, composed of equal parts under a single executive, and by the federalism of the United States during its early years as a confederation. In 1811–1812, the Provinces of Cartagena, Tunja and Antioquia adopted republican constitutions that reflected their enthusiasm for the US example, some following Pennsylvania, while others took Maryland, Massachusetts and Virginia as their templates. Bogotá, which led the State of Cundinamarca, diverged: its constitution was a kind of constitutional monarchy (with Fernando VII as 'King of the Cundinamarcans'), before it declared independence in 1813. Cundinamarca's president Antonio Nariño acknowledged the superiority of the Constitution of the United States over any other, but rejected the confederation of equal states favoured by New Granada's other states as completely unsuited to the region's society and circumstances.[62]

Clearly, the United States model had an uneven influence in Spanish America during Fernando VII's interregnum. Where Spain ruled, the monarchical Cádiz Constitution dominated. Where independent states were established, they created constitutions inclined towards republicanism and open to foreign influences, including, but not solely, that of the United States.[63] These proto-republics shared common features, reflecting, like Cádiz, the presence of political principles established by the American and French Revolutions. They differed, however, from Cádiz in significant respects. While the Spanish constitutional was monarchist, centralist and unicameralist, Spanish America's first independent governments tended towards republicanism, federalism and bicameralism.

By 1814, the Spanish and Spanish American revolutions started in 1808–1810 were largely defeated. With Fernando VII's restoration, the Spanish Cortes was abolished, and within a couple of years the insurgencies in Mexico and South America were forced to retreat. Ironically, at this crucial juncture, the United States did not fulfil the fears expressed by Spanish officials after the American Revolution; its governments admitted Spanish American refugees to US cities, and allowed privateering and arms supplies, but they refused to intervene against Spain.[64] In Spanish America, the spirit of the American Revolution was not dead, but it had changed its form. With the emergence of Simón Bolívar and José de San Martín as key military-political leaders, engaged in campaigns of continental liberation, US-style federalism was firmly rejected, and replaced by centralist regimes and constitutions that they believed more suited to the struggle against Spain and the restored monarchies of post-Napoleonic Europe. Nonetheless, although Bolívar rejected the model of the American Republic in favour of constitutions which blended British and Napoleonic influences, he, like other Spanish American Creoles, confronted the same underlying problem that had faced the 'Founding Fathers' of the United States in 1787: namely, how to create a state that was capable of rejecting and resisting European imperialism, while at the same time sustaining the privileges enjoyed by the descendants of Europeans but denied to indigenous and African descendants.[65] In that crucial respect, the American Revolution continued to serve as a model for the republics of Spanish America.

Notes

1 For a recent example, which provides an introduction to the wider historiography on Spain's political and military contributions to North American independence, see Thomas E. Chávez, *Spain and the Independence of the United States: An Intrinsic Gift*, Albuquerque: University of New Mexico, 2002. For Spanish intervention seen through the career of a key military and political actor, see Gonzalo M. Quintero Saravia, *Bernardo de Gálvez, Spanish Hero of the American Revolution*, Chapel Hill, NC: University of North Carolina Press, 2018.
2 For works which address the question: Mario Rodríguez, *La revolución americana de 1776 y el mundo hispánico: Ensayos y documentos*, Madrid: Technos 1976; Merle E. Simmons, *La revolución norteamericana en la independencia de Hispanoamérica*, Madrid: Mapfre, 1992; Anthony McFarlane, 'The American Revolution and the Spanish Monarchy', in Simon P. Newman (ed.), *Europe's American Revolution*, London: Palgrave Macmillan, 2006; Jaime E. Rodríguez O., 'Sobre la supuesta influencia de la independencia de los Estados Unidos en las independencias hispanoamericanas', *Revista de Indias*, LXX:250 (2010), pp. 691–714.
3 The pioneering work on Atlantic revolutions is Robert R. Palmer, *The Age of Democratic Revolution: A Political History of Europe and America, 1760–1800*, 2 vols, Princeton: Princeton University Press, 1959, 1964. For a revised restatement of the position which includes Haiti and Spanish America, see Wim Klooster, *Revolutions in the Atlantic World*, New York: New York University Press, 2009. For an emphatic endorsement of Palmer, see Jonathan I. Israel, *Democratic Enlightenment: Philosophy, Revolution, and Human Rights, 1750–1790*, Oxford: Oxford University Press, 2012, and Jonathan I. Israel, *The Expanding Blaze: How the American Revolution ignited the World, 1775–1848*, Princeton and Oxford: Princeton University Press, 2017.
4 Two works mark the historiographical shift: François-Xavier Guerra, *Modernidad e independencias*, Madrid: Mapfre, 1992; and Jaime E. Rodríguez O., *The Independence of Spanish America*, Cambridge: Cambridge University Press, 1998. For a synthesis, see François-Xavier Guerra, 'Lógicas y ritmos de las revoluciones hispánicas', in François-Xavier Guerra (ed.), *Las revoluciones hispánicas: Independencias americanas y el liberalismo español*, Madrid: Editorial Complutense, 1995.
5 McFarlane, 'American Revolution and Spanish Monarchy', pp. 29–41. On contemporary censorship in Spain, see Philip Deacon, 'Resisting Absolutism: Spanish Intellectual Freedom and its Enemies before 1812', in Stephen G.H. Roberts and Adam Sharman (eds), *1812 Echoes: The Cádiz Constitution in Hispanic History, Culture and Politics*, Newcastle upon Tyne: Cambridge Scholars Publishing, 2013.
6 Allan J. Kuethe and Kenneth J. Andrien, *The Spanish Atlantic World in the Eighteenth Century: War and the Bourbon Reforms, 1713–1796*, Cambridge: Cambridge University Press, 2014, pp. 287–304.
7 At the time that Gálvez was pushing for the introduction of key reforms, he, like all Spanish officials, was aware that Britain's war in its colonies was an unprecedented opportunity. Magallón expressed this mood when in 1776 he backed the immediate introduction of reform to the Spanish system for transatlantic commerce on the grounds that 'the troubles of the English nation with its colonies' provided an opportune moment to change: Stanley and Barbara Stein, *Apogee of Empire: Spain and New Spain in the Age of Charles III, 1750–1789*, Baltimore and London: Johns Hopkins University Press, 2003, p. 159.
8 Noted in his diary in November 1781: Francisco de Saavedra, *The Journal of Don Francisco Saavedra de Sangronis, 1780–1783*, ed. Francisco Morales Padrón, trans. Aileen Moore Topping, Gainesville: University of Florida Press, 1989, pp. 259–261.
9 Flórez to Gálvez, 11 July 1781: quoted in Israel, *The Expanding Blaze*, p. 437.

10 Anthony McFarlane, 'The Rebellion of the Barrios: Urban Insurrection in Bourbon Quito', *Hispanic American Historical Review*, 69:2 (1989), pp. 283–330.
11 David Brading, *The First America: The Spanish Monarchy, Creole Patriots, and the Liberal State*, Cambridge: Cambridge University Press, 1991, pp. 480–483.
12 Anthony McFarlane, 'Rebellions in Late Colonial Spanish America: A Comparative Perspective', *Bulletin of Latin American Research*, 14:3 (1995), pp. 313–339.
13 John L. Phelan, *The People and the King: The Comunero Revolution in Colombia, 1781*, Madison: University of Wisconsin Press, 1978.
14 Charles Walker, *The Tupac Amaru Rebellion*, Cambridge, MA: Harvard University Press, 2014.
15 Sergio Serulnikov, *Revolution in the Andes in the Age of Tupac Amaru*, Durham, NC: Duke University Press, 2013.
16 On reforms after 1783, see Kuethe and Andrien, *The Spanish Atlantic World*, chapter 9.
17 Saavedra, *Journal*, pp. 259–261.
18 José de Ábalos, 'Representación del Intendente Ábalos dirigida a Carlos III, Caracas, September 24, 1781', in Rodríguez, *La revolución americana de 1776 y el mundo hispánico*, pp. 54–63.
19 Ibid., p. 63.
20 Cited by Anthony Pagden, *Lords of All the World: Ideologies of Empire in Spain, Britain and France, c.1500 – c. 1800*, New Haven and London: Yale University Press, 1995, p. 194.
21 'Dictamen reservado que el Excelentísimo Señor Conde de Aranda dio al Rey Carlos III sobre la independencia de las colonias inglesas', in Rodríguez, *La revolución americana de 1776 y el mundo hispánico*, pp. 63–66.
22 For a recent expression of doubt, see José Antonio Escudero López, *El supuesto memorial del Conde de Aranda sobre la independencia de América*, Mexico City: UNAM, 2014.
23 This letter is reproduced in Escudero López, *El supuesto memorial*.
24 For this debate, see Anthony Pagden, *Lords of All the World*, chapters 6–7.
25 On the *Histoire Philosophique* and its intellectual impact on both sides of the Atlantic, see Jonathan I. Israel, *Democratic Enlightenment: Philosophy, Revolution, and Human Rights, 1750–1790*, Oxford: Oxford University Press, 2012, chapter 15. The 1781 edition focused specifically on the American Revolution.
26 Gabriel Paquette, 'Enlightened Narratives and Imperial Rivalry in Bourbon Spain: The Case of Almodóvar's *Historia Política de los Establecimientos Ultramarinos de las Naciones Europeas (1784–1790)*', *The Eighteenth Century*, 48:1 (2007), pp. 61–80.
27 For a sketch of Ábalos's career, see Manuel Lucena Giraldo (ed.), *Premoniciones de la independencia. Las reflexiones de José de Ábalos y el Conde de Aranda sobre la situación de la América española a finales del siglo xviii*, Madrid: Mapfre, 2003, pp. 23–26.
28 David Armitage, 'Declarations of Independence, 1776–2012', in David Armitage, *Foundations of Modern Political Thought*, Cambridge: Cambridge University Press, pp. 215–232.
29 Alejandro San Francisco, 'Independencia: Un concepto político y social en revolución, 1770–1870', in *Independencia: Iberconceptos II, tomo 4: Diccionario político y social del mundo iberoamericano*, edited by Javier Fernández Sebastián, Madrid: Universidad del País Vasco, 2014.
30 This document came to light in 1794, when the authorities searched private papers for subversive writings, but its title suggests that it might have been written during or soon after the War of American Independence. See Pedro Fermin de Vargas, *Diálogo entre Lord North y un filósofo*, cited by Carlos Villamizar Duarte, in 'Libertad', *Iberconceptos II, tomo 5: Diccionario político y social del mundo iberoamericano*. Vargas was a junior official in the administration of New Granada

and a member of a circle of *ilustrados* who engaged in intellectual debates in Bogotá during the 1780s. In public, Vargas's criticism of Spain was confined to advocating policies designed to remove monopolies and other impediments to the economic development of New Granada: see his 'Pensamientos políticos sobre la agricultura, comercio y minas de Santafé de Bogotá' of 1791, in Pedro Fermin de Vargas, *Pensamientos políticos*, Bogotá: Universidad Nacional de Colombia, 1968. In private, he harboured more radical ideas, and subsequently fled the country for the United States. For further details on Vargas, see Rafael Gómez Hoyos, *La revolución granadina de 1810: Ideario de una generación y de una época, 1781–1821*, vol. 1, Bogotá: Temis, 1962, pp. 275–310.

31 There is a substantial historiography on Viscardo. For his writings, Juan Pablo Viscardo Guzmán, *Obra Completa*, 2 vols, Lima: Congreso de la República del Perú, 1998. For an interpretation of his work as an expression of Creole patriotism, D.A. Brading, *The First America*, Cambridge: Cambridge University Press, 1991, pp. 535–540; also Anthony Pagden, *Spanish Imperialism and the Political Imagination*, New Haven and London: Yale University Press, 1990, pp. 117–132.

32 Fidel J. Tavarez, 'Viscardo's Global Political Economy and the First Cry for Spanish American Independence, 1767–1798', *Journal of Latin American Studies*, 48 (2015), pp. 537–564.

33 For an introductory discussion of what constituted the Spanish Enlightenment, see the editor's introduction in Jésus Astigarraga (ed.), *The Spanish Enlightenment Revisited*, Oxford: Voltaire Foundation, 2015, pp. 1–17. For Spanish and Spanish American Enlightenment in the broader context of the Iberian world, see Brian Hamnett, *The Enlightenment in Iberia and Ibero-America*, Cardiff: University of Wales Press, 2017. On the limitations of the Spanish Enlightenment, see Javier Fernández Sebastián, 'Tolerance and Freedom of Expression in the Hispanic World between Enlightenment and Liberalism', *Past and Present*, 211 (May, 2011), pp. 159–166.

34 The classic accounts of the Enlightenment in Spain are Jean Sarrailh, *La España ilustrada en la segunda mitad del siglo XVIII*, trans. Antonio Alatorre, Mexico City: Fondo de Cultura Económica, 1957, and Richard Herr, *The Eighteenth Century Revolution in Spain*, Princeton: Princeton University Press, 1958. On new forms of economic association in Spanish America, see R. J. Shafer, *The Economic Societies in the Spanish World (1763–1821)*, Syracuse: Syracuse University Press, 1958. On the development of the 'public sphere' in Spanish America, see Victor Uribe-Uran, 'The Birth of a Public Sphere in Latin American during the Age of Revolution', *Comparative Studies in History and Society*, 42:2 (2000), pp. 437–448.

35 Jonathan I. Israel, *Democratic Enlightenment: Philosophy, Revolution, and Human Rights, 1750–1790*, Oxford: Oxford University Press, 2012, pp. 1–17.

36 On the Enlightenment and the American Revolution, see Israel, *Democratic Enlightenment*, pp. 442–479.

37 Anthony McFarlane, *Colombia before Independence: Economy, Society and Politics under Bourbon Rule*, Cambridge: Cambridge University Press, 1993, pp. 275–278.

38 For a full analysis of the circulation of books in New Granada and the evolution of reading linked to the Enlightenment, see Renán Silva, *Los ilustrados de Nueva Granada, 1760–1808: Genealogía de una comunidad de interpretación*, Medellín: Banco de la República, Eafit, 2002, chapters 4–5. On the circulation of books and enlightened reading in both New Granada and Venezuela, see Clément Thibaud, *Libérer le Nouveau Monde: La fondation des premières républiques hispaniques (Colombia y Venezuela 1780–1820)*, Bécherel: Les Perséides, 2017, pp. 168–177.

39 For a review of the Enlightenment in New Spain and Peru: Hamnett, *The Enlightenment in Iberia and Ibero-America*, chapters 5–7; for the Río de la Plata: José Carlos Chiaramonte, *La Ilustración en el Río de la Plata: Cultura eclesiástica y cultura laica durante el Virreinato*, Buenos Aires: Punto Sur, 1989, pp. 51–116;

for a major study of the Enlightenment in New Granada, and its political implications, see Renán Silva, *Los ilustrados de Nueva Granada, 1760–1808*. For an important study of the historical debate, see Jorge Cañizares-Esguerra, *How to Write a History of the New World*, Stanford: Stanford University Press, 2001.
40 Israel, *Democratic Enlightenment*, pp. 530–532.
41 Finestrad was a Spanish friar who led a Capuchin mission to re-educate people in the Comunero rebel zone following the rebellion, and wrote an account of it in Joaquín de Finestrad, *El vasallo instruido en el estado del Nuevo Reino de Granada y en sus respectivas obligaciones* (transcription and introduction by Margarita González), Bogotá: Universidad Nacional de Colombia, 2001. On the influence of subversive foreign books, see pp. 42–43. Finestrad's central contention, however, was that the main cause of rebellion was lack of proper religious education and discipline among New Granadans, which led to them to their mistaken belief in a right to rebellion against 'bad government': see pp. 115–130.
42 Francisco de Saavedra, *Los Decenios (Autobiografía de un sevillano de la Ilustración)*, ed. F. Morales Padrón, Sevilla: Ayuntamiento de Sevilla, 1992, p. 207.
43 'Copia de la representación dirigida al Excmo Señor Don Pedro Acuña y Malbar, 19 de abril de 1793': Archivo General de Indias, Sevilla (AGI), Estado 53, no. 84, fols. 93–99; quotations from folio 84.
44 On the 1794 conspiracy, see Anthony McFarlane, 'Science and Sedition in Spanish America: New Granada in the Age of Revolution, 1776–1810', in Susan Manning and Peter France (eds), *Enlightenment and Emancipation*, Lewisburg: Bucknell University Press, 2006. On Nariño's library, Guillermo Hernández de Alba, *El proceso de Nariño a la luz de documentos inéditos*, Bogotá: Editorial ABC, 1958, p. 60.
45 Manuel del Socorro Rodríguez, Santafé de Bogotá, 19 September, 1796: AGI, Estado 53, no. 84, fols. 69–86; quotation from fol. 70.
46 Peggy K. Liss, *Atlantic Empires: The Network of Trade and Revolution*, Baltimore: Johns Hopkins University Press, 1983, pp. 156–168.
47 Thibaud, *Libérer le Nouveau Monde*, pp. 93–97.
48 John Lynch, 'British Policy and Spanish America, 1783–1808', *Journal of Latin American Studies*, 1:1 (1969), pp. 1–30; Thibaud, *Libérer le Nouveau Monde*, pp. 145–151.
49 Anthony McFarlane, *War and Independence in Spanish America*, New York: Routledge, 2014, pp. 29–31.
50 For example, in Chile and Venezuela: see Simon Collier, *Ideas and Politics of Chilean Independence*, pp. 36–39; Thibaud, *Libérer le nouveau monde*, pp. 110–112.
51 Valentín de Foronda, 'Carta sobre lo que debe hacer un príncipe que tenga colonias a gran distancia', Philadelphia, 1803, in Rodríguez, *La revolución americana de 1776 y el mundo hispánico*, pp. 46–54. José Ignacio de Pombo, *Comercio y contrabando en Cartagena*, Bogotá: Universidad Nacional de Colombia, 1986, and Sergio Elías Ortiz (ed.), *Escritos de dos economistas coloniales*, Bogotá: Banco de la República, 1965.
52 On neutral commerce and contraband in New Granada, see McFarlane, *Colombia before Independence*, pp. 298–307. On the wider effects of war on Spanish commerce, see Adrian J. Pearce, *British Trade with Spanish America, 1763–1808*, Liverpool: Liverpool University Press, 2007.
53 José M. Portillo Valdés, *Crisis Atlántica: Autonomía e independencia en la crisis de la monarquía española*, Madrid: Marcial Pons, 2006, p. 56.
54 For a full discussion, see José Carlos Chiaramonte, *Nation and State in Latin America*, trans. Ian Barnett, New Brunswick and London: Transaction Publishers, 2012, especially chapter 3.
55 Joaquín Varela Suances, 'Los modelos constitucionales en las Cortes de Cádiz', in Guerra (ed.), *Las revoluciones hispánicas: Independencias americanas y el liberalismo español*.

56 On the significance of tradition in Spain's first constitutional debates, see Brian Hamnett, 'The Medieval Roots of Spanish Constitutionalism', in Scott Eastman and Natalia Sobrevilla Perea (eds), *The Rise of Constitutional Government in the Iberian Atlantic World: The Impact of the Constitution of 1812*, Tuscaloosa: University of Alabama Press, 2015.
57 Antonio Ávila, 'Pensamiento republicano hasta 1823', in José Antonio Aguilar and Rafael Rojas (eds.), *El republicanismo en Hispanoamérica: Ensayos de historia intelectual y política*, Mexico City: Fondo de Cultura Económica, 2002.
58 Natalia Sobrevilla Perea, 'Loyalism and Liberalism in Peru', in Eastman and Sobrevilla Perea (eds), *The Rise of Constitutional Government*.
59 Collier, *Ideas and Politics of Chilean Independence*, chapters 3–5, 8–9.
60 Marcela Ternavasio, 'The Impact of Hispanic Constitutionalism in the Río de la Plata', Eastman and Sobrevilla Perea (eds), *The Rise of Constitutional Government*, pp. 133–149.
61 Thibaud, *Libérer le nouveau monde*, pp. 217–221.
62 On adhesion to US-style federalism in New Granada, see Anthony McFarlane, 'Building Political Order: The First Republic in New Granada, 1810–1815', in Eduardo Posada-Carbó (ed.), *In Search of a New Order: Essays on the Politics and Society of Nineteenth-Century Latin America*, London: Institute of Latin American Studies, 1998. For a full analysis of the emergence of the early independent states, Daniel Gutiérrez Ardila, *Un Nuevo Reino: Geografía política, pactismo y diplomacia durante el interregno en New Granada (1808–1816)*, Bogotá: Universidad Externado, 2010, Part II. The early constitutions are reproduced in Manuel Antonio Pombo and José Joaquín Guerra, *Las constituciones de Colombia*, 2 vols, Bogotá, 1951: Biblioteca Popular de Cultura Colombiana; also Daniel Gutiérrez Ardila (ed.), *Los asambleas constituyentes de la independencia: Actas de Cundinamarca y Antioquia (1811–1812)*, Bogotá: Universidad Externado, 2010.
63 For a sceptical view of US influences on Spanish American constitution-making, see Jaime E. Rodríguez O., 'Sobre la supuesta influencia de la independencia de los Estados Unidos en las independencias hispanoamericanas', pp. 702–706.
64 Piero Gleijeses, 'The Limits of Sympathy: The United States and the Independence of Spanish America', *Journal of Latin American Studies*, 24:3 (1992), pp. 481–505.
65 On the underlying similarities of political positions taken by Creoles in North and South America, see Joshua Simon, *The Ideology of Creole Revolution: Imperialism and Independence in American and Latin American Political Thought*, Cambridge: Cambridge University Press, 2017, especially chapter 2.

3 The rise and fall of the Spanish–French Bourbon armada, from Toulon to Pensacola to Trafalgar

Larrie D. Ferreiro

The Bourbon Family Compacts

The Bourbon armada, the combined forces of the French *Marine Royale* and the Spanish *Real Armada*, had its roots in the Bourbon Family Compacts, a series of three treaties between France and Spain that lasted from 1733 until 1792. These treaties were the result of the War of the Spanish Succession (1701–1714), fought between two coalitions led by (respectively) Britain and France, over whether a Habsburg or a Bourbon would control the Spanish Empire. It ended with a Bourbon king, Felipe V, firmly ensconced on the Spanish throne. At the same time, the *Real Armada* was formed when Spain's nine previously separate fleets were combined into one centralized navy. Almost immediately upon the end of the war, France and Britain created the Anglo-French Alliance as a hedge against the newly upstart Spain. This period of relative peace lasted until 1731, when Britain entered into a new alliance with Austria, at the time France's adversary (Black, 1997). The young French King Louis XV knew that he needed a powerful partner to face the British–Austrian alliance. Spain had also found itself vulnerable against the same alliance, so it was perhaps inevitable that the two nations, united by a common adversary and by family ties (both were descended from Louis XIV; Felipe V was Louis XV's uncle) would join forces.

On November 7, 1733, the first Bourbon Family Compact between the two nations was signed in the Spanish palace of El Escorial outside Madrid. The treaty agreed that the two nations would "act in concert" to promote their mutual interests, and support each other in gaining new territories—the Duchy of Lorraine for France, and the Kingdoms of Naples and Sicily for Spain. The Treaty of El Escorial (the official title of the first Compact) was quite far-reaching, providing, among other things, that France would support Spain's claims on several Italian states and Gibraltar. Spain, emboldened by the Family Compact, immediately sent forces in 1733 and 1734 to capture the Italian islands of Ischia and Procida, and conquered the Kingdoms of Naples and Sicily. The only joint operation that France and Spain carried out under the First Family Compact was not naval but scientific; the Geodesic Mission to the Equator (1735–1744), in which French and Spanish scientists proved that the Earth was not spherical but rather flattened at the poles (Ferreiro, 2011).

The success of the Bourbon armada at the Battle of Toulon / Cap Sicié, 1744

The War of the Austrian Succession (1740–1748) brought France and Spain back into conflict with Britain over the control of the Habsburg throne. Spain had actually been fighting with Britain since 1739 over trade in the Caribbean—it was then called the War of Jenkins's Ear or *La Guerra del Asiento*—and was marked by Britain's failed assault on the Caribbean port of Cartagena de Indias. The entry of France, Prussia, Austria and a host of other nations widened the conflict throughout Europe. In the early years of the war, France and Britain were on opposing sides of the conflict but not yet directly at war with each other. In September 1743 Britain and Austria strengthened their alliance with the Treaty of Worms, which forced France to also strengthen its alliance with Spain. The Second Family Compact between Louis XV and Felipe V was signed at Fontainebleau on October 25, 1743, in which the two nations specified their war aims and reaffirmed their "perpetual alliance" (Kuethe, Andrien, 2014, 157–158).

Britain was already blockading the Spanish ports of Cádiz, Ferrol and Cartagena, and in 1742 established a blockade of the French port of Toulon, where a Spanish squadron under Captain-General Juan José Navarro had taken refuge after landing troops in Italy and subsequently being battered by storms. For almost two years the British fleet under Thomas Mathews kept the Spanish ships bottled up in port, while allowing French ships to come and go. On February 9, 1744, a war council between Navarro and his French counterpart, the elderly Vice-Admiral Court de La Bruyère, determined that French fleet based in Toulon would combine with the Spanish squadron to break the blockade together, even though France was not yet technically at war with Britain. The Bourbon armada was composed of 16 French ships, which would form the van and center, while the 12 Spanish ships, including the massive 114-gun *Real Felipe*, would form the rear. On February 19 at 2:00pm, the fleet of 28 ships set sail to give battle to the 31 British warships waiting for them off the Isles d'Hyères.

For several days, light winds prevented the two fleets from forming into proper lines of battle. Finally, on the evening of February 22, the British rear began to engage the Spanish rear, and continued through the following day. Navarro outgunned and outmaneuvered Mathews, though it was not until late afternoon that the two French squadrons were able to wear and join the battle, finally driving the British off and allowing Navarro and Court de La Bruyère to escape to Cartagena. France declared war on Britain soon afterwards. The Battle of Toulon / Cap Sicié was the first military success for the Bourbon armada, despite the fact that it had been formed not by strategic design but out of tactical necessity. Mathews was court-martialed for his defeat, while Navarro was given the title Marqués de la Victoria (Blanco Núñez, 2001, 190–203).

Ultimately, the War of the Austrian Succession finished largely status quo ante bellum, leading to another great war in just six years.

The failure of the Bourbon armada in the Seven Years War, 1761–1763

The Seven Years War began in 1754 as a series of skirmishes between French and British forces vying for control of the Ohio Valley in North America. Within two years it included Prussia, Austria, Russia and other European nations, while fighting spread across the globe. Starting in 1759, Britain won a stunning string of victories at sea and on land, decimated the French fleets and occupied their strongholds from Canada to the Caribbean to Asia. Spain was not in the war at this point, but became increasingly fearful that France and Britain would make peace and leave Spain helpless. France's navy, meanwhile, was being mauled by the British navy, which out-built and out-captured France's navy by a ratio of ten to one (Glete, 1993, vol. 2, 272).

In early 1761, Louis XV and the new Spanish king Carlos III agreed to revive their alliance against Britain. France's foreign minister Choiseul and the Spanish ambassador Grimaldi signed the Third Bourbon Family Compact in Paris on August 15, 1761. It provided for Spain to declare war on Britain the following year provided no peace had been concluded, while France promised to support Spain if attacked. Word of the secret Family Compact leaked to Britain, which in January 1762 pre-emptively declared war on Spain. During the remaining months of the Seven Years War, France and Spain made two attempts to form a joint Bourbon armada, neither of which went beyond the planning stage before the preliminary peace treaties were signed in November of that year (Dull, 2005, 200–204).

In March 1762 a French squadron under *chef d'escadre* Coubon-Blénac arrived in the Caribbean, and unable to attack Jamaica, proposed to the Spanish officials in Havana to use his squadron to help defend that crucial port from an impending British assault. The Spanish officials in Cuba rejected that offer, and within a few months Havana was in British hands. In April, Carlos III proposed to France a joint Bourbon invasion of Britain. The focus of planning was on their navies, for while Britain's coasts were protected by its "wooden walls" of warships, the island itself had only a smattering of regular troops and militia. If France and Spain could land troops, Britain could easily be overrun. The plan called for a squadron of 20 Spanish ships from Ferrol and Cádiz to attack and drive off British squadrons which had been blockading Brest and Rochefort. The French squadrons would then join to create the combined Bourbon armada that would escort 30,000 troops from Dunkirk and Calais to invade Britain. The Spanish government planned for the squadron to depart Ferrol on October 1. However, the British assault on Havana reordered Spain's priorities, while the French troops slated to invade Britain were instead called up to fight in Germany. By July 1762, plans for a Bourbon armada were called off (Dull, 2005, 224–226).

The final Treaty of Paris that ended the Seven Years War was signed on February 10, 1763, which resulted in Spain losing Florida, France losing Canada and giving Louisiana to Spain. Britain was now unchallenged as the dominant power in Europe and the world, and with the French and Spanish navies now decimated, there seemed little that they could do to regain their standing and their territories.

The policy of *Revanche* and rebuilding the Bourbon armada, 1765–1770

Almost before the ink was even dry on the Treaty of Paris, French military officers were spreading out across the south of England, gathering intelligence on the British navy and potential landing sites on the coast. This was part of comprehensive Bourbon strategy of *revanche* (revenge) against Britain, developed by Choiseul and Grimaldi (newly appointed as foreign minister), whose centerpiece would be a combined assault on England. The attempted assault in 1762 had failed because France and Spain could not coordinate their fleets in haste. This time, the two ministers believed, their advance planning would ensure success (Abarca, 1965).

Both Choiseul and Grimaldi knew it would take five or more years for both navies to rebuild a credible offensive capability against the British fleet. In addition to intelligence-gathering, they also planned to create an effective, unified Bourbon armada. At the beginning of 1763, France only had 47 ships of the line, while Spain had just 37 (84 ships combined), far short of the numbers needed to defeat the 145 ships of the British navy. Though both ministers committed to building more ships, they also recognized that this was insufficient to defeat the British navy. A wholesale reformation and integration of the navies on both sides of the Pyrenees was in order. In France, Choiseul issued a sweeping Naval Ordinance in 1765 that streamlined the bureaucracy, enforced a strict series of "rates" that standardized the types and dimensions of ships so they would maneuver and fight as one unit, attempted to tackle the ever-present problem of timber supply, and set up the world's first professional corps of shipbuilders, whose task was to use scientific principles in the design and construction of vessels, with the goal of making each ship better than its British counterpart (Ferreiro, 2007, 286–287; Scott, 1979, 22–24).

Grimaldi's task, on the other hand, was to rebuild the Spanish fleet along the same lines as the French fleet, so they could operate in unison. That meant importing not just French technology but also French know-how. In 1765 Grimaldi asked Choiseul to send French engineers who could bring both Spanish shipbuilding and naval artillery up to French standards. For the first request, Choiseul sent Jean-François Gautier, a mid-level shipbuilder, to be placed in charge of all Spanish ship construction. Gautier quickly discarded the older, sturdier Spanish designs and began constructing lighter, faster warships in the French mode, following the instructions from Choiseul's Naval Ordinance. The French shipbuilder fully understood Grimaldi's objectives: "My duty is to regard French and Spanish vessels as forming a single Armada" (Sánchez Carrión, 2013, 236).

For the second request, Choiseul dispatched, also in 1765, the Swiss-French artillery engineer Jean Maritz to Spain, where he established foundries that employed the same technique recently introduced in France of solid-casting the cannon and drilling the bore, which gave cannon greater power and precision. Maritz followed the new French guidelines for gun sizes and calibers, so that the older Spanish hodge-podge of naval guns was soon replaced by a standardized set of cannon that could fire more accurately and at longer ranges (Valdez-Bubnov, 2011, 312–319). These changes to hulls, masts and artillery meant that the new generation of Spanish warships would maneuver and fight identically to French ships of the line. Now, just a few years after the Treaty of Paris, France and Spain were well advanced in planning a war with Britain, and were on their way to having an armada that could accomplish it.

The war plan that was agreed to by both nations in 1767 called for a surprise assault by a combined fleet of 140 ships of the line (80 French, 60 Spanish) against Britain's fleet, which now numbered 120 ships of the line. The main force would escort a fleet of smaller landing boats to descend on Portsmouth and the Sussex coast, laying waste to critical parts of the naval infrastructure. The invasion would stop short of a full-out assault on London, which could frighten other Continental powers. Instead, French diversionary forces would attack Scotland, while Spanish forces would descend on Gibraltar with the aim of recovering the strategic territory it had lost years earlier (Das, 2009, 18–20).

Just as the two nations were well on their way to becoming ready for an assault on Britain, in 1770 a political crisis in the Falkland/Malvinas Islands put a halt to them. In that year, the governor of Buenos Aires sent a large amphibious force to remove the British garrison on the island. Britain geared for war, while Spain called on France to honor the Bourbon Family Compact by coming to its aid. King Louis XV came down firmly against it. The crisis was diffused the following year when Spain disavowed the military action. But the crisis soured Louis XV on the *revanche* strategy against Britain, while making Spain's Carlos III doubt the worth of the Bourbon Family Compact and indeed of any further dependence on France. The invasions plans were put on shelves in Versailles and Madrid.

The Bourbon Alliance floundered for several years, until 1774 when Louis XV died, and the 19-year-old Louis XVI succeeded him to the throne. At just the same time, the political situation in America was coming to a boil. The new king appointed Charles Gravier, Comte de Vergennes, as his foreign minister. Vergennes was committed to working with his counterpart Grimaldi to renew the close relationship with Spain. As it happened, a new conflict just brewing in the British colonies of America would provide the two Bourbon powers to re-establish their policy of *revanche* against Great Britain, and lead them directly into the War of American Independence (Ferreiro, 2016, 31).

The success of Bourbon armada in the War of American Independence, 1779–1783

The longest-lived and most successful employment of the Bourbon armada was actually in the service of another cause, the independence of the American colonies from Great Britain. In April 1775, the shots fired at the Battles of Lexington and Concord signaled the beginning of a war that had actually been brewing for several years. Taxes, the lack of any representation in Parliament and the increasing restrictions on trade all drove the American colonists to take up increasingly violent protests against the British policies. But America began the war stunningly incapable of fending for itself; it had no navy, little in the way of artillery, and a ragtag army and militia that were bereft of guns and even of gunpowder. Without the help of France and Spain, the Americans knew they could not survive. In 1775, its colonial leaders reported to a secret French envoy to Philadelphia that "they are convinced they cannot defend themselves without a seafaring nation to protect them, and the only two powers which are able to help are France and Spain" (Doniol, 1886–1899, vol. 1, 288).

The two Bourbon powers at first provided materiel support to the United States, which had declared independence in 1776, but by the following year it was apparent that the Americans could not win the war without directly military intervention. France agreed to an alliance with the United States in February 1778, after which it sent naval forces under the Comte d'Estaing to assist in the fighting. But during his campaigns in the summer and autumn of 1778, d'Estaing failed to recapture either Newport or Savannah as intended, which left the Americans despairing for a French–Spanish alliance. As George Washington told the Congress that November,

> The truth of the position will entirely depend on naval events. If France and Spain should unite, and obtain a decided superiority by sea ... France with a numerous army at command, might throw in what number of land forces she thought proper to support her pretensions, and England without men, without money, and inferior on her favorite element could give no effectual aid to oppose them. (Crackel, 2007, vol. 18, 149–152)

Spain had opted to stay out of the alliance in 1778—they still had a treasure fleet at sea carrying $50 billion equivalent in silver, and did not want to risk it being attacked by the British navy (Blanco Núñez, 2004, 117–120). But once it was safely in port at the end of the year, Spain was free to reactivate the mutual assurance clauses of the Bourbon Family Compact. The "Treaty of Defense and Offensive Alliance against England" between France and Spain was signed at the Palace of Aranjuez April 12, 1779. It was in fact a long list of Spanish demands punctuated by the occasional concession to French desires, and stipulated that Spain and France would make war against Britain with the "intent to acquire" Gibraltar and Minorca, cooperate in an invasion of Great Britain, and expel British forces from Florida (Hernández Franco, 1992, 178–179).

The Comte de Vergennes and his new Spanish counterpart the Conde de Floridablanca dusted off the invasion plans for Britain that had been developed a decade earlier, and now drew up a new invasion scheme. French and Spanish ships of the line would rendezvous at the northern coast of Spain, before turning towards Britain. Once sea control had been established in the Channel, smaller vessels would transport a 30,000-strong Army of Invasion from Brittany and Normandy for the amphibious descent, during which they would occupy the Isle of Wight and Gosport, then destroy the British fleet at Portsmouth (Patterson, 1960, 46–53).

France and Spain sent spies to Portsmouth and Gosport, where they found under-manned garrisons and weak defensive works. They also stepped up dockyard activities to get their ships into service. Spain was actually the more prepared of the two. Minister of the Navy Castejón and his chief shipbuilder Gautier had overhauled and improved the Spanish dockyard system, so that fast warships based on French design principles were steadily coming off the slipways (Sánchez Carrión, 2013, 118). Back in France, Minister of the Navy Sartine was rushing to achieve the number of ships needed for the naval campaigns. Most of the dockyards' efforts were directed at refitting older vessels, which averaged just half the cost of a new-construction ship—the 90-gun *Ville de Paris*, for example, was refit to carry 104 guns in order to face British three-deckers like the 100-gun HMS *Victory* (Villiers, 2013).

Both the French and Spanish navies were delayed by an even greater problem that afflicted even the vaunted British navy—lack of manpower. Under the flag of Lieutenant-General d'Orvilliers, the French fleet of 28 ships of the line, plus frigates and other vessels, assembled in early June at Brest. The fleet was short 4,000 sailors, which d'Orvilliers had to supplement with inexperienced army men drafted at the last moment, many of whom boarded the ships already ill from an epidemic which was just beginning to grip the French nation. On June 3 they set sail, arriving a week later at their rendezvous point at the Sisargas Isles just off the coast of Galicia in Spain. The 39 Spanish ships of the line at Ferrol and Cádiz, under the overall command of Captain-General Córdova also faced delays due to lack of qualified officers and the need to quickly draft inexperienced hands from the local population. The Cádiz fleet sailed in late June, but due to contrary winds did not reach the rendezvous until July 23. By then, Spain had issued its declaration of war against Britain. With the campaign now in motion, all sides girded for battle (Patterson, 1960, 160–229; Villiers, 1995; Alsina Torrente, 2006, 142–149).

France and Spain had prepared meticulously for this invasion as far back as 1765, when Choiseul and Grimaldi first envisioned a combined Bourbon fleet, and had exchanged shipbuilders and artillery engineers so that their ships and weapons could operate side by side. It was therefore astonishing, even by the standards of the day, that these preparations had not extended to developing a common system of communications between the fleets. The problem lay not in the language—all of the senior Spanish officers spoke French—but in the signal flags. D'Orvillier's chief of staff, the Chevalier du Pavillon, had drawn up the French fleet's signal book. A copy had been sent to Madrid back in March, but it did not reach Pavillon's counterpart, Córdova's chief of staff José de Mazarredo, until shortly before the Cádiz fleet weighed anchor. "I was very surprised to learn that the signal books had not been printed in Spanish, and that M. Mazarredo was obliged to copy them by hand since his departure from Cadiz," complained d'Orvilliers to Sartine. "I assure you that never before have two squadrons at sea had to improvise their signals, but that is what I have been forced to do" (Chevalier, 1877, 161). As soon as the Spanish fleet arrived, Pavillon set to work with Mazarredo, producing ten signal books in one week to distribute to the rest of the ships. Unfortunately, that left the French and Spanish commanders no time to train and exercise together before entering into battle.

With the two fleets joined into a single armada, they were arranged into seven squadrons. D'Orvilliers was in overall command of four combined squadrons while Córdova, aboard his massive 112-gun flagship *Santísima Trinidad*, led an all-Spanish "squadron of observation" which would operate in reserve to attack the British during battle. Two more squadrons would patrol the Azores to protect Spanish convoys returning from the Americas. On July 29 the combined armada of 150 vessels, larger even than the 128 ships of the original Spanish Armada of 1588, left the Sisargas Isles bound for the English Channel. Within days, the crews began succumbing to disease; within a few days, 80 were dead and 1,500 ill. The doctors were at a loss to explain it, some pointing to scurvy as the cause. It was, in fact, part of a massive dysentery outbreak, one of the largest on record until that time. On top of the epidemic, it took the armada a full two weeks fighting calms and contrary winds to round the Brittany peninsula, finally entering the English Channel on August 16th.

The British learned of d'Orvilliers' departure from Brest on June 12. On June 16, the 28 ships of the line in Channel Fleet departed Portsmouth under Vice-Admiral Hardy's flag flying above HMS *Victory*. Although like the French and Spanish, the British ships were under-manned and their crews sickly, they nevertheless sped west to the Scilly Isles to intercept d'Orvilliers before he could enter the Channel. But the long-anticipated showdown between the Bourbon and British fleets never came. Hardy's fleet patrolled back and forth for a month, though it was too far west to catch sight of d'Orvilliers when he arrived. When the armada was finally sighted off Plymouth on August 16, the coastal towns immediately girded for an invasion, issuing arms and calling up militia, while back in London stocks dropped sharply on the news. But the Bourbon fleet was steadily losing its ability to threaten the British population. Their resupply ships never made their rendezvous, leaving the armada increasingly short of victuals and water. Meanwhile, dysentery continued to ravage the crews. On the flagship *Ville de Paris* 307 men fell ill, one-third of its 1,100 crew, necessitating that a frigate be stripped of much of its crew just to keep the flagship operational.

On August 18, a gale from the east blew the armada out of the Channel. A week later they finally encountered Hardy's flotilla. D'Orvilliers attempted to engage the Channel Fleet. Hardy knew he was overmatched, so he avoided combat while continuing to lead the armada back east towards the safety of

Portsmouth, where on September 3 he moored to reprovision for battle. The same day, d'Orvilliers received orders from Versailles to end the campaign and return to Brest. The armada entered port a week later with 8,000 sick and dying sailors aboard, but with only one captured British ship to show for their efforts. Sartine and the other members of the French court immediately denounced d'Orvilliers' failure to engage Hardy's flotilla, but Pavillon leapt to his defense, pointing out that "the French vessels ... were really more hospitals than ships of war" (Villiers, 1995, 28). The French–Spanish invasion of Britain, which had been the centerpiece of the entire Bourbon strategy and the culmination of a 15-year naval buildup, had simply fizzled out.

Despite the failure of the invasion scheme, France and Spain were still committed to the joint Bourbon armada, for neither nation could take on the British navy by itself. Over the course of the next year they ironed out their operational difficulties, as 16 French ships of the line joined Córdova's fleet, making several sorties into the Atlantic in order to intercept British ships cruising off the Spanish coast. One of those sorties departed Cádiz on July 31, 1780 with 24 Spanish and 6 French ships of the line. Owing to good intelligence passed to him by Floridablanca, Córdova knew that a massive, lightly escorted convoy was en route to the East and West Indies, and went in search of them. In the pre-dawn darkness of August 9, Spanish frigates glimpsed a cannon flash and heard a boom one minute later, which Córdova's chief of staff Mazarredo argued must be the convoy just ten miles away, and not the Channel Fleet. Córdova duped the convoy into following him by using the stern lamp of *Santísima Trinidad*, which they mistook for their own escort, the 74-gun HMS *Ramillies*. Dawn saw the 55 merchantmen under the guns of the combined fleet, while the copper-bottomed *Ramillies* was able to outrun its pursuers, much to the dismay of the French captains whose uncoppered ships were left in its wake. The convoy returned to Cádiz with an enormous haul. It was the single largest loss of ships the British navy would experience in the war, with over 3,000 soldiers, 80,000 muskets and £1.6 million in gold and silver (worth $17 billion today) now in Spanish hands (Blanco Núñez, 2004, 134–136).

The next major action of the combined Bourbon navy, the Battle of Pensacola in 1781, shows how well coordinated the French and Spanish fleets had become. Their ships were regularly operating from one another's ports and being refitted in each other dockyards, both in Europe and the Caribbean. The problems of signals and tactics that had plagued the combined armada against Britain had long since been ironed out. The two fleets now operated together routinely, with French captains taking orders from Spanish fleet commanders and vice-versa. In January 1781, Chevalier de Monteil, in command of the French fleet based at Martinique, brought his nine ships of the line to the Havana dockyard to be careened and scraped. The Spanish governor of Louisiana, Bernardo de Gálvez, was also in the city at the same time, planning his assault on the capital of British West Florida at Pensacola. Monteil was eager to assist the Spanish action, and anxious to go into action before he was forced to return to Martinique to protect French commerce from British attacks.

The Spanish fleet in Havana was still under repair from a devastating hurricane just months earlier. Nevertheless, Gálvez was eager to press the attack and convinced the military leaders in Havana to mount an under-manned and under-gunned expedition, with the promise that reinforcements would come as soon as they were ready. Gálvez's fleet departed Havana on February 28, 1781 and began the assault of Pensacola on March 9. As the siege dragged on, Gálvez's troops ran low on ammunition and supplies; by mid-April the soldiers were down to three ounces of beans per day and were foraging for spent cannon shot. On April 19, he received word that 20 newly repaired ships had just arrived from Havana under the flag of the Spanish naval brigadier general José de Solano, including 8 French warships under Monteil who had agreed to postpone an assault on a British blockade in South America in order to join the invasion. The fleet brought cannon, mortars, siege tools and gunpowder. Most welcome were the battle-hardened troops under the leadership of General Cagigal, which included French-speaking troops from Flanders, and five regiments of French soldiers who had seen just action in the United States and in the Caribbean. The combined French–Spanish army began its assault on the fortress on April 24, backed by naval artillery from the combined fleet. On May 8, a fortuitous shot from a Spanish howitzer detonated a British ammunition magazine. Gálvez's combined army quickly overran the British stronghold and forced its commander to surrender all of West Florida. With Britain no longer a threat in the Gulf of Mexico and surrounding waters, Spain was able to offer temporary protection of the French Caribbean colonies to the newly arrived French fleet commander, Comte de Grasse. This allowed de Grasse to bring his entire fleet north to assist the combined French and American forces at Yorktown, and defeat the British at the Battle of Chesapeake Bay on September 5, 1781 (Quintero Saravia, 2018, 180–244).

At the same time the Battle of Pensacola was being waged, a combined Spanish–French armada was being prepared to re-take Minorca. The French naval Lieutenant-General Comte de Guichen arrived in Cádiz in early July to link up with Córdova, with whom he had already sailed during the attempted invasion of Britain two years earlier. Meanwhile, the Duc de Crillon was appointed to lead the amphibious force. Crillon was an ideal choice to lead a joint campaign; he had been a French lieutenant-general in the first part of the Seven Years War, before transferring with the same rank into Spanish service in 1762. As Crillon, Córdova, and Guichen made their final preparations for the assault, word came of the victory at Pensacola, which was celebrated with a 21-gun salute. On July 21 the massive fleet began departing the Bay of Cádiz; 58 ships of the line and 75 transports carrying 8,000 troops. Britain's navy was at that time spread across Europe, the Americas, the Caribbean and Asia; they had no more ships left to confront such a massive fleet, or to reinforce Lieutenant-General James Murray's garrison on Minorca.

Even if the British navy were spread thin, they were still a force to be reckoned with. Córdova and Guichen took a long, roundabout route to disguise their ultimate objective; London did not know that it would be Minorca until just days before the force landed near the capital of Mahón, on August 20, and Murray was caught so off guard that his 2,700 troops barely had time to retreat to the citadel of Fort San Felipe. Crillon established a blockade of the city, while further Spanish and French reinforcements arrived in October. Crillon now had 14,000 men to occupy the entire island and lay siege to San Felipe, whose garrison endured months of almost constant bombardment while succumbing to diseases like scurvy. When Murray finally hoisted a white flag in February 1782, only 600 men were fit enough to walk out unaided. The victors were appalled by the near-skeletons they had to carry out of the citadel and nurse back to health; the vanquished boasted that their captors could take little credit for seizing a hospital (Beerman, 1992, 249–260).

With the fall of Minorca, the only British stronghold left in the Mediterranean was Gibraltar. Britain had captured the Spanish promontory in August 1704 during the War of the Spanish Succession, and ever since then Spain had been trying to recover it. After Spain and France had joined forces in 1779 and carried the war to Britain, the Spanish also laid siege to Gibraltar in an attempt to starve the inhabitants out. Britain had managed to break the naval blockade and resupply the garrison several times, allowing them to hold out. Now the Spanish and French turned their attention to concluding the three-year-long blockade and siege by its capture. The fall of Minorca had freed up many thousands of Spanish and French troops to join the siege of Gibraltar and prepare for a grand assault to break the backs of the British occupiers, once and for all. In June 1782, the Duc de Crillon was back in Madrid to accept his commission and receive his orders to lead the assault against Gibraltar

The concept for the assault decided in Madrid was simple if also far-sighted: since the most vulnerable part of the Gibraltar fortification was its western side, facing the Bay of Algeciras, the Spanish would build and deploy a series of armored floating batteries to pummel the British defenses and open up a breach for an amphibious assault to follow. These batteries were warship hulks, stripped of their masts and built with reinforced roofs to shield against British gunfire. In a clever innovation to guard against the well-known use of red-hot shot (cannon balls which had been heated in a furnace prior to firing), the batteries were fitted with pump-fed seawater pipes which ran the length of the ship to continually wet down the wooden structures, in order to prevent them from catching fire.

On September 12, the 35,000 soldiers surrounding Gibraltar were supplemented with 39 ships of the line under Córdova and Guichen. That evening, Crillon held a *junta de generals* to decide on the attack. Several senior officers wanted to delay the assault until all the preparations were complete, but Crillon had received intelligence that a British relief convoy for Gibraltar was being prepared, and any delay in his attack could jeopardize the whole operation.

On September 13, 1782 the combined assault using the floating naval batteries and land-based artillery began. While the Bourbon artillery lobbed shells at dug-in British fortifications, the British artillery commanders were depressing guns to fire into Spanish trenches and firing red-hot shot at the vulnerable floating batteries, which began to smoke, catch fire and then explode one by one. Over 40,000 artillery rounds were expended during the day-long battle, almost one for every second of the fight. Yet when the smoke and wreckage cleared, the British garrison at Gibraltar remained intact, and would do so through the end of the war (Blanco Núñez, 2004, 154–160; Chartrand and Courcelle, 2008).

Just as Crillon had feared, the British navy had been preparing another convoy to supply the Gibraltar garrison, but unknown to him its departure had been delayed by weather and accidents. On September 11, 1782, 34 ships of the line and 31 transports bound for Gibraltar left Portsmouth. Above HMS *Victory* flew the flag of Admiral Richard Howe, who had until recently commanded the British naval forces in America. The fleet weathered storms en route, but as they approached Algeciras on the night of October 10, a particularly violent gale blew in from the southwest. When dawn came it was clear that the French and Spanish ships were unable to stop the British from entering the bay; many had broken their moorings and were scattered about, with some hove up on shore. Howe's fleet had remained intact and came unopposed into harbor to offload the much-needed provisions.

A week later, Howe's 34 ships departed Gibraltar. By then, Córdova and Guichen had collected 36 ships intact, and gave chase. Although Córdova's flagship *Santísima Trinidad*, was coppered, most of the Bourbon fleet was uncoppered, and this greatly slowed them down. Even worse, the difference in performance meant that Córdova's formation was ragged, as the faster coppered ships tried to match speeds with the slower uncoppered ones. By contrast, Howe's fully coppered fleet was able to solidly maintain its formation, and at first he was so confident in his ability to control the battle that he intentionally slowed down to engage his adversaries. When the two met off Cape Spartel in Morocco on October 20, 1782, they exchanged a few desultory rounds before Howe decided that engaging Córdova's larger force presented too great a gamble—after all, he had already accomplished his mission of resupplying Gibraltar—so he ordered a general retreat. Howe's coppered ships were able to open the gap between the two fleets as night fell, and by daybreak the combined Bourbon fleet was 12 miles behind and unable to catch up. The last major European battle of the War of American Independence ended with a whimper, not a bang (Blanco Núñez, 2004, 160–163).

What Howe, Córdova and Guichen could not know is that even as the Battle of Cape Spartel was being fought, representatives of their three governments were already at Versailles, hammering out the details of a series of peace treaties would end the war and secure the independence of the United States. These treaties were finalized just in time to prevent a massive Bourbon fleet, 40 ships of the line, from departing Cádiz in early 1783, which was intended rendezvous with more than 50 French and Spanish ships in the Caribbean to finally capture Jamaica (Tornquist, 1942, 123). That invasion would never come to pass. The Bourbon armada had successfully fought the British navy across the globe, and forced London to sue for peace.

When the fleets at Cape Spartel disengaged, the commanders and their sailors would have been able to see, across the Straits of Gibraltar on the horizon to their north, a Spanish cape named Trafalgar. Twenty-three years in the future, many of these same men and ships that sparred at the Battle of Cape Spartel would meet again at Cape Trafalgar, in a battle that would change the course of history.

The failure of the French–Spanish armada in the Napoleonic Wars and the Battle of Trafalgar, 1804–1805

The French Revolution, which began in 1789, was not a direct consequence of the War of American Independence, but rather of its own internal strife which had been brewing for decades. The Spanish government was fearful that the French Revolution would spread across the Pyrenees and to its own Caribbean colonies, and distanced itself from its erstwhile ally. The French Revolutionary Wars began against Austria in 1792, by which time the Bourbon Family Compact was effectively null and void. In February 1793, France declared war on a coalition of nations, including Britain and Spain (Renaut, 1922, 436–444). Spain fought against France for two years, then finding itself on the losing end of the conflict, switched sides in 1796 to join France in its fight against Britain, with the Second Treaty of San Ildefonso now taking the place of the Bourbon Family Compact since France was no longer a Bourbon monarchy but rather a republic.

But by then, both France and Spain had lost much of their naval strength. The Spanish navy lost the Battle of Cape St Vincent in 1797, despite outnumbering the British almost two to one. The French navy was also devastated a year later at the Battle of the Nile. The French navy's officer corps was hit particularly hard by the Reign of Terror; generally members of the hated aristocracy, they were imprisoned, guillotined, shot or exiled in disproportionate numbers compared with their army counterparts (Vergé-Franceschi, 1990). As in the previous wars, the French and Spanish navies would have to combine into a single Bourbon fleet to have any chance of defeating Britain.

They would soon have that chance. In 1804, after war had resumed, France and Spain once again united against Britain. Spain had already ceded Louisiana to France, and Napoleon sold the entire territory to the Americans in order to pay for the new war effort. A major part of that effort would be a planned invasion of Britain, drawn in part from the invasion plans of 1765 and 1779. In order for the assault to proceed, a combined French–Spanish fleet would have to first take control of the English Channel, before a flotilla of invasion barges would cross the narrow stretch to land in Kent. While

Napoleon's plan broadly resembled the previous ones, the scale would be vastly different; where the 1779 invasion had 30,000 troops on shore, Napoleon had mustered almost ten times that number between Boulogne and Bruges for this invasion (Das, 2009, xi).

The naval side of the assault failed before the invasion flotilla could even get underway. The two navies had learned some lessons from their previous experience but forgotten others. By now all ships were coppered, but as with the British invasion attempt 26 years earlier, the French and Spanish fleets had not trained together to perform complex battle maneuvers. In early 1805, Napoleon developed a complicated and ultimately unworkable strategy to have the fleets break out from their ports on the Atlantic and Mediterranean, evade the British blockade, race across the Atlantic to rendezvous in the Caribbean, then race back to the English Channel to support the invasion flotilla. As the spring and summer progressed, only the Toulon fleet was able to accomplish its breakout, and by August the necessary fleet rendezvous with the invasion flotilla had failed. In the fall Napoleon ordered the combined French–Spanish fleet to depart its base at Cádiz to transport troops for the planned invasion of Naples. Under French Vice-Admiral Pierre Charles Silvestre de Villeneuve and Spanish Captain-General Federico Gravina, 33 ships of the line sortied from Cádiz on the evening of October 20 and headed for the Straits of Gibraltar. Waiting for them in the offing were 27 ships under the flag of Vice-Admiral Horatio Nelson.

As the two fleets closed near Cape Trafalgar the morning of October 21, officers in both fleets would have recognized the scene. The Battle of Cape Spartel had been fought within sight of Trafalgar 23 years earlier. Robert Moorsom and Philip Durham had been junior officers at Spartel, and now commanded their own British ships of the line. In the Spanish fleet, Spartel veterans Federico Gravina, Antonio de Escaño, José Gardoqui and Ignacio María Álava were now flag officers, while Cosme Damián Churruca and Francisco Asedo commanded ships. The sense of *déjà vu* would have been all the stronger, as the flagships HMS *Victory* and *Santísima Trinidad*, along with HMS *Britannia, Rayo* and *San Justo* fought in both battles (Rodríguez González, 2005; Hore, 2015).

But there the comparisons ended. Where the Battle of Cape Spartel was inconclusive, the Battle of Cape Trafalgar was an overwhelming British victory that indelibly marked the century to come. Nelson decisively cut the French–Spanish battle line in two places and destroyed it in detail. By the end of the day, the British fleet had captured or wrecked two-thirds of the French and Spanish ships, while Nelson was fatally wounded and died a national icon. Napoleon was thereafter reduced to continental operations as he could no longer count on his navy to carry out any major overseas campaigns. The impact went far beyond the European sphere—after Trafalgar, Britannia unquestionably ruled the waves across the entire globe, as for the next hundred years, until the outbreak of World War I, no other navy would contest its command of the ocean.

The Bourbon armada in context

The Bourbon armada was originally formed as part of the Bourbon Family Compact, and was created due to inability of either France or Spain to defeat the British navy on its own. The First Family Compact, signed in a period of relative peace, did not result in any joint naval actions. The Second Family Compact was signed during the War of the Austrian Succession, and although the joint action under at the Battle of Toulon / Cap Sicié in 1744 was a success, this was not due to any advance planning, since the French and Spanish squadrons sailed and fought independently of each with little strategic coordination. The Third Family Compact initially brought no result during the Seven Years War; two attempts at creating joint Bourbon fleets were abandoned even before they were begun. However, the interwar buildup of the Bourbon armada from 1765 to 1778, emphasizing common shipbuilding and artillery standards, brought both navies to a high level of materiel readiness.

The War of American Independence showcased the capabilities and possibilities of the Bourbon armada. Although the first joint operation, the planned 1779 invasion of Britain, was a failure—in part due to haste, lack of operational planning or training, but mostly due to an unforeseen dysentery outbreak—the French and Spanish navies quickly learned how to operate together. Their ships regularly used each other's ports and dockyard facilities, operational orders and signals were unified, and even command structures appear to have been well integrated. Indeed, had the planned 1783 invasion of Jamaica taken place, the combined Bourbon fleet of almost 100 ships would certainly have captured Britain's most important naval base in the West Indies.

The failure of the French–Spanish fleet in 1805 at Trafalgar was largely due to the same problems that plagued the 1779 invasion—a haste and the lack of operational planning and training—but had the fleet not been decimated by Nelson, there is a good chance the combined armada would have gone on to overcome these difficulties and stood toe-to-toe against the British fleet.

This chapter has provided an overview of a little-studied aspect of naval warfare during the age of sail, coalition warfare between allied navies. Far more research can and should be done to clarify the political calculus of the joint Bourbon armada, the command structures used during the campaigns, signaling, communications and tactics employed, the relationships between French and Spanish officers, and the logistics and support infrastructure for the fleets. Two centuries before NATO was even conceived, the Bourbon armada demonstrated how effective a coalition can be against a common adversary.

4 José's secrets
Minister Gálvez's master plan for Spain's participation in the American Revolution

María Bárbara Zepeda Cortés

King Charles III appointed José de Gálvez to the so-called Secretaría de Estado y del Despacho Universal de Indias or "Universal Ministry of the Indies" in January 1776, approximately seven months after the Battle of Bunker Hill and five months before the Second Continental Congress issued its Declaration of Independence. With this designation, the monarch recognized Gálvez's expertise in Western Hemispheric affairs and left him in charge of addressing any challenges arising from the actions of the "insurgent colonists," as Minister Gálvez once called the American rebels.[1] A look into archival documents and endnotes of books related to Spain and the American Revolutionary War reveals copious references to José de Gálvez as Spain's top issuer of royal orders and main receiver of information generated by the international conflict.[2] His executive role in the Anglo-Spanish armed conflict of 1779–1783, and his own contributions to the American Revolution, however, have been eclipsed by historical accounts of the heroic military feats of his nephew, Bernardo de Gálvez,[3] and of the crucial diplomatic work of his colleague, the Spanish minister of state, José Moñino, Conde de Floridablanca.[4] This chapter shows that José de Gálvez was the main coordinator of strategic operations in the Americas before and during the Anglo-Spanish war and also a major designer and enforcer of Spain's successful plan of action in the American war of independence.

Gálvez's master plan included, among other features, buying time to make war preparations; lobbying to promote West Florida and Central America as Spain's top strategic interests in the conflict; placing his nephew and brother as governors of those key areas; creating a secret office in rich New Spain to secure funds and supplies; and appointing a personal agent to act as crown representative in the theater of the war. He carefully conceived his project to secure Spain and its allies' military supremacy over Britain, but also to benefit his own family. Indeed, Bernardo de Gálvez was the genius behind the conquest of Pensacola, the brightest Spanish military victory in the Anglo-Spanish war and one of the decisive battles in the annals of the American Revolution. In Central America, José's older brother and Bernardo's father, Matías de Gálvez, achieved impressive military feats against the British too. Neither Bernardo nor Matías could have succeeded in the resounding way they did without the efficient support of a state machinery mounted by José de Gálvez. An examination of the colonial minister's master plan for the war illuminates the critical role of both individual and group agency in the international conflict.

A grand plan for the war

Preparedness was José de Gálvez's first rule of conduct before the American Revolution. In his first month in office, he began assessing the nature of the conflict and addressing the dangers of an increased British military presence in the Americas. On February 28, 1776, Gálvez issued a royal order to the governor of Cuba, the Marqués de la Torre, requesting a full report on the island's defensive situation and urging preparedness for an eventual military mobilization.[5] He also asked Torre to deploy spies to "Pensacola, Florida, Jamaica, and other British colonies" to gather data on military developments, numbers of troops, and attitudes toward Spain on both sides of the conflict.[6] The same year, Gálvez orchestrated the shipment of militia uniforms and thousands of muskets from Spain to Cuba.[7] The consolidation of Havana's defenses was a sound measure to avoid a major embarrassment such as the British occupation of that port in 1762 during the Seven Years' War (1756–1763). Another reason for a reinforced Havana was to use it as a strategic base of operations and support to achieve the more ambitious military objectives Gálvez had in mind, namely the conquest of Pensacola Bay in West Florida and the expulsion of the British from the Atlantic coast of Central America. He pursued these two offensive goals upon assuming the colonial office, but he had sketched them almost two decades before.

Of relatively humble and provincial origins, José de Gálvez worked twenty years (1744–1764) as a lawyer at the Spanish court. His portfolio of cases included mainly commercial disputes, from which he acquired some expertise in Spanish American affairs. Gálvez became a minor representative of the *proyectista* tradition in eighteenth-century Spain around 1759, coinciding with Charles III's ascendancy to the throne. In his *Discurso y reflexiones de un vasallo sobre la decadencia de nuestras Indias españolas*, Gálvez made colonial policy recommendations for the new monarch.[8] This treatise identified the increased presence of the British in Central America as a danger for Spain's richest colony, New Spain. Gálvez denounced Britain for building small fortifications to protect contrabandists, whose ships traveled the coast from Campeche to the Bay of Honduras. He advocated the foreigners' expulsion by force. Even a costly military operation would be worthwhile, he remarked, because the precious woods and dyewood that the British extracted furtively could become valuable commercial assets for Spain. Moreover, Gálvez warned, Britain would be in an auspicious position to attack the "Mexican Empire" if it obtained French Louisiana as a result of the Seven Years' War.[9] Louisiana served at the time as a buffer zone between New Spain and the

British colonies of North America. Gálvez saw his fears confirmed when, in 1762, Spain joined the war, lost it, and exchanged West Florida for the liberation of Havana a year later. A British possession rubbed shoulders with the now-Spanish Louisiana. In his first year at the Ministry of the Indies, an empowered Gálvez began to move the human chess pieces across the Atlantic with the firm objective of making the Gulf of Mexico a Spanish lake again, if an armed conflict would allow it.

In mid-1776, José de Gálvez secured two consecutive appointments for his 30-year-old nephew, Lieutenant Colonel Bernardo de Gálvez. In May, Bernardo was named commandant of the infantry regiment (*regimiento fijo*) of the province of Louisiana, and in September, the king entrusted him with the governorship of the same province.[10] From his office in New Orleans, the minister's relative was in a position to assess, and perhaps even influence, the conflict next door. In Central America, José de Gálvez first replicated the measures he took in Cuba. In 1777, he dispatched from Spain a new army battalion for Guatemala. This move surprised an anonymous observer who thought that the British did not constitute a real danger to Spanish control in Central America because they were too busy with the rebellion of their North American colonies. The critic also argued that it was a warmongering measure that would only create anxiety among the Guatemalan population.[11] The increased number of troops in Central America required a military inspector.[12] In a political move that paralleled Bernardo de Gálvez's succession of appointments in Louisiana, Colonel Matías de Gálvez, the then 61-year-old brother of José, arrived in the Central American isthmus as general inspector of the enlarged Guatemalan army and militias in mid-1778. In January 1779, José de Gálvez informed the captain-general and president of the Audiencia (high court) of Guatemala, Martín Mayorga, that inspector Matías de Gálvez had been appointed his successor.[13]

While Gálvez set up his projected war scenarios by positioning his brother and nephew in Louisiana and Guatemala, at court, he played the card of buying time. Spain's ambassador in France, the Conde de Aranda, began talks with American delegates in Paris as early as late 1776. In January 1777, Aranda urged Charles III to enter the war, as it would be an opportunity to "annihilate England forever" and secure favorable terms for Spain with the new power he predicted would emerge in North America.[14] Although generally considered a war enthusiast,[15] the Spanish king was also prudent. In early February, Charles III consulted with his ministers about ending neutrality and joining the American colonists in their war against Britain. José de Gálvez was among those who provided feedback.

The Spanish cabinet rejected Aranda's suggestion, but each member had to argue his decision in writing. Gálvez's dictum is relevant as it is the only extant source disclosing his thoughts on the American Revolution. The minister of the Indies explained that he opposed the war due to the feeble position of the "insurgent colonists." The lack of a "stable form of government" [*constitución fija*] of the

American Congress and the uncertainty about their own future had led the Americans to seek the support of the powerful French and Spanish monarchies.[16] Gálvez believed that it would be "improper" and "imprudent" to enter the war but recommended adopting a defensive stance. After all, the British were making extraordinary military preparations, and Spain should also build up as much as possible to be ready for any surprise attack. He proposed that France and Spain give secret military aid to the insurgents. Granting the Americans "as much aid as we can," he wrote, had the "important goal" of prolonging the conflict so that "both sides annihilate each other." He suggested support in the form of arms, ammunition, and money "which is the main source of strength [*principal nervio*] of power." In his closing statement, Gálvez stressed preparedness: "Justice and Divine Providence will help us as long as we do our part with the due constancy and diligence."[17]

A couple of weeks after the antiwar dictum of Charles III's ministers, Gálvez moved quickly to implement his proposal.[18] On February 20, 1777, he sent a confidential royal order to Louisiana's governor that mandated extending secret aid for the rebels. On this point, Caughey writes that "much of [Bernardo de] Gálvez's assistance [to the Americans] was given before Spain had entered the war against Britain."[19] José de Gálvez's plan included the shipment of antimalarial cinchona bark (quina), other medicines, woolen cloth, gunpowder, and muskets by the crown to New Orleans, disguised as merchandise that a private Spanish merchant (in actuality a secret crown agent) would sell discreetly to an agent of General Charles Lee. Aid arrived in New Orleans in May, but the operation aroused suspicions. Bernardo de Gálvez dismissed his uncle's chosen agent and fixed the whole operation with a complicated scheme that mixed truthfulness and falsehoods and customized the secret delivery of each of the products. Minister Gálvez approved his nephew's actions in October 1777.[20]

France announced its support of the American rebels in January 1778, prompting Charles III to consult his ministers for a second time. But once again, the cabinet advocated neutrality. In contrast to the calmed tone Gálvez had employed in his 1777 antiwar dictum, his language now conveyed urgency. Above all, the colonial minister stressed that Spain had powerful reasons to buy time. He proposed mature reflection before joining a war "that may be seen now as unavoidable." Gálvez strongly criticized the "inconstancy of Versailles." Because France had acted on its own, without consulting Spain, he opined, "we are free to take our own prudent measures and avoid being carried down the precipice." The French would understand if Charles III avoided involvement because Spain had much to lose if the British attacked its American possessions. Gálvez explained that currently the Spanish forces were scattered, and a fleet loaded with silver had either departed or was about to depart from Havana. He stated, "We must make the impossible to prolong peace and avoid the war until our America and its principal sites [*plazas*], currently under fortification, are in a better defensive state." Gálvez suggested that

Spain could offer itself as a mediator in the conflict while, at the same time, the crown could quietly send at least five extra army regiments to Puerto Rico, Havana, and New Spain. He ended with the need to issue a general warning about the imminent danger of war to all viceroys, captain-generals, and governors in the empire so they could start preparing defenses "and offenses, if possible."[21] Once again, Gálvez proposal favored neutrality but stressed preparedness.

The memoirs of a courtier recorded that Spain finally joined France in the war against Britain when the French ambassador in Madrid, the Comte de Montmorin, managed to speak privately with Charles III in early 1779. This time the cabinet could not dissuade Charles.[22] On April 12, Minister Floridablanca and Montmorin signed the Treaty of Aranjuez, sealing the alliance. Historiography has traditionally overlooked Gálvez's influence in this diplomatic process, giving all the credit to Floridablanca.[23] But José de Gálvez had been acting on his master plan for three years, and when the moment of declaring war arrived, he was there to make sure his project would be executed. The colonial minister signed as witness in the power of attorney that Charles III extended to Floridablanca to negotiate the terms of the agreement with France's representative.[24] Moreover, Article 7 of the treaty listed Spain's strategic objectives as: 1) the recovery of Gibraltar; 2) the conquest of Mobile; 3) the reconquest of Pensacola and East Florida; 4) the expulsion of the British from the Bay of Honduras and the enforcement of the Treaty of Paris of 1763 that prohibited British establishments in the coast of Central America; 5) the revocation of permits to British loggers to cut dyewood in the coast of Campeche; and 6) the restitution of Menorca.[25] It is evident that points 2 to 5 had Gálvez's influence all over them. After both monarchs ratified the alliance, on June 21, 1779, Spain entered the conflict as an ally of France. Gálvez's "unavoidable war" had begun and he was ready to fight it from his ministerial trench.

The minister's personal weapons

As one of Gálvez's contemporaries explained, "The first predicament in all wars ... is the scarcity of [financial] means to sustain them."[26] In August 1779, the minister of the Indies opened a steady flow of silver *pesos* from rich New Spain by stripping Viceroy Martín de Mayorga of his power to deal with finances and by giving the economic reins of the viceroyalty—that is, the *superintendencia* of the royal treasury office—to one of his closest associates in Mexico, merchant-bureaucrat Pedro Antonio de Cossío y Cossío (1721–1791).[27] Cossío was a wealthy merchant resident of Veracruz, who, in the times of the Gálvez's visitation of New Spain, had become a fellow advocate of reform. In 1767, Gálvez named him administrator of the Veracruz customs. The trader stayed in that position until his unexpected wartime promotion of 1779. Cossío's appointment was secret, however. Only he, Viceroy Mayorga, Gálvez, and Charles III knew that he headed the superintendencia. The colonial minister instructed Mayorga to sign all of Cossío's resolutions as if they were his own.[28]

In 1785, Cossío reminisced that Gálvez had entrusted him to go to Mexico City to work on grave matters, particularly to make sure "there was sufficient capital (and there was) to sustain the war in this America and the Barlovento [Caribbean] islands."[29] Gálvez's plot worked well because during Cossío's short tenure as *superintendente*, the viceregal treasury revenues increased considerably. According to the merchant-bureaucrat, between March 1780 and April 1783, he supported the war effort with 52 million *pesos* remitted from New Spain. It is an impressive figure that coincides with the official government records.[30] Cossío's confidential letters to Gálvez in this period devote entire sections to information about his secret mission of securing funds for Matías and Bernardo de Gálvez's military operations. In November 1780, he remarked that New Spain "has aided and will continue aiding Guatemala and Louisiana with anything they ask."[31] In fact, at one point in 1780, Matías de Gálvez had written Viceroy Mayorga not to send more money because the 600,000 *pesos* he had received were enough.[32] In early 1781, Cossío informed the minister that "streams of silver and food supplies had left New Spain." Later he added that "there has been no sparing of aid for those places where Don Matías and Don Bernardo" were operating. Referring to Matías de Gálvez's successful defense of the Immaculate Conception fortress in Nicaragua's San Juan River in January, the secret superintendente commented that the military victory had been possible "with the help of God, [aid] *sent from this kingdom*, and [Matías de Gálvez's] great spirit."[33] No doubt, Cossío became José de Gálvez's secret weapon to drain New Spain's treasury to succeed in his carefully prepared, personal war strategy. Yet the viceroyalty's capital remittances to Havana reached their maximum level only after November 1781, when Gálvez's second personal weapon, Francisco de Saavedra, pushed Cossío "to do the impossible," in the superintendente's own words.[34]

Both Matías and Bernardo de Gálvez began to reap successes early in the war. Bernardo's conquest of British-occupied Baton Rouge earned him the prestigious army rank of *mariscal de campo* and the special commission of leading the invasion of Pensacola.[35] He also captured Mobile, one of Spain's objectives for the war and an advanced post for the Pensacola operation. With the reputation of his family at stake, Minister Gálvez used yet another ace up the sleeve to secure a victory: he extended his reach to the theater of war through the appointment of a personal representative. Francisco de Saavedra y Sangronis (1746–1819), a future prominent Spanish statesman of the 1790s and early 1800s,[36] left his military career when his friendship with Bernardo de Gálvez earned him a job as an officer at the Ministry of the Indies in 1778. There, Saavedra gained José de Gálvez's admiration with his efficient work in the drafting of the *Comercio Libre* (intraimperial free trade) law. In 1780, the minister proposed him as crown agent for the war. Saavedra's narrative of his appointment reveals Gálvez's agency and describes the multiplicity of tasks entrusted to him:

Given the way the war unfolded, the Americas had to be the main scenario, [therefore] Don José de Gálvez thought that an individual knowledgeable of the situation in Europe and of the cabinet's projects ... should travel there and] attend the military junta meetings to communicate the thoughts of the court; serve as a mediator between the different opinions of those in charge; deal with the generals of the allied nations; make sure money flowed between the different theaters of war; and go where the need and the public good demanded it.[37]

On a single day—June 22, 1780—Gálvez communicated his plan to Saavedra, then to Floridablanca, and both ministers consulted the king, who approved the motion. Saavedra's decisions would have the weight of royal orders.[38] It was an impressive delegation of power.

Gálvez micromanaged Saavedra's mission's departure. He dispatched confidential orders announcing the coming of the special emissary to those in charge of the Spanish military operations in Havana. To the Spanish American treasuries he mandated that all money requests that Saavedra signed be granted. For example, Gálvez ordered Cuba's treasury intendant to help his envoy "with all that he asks" and provide him access to Havana's accounts.[39] Before leaving Aranjuez, Saavedra was reminded "by word" (Gálvez's?) of his goals: he had to make sure the expedition to Pensacola was executed; send promptly and securely as many funds as possible to Spain; help Matías de Gálvez expel the enemy from Guatemala's coast; and "facilitate a joint Franco-Spanish land and sea expedition to conquer Jamaica or any other important operation dictated by the circumstances."[40]

Saavedra could not reach Havana until late January 1781.[41] Once in Cuba, José de Gálvez's envoy found the army and navy generals busy organizing the third (and final) expedition to Pensacola.[42] The situation was not ideal. Havana had debts and needed funds; Mexico had only sent 1.7 million *pesos*. The treasure fleet was docked at the port carrying 4 million *pesos*, also from New Spain, but destined for Spain, therefore it was capital that could not be touched. There were not enough ships to bring food provisions from Veracruz. Diseases had ravaged the rank and file of the Spanish Army of Operations, and five months after reaching Havana only 3,000 of the original 8,000 soldiers who left Cádiz were fit to fight. The devastating October 1780 hurricane had left most of the Spanish warships in need of repairs, and the navy lacked seamen. Matías de Gálvez asked for remittances of ships and men to Central America; he had received money and food supplies, but it was not enough. The members of the junta directing operations fought with each other over the details of the next military objective. Saavedra's friend, Bernardo de Gálvez, kept requesting a large number of men for Pensacola because he could not risk an expedition "that was going to decide his reputation and his fortune, and that had both his protectors and his enemies waiting for results."[43]

On his first participation on the generals' junta, Saavedra placed José de Gálvez's strategic interests at the forefront. He stressed that "the king wanted an offensive and vigorous war as the way to reach peace" and asked the generals to concentrate on the conquest of Pensacola first, on giving aid to Guatemala second, and then on dispatching the treasure fleet to Cádiz and situating the Spanish forces in Saint Domingue for an eventual Franco-Spanish attack on Jamaica.[44] In mid-February, Saavedra informed Gálvez that New Spain, Havana, and even New Granada were assembling aid for "Don Matías," then fighting in Nicaragua. He added, "As Your Excellency told me, every fifteen days there will be a ship sailing from the Batabanó [Cuba] to the Bay of Honduras" loaded with aid.[45] The Pensacola expedition set sail in late February, and Saavedra visited the war front in April to stay there until the mission succeeded. He left Havana along with 1,600 reinforcements and supplies sent after news of British ships coming to rescue their West Florida possession reached Cuba. In his memoirs, Saavedra wrote that when he encountered Bernardo de Gálvez in the Spanish military camp outside the port of Pensacola, he never left his side "as his uncle Don José had asked [him]" to do.[46] Pensacola surrendered in early May. Minister Gálvez's top strategic objective had been accomplished and, after his repeated shows of bravery, his nephew was, in the eyes of all, a hero.

A few days after the capture of Pensacola Saavedra returned to Havana and found news of another lobbying success of José de Gálvez at the court: Bernardo de Gálvez had been named head of the Spanish Army of Operations in early 1781. The need of an advocate on Bernardo's behalf in junta meetings was gone. Minister Gálvez thus relieved Saavedra of one of his responsibilities now that his nephew had "independent command" and was in charge of preparing the next campaign. Nevertheless, he encouraged Saavedra to remain on Bernardo's side.[47] In his enthusiastic response letter to the good news of Pensacola, the minister thanked his envoy for his report and participation in one of "the most risky and glorious [military] enterprises in the annals of all nations." He added that he had read Saavedra's chronicle of the conquest to the king and His Majesty had heard it with gusto. Gálvez informed Saavedra that the monarch had rewarded his zeal, energy, and efficiency with a prestigious pensioned knighthood and Cross of the Order of Charles III.[48]

Another aim of Saavedra's mission was to ensure that funds circulated efficiently between theaters of war. Because of Saavedra's pressure, in only six months (from November 1781 to May 1782), New Spain remitted 9 million *pesos* in cash to pay Havana's debts, support France's military objectives, and help with the preparations of the ambitious joint conquest of Jamaica. Saavedra began to shuffle war funds in the summer of 1781 when he started more serious talks with the allied French generals. In Guárico, Saint Domingue (present-day Cap-Haïtien), Saavedra discussed military objectives with Admiral Comte de Grasse. At the time, Grasse was organizing a large expedition to North America to help the rebels fight Lord Cornwallis and he requested money and ships from the Spanish. Saavedra explained that Spain could not pledge its own ships because it had not officially recognized the independence of the Anglo-Americans, but it could certainly transfer capital to its ally.[49] Gálvez's delegate traveled to Havana immediately, and on August 8 he raised a loan of half a million *pesos* in six hours among the city's merchants and shipped the funds to Grasse's expedition. Saavedra's overconfidence came from the safety net that rich New Spain represented. As historian James Lewis argues, this transference of funds contributed to the British defeat at Yorktown, the battle that marked the beginning of the end of the American Revolution.[50]

Jamaica was the next war objective if the Franco-Spanish expedition gathered enough resources. Saavedra traveled to Mexico City in November 1781 to request the viceroy (read, Cossío) 9 million *pesos*.[51] Cossío readily prepared 3 million *pesos* that left to Havana with Saavedra that December. He promised 3 million *pesos* more in February and the final 3 million in May. Cossío then negotiated interest-free loans with individual merchants and obtained a couple of interest-bearing loans from the Mexico City *consulado* (merchant guild) and the Mining Tribunal.[52] Under pressure, Cossío confessed his worries to Gálvez: "both Matías and Bernardo are in campaign in their respective sites, pray God will continue helping them so that this war ends [soon] because it cannot be supported any longer." But he quickly added words of comfort: "Do not worry yourself about aid to these two heroes."[53] In May 1782, the secret superintendente reported that that year he had sent 9 million *pesos* in cash to Havana. He still needed to send 2 million *pesos* more and told his boss, "I will do the impossible, so you don't have to worry."[54]

The massive transfers of funds of 1782 happened when the war was coming to an end. The Saavedra–Bernardo de Gálvez duo traveled to Guárico to organize the Jamaica expedition, but the April 12 defeat of the large fleet of Grasse in Martinique against Admiral Rodney ended all Franco-Spanish aspirations. Saavedra carried the bad news to Europe and that ended his brilliant mission as crown representative. That May, Matías de Gálvez's forces achieved their final success when they captured the British-occupied island of Roatán. In October, José de Gálvez secured for his brother the appointment of viceroy of New Spain. On the same day, Gálvez issued an order of retirement for Cossío, he was no longer needed, and in addition, his public position as viceregal secretary "who improperly exceeded his [offices'] prerogatives" had earned him influential enemies in Mexico City in addition to corruption accusations.[55] The Treaty of Paris of 1783 granted most of Gálvez's strategic wishes. The Gulf of Mexico was again a Spanish lake when the British ceded East Florida too. The only point in his plan that could not be secured was that the foreigners were allowed to keep cutting dyewood on the coast of Campeche.

Conclusion

In addition to Gálvez and Floridablanca, the other members of Charles III's cabinet directly involved in the war effort were the Conde de Ricla, minister of war; Miguel de Muzquiz, of the treasury (and also of war at Ricla's death in 1782); and Pedro González de Castejón, of the navy. In the historical sources reviewed for this chapter, only Floridablanca is mentioned a few times, and González de Castrejón appeared once giving orders to the Spanish treasure fleet via José de Gálvez. The remaining question is, of course, how much influence Gálvez had on royal decisions.[56] Here, I suggest that the minister of the Indies practically molded Spanish participation in the American Revolution. It is remarkable that he initiated war preparations in 1776, while publicly advocating before the king that entering a conflict with Britain was imprudent and unadvisable. He also proposed and coordinated the delivery of covert aid to the American rebels. Next, Gálvez shaped Spain's goals for the war in the Americas according to his own strategic and personal interests. For a colonial minister invested in the modernization of the Spanish Empire, it makes sense that a high priority was to protect Spain's most profitable possession, New Spain. Banishing all foreign powers from the Gulf of Mexico was worth it because, precisely in the early 1780s, under the combined command of Cossío and the Mexico City Mint director, Fernando José Mangino (another ally of Gálvez), that viceroyalty began to coin 20 million *pesos* annually.[57]

Gálvez found a way to glorify his family through a conflict he thought was inevitable.[58] He sent his young and brave nephew Bernardo and, perhaps even more riskier, his older brother Matías to his predesigned war scenarios. Both felt the pressure of their assignments, but with the right support secured by José, and their own military talents, they led the Spanish troops to brilliant victories from 1779 to 1782.[59] Their military accomplishments increased the collective prestige of the family and the individual power and influence of Gálvez at the Spanish court. In 1780, José became a member of the prestigious Council of State. In 1783, the king rewarded the minister with a Grand Cross of the Order of Charles III and named Bernardo first Conde de Gálvez. It was the family's first title of Castile. That same year Matías became viceroy of New Spain.

Historians have not assessed José de Gálvez's role in the American Revolution before because many of his actions occurred behind closed (Cossío) or partially closed (spies, covert aid to American rebels, Saavedra) curtains of secrecy. Gálvez was also careful to always speak on behalf of Charles III. Even on a private letter, he reminded Saavedra of the monarch's interests instead of his own. Thus, while speculating on Bernardo's next steps in June 1781, Gálvez wrote that he hoped that at this time "my nephew ... would have taken as his next goal to expel the English from the Coast of Guatemala and the islands in the Bay of Honduras, because, after the conquest of Pensacola, it is the main objective that the king has proposed to do in this war."[60] With his power, careful planning, and thoughtful use of "personal weapons/extensions" such as Cossío and Saavedra, José de Gálvez shaped the Anglo-Spanish war to an extent this chapter only begins to uncover.

Notes

1 José de Gálvez, dictum, El Pardo, February 2, 1777, Archivo Histórico Nacional, Madrid (hereafter cited as AHN), Estado, leg. 3884, exp. 3, f. 16. Gálvez (1720–1787) was the central architect of the Bourbon reforms in the Spanish Empire. This state-led modernization effort sought to increase colonial revenue to enhance Spain's position in the concert of Europe through the renewal of the empire's economy, administration, defense, and general levels of social wellbeing. His career in the colonial administration began in the 1765–1771 period with his appointment as visitor-general of New Spain (modern Mexico). The expertise he gained overseas was crucial for his nomination as minister of the Indies. During his ministry (1776–1787), imperial modernization advanced at a fast, relentless pace. For biographical outlines of Gálvez, see H. I. Priestley, *José de Gálvez, Visitor-General of New Spain (1765–1771)*, 1–12 and Gonzalo M. Quintero Saravia, "Bernardo de Gálvez y América a finales del siglo XVIII," 99–123. On Gálvez as a reformist, María Bárbara Zepeda Cortés, "Empire, Reform, and Corruption: José de Gálvez and Political Culture in the Spanish World, 1765–1787." I am currently writing the first modern biography of this Spanish minister.
2 For example, José de Gálvez appears 1,140 times in a catalogue of documents on the American Revolution housed in Seville's Archivo de Indias: Purificación Medina Encina, ed., *Documentos relativos a la independencia de Norteamérica existentes en archivos españoles*, 1:936.
3 The United States recognizes Bernardo de Gálvez (1746–1786) as a hero of the American Revolution. In 2014, the U.S. Congress conferred honorary citizenship on him, a distinction he shares with seven others, including Lafayette, Churchill, and Mother Theresa. On this figure, see Quintero Saravia, *Bernardo de Gálvez: Spanish Hero of the American Revolution*; and John Walton Caughey, *Bernardo de Gálvez in Louisiana, 1776–1783*.
4 For an emphasis on Floridablanca's diplomatic work in historiography, see the work of Benjamin Lyons in this volume; Thomas Chávez, *Spain and the Independence of the United States: An Intrinsic Gift*, 70–88, and 126–27; Larrie D. Ferreiro makes Floridablanca the "administrative head" of the "vast empire"; Ferreiro, *Brothers at Arms: American Independence and the Men of France and Spain Who Saved It*, 78–80.
5 Allan Kuethe, *Cuba, 1753–1815: Crown, Military, and Society*, 96–97. For Torre's detailed report, see summary of Torre to Gálvez, Havana, May 11, 1776, Archivo General de Indias, Seville (hereafter cited as AGI), Santo Domingo, leg. 1226, in Medina Encina, *Documentos*, 1:68–69.
6 Kathryn Abbey, "Efforts of Spain to Maintain Sources of Information in the British Colonies before 1779," *Mississippi Valley Historical Review* 15, no. 1 (June 1928): 57. Gálvez recommended that the secret agents posed as private merchants or even smugglers. These agents and spies crisscrossed the Atlantic coast from New York to Havana and also used the Mississippi river lines of communication, becoming a veritable network of informants working for Gálvez; relatively well-known names are Miguel Antonio Eduardo, Juan Elegio de la Puente, Juan de Miralles, and Francisco Rendón; Light Townsend Cummins, *Spanish Observers and the American Revolution, 1775–1783*.
7 Kuethe, *Cuba*, 97.

8 The information on Gálvez's early years comes from my current biography project. On Gálvez as a *proyectista*, see Allan Kuethe and Kenneth Andrien, *The Spanish Atlantic World in the Eighteenth Century: War and the Bourbon Reforms, 1713–1796*, 204–5. A genre of treatises addressed to the monarch prescribing policy change and administrative renewal, the *proyectos* were popular in the eighteenth century. These essays typically circulated among members of the Spanish elite interested in public affairs. Two copies of Gálvez's treatise survived, one at the library of Madrid's Royal Palace and the other at the Archivo de Indias in Seville. There is no evidence of the wider impact of his ideas beyond what I examine in this chapter. For the modern transcription utilized here, see Gálvez, "Discurso y reflexiones de un vasallo sobre la decadencia de nuestras Indias españolas," in *La política americana de José de Gálvez: según su "Discurso y Reflexiones de un Vasallo,"* ed. Luis Navarro García, 123–63.
9 Gálvez, "Discurso," 127–30.
10 Francisco de Saavedra, *Los decenios (autobiografía de un sevillano en la Ilustración)*, ed. Francisco Morales Padrón, 107; Caughey, *Bernardo de Gálvez*, 61 and 67; Quintero Saravia, *Bernardo de Gálvez*, 78. For a contemporary criticism of the appointment, see anon., "Apuntes sucintos y prácticos de la América española para quien más interesa en su mejor gobierno," Madrid, ca. 1776–1777 (hereafter cited as "Apuntes"), AGI, Estado, leg. 42, no. 3, paragraph 165.
11 "Apuntes," paragraphs 315–16.
12 Light Townsend Cummins, "The Gálvez Family and Spanish Participation in the Independence of the United States of America," *Revista Complutense de Historia de América*, no. 32 (2006): 185.
13 José Joaquín Real Díaz and Antonia Heredia Herrera, "Martín de Mayorga (1779–1783)," in *Los virreyes de Nueva España en el reinado de Carlos III*, ed. José Antonio Calderón Quijano, 2:28 and 31.
14 Luis M. Farías, *La América de Aranda*, 205.
15 Saavedra, *Los decenios*, 114; Kuethe and Andrien, *The Spanish Atlantic World*, 237.
16 Real Academia Española, *Diccionario de la lengua castellana* (Madrid: Joaquín Ibarra, 1780), s.v. constitución. Gálvez's views coincide with Ferreiro's provocative reinterpretation of the U.S. Declaration of Independence as a last-minute device to attract France and Spain as allies of the American cause; Ferreiro, *Brothers in Arms*.
17 Gálvez, dictum, El Pardo, February 2, 1777, AHN, Estado, leg. 3884, exp. 3, f. 16. Chávez describes Floridablanca's policy before Spain entered the war as one of patience. An important piece of evidence he shows comes from two letters to Aranda from December 1776 and January 1777; Chávez, *Spain*, 75. Floridablanca became minister of state until February 19, 1777, after Charles III's first consultation to his cabinet. Therefore, in early 1777, high politicians at the Spanish court such as then Ambassador Floridablanca and Minister Gálvez disagreed with Aranda's aggressive approach and shared a cautious stance toward the developments in North America.
18 Gálvez had acted on this plan before. In December 1776, the minister informed the governor of Louisiana that "through all available means" Havana would send "aid in arms, ammunition, clothing, and quinine asked for by the English colonies;" Gálvez to Louisiana governor, December 24, 1776, transcribed in James A. Robertson, "Spanish Correspondence Concerning the American Revolution," *Hispanic American Historical Review* 1, no. 3 (1918): 304. Beerman also argues that Spain began providing secret aid to the American rebels since 1776; Eric Beerman, *España y la independencia de Estados Unidos*, 21–23.
19 Caughey, *Bernardo de Gálvez*, 85.
20 Ibid., 88–90. On secret crown agent Miguel Eduardo, see Cummins, *Spanish Observers*; Chávez, *Spain*, 91–93.

21 Gálvez, dictum, El Pardo, January 23, 1778, AHN, Estado, leg. 4199, exp. 2. On Madrid's mediation attempts in the conflict, see Beerman, *España*, 40; Chávez, *Spain*, 129–32.
22 Saavedra, *Los decenios*, 114.
23 George L. Rives, "Spain and the United States in 1795," *American Historical Review* 4, no. 1 (1898): 64; José Antonio Escudero, *Los orígenes del Consejo de Ministros en España: La Junta Suprema de Estado*, 1:367; Beerman, *España*, 41–42; Chávez, *Spain*, 8–9; Cummins, "The Gálvez Family," 182.
24 Charles III, "authorized power to sign a convention on behalf of the Conde de Floridablanca," Aranjuez, April 10, 1779, AHN, Estado, leg. 3373, exp. 7.
25 "Tratado de alianza defensiva y ofensiva celebrado entre las coronas de España y Francia contra la de Inglaterra," Aranjuez, April 12, 1779, in *Tratados, convenios y declaraciones de paz y de comercio que han hecho con las potencias estranjeras los monarcas españoles de la Casa de Borbón*, ed. Alejandro del Cantillo, 552–54.
26 Saavedra, *Los decenios*, 116.
27 I have studied this case elsewhere: Zepeda Cortés, "Trumped by Politics: Adventures and Misadventures of a Merchant-Bureaucrat in Bourbon Mexico" (unpublished article). The royal treasury *superintendencia* office was a prerogative of viceroys in Spanish America since the 1750s. Mayorga remained in charge of the viceroyalty's civil, justice, and military affairs.
28 Gálvez, *resolución*, August 12, 1779, and Gálvez to Mayorga, San Ildefonso, August 14, 1779, both in AGI, Mexico, leg. 1510. Gálvez gave Cossío the front office of viceroy's secretary to hide his secret appointment from the public.
29 Cossío to Gálvez, Veracruz, January 29, 1785, AGI, Mexico, leg. 1878.
30 Ibid. and Zepeda Cortés, "Trumped by Politics."
31 Cossío to Gálvez, Mexico City, November 26, 1780, AGI, Mexico, leg. 1511.
32 Mariana Rodríguez del Valle and Ángeles Conejo Díez de la Cortina, "Matías de Gálvez (1783–1784)," in *Los virreyes de Nueva España*, 2:230–31, n. 32.
33 Cossío to Gálvez, Mexico City, February 20–24, 1781, AGI, Mexico, leg. 1511, my emphasis.
34 Cossío to Gálvez, May 16, 1782, AGI, Mexico, leg. 1511.
35 Matías de Gálvez also obtained the *mariscal de campo* rank in early 1781; Zepeda Cortés, "Empire," 165.
36 On his leadership during Napoleon's invasion of the Iberian Peninsula; Gonzalez-Silen, "Holding an Empire Together: The Spanish Resistance and Caracas in the Early Years of the War against Napoleon".
37 Saavedra, *Los decenios*, 118.
38 Saavedra explained, "the president of the junta of military generals in Havana was told that they should…obey what I said as if my words were the king's orders communicated by his secretaries of state"; ibid. Also, Ángel López Cantos, *Don Francisco de Saavedra, segundo intendente de Caracas*, 3.
39 Gálvez to Juan Ignacio de Urriza, June 20, 1780, cited in Chávez, *Spain*, 178.
40 Saavedra, *Los decenios*, 119.
41 On the vicissitudes of his voyage, see ibid., 119–36.
42 Saavedra to Gálvez, no. 3, Havana, February 15, 1781, Fondo Saavedra, Universidad de Granada, Granada (hereafter cited as FS), box 32, exp. 1. Two expeditions had been aborted in 1780.
43 Saavedra, *Los decenios*, 138, 140–41.
44 Ibid., 142.
45 Saavedra to Gálvez, no. 4, Havana, February 15, 1781, FS, box 32, exp. 6.
46 Saavedra, *Los Decenios*, 150–51.
47 Gálvez to Saavedra, Aranjuez, June 12, 1781, FS, box 32, exp. 6.
48 Gálvez to Saavedra, San Ildefonso, August 31, 1781, FS, box 14, exp. 16.

49 Saavedra, *Los decenios*, 159 and 162.
50 James Lewis, "Las Damas de la Havana, el Precursor, and Francisco de Saavedra: A Note on Spanish Participation in the Battle of Yorktown," *The Americas* 37, no. 1 (1980): 83–99.
51 Saavedra's memoirs do not reveal he knew Cossío was the viceroyalty's acting superintendente of the treasury; Zepeda Cortés, "Trumped by Politics."
52 Ibid.
53 Cossío to Gálvez, Mexico City, February 4, 1782, AGI, Mexico, leg. 1511.
54 Cossío to Gálvez, Mexico City, May 16, 1782, AGI, Mexico, leg. 1511.
55 Zepeda Cortés, "Trumped by Politics."
56 Chávez thinks Gálvez only had "some influence" on the king's decisions; Chávez, *Spain*, 125.
57 Cossío to Gálvez, Mexico City, January 16 and February 4, 1782, AGI, Mexico, leg. 1511. On Mangino, Zepeda Cortés, "Empire," chap. 1.
58 On Gálvez's nepotism in relation to the Anglo-Spanish war, see Caughey, "Bernardo de Gálvez," 61; Quintero Saravia, *Bernardo de Gálvez*, 120 and 125. For the historiography and practice of José de Gálvez's nepotism, Zepeda Cortés, "Empire", chap. 3.
59 See Saavedra's comment regarding Bernardo de Gálvez's anxiety before the conquest of Pensacola above. The British struck first in Central America and took the fortress of Omoa (in Honduras) in October 1779. In response, Matías de Gálvez "led one of the most daring forced marches" of the Anglo-Spanish war: with one thousand men he traversed rainforests and mountain ranges and managed to reconquer the stronghold after a short siege in late November; Cummins "The Gálvez Family," 186. Calderón Quijano contends that the fall of Omoa greatly embarrassed Matías and the real motive for the amazing forced march was to prevent the bad news from reaching his powerful brother; cited in Isidoro Vázquez de Acuña, *Historial de la Casa de Gálvez y sus alianzas*, 1214.
60 Gálvez to Saavedra, Aranjuez, June 12, 1781, FS, box 32, exp. 6.

5 "Foreseeing what great occasions might come"
American independence and Spanish naval reformers

Manuel Lucena-Giraldo

The Spanish intervention in the American Revolution and Independence has been neglected—with important exceptions—until recently in the general historical narrative. Aspects related to the history of science and technology have been almost completely absent.[1] Although explanations in history are never simple, it is not difficult to perceive the influence of the Black Legend, the negative, stereotypical vision of the Hispanic past, to explain such a circumstance. Spanish intervention in the American quest for liberty was almost by definition an impossibility, because Spain could not be imagined as a relevant or decisive support of the founding fathers, or as a power with some merit or debt to reward at the beginning of the great American nation. More than 3 million *pesos* are a recent calculation of direct Spanish help for rebels during the war. Other historians point out it was equivalent to twice the annual peacetime defense expenditures of the metropolitan treasury at Madrid.[2] After 1783, the existence of common borders between the Spanish monarchy and the new, aggressive, and independent republic did not help. Reports and letters about American "ingratitude," surprise and even anger from Spanish ministers, after the arrival of American petitions about navigation of the Mississippi River, right of trade, or access to the port of New Orleans, are common in Spanish archives.[3] The famous but sadly not especially influential "Reserved instruction for the State Council" from the count of Floridablanca, prepared for the government of the future king Charles IV in 1788, specified the importance "of a human barrier to protect Spanish Louisiana against American colonists, depending on the United States trying to extend very fast in those regions and vast territories."[4]

It is interesting to remark historical realities could be the opposite of stereotypes coming from the past, operating in the present and shaping the future. It is not only the so-called *Iberian Turn* in the history of science of the Early Modern Period. That is, the recognition of the importance in the first globalization of scientific institutions of the Spanish–Portuguese monarchy in the Renaissance and the Baroque. It changed ideas and presumptions about foundation of global science after 1500.[5] It is a new historical perspective from reforms in European overseas empires, and reaction in the American kingdoms and colonies, north and south.[6] There is a different framework to integrate a global explanation, developed through changes at big and small scales. It is certain that one of the best generations of Spanish scientist of all times lived and fought at the time of the War of American Independence. Commemoration of the bicentenary of the Museo del Prado is celebrated in 2019. Few people remember the admirable classic building at the center of Madrid was planned by Juan de Villanueva in 1785 and built to be a section of the Spanish Academy of Sciences. An imperial machine, not a courtier turned public institution dedicated to the celebration of the human spirit through painting and fabrication of the image of a monarchy in transition from empire to nation.

Perfidious Albion

Wars are now, as then, about technology. In this chapter, I examine the role played by the Spanish Navy, the Real Armada, and particularly the figure of José Solano y Bote, in support of the American rebels, and some of the less obvious consequences of that participation. At the same time he was contributing to the war effort, he was implementing in command of the Armada new ideas, an approach to scientific leadership established long before. He was not a novice but rather an expert in imperial conflicts and boundaries. Solano took part in expeditions sent to settle the frontiers of the Spanish Empire in what is now Venezuela in 1754 and Santo Domingo in 1776. Foreseeing what great occasions might come, we can understand to what extent the changes in Spanish imperial policies by the 1780s, what we can define as counter-reformism, or the reform of the Bourbon reforms in Spanish America, can be at least in part related to the victory of the Bourbon coalition in the war against the British, and the lessons learned at that time. Because the War of American Independence was, above all, a conflict between empires.

The war against the British was always popular in Spain and Spanish America. Gibraltar, the North Atlantic and the Caribbean were other important fields of battle at the same time the War of American Independence was been fought. In fact, it was the last serious attempt of Spanish forces to occupy Gibraltar. In the court, political atmosphere by the 1770s was toxic. Contrary to what happened in Madrid in 1766, at the infamous Esquilache Mutiny, when the "Italian" minister marquis of Squilace was expelled from power, and King Charles III escaped to Aranjuez to save himself from the mob, after 1779 the decisions of the Spanish political imperial elite and popular feelings were quite the same. It was not a case of *galofilia*, a love for foreigners and fashion coming from France extended between the aristocracy and pretentious people, versus *galofobia*, a disdain for French fashion and language extended between the "popular element" which, in due course, would explode with justified anger and violence in May 1808, with the Napoleonic invasion of Spain.[7] Against "Perfidious Albion," there was no disagreement. After the wars against the British were lost with terrible results for Spain in 1713 and 1763, with another in 1742 without a clear winner, naval officers, merchants and policy makers from ports like Cádiz, Barcelona, Veracruz or Havana saw an opportunity for revenge. The American Revolution was the ideal scenario. Gibraltar was always a pain in the neck. But in order to understand what represents the American rebellion as imperial opportunity, in particular for Spanish policy reformers and Army and Navy officers, it is important to take into account recent historiographies.

The War of American Independence was not one war, but several wars. It was not only American, but a war in the Americas, and especially in the Caribbean. The independence of 13 British colonies giving birth to United States is a well-known result. Historians guess very well the past. But from the beginning, it was an extremely contradictory and politically dangerous event, as depicted by the ministers of the Catholic King, Charles III of Spain and the Indies. Contemporary debates matter. Are the enemies of your enemies always your friends? To what extent was it fair, not to say prudent, to help the American rebels against their British king, your enemy? What about the possibility of extension of a rebellious attitude between Spanish Americans? In the middle of the war, anti-reformist rebellions began in the Andes, in the viceroyalties of Peru and New Granada, against new monopolies and taxes at the core of Bourbon reforms. Although multitudes shouting "Long live to the king, down with the bad government," cannot be presented as a proclamation of revolutionary modern ideas, fear of rebellion of Tupac Amaru in Peru, Tupac Catari in Upper Peru, or the Comuneros in New Granada, was widespread in the imperial government. And for good reasons. Visitador Areche was substituted in 1782 by Jorge de Escobedo after cruelty and mismanagement of the upheaval. Santafe de Bogotá was saved in 1781 thanks to the intervention of Archbishop Antonio Caballero y Góngora, who became the next viceroy. The Spanish ministers planning how to help, albeit in a covert way American rebels, Floridablanca or Gálvez, were at the same time suffocating the revolts.[8]

Fear of repeating history was menacing them. But the Spanish empire this time was not so ill-prepared. Following the Seven Years War and the British capture of Havana and Manila in 1762, the Spanish Crown designed a comprehensive military reform for Spain and key areas of the empire. In Spanish America, this program was first implemented in Cuba and later extended to other strategic dominions. The Caribbean would be a key scenario of future wars.[9]

Some of the elements of new, comparative and integrated historiographies of independence and the Atlantic World are related to the importance of the Haitian Revolution, which began in 1789 and finished with the proclamation of the first "Black Republic" of the history of the world in 1804, with extremely important political and social effects in the region.[10] After the imperial crisis in April 1810 in peninsular Spain, when the fall of Cádiz at the hands of the French Army and the end of resistance of Spanish patriots seemed a matter of weeks, the crisis extended from the European center of the empire to the American periphery, without remedy. The configuration of three types of war in Spanish America after 1810, as established by Clément Thibaud, first civic between cities, until 1812, with some patriots for revolution and, in the end, independence, some royalist; secondly a civil war, until 1815, a social and ethnic conflict mainly fought with irregular militias and guerrillas; and, finally, the imperial and patriotic war, until 1825, "Americans" versus "Spanish," in different versions, a war made mostly by professional armies and soldiers, a good number of them unemployed veterans of the Napoleonic wars in Europe, offer new ways to compare and explain.[11]

The War of American Independence –the first in the continent with such a consequence—shows one possible way of solving imperial constitutional mismanagement, or lack of adjustment, after the poisonous British victory of 1763. But it is important to remark not only the British, the winners of a war with two names, the Seven Years War, or the French and Indian war, quite remarkably, but the French, almost expelled from the Americas, and their allies, the Spanish, who came to terms with the limitations of an empire coming almost without changes from the sixteenth century—based on the occupation of cities, the actions of legal bureaucracies, and the control of trade—suffered the huge effect of rebellion in the 13 British North American colonies after 1776. If there is a global history of the American independence, and I think there is one, 30 years before, and far away, in the Amazon, something influential happened.

An expert in frontiers

In 1746, negotiations between the crowns of Spain and Portugal started to settle their boundary disputes in the Americas and Asia. From these deliberations emerged a reevaluation of historical and diplomatic traditions, Jesuit cartography, and arguments emphasizing observation and measurement to support political positions. Both sides acted upon presumptions based in new ideas about imperial reform, which asserted the extension of power of the crowns to the South American frontier. Both sides therefore agreed that Portugal could legally control the Amazon, and Spain, the River Plate.[12] In the middle of these negotiations, Jorge Juan and Antonio de Ulloa, two Spanish naval officers, scientists, and veterans of the expedition sent to Quito to measure the length of a degree latitude at the Equator, published their *Dissertacion historica y geographica sobre el meridiano de demarcación* (1749). This important book about history of boundaries marked the beginning of a Spanish American scientific literature on the subject of geometric and geodetic measurement. As a result of the Treaty of Madrid, signed in 1750 and represented in the so-called "Mapa das Cortes," Spanish and Portuguese commissioners organized two expeditions to carry out the demarcation in South America. The expedition to the Orinoco in the charge of José de Iturriaga was to settle the boundary in the north, from Guiana to the Jauru River. The expedition of Gaspar de Munive, fourth Marqués de Valdelirios, operated in the south up to the Castillos Grandes mountains in Uruguay. Each expedition was composed of three groups, or parties, of Spanish and Portuguese commissioners assigned to explore; to mark part of the border; to measure latitude, longitude, and temperature; to prepare maps and charts, and other tasks related to botany, mining and increase of population.

On the other side of the world, an officer of the Spanish Navy, José Solano y Bote, was by 1751 escaping from London. He had been practicing industrial espionage in Deptford shipyards with the scientific and Spanish naval officer *par excellence* Jorge Juan, and very much enjoying the experience.[13] Shortly after joining the Spanish Navy in 1742, Solano took part in the Battle of Toulon (1744), where the Spanish fleet defeated the British. As a result of his outstanding performance, he was promoted to the rank of "alférez de fragata." In 1754, he was promoted again and sent to the Americas as a fourth commissioner of the Orinoco expedition. What is important is the personal evolution of José Solano to become one of the most efficient officers in the expedition. On the one hand, he managed to put into practice scientific knowledge with clear results in cartography, maps and botany.[14] On the other, the implementation of new imperial policies related to the control of the territory were from the beginning entangled with the border expedition. Not everyone managed to understand that times had changed. He did. In order to fulfill the principal task, to plant obelisks and marks signaling the border, it was necessary first to organize the frontier. So he came to terms with regional powers, indigenous peoples, foreigners or different missionaries, enemies and collaborationists of the new order. As expressed by a key minister, José de Carvajal, then in charge of foreign affairs, "we do not adjust not doing trade nor war," and so lose everything. The direct presence of men of the king, *españoles del rey*, had to make a difference.

After London, Solano spent seven years, from 1754 to 1761, exploring the Orinoco River and tributaries, north and south to the Amazon, west to New Granada and east to the Guianas, as well as making several trips to Bogotá, in pursuit of additional funding and help from viceroy José Solís Folch de Cardona to support their efforts. He was in charge of a team of geographers and astronomers that drew many sketches and maps from the middle and upper Orinoco. They explored the link between Orinoco and Amazon rivers. In fact, Spanish under his command arrived to Mariuá, the meeting place with the Portuguese in the Negro River, with three years of delay. When he concluded his assignment in 1761, he was promoted to the rank of "capitán de navío." In 1762, in the new war with England, he took the command of the "Rayo," a 100-gun ship or *navío*, built in Havana. If the administration of the empire was a problem, Solano was part of the solution. After the French and Spanish ominous defeat, he was appointed governor of Venezuela, from 1763 to 1770, and later served as governor and captain-general of Santo Domingo, from 1770 to 1779. Brilliant and efficient, he wrote that he decided to return to his "natural job and inclination" in the Real Armada. It was the right time and he would be, as accustomed, in the right place. Almost three years after the declaration of independence of the

American rebels, on April 3, 1779, the Spanish government sent to London some proposals of mediation and truce. At the beginning of May, as expected, the British explained that these were unacceptable. It was war. Solano was in months second in command of a squadron in the English channel, "losing his time" in his own words, due (as seen by himself) to badly planned French strategies of invasion.

Master and commander

The main goals of Spain were, as in the Seven Years' War, the recovery of Gibraltar and Menorca from the British, who had claimed them since 1704, and to damage British trade through the actions of privateers. The siege of Gibraltar, June 16, 1779 to February 7, 1783, was the longest lasting Spanish action in the war. Despite the larger size of the besieging French–Spanish army, at one point numbering 33,000 soldiers, the British under George Augustus Elliott were able to hold out in the fortress. They were resupplied by sea three times. Admiral Luis de Córdova y Córdova was unable to prevent Howe's fleet returning home after resupplying Gibraltar in October 1782. The recovery of Menorca in 1781 met nevertheless with success. Menorca surrendered the following year, and was restored to Spain after the war, nearly 80 years after it had been captured by the British. In 1780 and 1781, the fleet of Luis de Córdova captured America's-bound British convoys, doing much damage to British military supplies and trade. Solano knew a key element of the imperial war was the Caribbean, a geography of his vast experience. But he was ordered to stay in Brest, the French Navy main port in the Atlantic. From Brest to Cádiz, he followed the movements of Admiral Rodney who, after Gibraltar, departed for the West Indies. In February 1780, he was in charge of a squadron of eight ships to Havana, *without wine on board*. He had it offloaded to ensure that his men would be ready for battle. Two divisions, 18 ships, 8,000 thousand men and artillery were en route to Cuba, where they arrived by August.

A well-known history explains Solano then had his finest hour in the Siege of Pensacola, when he came to support Bernardo de Gálvez in March 1781, with almost 4,000 men and 36 ships.[15] Although the purely military events are well known, it is important to remark the transfer of scientific strategies by Solano in the command of the Spanish Armada during the War of American Independence. As soon as he was in charge, he realized the empiricist approach prevailed. Not anymore. Combination of tactics and scientific procedures were updated. An impossible and dangerous combination of maps and charts used in the different ships was substituted by a common work from a pilots committee. They produced a general map of the region, an *Atlas de la América Septentrional*. After the war, in 1787, a map of the Caribbean coast and islands was drawn by the pilot of the fleet José de San Martín. He explained it was done under Solano's command. The information from first and second pilots of the Armada, and the collection of geographical positions support the initiative. It sounds easy and logical, but it was difficult and even a matter of discussion. It was a moment of debate between scientific officers and traditional officers, accustomed to improving their careers through battles and war, "more accustomed to rum than equations," as Cesáreo Fernández Duro put it.

It was a false debate. Without proper maps, cartography, engineering and scientific institutions, no imperial politics was possible. Admiral José de Mazarredo and the newly appointed Antonio Valdés, Minister of the Navy after 1783, until his dismissal in 1795, a key modernizer of the Spanish Armada, shared Solano's opinions and ideas. They put into practice the most important Spanish cartographical project of the time, the *Maritime Atlas of Spain, 1783–1788*, under the direction of Vicente Tofiño. Proper scientific methods to develop maps, delineation of the coast, a team with collaborative tasks, a sense of duty fulfilled in a professional career in the service of the State, were taken into account in the organization. From the Caribbean to the Mediterranean, and back. After 1792, the model was replicated in the Caribbean, with the expedition of the American Atlas, based in two divisions in the charge of Cosme de Churruca (until 1795 in the Antilles) and Joaquín Francisco Fidalgo (until 1810 based in Cartagena de Indias, the Armada's base in the region). It is easy to realize there was a coincidence of planning and objectives, from Solano's fleet in the War of American Independence, to the Atlas of Spain and lastly the American Atlas in the Caribbean.

Learning for Spain from the War of American Independence and constitutional debate of course did not stop. Everything seemed connected. The Captain-General of Venezuela, Luis de Unzaga, from 1777 until 1782, coming from Louisiana, who in fact helped with some military equipment the American rebels, informed by 1781 about the extension of rumors in Caracas of the presence of Tupac Amaru's nephew in Venezuela. Although a proper search did not find him, you never know. In the middle of the War, reforms of Spanish empire and evaluation of the worst effects continued into effect. Probably the minister Count of Aranda, on the one hand, and José de Abalos, first intendant of Venezuela, on the other, wanting to avoid something similar to "a republic of colonists" in Spanish America, recognized that changes were necessary. In two separate proposals, they outlined a solution for the empire, "federal" in their nature. In order to increase loyalty, they proposed sending members of the royal family to the kingdoms of the Indies, based in Mexico and Lima, equivalent to updating the dynasty and combating lack of faith. They knew it was necessary to gain time. It could be through this formula, avoiding the risks of eroding the ancient constitution, as happened in British America with terrible consequences.[16] It was necessary in any case to modify the reforms, especially after 1787 with an economic crisis in the Spanish Atlantic. A sense of devolution of powers and trust was fulfilled after the extension of new measures to reinforce the participation of Spanish American creoles in the business of empire: commercial consulates, scientific expeditions, internal free trade. At the same time, it was evolving a sense of an Atlantic

Spanish nation, in both hemispheres. From 1787 to 1792, the institutional culmination of the Bourbon reforms, the ministers of justice and the navy unified; that means, dealing at the same time with affairs American (the old kingdoms of the Indies) and Spanish (the old peninsular kingdoms), marking the peak of the political experiment.[17]

Lessons of the War of American Independence were learnt. The effect of imperial reforms in Spanish and British America was the opposite. In this last case, the result was American independence. In the Spanish, after the elimination of strongly reformist and anti-creole elements, there was a return to forms of traditional constitution and pactism after 1783.[18] It was a lesson taken in part from the American independence, which served as a regional catalyst. The Spanish Atlantic managed to survive unified until 1810, throughout the French Revolution, the Haitian Revolution and almost constant warfare. After 1808, with the French invasion of the peninsula (European Spain, properly named as such), everything changed. It began an imperial war against the Napoleonic invasion. Spanish American men and money supported the Spanish patriots' resistance. José de San Martín, founding father of Argentina, was a part of the command in the Battle of Bailén, the first defeat of a Napoleonic army in open field, in the hot Andalusian summer of 1808. Loyalty would endure until April 1810. Until exactly the moment when social order was at the risk of collapsing and turned the Haitian nightmare into a Spanish America reality through an imposing French revolutionary government. Meanwhile, step by step, from neutral to non-belligerent flag, smuggling or by proper legal commerce, the United States was trading and making the best of the worst circumstances.[19] The American miracle began when the only free trade of the Napoleonic era made possible the transformation of a country from merchants and traders into another of industrialists. Some of the links and routes used came from the old times of war and camaraderie.

Notes

1 A recent general approach, Juan Marchena and Justo Cuño, eds., *Vientos de guerra. Apogeo y crisis de la Real armada (1750–1823)* (Aranjuez: Doce Calles, 2018), I, 87–121; III, 317–379.
2 José María Lancho, "La ayuda financiera española a la independencia de los Estados Unidos," *España y la independencia norteamericana* (Madrid: Instituto de Historia y Cultura Naval, 2015), 116; Carlos Marichal, "Las guerras imperiales y los préstamos novohispanos, 1781–1804," *Historia Mexicana*, 34:4 (1990): 881–907.
3 *Documentos relativos a la independencia de Norteamérica existentes en archivos españoles*, Rosario Parra Cala, ed. (Madrid: Ministerio de Asuntos Exteriores, 1976), VII, General Archive of the Indies, documentation about Louisiana and both Floridas (1778–1817), 490.
4 *Gobierno del señor rey don Carlos III o Instrucción reservada para la junta de Estado que creó este monarca, dada a luz por Don Andrés Muriel* (París: Girard Hermanos, 1838), 191.

5 Jorge Cañizares Esguerra, *Nature, History and Nation: Explorations of the History of Science in the Iberian World* (Palo Alto: Stanford University Press, 2006), 14–46.
6 For a brilliant pioneering effort, see Gabriel Paquette, *Imperial Portugal in the Age of Revolutions: The Luso-Brazilian World, c. 1770–1850* (Cambridge: Cambridge University Press, 2013), 1–16.
7 Manuel Moreno Alonso, *La guerra del inglés en España (1808–1814)* (Madrid: Sílex Ediciones, 2019), 15–45.
8 David Cahill, "Taxonomy of a Colonial 'Riot': The Arequipa Disturbances of 1780," John R. Fisher, Allan J. Kuethe and Anthony McFarlane, eds., *Reform and Insurrection in Bourbon New Granada and Peru* (Baton Rouge: Louisiana State University Press, 1990), 255–291.
9 Mónica Ricketts, "The Rise of the Bourbon Military in Peru, 1768–1820," *Colonial Latin American Review*, 21:3 (2012): 413.
10 Lester D. Langley, *The Americas in the Age of Revolution, 1750–1850* (New Haven: Yale University Press, 1996), 122–147; Gabriel Paquette, Manuel Lucena Giraldo, Gonzalo M. Quintero Saravia, Oriol Regué-Sendrós, "Introduction: New Directions in the Political History of the Spanish-Atlantic World, c. 1750–1850," *Journal of Iberian and Latin American Studies*, 24:2 (2018): 1–8.
11 Clément Thibaud, *Repúblicas en armas. Los ejércitos bolivarianos en la guerra de Independencia en Colombia y Venezuela)* (Bogotá: Instituto Francés de Estudios Andinos-Editorial Planeta, 2003), 3–7.
12 Manuel Lucena Giraldo, *Laboratorio tropical. La expedición de límites al Orinoco, 1754–1761* (Caracas: Monte Ávila-CSIC, 1993), 79.
13 Nuria Valverde, *Un mundo en equilibrio. Jorge Juan (1713–1773)*, (Madrid: Marcial Pons, 2012), 111–135.
14 Kenneth Nyberg and Manuel Lucena Giraldo, "Lives of Useful Curiosity: The Global Legacy of Pehr Löfling in the Long Eighteenth Century," in Hanna Hodacs, Kenneth Nyberg, Stéphane Van Damme, eds., *Linnaeus, Natural History and the Circulation of Knowledge* (Oxford: Voltaire Foundation-University of Oxford, 2018), 223–228.
15 José Luis Santaló Rodríguez de Viguri, *Don José Solano y Bote. Primer marqués del Socorro, capitán general de la Armada* (Madrid: Instituto histórico de marina, 1973), 95–107; Carmen de Reparaz, *Yo solo. Bernardo de Gálvez y la toma de Panzacola en 1781* (Barcelona: Serbal, 1986), 272; Gonzalo Quintero Saravia, *Bernardo de Gálvez: Spanish Hero of the American Revolution* (Chapel Hill: University of New Carolina Press, 2018), 180–245.
16 Manuel Lucena Giraldo, ed., *Premoniciones de la independencia de Iberoamérica. Las reflexiones de José de Abalos y el conde de Aranda sobre la situación de la América española a finales del siglo XVIII* (Madrid: Fundación Mapfre Tavera-Secretaría de Cooperación Iberoamericana-Doce Calles, 2003), 23–28.
17 Jacques Barbier, "The Culmination of the Bourbon Reforms, 1787–1792," *Hispanic American Historical Review*, 57: 1(1977): 51–68.
18 John H. Elliott, *Empires of the Atlantic World: Britain and Spain in America, 1492–1830* (New Haven: Yale University Press, 2006), 292–325.
19 Manuel Lucena Salmoral, "El comercio de los Estados Unidos con España y el Caribe a comienzos de la presidencia de Madison: 1809," *El comercio del Caribe con España a comienzos del siglo XIX* (Caracas: Italgráfica, 1983), 215–220.

6 The Spanish slave trade during the American Revolutionary War

Emily Berquist Soule

It is well known that Spain joined France in war against Britain on June 21, 1779, largely to pursue its own geopolitical goals—not to support the rebel American colonists. In Europe, the Spanish hoped to recover Gibraltar and Minorca, both of which had been lost during the War of Succession in Spain. In North America, they sought to recoup Florida (lost to the British in 1763 during the Seven Years War) and to fortify their sovereignty in Mississippi and Louisiana. They also hoped to expel the British from the Bay of Honduras and Campeche, Mexico, where they had been almost constant interlopers in valuable lumber trades.[1] While these concerns are the most widely studied goals of Spain's involvement in the American Revolution, they were not the only ones. Also at stake was the volatile and complex relationship the Spanish and the British had forged through the trade in African captives, a relationship that had existed in both official and illegal forms since the start of the seventeenth century.[2] Placing the slave trade at the center of Spain's involvement in America's war for independence reveals that there were additional theaters of engagement, and that these were linked not only to Spain's resentment over British dominance in the slave trade but also to its longstanding enmity against Britain's ally Portugal. Yet at the same time, the contest over the commerce in African captives defied global tensions, particularly when demand for slaves on the ground took precedence over declarations of war and imperial prohibitions on trade. Although it is undeniable that as Gabriel Paquette argued, "war with England ... was the most constant factor in Spanish foreign affairs" in the eighteenth century, in the dawning age of global capitalism, market forces often belied foreign relations—particularly when it came to the slave trade.[3]

Despite their mutual antipathy, the Spanish and the British had previously forged a mutually convenient relationship through Atlantic slavery: the British offered slaves for sale and the Spanish Americans eagerly purchased them. At times, these exchanges were sanctioned by their governments, in other instances they were expressly forbidden. Britain's role as the major supplier of slaves to Spanish America began after the conclusion of the War of Spanish Succession in 1713, when London won the exclusive right to supply African slaves to the Spanish colonies via the *asiento* monopoly contract with the

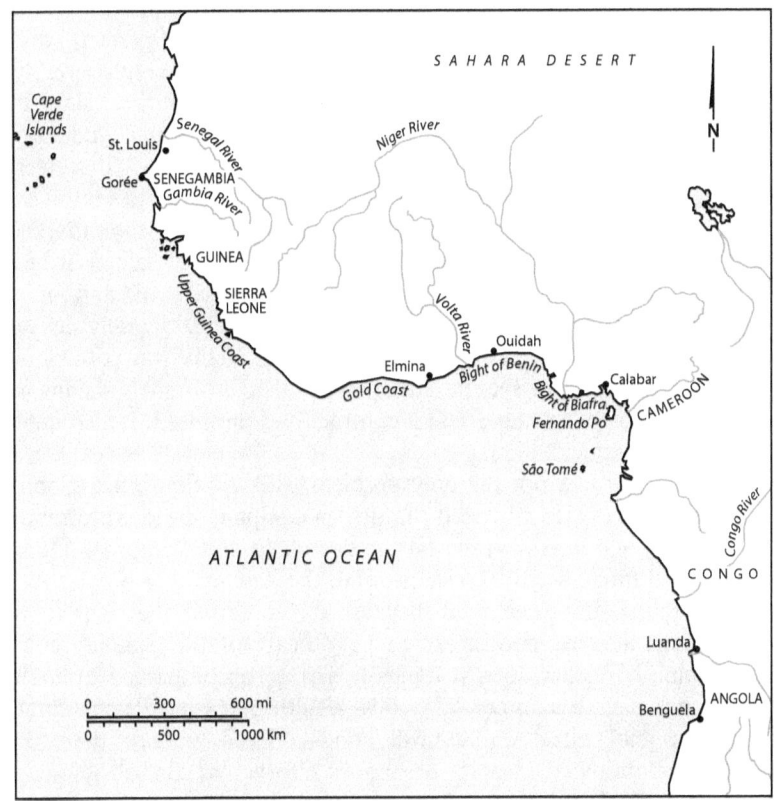

Map 6.1 The West African Coast in the Era of the Slave Trade

Spanish Crown. England's newly formed South Sea Company agreed to import 4,800 *piezas de Indias*,[4] or African slaves, to Spanish America annually for a 30-year period, paying the Spanish Crown £34,000 yearly for the privilege.[5] The British ran this trade through the West Indies, using chiefly Jamaica and Barbados as depots where slaves could be sorted and assessed before being sold to Spanish American traders.[6] This was a key component of what scholars like Gregory O'Malley have characterized as the intra-American slave trade, whereby slaves were captured in Africa, disembarked in British America, and then moved again to a final point of sale elsewhere in the Americas. The South Sea Company ran both a transatlantic and an intra-American trade during the 26 years it held the asiento, ultimately delivering over 60,000 captives to Spanish American buyers. This was, of course, a staggering number, but one quite small by British or French slaving standards, and far below what the original contract had promised. It also failed to meet Spanish demand.[7]

Failure to deliver was not the only problem with the South Sea Company asiento. The contract also allocated the British company the right to send one 500-ton ship to each annual trade fair at Portobelo and Veracruz. Although one single vessel might seem inconsequential, the Annual Ship was, as Adrian Pearce has argued, unprecedented, because it "conferred the right to trade openly in manufactured goods, at the very heart of the Spanish colonial trading system."[8] Furthermore, it typically arrived accompanied by multiple ships to restock it with commercial goods, resulting in what Pearce describes as a "catastrophic" effect on Spanish goods offered for sale there. Here, market forces dominated in spite of Spain's efforts: the British goods were simply more desirable to Spanish buyers, as they were typically less expensive and of better quality.[9]

An additional cause for Spanish concern about the asiento was how it allowed the British to establish commercial inroads in Spanish America. In the process of setting up distribution centers for the South Sea Company in Mexico City, Lima, Buenos Aires and nine other major cities in Spanish America, the British received what has been referred to as "hands on training ... in the categories of merchandise Spain's colonial consumers preferred, in the terms and methods of repayment, and in the export stapes available ... and perhaps most valuable, one on one commercial contacts."[10] Upon the termination of the asiento in 1738, English merchants in the West Indies readily "transformed Jamaican harbors into entrepôts with well-supplied warehouses."[11] This expertise would prove invaluable for generations.

But perhaps most importantly, the asiento was notorious for generating contraband trade in slaves—the exact opposite of what a monopoly contract was intended to do. Since the South Sea Company was never able to meet the agreed quota of slave imports, additional demand was satisfied by contraband British traders who surreptitiously operated along the Company's routes. Some of these trans-imperial smugglers delivered their captives to ports in Spanish territory under cover of darkness. Others attempted to blend in with licensed traders, passing off their human wares as properly taxed. Of course, this unsanctioned branch of the intra-American trade violated the principles of the asiento contract, and it therefore provoked the attention of the Spanish *guardacostas*, who began to board British ships in search of contraband slaves. The most infamous of these episodes took place in 1731 when British captain Robert Jenkins claimed Spanish naval officers cut off his ear during an altercation aboard his vessel. Returned to the House of Commons seven years later, he pulled the long-dead ear from his pocket, dramatically brandishing it as evidence of Spanish atrocities. By 1739, the Company's contract was revoked and Spain and Britain were at war; the conflict tellingly recognized as the War of Jenkins' Ear by the British, and the *Guerra del Asiento* by the Spanish.[12] The fighting endured for nine more years. During this time, all official trade between Spain and Britain was cut off.

Nevertheless, demand for slaves in Spanish America remained high, exacerbated by the fact that Spain had given up direct access to markets in Africa centuries ago, upon signing the Treaty of Alcaçovas in 1479.[13] Despite the prohibition on Spanish–British trade, British smugglers continued to surreptitiously deliver African slaves to Spanish purchasers, particularly from Jamaica. They employed a variety of tactics. Foreign ships could claim distress at sea in order to gain access to Spanish American ports, where they would then sell their human cargoes under cover of darkness. Others sent small crafts with just a few slaves at a time, because these were less likely to be detected by Spanish authorities. Most sales were conducted in hard cash or in barter in order to eliminate any written evidence of smuggling.[14] By 1748, the War of Jenkins' Ear was over. In early peace negotiations, the British pushed to reinstate the asiento, but as the parties finalized their agreement in 1750, Britain decided to give up the remainder of the contract in return for a payment of £100,000.[15]

Although the loss of the asiento meant that British traders could no longer officially enter Spanish American ports, the trans-imperial slave trade did not end. Instead, Spaniards and Spanish Americans began arriving in the British West Indies in record numbers to purchase slaves and other goods, doing so in flagrant violation of Madrid's continued official policy of tightly controlled mercantilism.[16] The British Free Port Act of November 1766 only stimulated this dynamic when several ports in Jamaica and Dominica were declared open to all foreign ships for seven years.[17] Although the act stipulated that foreign traders could not import sugar, molasses, coffee, tobacco, or manufactured goods to trade with in the West Indies, they were, of course, welcome to bring Spanish silver.[18] The British, for their part, recognized the realities of the West Indian market and were prepared to use those to their advantage. However, according to Spanish law, direct trade between the Spanish and British remained was still illegal.

Even though Spanish officials were quite willing to look the other way when Spanish buyers purchased African captives from British traders at Jamaica and Dominica, such transactions nevertheless hurt the empire's bottom line. When the British served as middlemen, the Spanish Crown lost valuable tax revenues. With each illicit slave transaction the Spanish failed to receive the *derecho de marca* or branding tax levied on slaves imported through official asiento routes.[19] Those who smuggled slaves also avoided paying the traditional import tax of 40 pieces of eight on each slave *pieza*.[20] Were the Spaniards to mount and execute their own trade in slaves, these taxes and duties would be paid directly to the Spanish Crown.

By the second half of the eighteenth century it was clear that wars, monopoly contracts, and legislative bans had failed to curtail the unsanctioned yet thriving relationship between British slave traders and Spanish American buyers, and Spain had the most to lose. Spain's need to directly provision slaves to its subjects only became clearer after Spain entered the Seven Years War against Britain in January 1762. That summer, the British invaded and captured Havana, then proceeded to sell no fewer than 3,500 African slaves to the eager Cuban planters in just 10 months.[21] Though Havana was returned to Spanish control the following year, it was by then abundantly clear that slaves were key to Cuba's financial future.[22] Soon thereafter, Spanish administrators unfurled a series of initiatives designed to develop the traffic without relying on the British, including creating their own limited trading companies to import slaves via third parties and directly from Africa; lifting some of the most onerous taxes and duties on international trade; and at the local level, forming specific plans about how to increase the volume of slave imports.[23] Even this was not enough. The contraband trade in slaves continued to dominate Spanish Caribbean markets, enriching mainly British smugglers. British merchants also continued to use the trade as an instrument through which to penetrate the closed Spanish economic system, offering Spanish American consumers the manufactured goods that were chronically undersupplied via the official mercantile system.[24] By all measures, British dominance in Atlantic trade appeared unshakable. Only with the outbreak of the American Revolutionary War would this troubled symbiosis be endangered, offering the Spanish renewed opportunity to claim a much greater role in the Atlantic trade in slaves.

The slave trade and the American Revolution in the greater Atlantic

Though slave labor was becoming increasingly central to the Spanish American economy in the Bourbon period, Spanish theorists and reformers were for the most part rather quiet on the subject. In fact, the high-profile Spanish reformers of the period issued very little public comment regarding the slave trade. Pedro Rodríguez de Campomanes' *Reflexiones sobre el comercio Español a Indias* (1762) argued that after liberalizing the import of slaves to their American colonies, the British and the French had enjoyed much greater financial returns that the Spanish should hope to imitate.[25] He also found Portugal's African colonies and direct access to slave markets admirable.

Spain's lack of African territory and market connections, Campomanes was certain, had meant that the supply of slaves to Spanish America had always been "precarious" and "second rate."[26] He also saw significant need for improvement in the asiento system itself. It made slaves more expensive, he argued, without guaranteeing a reliable supply of forced labor. (The Portuguese, the French, and the English, he noted, had all failed to meet the terms of their asiento contracts.)[27] They had, however, benefited from the opportunity to engage in contraband trade, so much so that "their [slave] factories were really trading houses."[28] Another problem with the trade in slaves to Spanish America was that the Spanish themselves did not produce any of the manufactured goods that traders used to purchase slaves in Africa—Spain should begin to produce these items itself, he concluded. Finally, Campomanes suggested that the Spanish transform one of the Canary Islands into a "general factory of slaves" where French, English, Dutch and Portuguese merchants could sell captives to Spanish traders, who could then easily ship the Africans to America, or wherever they were needed.[29] "This trade is of much importance to the [Spanish] state," he concluded. "Without a great supply of slaves, especially for the mines, the islands, and for lumber in Campeche [and] Honduras, we will not be able to make our colonies flourish."[30]

As Campomanes noted, the British were well aware that slavery and the slave trade were integral parts of profitable American colonies. It is therefore not surprising that the American revolutionaries themselves also recognized that the slave trade had key financial and symbolic value in their war against Britain. The First Continental Congress in October 1774 called for an end to British slave imports, a position confirmed by the Second Continental Congress in 1776. In drafting the Declaration of Independence, Thomas Jefferson intended to include an indictment of George III's involvement in the transatlantic slave trade; but Southern delegates, ever mindful of their slaveholding constituents, insisted the phrases be deleted.[31] Instead, the Americans declared a temporary moratorium on slave imports from Britain and her territories, gesturing towards implied moral superiority over the British while continuing to conduct their own trade in African slaves. The real importance of outlawing British slave imports to the American colonies was to harm British finances through shutting off the traffic. The measure was intended to work both ways—Americans were similarly prohibited from selling their captives to buyers in the British West Indies. However, American traders soon found a ready complement of buyers in Spanish America. Rhode Island merchants led the way in establishing new trade routes between Anglo and Spanish America, forging the deepest inroads in Cuba.[32]

For its part, although Spain maintained a stance of official neutrality in the war until 1779, it recognized much earlier that the American Revolution offered a welcome opportunity to gain geopolitical advantage over the British in the Americas. Spain quietly funneled money to the American rebels. José de Gálvez used the occasion to establish a network of informants who could report on the progress of the war.[33] The Spanish also took advantage of the conflict to attack British ships in the West Indies whenever possible—commandeering as many as 250 vessels in 1776 alone.[34] Since British vessels were now prohibited in Spanish territory, the Spanish were free to seize slave ships as prizes, and then sell their captives in Spanish markets.[35] Spain's fresh alliance with France also allowed for new potential sources of slaves: in January 1780, Madrid officially granted all of the inhabitants of its American territories (with the exception of the silver-producing regions of Río de la Plata, Chile, and Peru) express permission to "provision themselves with slaves from the French colonies during this war." Such expeditions were to be made on Spanish ships, slaves were to be taxed at the usual rate of 6 percent, and traders were not permitted to return with anything other than the slaves themselves on their ships.[36] Although they were not able to sell vast quantities of slaves to the Spanish, at least some French also found their new slave trading partnership to be more lucrative than selling captives to Saint-Domingue, where slave prices had fallen after wartime naval hostilities made it extremely difficult, if not impossible, for French planters on Saint-Domingue to ship their sugar back to Europe. As a result, there was less of a demand for slaves on the island, and their prices fell. Therefore, French slave traders looked for more lucrative markets, which they found in the nearby Spanish Caribbean. The French sold no fewer than 7,000 slaves to Cuba alone from 1781 through 1783.[37]

Though French slave traders were able to meet some of the ever-increasing demand of Spanish slave buyers, Spanish bureaucrats throughout the empire also realized that Spain needed more control over the supply of captives to the American colonies. For example, while serving as governor of Louisiana in 1777, Bernardo de Gálvez authorized the direct import of slaves to the colony from the Gulf of Guinea.[38] Four years later from Peru, Visitador General José Antonio Areche cautioned that "the shortage of this product [slaves] would be ruinous and destructive of our inhabitants, and of the towns, settlements, and fields of the coast of this Kingdom." He therefore proposed that Peruvian traders be permitted to travel to "Senegal and other coasts" to procure captives, or else to Brazil to make their purchases.[39] Suggestions also arrived in Madrid from private citizens. In 1783, Josef Antonio de Campos proposed that the crown allow the import of no fewer than 16,000 slaves to America on foreign ships, as long as they flew the Spanish flag while at port and did not carry any other merchandise besides human cargo.[40] From Santo Domingo in 1785, Antonio Sánchez Valverde recommended that the Spanish open local ports to foreign slave traders, reasoning this would result in a greater supply of slaves at lower prices and that the British ships would fill their holds with local wood and agricultural products for the return trip, thereby benefiting the Dominican economy twofold.[41] These petitions, and dozens of others like them, signal just how deeply involved individuals across the empire found themselves in slave labor and the slave trade.

Similarly, the Spanish Crown envisioned and enacted policies it hoped would promote an independent trade in African captives. In 1740, the Royal

Havana Company was authorized to purchase slaves from foreign traders and sell them in Cuba. In 1765, four Spanish merchants formed the Cádiz Company, which imported slaves to the Spanish Caribbean until 1769. But by the late 1770s, geopolitical machinations in South America resulted in an unprecedented opportunity for Spain to begin its own trade in slaves from sub-Saharan Africa – its first legal opportunity to do so since 1479.[42]

The path to Spanish territory in Western Africa's Bight of Biafra was a circuitous one that began in South America, where Portugal and Spain had already experienced decades of disagreements, skirmishes, and even military campaigns in the disputed Spanish–Portuguese borderlands in Río de la Plata. These so-called "Debatable Lands" (today the Brazilian states of Paraná, Santa Catarina, and Rio Grande do Sul, as well as the nation of Uruguay) had been in dispute ever since the Iberian powers had drawn an imaginary line to divide their sovereignty over the globe with 1494 the Treaty of Tordesillas. This agreement split the contested Río de la Plata territory, but Spain and Portugal thereafter disputed the exact location of the line of division. They continued to battle over the Debatable Lands throughout the colonial period, sometimes through military conflicts and other times through repeated treaty negotiations.[43]

Though this Iberian rivalry in South America is often dismissed as a relatively insignificant "boundary dispute," placing it within the context of the American Revolutionary War highlights how both Spain and Portugal understood their relationships with Britain as central to their diplomatic strategy and geopolitical engagements in the 1770s. Portugal saw Britain as its solid ally, with Secretary of State Marques de Pombal certain that the Anglo-Luso Methuen Treaty of 1703 stipulated that "Portugal was entitled to British aid should Spain attack."[44] When Britain began to commission and build more warships in preparation for war against the American colonists in 1776 and 1777, Pombal somewhat myopically viewed these efforts "as evidence of British support" for boundary disputes with Spain in South America. (The British, as we shall see, thought otherwise.)[45] For their part, the Spanish wanted to best the Portuguese in the increasingly strategic Río de la Plata region, and they were quite concerned with making sure the British could not aid their Lusophone allies there. Therefore, Madrid matched France's donation of 1 million livres tournois to the American rebels, "so as to prolong the American war and prevent the British from helping Portugal," as one diplomatic historian of the war has argued.[46] In fact, Anglo-British tensions ran so deep Spain only agreed to enter the war against Britain after a tentative promise that were England to be bested, Spain and France would together invade Portugal in order to once again place the entire Iberian Peninsula under Spanish (and Bourbon) rule.[47] Though this scheme was decidedly unrealistic, it encapsulates just how deep Spanish resentment towards Portugal ran.

While a land invasion of Portugal was one of the lofty goals of Spanish geopolitical strategy during the war, concerns on the ground in Latin America were more immediate. Though protecting the silver mined at the *Cerro Rico* of Potosí was foremost in the minds of Spanish imperial administrators, the economy of southern Spanish America was not solely based on silver. This meeting place between Portugal and Spain was also one where "land was plentiful but labor was dear."[48] With abundant land, agriculture offered economic opportunity. Therefore, black African slaves eventually became what one scholar has called the single "most important object of trade" in the area.[49] Here again, conditions on the ground favored an intra-American slave trade instead of one conducted directly from Africa. Alex Borucki has demonstrated how the Portuguese sold and the Spanish purchased African captives in the Portuguese town of Colonia do Sacramento, conveniently situated directly across the river Plate from Buenos Aires.[50] Colonia had long been an overlooked outpost, but by the eighteenth century, along with Buenos Aires and Montevideo, it was transformed into a vital port complex where Spanish, Portuguese, and British merchants bought and sold their wares in the three neighboring cities. Even though the Portuguese Crown had outlawed the sale of slaves to foreigners in 1751, and the Spanish were not permitted to trade outside of their own empire in times of peace, Iberian neighbors in the region enthusiastically continued trading with one another—especially for black African slaves.[51] Indeed, the ease with which they flouted international accords to sell and buy slaves reflects how the Spanish, British, Portuguese and Americans continued to engage in the trade despite official prohibitions on all sides. When it came to the traffic in slaves, the realities of free market demand were fast outpacing the older mercantilist restrictions European crowns sought to maintain.

Similarly, wresting control over the Río de la Plata slave trade from the Portuguese likely factored into King Carlos III's 1776 decision to mount a major military expedition against Portuguese interests in the region. Not coincidentally, he was well aware that Portugal's longstanding ally, Britain, was otherwise occupied in the hemisphere, and unlikely to come to the aid of their Iberian partners. At the king's bidding, a Spanish naval armada departed Cádiz for South America on November 13, 1776, in a massive expedition with no less than 116 ships; 10,000 troops; 8,500 sailors; and supplies to last half a year. On February 20, 1778, the expedition arrived at Santa Catarina harbor, only to find at daybreak that the fortress had been abandoned by the Portuguese.[52] In May of the following year, the Spanish sent Pedro Antonio Cevallos, the recently appointed Viceroy of Buenos Aires, to conquer Colonia.[53] With over 10,000 Spanish troops under his command, Cevallos easily bested the Portuguese, seizing Colonia and displacing over 1,000 Brazilians in the process.[54] Conveniently, Cevallos' campaigns also served as a deterrent for any future British-Portuguese attacks against Spanish interests in the area. This opened the door for the Spanish to establish what they hoped would become definitive sovereignty in the area.[55]

Although small skirmishes between the Iberian powers continued, on October 1, 1777, Spain and Portugal signed what they both hoped would become the definitive agreement delineating territorial limits in the region, the Treaty of San Ildefonso. Under its terms, the Portuguese ceded Colonia do Sacramento and its environs to Spain, as well as the contested territory of the Jesuit Missions. As a sign of goodwill, Spain gave up some of its claims in the region as well, including the Lago dos Patos lagoon and Santa Catarina island. In return, Spain received from Portugal what would become its first legally recognized possessions in sub-Saharan Africa, two tiny volcanic islands in the Gulf of Guinea's Bight of Biafra called Fernando Pó and Annobón. Although the Spanish knew few specifics about the territory in question, they were well aware of the region's centrality to the slave trade throughout the eighteenth century—at least 950,000 Africans were captured and exported from the Bight of Biafra between 1730 and 1807. By the 1780s, the Bight of Biafra alone accounted for 20 percent of all enslaved Africans destined for the Americas, the majority of whom were boarded onto British or American ships.[56] These numbers, of course, do not account for illegal enslavement and contraband trading in the area, which was by design completed off-record.

Another important indication of the volume of the Biafran trade was that the British were also keenly interested in the area. British contraband traders were ubiquitous in the Gulf. Many were suspected of furtively exchanging their captives with Spanish slavers who were, until the 1778 accords at least, also in the area clandestinely.[57] In fact, from 1759 to 1779, at least 581 English ships dropped anchor on the neighboring Portuguese Island of São Tomé (while records show only 294 Portuguese ships arrived).[58] Many of these were, of course, slaving ships. As early as 1765, a group of British slave merchants had inquired as to whether the Portuguese would consider granting them official trading rights on Fernando Pó. They were, unsurprisingly, displeased when in 1777, the Portuguese gave the island to Spain instead,[59] cutting off their access to the Northern portion of the island, where British traders often went "to purchase rations for the slaves they buy in Old and New Calabar."[60]

With so much at stake, it seems almost predetermined that Portugal's transfer of Fernando Pó and Annobón to Spain would set off a series of events highlighting the strategic importance of the transatlantic slave trade during the American Revolutionary War. The Spanish were eager to seize new opportunities in order to directly provision their territories with slaves, and volatile relations with both England and Portugal offered a unique chance to do so. Bested by the Spanish in the Río de la Plata, the Portuguese had to part with some of their territory in the Bight—but as we shall see, they did not do so entirely willingly or without incident. Jealous that their supremacy in the West African slave trade was being challenged by a newcomer to the global economy of the slave trade, the British retaliated however they could in the African theater. Once Spain declared its support for the American revolutionaries in June 1779, the British clapped back against the Spanish where they could do so with the greatest impunity and with the most possible financial gain—in the Bight of Biafra.

The slave trade in the Bight of Biafra during the American Revolution

In the complex Atlantic relationship among Spain, Portugal, and Britain, the Río de la Plata and the Bight of Biafra became theaters of war. To some extent, this reflects the reticence of Spain and Britain to deepen their own direct military conflict: in the early years of the war, Spain preferred to financially support the American revolutionaries instead of directly waging war against Britain. Instead, military engagement focused on geopolitical hotspots of lesser importance. Scholars on both sides of the Atlantic have recognized that this is why the Spanish–British conflict was fought over better-known European or American territories, like Gibraltar and Florida. However, the Bight of Biafra and the slave trade should be considered in our understanding of how, where, and why the Spanish participated in the war. What took place there reminds us that the slave trade was quickly becoming one of the most important financial and geopolitical institutions in a rapidly globalizing Atlantic world.

In the 1777–1778 negotiations to end the Debatable Lands conflict and hand over what would become Spain's first legally recognized territories in sub-Saharan Africa, the two tiny volcanic islands of Fernando Pó and Annobón, the Iberian powers agreed that both parties could use the islands for supplies or safe harbor.[61] They also promised to collaborate in promoting an "open and free commerce and trade in slaves" in the Bight.[62] Next, Spain decided Fernando Pó and Annobón would be administered through the newly created Viceroyalty of Río de la Plata—possibly an indication of their intention to use the islands to provide slaves for the booming slave markets there, where almost 70,000 captives would arrive between 1777 and 1812.[63] Linking the Gulf of Guinea islands to the Río de la Plata also proved convenient in terms of manpower: instead of mounting new military forces to settle the desired slave entrepôts in the Bight, the Spanish could repurpose the military leaders, soldiers, ships, and armaments from the now-settled conflict in South America to the Gulf of Guinea. The effort was overseen by Viceroy Cevallos; who simply transferred the troops and materials he had managed during the campaign against the Portuguese. Conde Felipe de Argelejo, who would become captain of the Fernando Pó mission, had also participated in earlier campaigns in South America.[64]

With the Spanish empire's South Atlantic economy of slavery expanding so rapidly that from 1778 to 1810, the slave population of Buenos Aires doubled, there was little time to waste.[65] On April 17, 1778, the *Santa Catalina*, the *Nuestra Señora de la Soledad* and the *Santiago* lifted anchor at Montevideo and headed to the Gulf of Guinea. Although most of the soldiers and sailors did not yet know it, their objectives were two: to establish a Spanish slave trade there, and to settle a harbor and provisioning station for Spanish ships sailing to and from the Philippines via the Cape of Good Hope. Captain Argelejo and his men were to set up provisional settlements on both islands. In anticipation of conflict with the British, who had long been the most numerous traders in the Bight, the expedition's instructions also stipulated that Argelejo take special care that "no one discover the secret of [the mission's] destination or objectives" prior to their arrival.[66] Eleven days later, Argelejo read a second, secret set of instructions stipulating the military details of the expedition. They specified that Spain's new settlements on the islands would be defended by no fewer than 100 troops, 20 artillerymen, and whatever ammunition these required. The logistics would be coordinated by Viceroy Cevallos in Buenos Aires.[67]

The Spanish expedition arrived at the Portuguese island of El Príncipe on June 29, 1778, dropping anchor on what Argelejo later described as a striking beach of pebbled sand dotted with brilliant purple coral.[68] Once the ships were secured, Argelejo led a small party to visit the island's governor, Josef Esquerra, planning to inform him "of the peace celebrated between the two nations, of which he did not know." Argelejo presumed this would be followed by an "immediate handover" of Fernando Pó and Annobón.[69] After delaying an hour, the Portuguese returned to tell Argelejo and his party that the governor was nowhere to be found, and furthermore, they had not heard anything about transferring two of Portugal's four Biafran islands (the others were São Tomé and El Príncipe, where the Portuguese had focused their settlements) to Spanish sovereignty. Even on that first day, the Portuguese "seemed distrustful," Argelejo later recorded in his diary—particularly because they immediately began moving their artillery around the Spanish vessels. Argelejo soon learned that Portugal had assigned new officials to administer the Biafran territories, and the men were still making their way from Lisbon. It would be three months before they appeared. In the meantime, the Spanish ships waiting in harbor used up their precious supplies, and many of the troops fell ill in the notoriously insalubrious climate, known for malaria, yellow fever, and trypanosomiasis (a slowly developing but lethal malaise caused by tsetse fly bites).[70]

While languishing at port in El Príncipe, the Spanish received news from Europe via the *Boussole*, a French slaver that had taken on 600 captives at Ouidah. The French recommended the Spanish "take precaution" with the English, because France's recognition of the American colonies' independence had made the situation in the Gulf of Guinea "really complicated."[71] (Although Spain and France were bound by the Bourbon Family Compact to act as allies, Spain at this moment had not yet declared war against England.) This news was surely disturbing, yet the more pressing problem seemed to be Portuguese stonewalling. The officials of El Príncipe did not want to allow foreign ships into port. They claimed they could take no action until receiving directions from Lisbon. Argelejo tried plying them with a lavish offering of Spanish sherry, tobacco, figs, chocolate, cheese, and "a dozen cow tongues." In return, he received 24 hens, some local produce, and a curt notice that the Portuguese "did not have, and could not send, anything else."[72]

The wait continued. On August 1, 1778, an English slaver coming from Malabar docked at São Tomé. When a Spanish official boarded the vessel in search of news, the English "had the audacity to tell him that they were surprised to see our flag in these seas, [and] that we would have a bad time if we sailed on a warship" in the Bight.[73] Just nine days later, the predictions turned out to be accurate: the Spanish packetboat *Santiago* was held up by a British blockade in São Tomé harbor. Three British ships armed to the hilt with cannons and soldiers blocked its departure for almost two months.[74] Problems with the Portuguese officials persisted as well. By the middle of August, Argelejo was convinced that the Portuguese had in their nature "to oppose just to cause problems," that "their promises meant nothing," and "their word was no good."[75] By September, the townspeople of São Tomé had also turned against the expedition's troops and settlers, "insulting them and singing ironic songs with jokes about the Spanish."[76] Soon thereafter, Argelejo came to the realization that Madrid had been "badly informed about the state and situation of these islands" by the Portuguese. Not only had the Portuguese given the Spanish inaccurate information about the resources, population, and geography of Fernando Pó and Annobón, but both islands, Argelejo wrote with some exaggeration, "had never had Portuguese settlements, or any garrison."[77] The Portuguese had promised populated islands with infrastructure and compliant inhabitants. Soon, the Spanish would see for themselves just how deeply they had been deceived.

The Portuguese officials entrusted with the transfer finally arrived on El Príncipe on October 4. On October 14, 1778, the Spanish departed for Fernando Pó, where they landed ten days later. Seeing no signs of inhabitants, Argelejo performed the usual ceremonies of possession. Afterwards, the Spanish returned to São Tomé for rest and provisions, and on November 10, they set sail for Annobón. Just four days into the journey, Argelejo died of fever.[78] His second-in-command, Lieutenant Colonel Joaquín Primo de Rivera, assumed control, leading the group of Spanish soldiers and their Portuguese escorts when they first set foot on Annobón on November 29, 1778. Ringing church bells heralded their arrival. But instead of smiling locals welcoming them with refreshments, the Spanish must have been surprised to be greeted by "a great many men and women who stopped us at every step, telling us with their screams and their threats the repugnance they felt upon seeing us enter their town."[79] Matters did not improve. As the day went on, the newcomers were subject to aggression, insults, and humiliation, topped off with an uncomfortable incident when as the Spanish were boarding their ship, the women of the town gathered on the beach, supposedly deciding to wash themselves "from the waist down" at that very moment. Shortly thereafter, they all turned around, and as Commander José Varela later recalled, "showed us their backsides, and then went running back to the town." Privately, he later commented that he found the entire episode to be a "disagreeable spectacle."[80]

Just a few hours after this incident, Primo de Rivera realized it would be impossible for the Spanish to take effective control of Annobón. Despite Portuguese promises of an established town with docile inhabitants, it turned out that the town of San Pedro contained only shabby wooden houses with thatched roofs, and it had no European authorities, religious or otherwise. To make matters worse, "the inhabitants did not recognize the King of Portugal as their sovereign, nor did they want to obey his orders." How could the Spanish take over the island from the Portuguese if the Portuguese themselves were not recognized as authorities? At that point, Primo de Rivera and Varela were forced to admit to admit their intentions were "completely frustrated, we no longer had even the smallest hope of establishing ourselves on Annobón."[81]

With the plans to settle a slaving colony on hold, Varela returned to Spain for further instructions. Primo de Rivera arrived back on São Tomé on December 3, 1778, where he would wait to hear from Madrid. The expedition personnel would languish there for over one year, their health worsening and supplies dwindling all the while. Though on the ground, it seemed the Fernando Pó mission had been forgotten, on January 9, 1779, King Carlos III decreed from Madrid that the objective remained "to acquire settlements that with expense and effort will provide us entry into the trade in black slaves, which only we [The Spanish] do not have, and which we therefore need more than any other nation."[82] In March, José de Gálvez ordered supply ships to depart from Tenerife to bring vital supplies to the Spanish in the Bight, but by September, the ships were yet to depart – they were needed for other theaters of Spain's involvement in the American Revolutionary War.

The situation in the Gulf of Guinea quickly worsened when on June 21, 1779, Spain declared war against England in support of the American revolutionaries. The declaration endangered all Spanish maritime traffic throughout the Atlantic basin, imperiling merchant vessels, the silver transport vessels, and of course, slave ships. As anticipated, in September 1779, the British extracted revenge in the waters off West Africa, seizing two of the Fernando Pó expedition's ships: the warship *Soledad* and the *Santa Engracia*, blockading them at São Tomé,[83] where they would remain, unable to freely depart until November 21, when the *Santiago* arrived and rescued them.[84]

It was not until November 30 that the Spanish expedition left São Tomé again, headed again to Fernando Pó for a second attempt at settlement there. The ship arrived on December 7 and the crew disembarked two days later, but their run of bad luck continued. They faced interference and blockades by other European powers who were none too happy about added competition in the already crowded slave trade; a smallpox outbreak among the crew and the slaves they had purchased; a severe lack of supplies that brought the crew near starvation; and continued attacks and affronts from the locals. By June, no fewer than 85 members of the Spanish expedition had died on the island, and dozens more were sick in the rudimentary hospital hastily erected there. What little medicine remained to treat them had gone bad, and given their poor diet, scurvy was rampant.[85] The men left on Fernando Pó saw themselves as forgotten and abandoned on a distant outpost, under continuous threat from the "wild blacks" whom they feared at any moment might recognize their vulnerability and "come down [from the mountains] and crucify us."[86] On September 24, 1780, Sargent Gerónimo Martín spoke for many of the men when he declared simply: "I believe our rescue is impossible."[87] Unable to endure the deprivation and isolation any longer, later that day he and 27 others arrested and tied up captain Primo de Rivera, then commandeered the ships to leave the island. Upon arriving back at São Tomé, they were intercepted by Portuguese officials. The captain was freed and the mutineers incarcerated. Then all were forced to wait yet again, for more than a year this time. The sicknesses and deaths continued. The British were also close by, with three of their frigates stationed at São Tomé, ready to attack the weakened Spanish. In the dark of night on September 23, 1781, they sent a launch with armed men to the Spanish convoy, in what one member of the expedition later described as an attempt "to kill us and make off with the ship." The sailors fought them off, ultimately slaying over 30 British soldiers in the process.[88] By November of 1781, Miguel de Luca, the slave merchant who the Spanish had appointed to oversee the mission's slaving efforts, wrote to José de Gálvez to express the "irredeemable misfortune" he had endured with the Fernando Pó settlement because of his own failing health, but also due to "the ill-fated mishaps of the expedition, all of which counter the Royal aims of the King."[89]

On December 30, 1781, the few crew who remained set sail to cross the Atlantic and return to Spanish America. After a February arrival in Bahia, Brazil, where the expedition had been forced to stop in order to complete repairs on their ships, Primo de Rivera received a royal order reminding him of his duty to form a Spanish settlement on Fernando Pó that would serve as a depot providing slaves to Spanish America. Needless to say, the instructions went unheeded. But the conflict was not over: while the Spanish waited for the repairs on their vessels at Bahia, a British convoy of 3 war ships, a supply ship, and 10 merchant ships (also armed) sailed into the harbor on November 9, 1782, carrying no fewer than 2,200 seamen and almost 150 cannon. Primo de Rivera immediately wrote to Viceroy Vertíz, advising him that "I will try to facilitate our departure without risk from this squadron, but ... please recognize that the delay could be significant."[90]

It wasn't until January 1784 that the Spanish were able to depart. By the time the repairs had been completed and the *Santiago* and the *Carmen* dropped anchor at Montevideo, only 32 of the original Spanish soldiers and crew were still alive. They were accompanied by 24 royal slaves who had also survived the voyage to and from the Bight, and all the incidents in between.[91] After a lengthy trial in Montevideo, José de Gálvez recommended that Gerónimo Martín and his fellow mutineers be put to death, but Primo de Rivera intervened on their behalf, responding that "this case does not seem worthy of this ... sentence."[92] His petition saved their lives, but Spain's mission to establish a slave trade in the Gulf of Guinea had been a disastrous failure of epic proportions – a story of mishaps and misfortunes, but also one that reveals the Spanish Crown's desperation to forge a stake in the lucrative trade in slaves, a business they knew would be key to the future survival of their empire.

*****

Although Spanish actions—particularly supply chain problems and the mutiny—and local resistance from both the natives and the Portuguese in the Bight ultimately doomed the Fernando Pó expedition, placing the story in the broader context of the American Revolutionary War demonstrates that conflicts with Britain and Portugal followed the Spanish to the Bight, and undoubtedly contributed to the expedition's failure. Although the Portuguese and the Spanish were ostensibly at peace after the 1778 treaty, the actions of Portuguese officials in West Africa suggest otherwise. The treaty proved generous to the Spanish, providing them with territories and assistance necessary to fully engage in the direct trade in African slaves for the first time since its beginnings in the fifteenth century. The Portuguese, however, showed scant enthusiasm for such a plan. Even though official Portuguese policy on the slave trade in the region changed after Pombal fell from power in February 1777, this was not immediately apparent in the Bight of Biafra. When confronted with Spanish interlopers now claiming official possession of what had long been theirs, Portuguese officials employed their best techniques of stonewalling—refusing the transfer of sovereignty, giving misinformation, inciting the locals, and causing delay after delay—engendering a diplomatic cold war of sorts in the Gulf, where they managed to largely impede the Spanish from accomplishing their stated objective without engaging in direct conflict.

Bound by no such treaty of friendship, the British saw the slave trade in the Bight as their exclusive province—which it had largely been for the 1759–1779 period, when English ships outnumbered Portuguese ships in their own territory almost two to one.[93] In attempting to hamper Spanish efforts to set up their own slave trade in the Bight of Biafra, British traders were protecting their own interests. The arrival of Spanish warships heightened the conflict. Once Spain abandoned its official stance of neutrality, the British attacked Spanish ships in the Gulf of Guinea. This proved much more convenient than direct engagement in Spanish America—a much more serious affront likely to engender much deeper consequences. Instead, in this distant arena, Spain was all the more vulnerable, and Britain all too happily exploited its weaknesses.

Despite their conflicts, the Portuguese, the British, the Americans, the Spanish, and indeed all other European powers in the region shared one common goal: to control the competition for slaves in the region and to enjoy the lion's share of its profits. The American Revolutionary War, however, upended slave trading relationships all around. One anonymous informant whose report on the slave trade in Spanish America arrived in the hands of Spanish Ministers Floridablanca and Gálvez put it quite plainly: "the trade in slaves has suffered interruption during the War."[94] Without access to captives traded by the British, the Spanish moved their search for captives to their newly acquired territories in Biafra. In return, Portugal and Britain jealously protected what they believed was their slaving territory—

no matter what Spanish–Portuguese treaties said. Although Primo de Rivera's return to Montevideo momentarily marked the end of Spain's settlement attempts in the Bight of Biafra, the Spanish Americans' desire to purchase black African captives would only grow as the eighteenth century gave way to the nineteenth and plantation slavery boomed in the Spanish Caribbean.

After the American Revolutionary War, the Spanish also came to realize the importance of their own involvement in the transatlantic trade in slaves. They began to enact policies, develop geopolitical strategies, and make financial arrangements that reflected the increasing strategic importance of the slave trade. For instance, in 1789 the Spanish Bourbons decided that the most efficient way to ensure a sufficient slave population was to allow Spaniards in the Caribbean and Venezuela to trade directly with foreign merchants for slaves. Within several years, the decree was extended to allow direct importation of slaves to Cartagena, Río de la Plata, Lima, Guayaquil, and Panama.[95] The Spanish empire became increasingly involved in the slave trade, with 405 Spanish vessels making slave trading voyages between 1789 and 1817, resulting in a total of 92,464 slaves disembarking under the Spanish flag in mainland Spanish America.[96] While only a small portion of these came from Fernando Pó and Annobón, more broadly the failed attempt to create a Spanish slave entrepôt in West Africa had highlighted that without a sufficient supply of slave labor, Spain's great American empire would be imperiled.

Furthermore, examining the Spanish Atlantic slave trade during the American Revolutionary War reminds us how the Spanish Crown designed slave trade policies around geopolitical alliances and conflicts, at times breaking with the British and the Portuguese, and in other instances forging close connections over the trade in human captives. As Spain expanded into new geographical contexts with new promises of profit, international conflicts over the slave trade were only heightened. Although Spanish administrators exhorted their imperial subjects to likewise manage their slave purchasing decisions in light of global geopolitics, on the ground, supply, demand, and profit reigned. Even in 1782, deep into Spain's involvement in war against Britain, Spaniards continued to petition their king for permission to import slaves from the British Caribbean to Havana, reasoning that slaves were as necessary for the island's survival as foodstuffs, which had already been arriving from the British Caribbean in wartime.[97] With the imperial powers seated thousands of miles away in Madrid, commercial interest on the ground trumped imperial dictates. Spanish buyers needed slaves, and British traders needed buyers. This relationship continued, legally or illegally, throughout the eighteenth century and beyond. As the case of the Spanish slave trade during the American Revolutionary War so clearly demonstrates, in both the official relationships forged through diplomacy and trade and in the informal connections fostered in the Americas between sellers and buyers, the slave trade stood unmistakably at the center.

Notes

1 The author would like to gratefully acknowledge the historical expertise and bibliographic suggestions of Alex Borucki, Trevor Burnard, Gregory O'Malley, Gabriel Paquette, Fabricio Prado, Jim Sidbury, and Gonzalo Quintero Saravia for this piece, as well as Christopher Leslie Brown, whose talk at the Huntington Library in 2017 first inspired me to consider the role of Fernando Pó and the Spanish Atlantic slave trade through the prism of the American Revolutionary War. Support for research and writing of this project was generously funded by a Franklin Research Grant from the American Philosophical Society, a Beveridge Grant from the American Historical Society, and a Research Grant from the Office of Research and Sponsored Projects at California State University, Long Beach. Thanks also to my research assistant Carlos Mayerstein for his work inventorying relevant documents from Argentina.

"Tratado de alianza defensiva y ofensiva celebrado entre las coronas de España y Francia contra la de Inglaterra; firmado en Aranjuez el 12 de abril de 1779," in Alejandro del Cantillo, ed., *Tratados, convenios y declaraciones de paz y de comercio:que han hecho con las potencias estranjeras los monarcas españoles de la casa de Borbón: desde el año de 1700 hasta el día* (Madrid: Alegria y Charlain, 1843), 552–554.

2 Gregory O'Malley argues that "in the foundational decades of slavery in English America (ca. 1619–1700) the dispersal of Africans was more haphazard, often taking place, not on merchant ships, but rather on the vessels of pirates and privateers." *Final Passages: The Intercolonial Slave Trade of British America, 1619–1807* (Chapel Hill: University of North Carolina Press, 2014), 85–86.

3 Gabriel B. Paquette, *Enlightenment, Governance, and Reform in Spain and Its Empire, 1759–1808* (New York: Palgrave Macmillan, 2008), 37.

4 For much of the sixteenth century, one pieza meant one individual slave. But some time during the seventeenth century, "the term 'pieza' evolved in a way that enabled royal officials to tax enslaved children at adjustable rates based on the value of one healthy, adult captive." David Wheat, *Atlantic Africa and the Spanish Caribbean, 1570–1640* (Chapel Hill: University of North Carolina Press, 2016), 101.

5 Eliga H. Gould, *Among the Powers of the Earth: The American Revolution and the Making of a New World Empire* (Cambridge: Harvard University Press, 2012), 59.

6 See chapter 6 of O'Malley.

7 Ibid., 221

8 Adrian J. Pearce, *British Trade with Spanish America, 1763–1808* (Liverpool: Liverpool University Press, 2007), 21.

9 Ibid., 22

10 On South Sea Company infrastructure in Spanish America, see Peggy K. Liss, *Atlantic Empires: The Network of Trade and Revolution, 1713–1826* (Baltimore: Johns Hopkins University Press), 9–10 and Stanley J. Stein and Barbara Stein, *Apogee of Empire: Spain and New Spain in the Age of Charles III, 1759–1789* (Baltimore: Johns Hopkins University Press, 2003), 295.

11 Stein and Stein, 296.

12 O'Malley, 263.

13 For early Iberian disputes over Africa and slavery, see Emily Berquist Soule, "From Africa to the Ocean Sea: Atlantic Slavery in the Origins of the Spanish Empire," *Atlantic Studies: Global Currents* 15:1 (January 2018), 16–39.

14 Pearce, 26–29.

15 Pearce, 29.

16 Ibid. Also see Gould, 59.

17 Frances Armytage, *The Free Port System in the British West Indies: A Study in Commercial Policy, 1766–1822* (London: Longmans, Green & Co., 1953), 13.

18 Pearce, 51.

19 This tax was levied at the moment slaves were branded upon landing at their Spanish American destination. See James Ferguson King, "Evolution of the Free Slave Trade Principle in Spanish Colonial Administration," *The Hispanic American Historical Review* 22:1 (February, 1942), 34.
20 Ibid., 36
21 See Alex Borucki, David Eltis, and David Wheat, "Atlantic History and the Slave Trade to Spanish America," *The American Historical Review* 120:2 (April 2015), 450.
22 Elena Schneider, "African Slavery and Spanish Empire: Imperial Imaginings and Reform in Eighteenth-Century Cuba and Beyond," *Journal of Early American History* 5 (2015), 20–21.
23 For an overview of these initiatives, see Emily Berquist, "Early Anti-Slavery Sentiment in the Spanish Atlantic World, 1765–1817," *Slavery & Abolition* 31:2 (June 2010): 181–205, as well as Rolando Melaffe, *Negro Slavery in Latin America* (Berkeley: University of California Press, 1975), and Schneider.
24 O'Malley has concluded that "British securing of the asiento was…part of an effort to co-opt all European trade with Spanish America," because "the slave trade was entangled with other branches of commerce," 222.
25 Pedro Rodríguez de Campomanes, *Reflexiones sobre el comercio Español a Indias* (1762) (Madrid: Alisal, 1988), 336.
26 Ibid., 94
27 Ibid.
28 Ibid., 94–95
29 Ibid., 335
30 Ibid., 336
31 Don E. Fehrenbacher, *The Slaveholding Republic: An Account of the United States Government's Relation to Slavery* (New York: Oxford University Press, 2001), 16–17.
32 Leonardo Marques, *The United States and the Transatlantic Slave Trade to the Americas, 1776–1867* (New Haven: Yale University Press, 2016), 13–53.
33 Anthony McFarlane, "The American Revolution and the Spanish Monarchy," in Simon P. Newman, ed., *Europe's American Revolution* (New York: Palgrave Macmillan, 2006), 32.
34 Trevor Burnard and John Garrigus, *The Plantation Machine: Atlantic Capitalism in French Saint-Domingue and British Jamaica* (Philadelphia: University of Pennsylvania Press, 2016), 200.
35 Ibid., 200–208.
36 Orden general declarando las condiciones con que Su Majestad ha concedido a sus vasallos de America el permiso de proveerse denegros de las colonias Francesas durante la actual Guerra, por haber finalizado su contrato la Compania de Negros. El Pardo, 25 de Enero de 1780. Sevilla: Archivo General de Indias, Indiferente 2820B.
37 Borucki, Eltis, and Wheat, 444–445. However, beyond this data there is very little information available. For instance, the forthcoming *Final Passages: The Intra-American Slave Trade Database* (which will be attached to the larger Voyages database project, Alex Borucki and Gregory O'Malley, eds.,) lists only a handful of slave voyages departing from the French Caribbean to sell their captives at Spanish Caribbean markets. Also see Gregory O'Malley and Alex Borucki, "Patterns in the Intercolonial Slave Trade across the Americas before the Nineteenth Century." *Revista Tempo* 23:2 (May/August 2017), 315–338.
38 Gonzalo M. Quintero Saravia, *Bernardo de Gálvez: Spanish Hero of the American Revolution* (Chapel Hill: University of North Carolina Press, 2018), 115.
39 Jose Antonio de Areche to José de Gálvez, Lima, 23 November, 1781. Seville: AGI, Indiferente de Negros 2820B.
40 Josef Antonio de Campos to King Carlos III, Madrid, 16 August 1783. Seville: Archivo General de Indias, Indiferente 2820B.

41 Antonio Sanchez Valverde, *Idea del Valor de la Isla Española* (Trujillo, Dominican Republic: Editora Montalvo, 1947), 174–178.
42 See Berquist Soule, 16–39.
43 Dauril Alden, *Royal Government in Colonial Brazil* (Berkeley: University of California Press, 1968), 59–135.
44 H.M. Scott, *British Foreign Policy in the Age of the American Revolution* (Oxford: Clarendon Press, 1999), 212.
45 Ibid., 213, 222
46 Jonathan R. Dull, *A Diplomatic History of the American Revolution* (New Haven: Yale University Press, 1985), 70.
47 W.N. Hargreaves-Mawdsley, *Eighteenth-Century Spain, 1700–1788: A Political, Diplomatic, and Institutional History* (Totowa, NJ: Rowman & Littlefield, 1979), 128.
48 Alex Borucki, *From Shipmates to Soldiers: Emerging Black Identities in the Río de la Plata* (Albuquerque: University of New Mexico Press, 2015), 2–3.
49 Ibid.
50 Ibid. Also see Fabricio Prado, *Edge of Empire: Atlantic Networks and Revolution in Bourbon Río de la Plata* (Berkeley: University of California Press, 2015), 32.
51 Alex Borucki, "The Slave Trade to the Río de la Plata, 1777–1812: Trans-Imperial Networks and Atlantic Warfare," *Colonial Latin American Review* 20:1 (April 2011), 91. The demand was so great that no fewer than 70,000 captives were brought to Montevideo and Buenos Aires from 1777 to 1812, with 6 out of 10 being imported through Portuguese ports in Brazil. Ibid., 4. A similar argument is made by Fabricio Prado in a forthcoming *Colonial Latin American Review* article on "Inter-American Networks."
52 Alden, 224–245.
53 Ibid., 68.
54 Prado, 34.
55 Alex Borucki, "Across Imperial Boundaries: Black Social Networks across the Iberian South Atlantic, 1760–1810," *Atlantic Studies: Global Currents* 14:1 (2017), 4.
56 Carolyn A. Brown and Paul E. Lovejoy, "The Bight of Biafra and Slavery," in *Repercussions of the Atlantic Slave Trade: The Interior of the Bight of Biafra and the African Diaspora*, Brown and Lovejoy, eds. (Trenton: Africa World Press, 2011), 4–5.
57 Gabriel B. Paquette, *Imperial Portugal in the Age of Atlantic Revolutions: The Luso-Brazilian World, c. 1770–1850* (Cambridge: Cambridge University Press, 2013), 30.
58 Ibid.
59 Ibrahim K. Sundiata, *From Slaving to Neoslavery: The Bight of Biafra and Fernando Po in the Era of Abolition, 1827–1930* (Madison: University of Wisconsin Press, 1995), 18.
60 "Descripción de la Isla de Fernando Poo, hecho por el Capitan de Fragata de la Marina Real Española, Don José Varela, 1780." Simancas: AGS, Estado 7411-2.
61 For more on the failed mission, see Manuel Cencillo de Pineda, *El Brigadier Conde de Argelejo y su Expedición Militar a Fernando Poo en 1778* (Madrid: Instituto de Estudios Africanos, 1948) and Dolores Garcia Cantús, *Fernando Poo: Una Aventura Colonial Española* (Barcelona: Ceiba, 2006).
62 Tratado de Amistad, Garantia y Comercio, Ajustado y Concluido entre el Rei. N. S. V La Reina Fidelisima y ratificado por Su Majestad en el Pardo a 25 de Marzo de 1778. En el cual se revalidan y explican los demas tratados precedentes que subsistían entre las Coronas de España y Portugal, cediendose a favor de la primera algunos Territorios y Derechos. (Madrid: Imprenta Real de la Gazeta, 1778.)
63 Borucki, 2015, 2; Borucki et al., 2015, 433–434.

64 Luis Ferlan, "Notas sobre la expedición del Conde de Argelejo y la presencia Española en el Golfo de Guinea (1778–1783)." VI Simposio de Historia Maritima y Naval Iberoamericana, Lima, Peru, 19–23 November, 2001, 6.
65 Borucki, 2011, 85.
66 "Instrucción que debe observarse para proceder a tomar posesion de las Islas de Annobón y de Fernando del Pó." San Ildefonso, 9 October 1777. Simancas: Archivo General, Estado 7411–1.
67 "Instrucción reservada para proceder a tomar Posesión de las Islas de Annbon y de Fernando del Pó." San Lorenzo el Real, 20 October 1777. Simancas: Archivo General, Estado 7411–2.
68 Conde de Argelejo, "Extractos de los puntos más precisos sacados de mi Diario," Sevilla: Archivo General de Indias: Buenos Aires, 41.
69 Ibid.
70 Sundiata, 4.
71 Conde de Argelejo, "Extractos de los puntos más precisos sacados de mi Diario," Sevilla: Archivo General de Indias: Buenos Aires, 41.
72 Ibid.
73 Ibid.
74 Ibid. Dolores García Cantús notes that the Santiago finally left for Spain on September 27, 1778, 26.
75 Conde de Argelejo, "Extractos de los puntos más precisos sacados de mi Diario." Sevilla: Archivo General de Indias: Buenos Aires, 41.
76 Ibid.
77 Conde de Argelejo, "Extracto de todo el trabajo y noticias adquiridas conducentes a mi Instrucción, y fines de la Corte en la Posessión de las Islas de Annobón y Fernando Pó." Sevilla: Archivo General de Indias: Buenos Aires, 41.
78 For narratives of the expedition, see Cantus and Cencillo Pineda.
79 "Don Joseph Varela Ulloa da cuenta de su viaje," Cádiz, March 12, 1779. Sevilla: Archivo General de Indias, Buenos Aires 41.
80 Ibid.
81 Ibid.
82 "El Pardo, 9 de Enero de 1779." Simancas: AGS Estado 7411–1.
83 "To Miguel de Luca, 16 October, 1780." Simancas: AGS Estado 7411–2. The letter reports the ships were captured on September 18, 1779.
84 "Bartolome Casabuena to José de Gálvez, Santa Cruz de Tenerife, 28 November, 1779." Sevilla: AGI, Buenos Aires 41.
85 "Primo de Rivera, Oficio, Fernando del Pó, 6 Junio 1780." Simancas: AGS Estado 7411–2.
86 "Declaration of Mauricio Pechuan, Sumaria Formada al Sargento Gregorio Martín, Padre Cuoto y Consortes, por el levanitmiento de Fernando Póo, 1784." Ibid.
87 "Gerónimo Martín to Joaquín Primo de Rivera, 24 Septiembre, 1780." Simancas: AGS Estado 7411–2.
88 Cencillo de Pineda, 162.
89 "Miguel de Luca to José de Gálvez, São Tomé, 8 Noviembre 1781." Simancas: AGS Estado 7411–2.
90 "Primo de Rivera to José de Vertíz, Bahia de los Santos, 29 November, 1782." Archivo General de la Nación, Buenos Aires: IX 10–10–1.
91 "Relación que manifiesta los individuos que han conducido a este Peruto el Navio Santiago, y la Fragata Carmen, relativos a la Expedición que salió de el en Abril de 1778 con destino al Golfo de Guinea." Simancas: AGS Estado 7411–2.
92 "Primo de Rivera to José de Gálvez, Montevideo, 15 Febrero, 1783." Simancas: AGS Estado 7411–2.
93 Paquette 2013, 30.

94 "Anonymous report on the Slave Trade," no date. Sent from Conde de Floridablanca to José de Gálvez on 23 February, 1783. Seville: Archivo General de Indias, Indiferente 2820B.
95 King, 50–52.
96 These statistics are in stark contrast to the only 11 voyages producing 3,537 slaves from 1765 to 1789. "The Atlantic Slave Trade Database," Emory University, http://slavevoyages.org/tast/index.faces.
97 "El Conde de Prasca en nombre del Marques de la Casa Enrile, Aranjuez, 5 May, 1782." Seville: Archivo General de Indias, Indiferente 2820B.

7 Spain's bid for the American interior?
The imperial contest over the revolutionary Great Lakes

John William Nelson

During the early morning of February 12, 1781, Captain Eugenio Pouré and sixty Spanish militia crossed the iced-over Saint Joseph River to surprise a British outpost. They had traversed the river routes north from St. Louis, over 400 miles, gaining support along the way from Indigenous allies and French residents of the Illinois Country. Without firing a shot, the detachment of Spanish soldiers and their allies seized Fort Saint Joseph, near present-day Niles, Michigan, raising the Spanish flag over the Great Lakes for the first and only time. The Spanish took several British traders into captivity, looted the fort's storeroom, distributed supplies to the local Potawatomis, and fled back up the river. Later accounts in Madrid boasted that the troops conducted an elaborate ceremony, in which they "took possession, in the name of the King, of that place and its dependencies," but the invaders did not linger long.[1] Local Indians' loyalties to the British, and enemy forts to the north and east made the spot untenable for any long-term occupation. The post's capture nevertheless brought the fight back to British soil and away from Spanish-held St. Louis and its subsidiary settlements along the eastern shore of the Mississippi.

Like the handful of British traders who woke to find Spanish soldiers at their gates that morning, historians of the American Revolution might find themselves caught off guard by the appearance of a Spanish show of force along the Great Lakes frontier. Even those familiar with Spain's efforts during the American Revolution typically think of the larger military campaigns waged against the British-held Floridas, or Gibraltar, rather than the North American interior.[2] In recent decades, the St. Joseph raid has remained the purview of public historians and archeologists who have preserved the memory of the event at a local level.[3] The last scholarly article to deal with the Spanish expedition to Michigan came out in 1985. Since then, few monographs covering the revolutionary frontier even mention the episode.[4] Even as scholars have begun to explore the entangled borderlands of the British and Spanish empires in North America, the raid has remained understudied.[5] Generations of earlier historians had dismissed this event as nothing more than a "mere plundering foray" along the frontier. So far, modern scholars have mostly followed suit.[6]

Yet the capture of Fort St. Joseph offers a striking example of the wider Spanish influence in the Illinois Country and lower Great Lakes both during the Revolutionary War, and after. Historians have demonstrated the importance of Spanish relations with Native peoples in the southeast and Gulf Coast, but the impact of Spanish actions extended much further north.[7] Far from a bit player in the riverine interior, Spain exerted real sway over the Indigenous politics of the upper Mississippi and lower Great Lakes. Threats of Spanish actions northeast of St. Louis animated British officers from Michilimackinac to Montreal during the war, and after peace came, similar fears of Spanish influence in the Northwest troubled American officials. Part of a larger history of Spanish activity in the Illinois Country and Upper Mississippi, the raid on Fort St. Joseph demonstrates Spain's continued significance in what would become the Old Northwest of the fledgling United States.[8]

Spanish and British officials had resided as uneasy neighbors in the Illinois Country since 1762. Though most of the European population in the area remained ethnically French, Spain had taken formal possession of the Mississippi River's western bank following the defeat of France in the Seven Years War. Fur traders founded St. Louis in 1764 across the river from the older French settlement of Cahokia. As Spanish officials established their authority there, the settlement became the center of commerce and government in "Spanish Illinois." In a geopolitical sense, Spanish authorities viewed the upper Mississippi as a key buffer against British incursions from the north. St. Louis sat upriver, as a vanguard to any British advances towards New Orleans, while the lower Mississippi acted similarly as a bulwark protecting Spanish colonial centers to the south and west.[9]

Initially, most of the friction between Spanish and British officials in the Illinois Country stemmed from trade rivalries and riverine access. Though Spain claimed sovereignty over the entire western shore of the Mississippi, prohibiting British and French traders from entering their territory proved a constant challenge. Bernardo de Gálvez, the Spanish governor of Louisiana, charged a succession of lieutenant governors sent to Spanish Illinois "to prevent the English from entering said rivers, and to see to it that they do not entice our Indians."[10] Spanish officials did the best they could, recruiting traders to patrol the rivers and authorizing them to capture any British traders and confiscate their goods. In March 1773 for instance, a prominent St. Louis trader, Pierre Laclède, intercepted Jean-Marie Ducharme, a Montreal merchant trading illegally with the Little Osage Indians along the Missouri River. Ducharme escaped with a bullet in his thigh, but Laclède seized his two canoes full of goods and several of his employees, taking them into custody on behalf of the Spanish government.[11] Such successful encounters remained rare for the Spanish, however. The multiple river routes connecting Spanish territory with the Great Lakes trade networks proved difficult to police, and traders like Ducharme continued to operate in both British and Spanish domains.

Indians, far from bystanders in such rivalries, satisfied themselves by playing the two European powers off one another. To taunt Spanish officials, Osage and Missouri Indians planted an English flag along the riverbank during their first visit to the newly built Spanish fort, Carlos III, in 1768. Meanwhile, Indians intentionally wore Spanish gorgets when meeting with British officials at Great Lakes posts. Pedro Joseph Piernas, the Spanish Lieutenant Governor of Upper Louisiana, saw such formal symbolism as key to Native relations, and even suggested that if he had some spare Spanish flags to distribute to his Indian allies, he might be better able to promote Spanish interests among the Native peoples.[12] In a precarious borderland where neither British nor Spanish officials enjoyed a monopoly over Indigenous relations, such symbolic gestures of influence proved vital to maintaining order.[13]

Spanish officials nevertheless commanded wide-reaching influence among the region's Indians, even beyond their own territorial claims on the western side of the river. Francisco Rui, commandant of the Illinois in 1769, reported a wide distribution of diplomatic presents among Native leaders. Spanish generosity extended to the "Ylinneses," members of the Illinois confederacy just across the Mississippi, but also Indigenous nations further afield, including Piankeshaws, Weas, Kickapoos, Mascoutens, and Miamis from the Wabash River Valley and Ojibwas, Potawatomis, and Odawas "of the river San Joseph and of that of Ilinneses." Worse yet, from a British perspective, Rui reported that "besides the above named tribes" some Indians from as far as British-held Detroit "are wont to come."[14] This diplomatic overreach disturbed and infuriated the British, as they struggled to maintain precarious alliances with many of the Great Lakes tribes after Pontiac's War.

Despite such commercial and diplomatic tensions, neither side proved willing to engage in open hostility through most of the 1770s. While the fur trade generated a significant amount of wealth for individual traders, neither imperial power saw the upper Mississippi Valley as a territory worth risking a war over. Even after American insurgents launched their revolution in 1776 and France joined the war against Britain in 1778, Spanish officials in the northern borderlands continued to avoid open aggression against their British rivals.

Spanish Illinois remained far removed from Britain's colonial revolt until George Rogers Clark, acting on behalf of revolutionary Virginia, led an expedition against British Illinois during the summer of 1778. Taking the British garrisons in the region by surprise, Clark's forces seized Fort Vincennes, Kaskaskia, and Cahokia. Now de Leyba, the Spanish Lieutenant Governor, found the American revolutionaries directly across the river from his St. Louis *azile*. Though instructed to keep his dealings secret, de Leyba began corresponding with the American commanders across the river almost immediately. George Rogers Clark wrote to de Leyba that July, thanking him for his treatment of the American emissaries in Cahokia and for the numerous speeches de Leyba had made to the region's Indians "in favour of us."[15] de Leyba approved shipments of supplies for the Americans, and even entertained Clark as a guest in St. Louis.[16]

British commanders in the Great Lakes, such as Arendt Schuyler DePeyster at Michilimackinac, were aware of Spanish aid to the American forces operating in Illinois. Yet they remained cautious not to spark open conflict with the Spanish while the two countries remained formally at peace. But with the declaration of war between Spain and Great Britain in June of 1779, British officials began to prepare for a grand sweep of the upper Mississippi Valley as a general plan to drive the American rebels and Spanish rivals from the west.[17]

The thrust of these plans centered on Spanish St. Louis, which was easily accessible through the river routes leading from the Great Lakes. Patrick Sinclair, the British Lieutenant Governor for the western Great Lakes, appointed Emanuel Hesse, a trader at Prairie du Chien on the Mississippi, to coordinate and lead the allied Indian and British forces for the campaign against St. Louis. Sinclair offered an incentive to other traders to join the expedition as well, offering monopoly licenses for the fur trade of the region should St. Louis and the west bank of the Mississippi fall into British hands. Jean-Marie Ducharme, among others, volunteered in hopes of this bounty.[18] The main contingent of British and Dakota allies assembled near the Wisconsin-Fox portage during the winter of 1780, while smaller supporting forces under Charles Langlade assembled at the Chicago portage. de Leyba received word of the gathering British and Indian forces in late March from a sympathetic trader fleeing the upper Mississippi.[19]

To defend St. Louis against the allied British and Indians, de Leyba dismantled the dilapidated Fort Carlos III and moved the five cannons to the outskirts of the city. He summoned all *voyageurs* and fur traders in from the surrounding area to augment his small force of defenders. He outfitted two bateaux, equipped with armed crews of militia and swivel guns, with which he planned to defend against any waterborne attacks along the Mississippi River. He also had a series of defensive trenches dug along the northern and western edges of town and began construction on four stone towers to house the artillery.[20]

Despite only completing one tower by late May, the Spanish proved ready for the British and their allied Indians when they arrived on May 26, 1780. The main force of British traders and allied Indians attacked the trenches on the northern and western sides of the town, skirmishing throughout the day with Spanish defenders. Hesse, in the meantime, sent Ducharme with a smaller contingent to the eastern bank of the river to take American-held Cahokia. The British and Indians were surprised to find St. Louis so well prepared for the attack, and with artillery and musket fire, de Leyba's defending forces managed to keep the British and Indians at bay. On the eastern shore of the river, American reinforcements arrived to drive back Ducharme's advance against Cahokia.[21] Parties of Indians captured and killed many people in the outlying settlements throughout the day, but even with their numerical advantage, the British proved unable to take St. Louis.[22]

With attacks on both sides of the Mississippi repulsed, the British offensive unraveled. Many of the Indians allied to the British fled up the Illinois River Valley, meeting Charles Langlade and his small rearguard near the Lake Michigan shoreline. The Dakota and the British traders in command likewise ascended the Mississippi. Writing to his superiors after the battle, Sinclair blamed the defeat on disloyal Sauk and Mesquaki Indians who had reluctantly joined the offensive, and the two traders, Jean-Marie Ducharme and Joseph Calvé, who he suspected of mixed loyalties at best.[23]

Meanwhile, in St. Louis, de Leyba degenerated quickly from a prolonged illness, and relinquished command to Lieutenant Silvio de Cartabona, who sent the official report of the battle back to New Orleans. de Leyba died that June, and throughout the summer, residents of St. Louis continued to write to Governor Gálvez in New Orleans asking for more support against the threat of attacks from the Indians and British. Summing up Spanish fears and ambitions in St. Louis in July of 1780, Picoté de Belestre pleaded with the governor to "send a commandant this autumn with aid" who would help St. Louis not only resist further attacks from the British but "to seek them at their home, and take away from them the desire to possess the Missouri."[24] The people of St. Louis desired to go on the offensive against the British. Governor Gálvez did not ignore such requests. On September 24, 1780, Francisco Cruzat returned to St. Louis to begin his second term as Lieutenant Governor there.[25]

After the British campaign against St. Louis crumbled, some adventurous French *habitants* in the Illinois Country saw a chance to capitalize on the retreat. Rallied by an independent French officer, Augustin Mottin de la Balme, nearly a hundred French volunteers ascended the Wabash River and raided a British trading post and Miami town in November 1780. The settlement and trading post lay abandoned at the time of the raid. After three days of pillaging, the force marched on to attack another Miami settlement on the nearby Eel River. En route, returning Miami Indians ambushed the volunteers, killing de la Balme and scattering the remaining French.[26] That same season, Jean-Baptiste Hamelin led a band of volunteers up the Illinois River to the southern shore of Lake Michigan, and then east to attack the British post at Fort St. Joseph. Hamelin's force took the fort easily, as the local Potawatomis had dispersed for their winter hunt. After looting the post and capturing several British traders, the small force fled west along the lake, taking "at least fifty bales" of furs and supplies with them. Dagneau de Quindre, whom the British had recently appointed Indian agent in the area organized a party of Potawatomis to pursue the raiders. The British and Indians caught up to Hamelin's force near the Calumet River. They surrounded them, killing four men and capturing seven more, whom the Potawatomis took as captives.[27]

These disastrous raids and counterraids along the Calumet and the Wabash Rivers in the last months of 1780 vexed imperial officials in both the Great Lakes and St. Louis. Likewise, Indigenous headmen were unsure which side to back, since neither the British nor the American, French, and Spanish contingents looked to hold any advantage. DePeyster and Sinclair continued to fret over possible enemy advances up the Illinois and Wabash Rivers. The British also continued to suspect the region's French inhabitants of divided loyalties and constantly feared their Native allies' defection to the Spanish and American causes. Sinclair made efforts to address these threats by relocating the local French families from strategic sites along Lake Michigan's southern shore, such as the St. Joseph River Valley and Trail Creek. Such exertions by the British, though often misguided, or unfounded, revealed British vulnerability along the Great Lakes frontier by late 1780.[28]

Meanwhile, Cruzat remained convinced a second British attack on St. Louis would prove forthcoming in the spring. At least 200 Canadians remained assembled at Michilimackinac in anticipation of another expedition setting out in the spring, and even the British held hopes to relaunch their drive south.[29] In late November 1780, the Anishinaabe headmen Nakiowin and Sigenauk, known as Naquiguen and El Heturno to the Spanish, came to St. Louis to persuade Cruzat to take the offensive against the British upriver. These two headmen wanted to launch a joint attack with the Spanish against the British supply depot of Fort St. Joseph, near the southeastern end of Lake Michigan. Cruzat feared looking weak in front of his Native allies, and in addition, an expedition with the Anishinaabeg would help shore up loyalties and weaken the British ability to mount another campaign of their own. Cruzat's best intelligence also suggested that a fur trader named Duguét, a Montreal merchant allied with the British, had resupplied Fort St. Joseph with military stores that could be used to support a second offensive against St. Louis.[30] Attacking the post and capturing or destroying the supplies would go a long way towards preventing another desperate defense of St. Louis itself.

Cruzat endorsed the Indians' plan and dispatched Captain Eugenio Pouré with sixty-five militia to attack the British. He also sent Louison Chevalier, a *Métis* fur trader who had grown up in the St. Joseph area and maintained kinship ties with the local Potawatomis. Chevalier served as interpreter for the expedition.[31] The party set out for the mouth of the Illinois River on January 2, 1781. More volunteers joined at Cahokia. Further up the river Jean-Baptiste Maillet's command of twelve men, forward scouts for the Spanish, also fell in with the expedition. The Spanish linked up with their Native allies and somewhere upriver from Peoria, the force abandoned their boats and began to trek over the frozen waters of the Illinois, and then the Kankakee Rivers.[32]

Pouré's combined force arrived near Fort St. Joseph on February 11, 1781 and a young Potawatomi, La Gesse (the Quail) ventured to the nearby Indian towns to negotiate their agreement not to interfere with the Spanish attack. La Gesse and Chevalier offered to share half the plunder from the raid with the local headmen. That a fellow Potawatomi, La Gesse, and a local *Métis* trader, Chevalier, led the negotiations proved significant in convincing the St. Joseph Indians not to intervene on behalf of the British, whom they had previously supported. They may have been even more willing to cooperate since Sigenauk and Nakiowin, fellow Anishinaabeg, had accompanied the Spanish northward. The St. Joseph Potawatomis promised they would not interfere. Local politics and personal relations played a direct role in their sudden neutrality.

The next morning, Pouré's force crossed the river and seized the fort without much resistance. There were no British soldiers present when they attacked, but Pouré's force captured the trader Duguét and his seven employees. The Spanish also distributed the trade goods at the fort to the local Potawatomis, as promised. Inspecting the fort's stores, however, Pouré's men found a large supply of food and other goods, which they suspected "the enemy had there in storage, without doubt for some expedition they had planned against us." These foodstuffs, comprising 300 sacks of corn and a large quantity of tallow, they destroyed to prevent them being used in the future.[33] This cache of fur trade rations proved enough to convince the Spanish that the raid had been a necessary endeavor to protect against further British attacks.

The Spanish orchestrated a formal show of their capture as well. Duguét surrendered the British flag that had been flying over the fort and Pouré replaced it with a Spanish one to signify their victory. Pouré drew up an "Acte de Possession," claiming to "annex and incorporate" the "Post of San Joseph and its dependencies," along with the St. Joseph and Illinois Rivers, on behalf of the King of Spain, which Pouré and his militia officers then signed.[34] Though Pouré's force never intended to hold the post, their efforts exhibited a formality meant to legitimize Spanish influence among the Indians of the Great Lakes and Illinois Country. Pouré hoped his demonstrations would sufficiently awe the local Indians and underscore Spanish power as an ally.[35] A Spanish show of force along the St. Joseph, with no resistance from the British traders at the fort, further emphasized English weakness—something Pouré and Cruzat no doubt hoped would deter local Indians from future alliances with the British.

The following day, Pouré's force withdrew back the way they had come. Lieutenant Dagneau de Quindre, the British agent active in the area, arrived on the scene too late. He tried to rally the local Potawatomis for a pursuit but, true to their agreement with La Gesse and Chevalier, they declined. Instead, they offered to accompany de Quindre to Detroit to report how the fort had fallen to the Spanish. Traveling to Detroit in early March, the St. Joseph Potawatomis made excuses for why they had failed to protect their British traders. Many of the fighting men had been away on a hunt, and the St. Joseph towns could not mount a force "sufficient to oppose one hundred white People and Eighty Indians." Furthermore, the expedition had been "led by Seguinack and Nakewine, who deceived them [the Potawatomis] by telling them that it was the Sentiment of the Indians in general to assist the French and Spaniards." DePeyster, now commanding at Detroit, became angered by the report and the excuse. He warned the Potawatomis against any friendship with the Spanish. He cited black legend examples from earlier Spanish conquests in "an Indian Country the other side of the Missisipi" where during "the time of your ancestors" the Spanish killed thousands of Native people to acquire gold and silver. He concluded his response to the Potawatomis by demanding they "return to St. Josephs and bring me the chiefs Seguinac and Nakewine" who he viewed as renegades of their nation.[36] DePeyster's demands came too late, and the reluctant Potawatomis never attempted to overtake the two errant headmen or their Spanish allies. Days earlier, on March 6, 1781, the Spanish expedition had safely returned to St. Louis and Captain Pouré presented the captured British colors to Cruzat.

Back in St. Louis, Lieutenant Governor Cruzat recognized the diplomatic, as well as strategic, success his men had won along the St. Joseph. The following August, Cruzat wrote to his superiors in New Orleans and Havana to report Pouré's success along the St. Joseph. He outlined the victory as twofold. First, in destroying enemy supplies he believed Pouré had detracted from the British ability to launch a second campaign against St. Louis. Second, the Spanish show of force along the Great Lakes meant Indians "of those districts who are our enemies have been intimidated and obliged by this event to maintain themselves neutral."[37] For Cruzat, the raid on St. Joseph represented both a military and political victory. Strategically Pouré's forces may have curbed a key British supply depot, but more importantly, the Spanish had demonstrated strength to their Indian allies and pacified Britain's Native auxiliaries.

The raid against St. Joseph had originated not as some grand geopolitical design for territorial expansion, but as a desperate local response to regional threats in Spanish Illinois. Cruzat had followed the suggestion of his Indigenous allies, going on the offense only to ensure the continued defense of St. Louis and to appear strong for the sake of Native alliances. However, those in the metropole interpreted this fringe action as a significant boon to Spanish claims in North America. As news of Pouré's raid traveled across the Atlantic, many interpreted this diplomatic victory not in regional, Indigenous terms, but in geopolitical claims to the North American interior during the waning days of the war. The *Gaceta de Madrid* boasted of the raid on March 12, 1782, offering a full account of the Spanish formalities of possession. Newspapers in Brussels, Luxembourg, Italy, and across Europe followed, reporting the Spanish sack of Fort St. Joseph, and suggesting further Spanish claims to the interior.[38]

The geopolitical implications of the Spanish raid worried American officials. John Jay, serving in Madrid as the Continental Congress's representative to the Spanish court, saw the significance of the incident. He sent a translated copy of the newspaper report back to Congress noting "the ostensible object of this expedition" and "the formalities with which the place, the country and the river were taken possession of" as a clear problem for American territorial negotiations.[39] To Americans concerned with holding onto the trans-

Appalachian west in any future peace negotiations, the Spanish raid complicated matters in the Great Lakes country.

While it seems unlikely that Cruzat ever entertained such grandiose ambitions when he sent the expedition against St. Joseph, European and American reactions to the raid demonstrate its significance at the highest diplomatic levels. As early as 1780, Chevalier de la Luzerne, the French minister to Congress, warned the Americans that Spain considered all lands west of the Appalachian Mountains available for "making a permanent conquest for the Spanish crown."[40] Spanish officials in Madrid and Paris contemplated the daylong occupation as a sign of conquest, while American diplomats like Jay and Franklin worried about what the attack would mean for U.S. ambitions in the west. Indeed, the raid had a lasting effect in that it fed American fears about Spain's influence in the Illinois Country and Upper Mississippi during the decades following the revolution. For American officials along the frontier, the raid demonstrated Spain's continued capability to intervene in events on both sides of the Mississippi River going forward.

Spain's incursions into the region haunted American officials in the decades to come. Though Spain's imperial claims to the Illinois Country went no further during the peace negotiations, the Spanish in St. Louis would continue to exert their influence over the lands, peoples, and waterways of the Illinois Country throughout the 1780s and 1790s. Navigation of the Mississippi River—controlled by Spanish Louisiana—continued to plague U.S.–Spanish relations in the west.[41] And while American commerce remained blocked by Spanish officials in St. Louis, American authorities worried over continued Spanish trade flowing through American lands by way of the Illinois River.[42] Governor Arthur St. Clair, who ventured as far as Kaskaskia in 1790, reported back to President Washington that the Illinois Country remained tied to Spanish holdings across the Mississippi through both commerce and kinship networks that spanned the international border. St. Clair described relations from one riverbank to the other as "still very intimate," which allowed for the flourishing of illicit trade and intercourse that the Americans seemed incapable of taxing or monitoring.[43] Meanwhile, Spanish officials at St. Louis continued to send emissaries among the tribes of the Illinois and those villages near Chicago—"particularly the Pottawautamys" who received wampum belts that same year from the Spanish.[44] Given the close ties Sigenauk and Nakiowin's Milwaukee settlements maintained with St. Louis during the American Revolution, it is not surprising the Spanish upheld diplomatic relations with the Potawatomis and other Anishinaabe settlements in the Great Lakes during the following decades.

The Spanish raid against Fort St. Joseph proved much more than a foray aimed at plunder. In the Illinois Country, Spanish officials contended within a world of competing Indigenous politics and exerted a real influence throughout the interior, both during, and after, the revolutionary years. Spanish officials in St. Louis conducted the expedition as part of an ongoing effort to maintain Indigenous ties in the upper Mississippi, and to blunt further British advances against Spanish territory. The raid fit within a broader Spanish strategy which saw the Mississippi River Valley as the first line of defense against Anglo-American incursions. This strategy held important implications for both Spanish involvement in the American Revolution and Spanish-American tensions along the Mississippi River after the war. Studying the raid as part of an enduring contest for influence in the region reveals the complex borderlands nature of the upper Mississippi and Great Lakes theatres during the American Revolution, and Spain's key role in that history.

Notes

1 Jared Sparks, ed., "Gaceta de Madrid, March 12, 1782," in *Diplomatic Correspondence of the American Revolution*, 12 vols. (Boston: Nathan Hale and Gary & Bowen, 1829), 8:76–78.
2 For Spanish campaigns in the Floridas, see Gonzalo Quintero Saravia, *Bernardo de Gálvez: Spanish Hero of the American Revolution* (Chapel Hill: The University of North Carolina Press, 2018); Kathleen DuVal, *Independence Lost: Lives on the Edge of the American Revolution* (New York: Random House, 2015). For Gibraltar and the Mediterranean, see Brendan Simms, *Three Victories and a Defeat: The Rise and Fall of the First British Empire, 1714–1783* (New York: Basic Books, 2009), 615–662. See also Larrie Ferreiro, *Brothers at Arms: American Independence and the Men of France & Spain Who Saved It* (New York: Alfred Knopf, 2016).
3 See, for example, the Niles History Center website: http://www.nilesmi.org/departments_and_divisions/niles_history_center/index.php/visit/fort-st-joseph-museum; in recent years, Dr. Michael Nassaney of Western Michigan University has coordinated an archeological project and public education program at the fort site. See Michael Nassaney et al., "Fort St. Joseph Annual Report" (Kalamazoo, MI: January 2018).
4 Stanley Max, "A Re-Evaluation of the Spanish Raid on Fort St. Joseph, Michigan, in 1781," *The Great Lakes Review* 11, no. 1 (1985): 12–22; The St. Joseph expedition garners brief mention in two recent works, Alan Taylor, *American Revolutions: A Continental History, 1750–1804* (New York: W.W. Norton & Co., 2016), 266; it appears in DuVal, *Independence Lost*, 186–187, but is attributed to de Leyba, who was dead by 1781.
5 For entangled histories of the British and Spanish Atlantics, see Eliga Gould, "Entangled Histories, Entangled Worlds: The English-Speaking Atlantic as a Spanish Periphery," *The American Historical Review* 112, no. 3 (2007): 764–786; Jorge Cañizares-Esguerra, ed., *Entangled Empires: The Anglo-Iberian Atlantic, 1500–1830* (Philadelphia: University of Pennsylvania Press, 2018).
6 For earlier historiographical debates over the significance of the raid, see Clarence Alvord, "The Conquest of St. Joseph, Michigan, by the Spaniards in 1781," *Missouri Historical Review* 2 (1908): 195–210; Frederick Teggart, "The Capture of St. Joseph, Michigan, by the Spaniards in 1781," *Missouri Historical Review* 5, no. 4 (July 1, 1911): 214–228; Lawrence Kinnaird, "The Spanish Expedition against Fort St. Joseph in 1781: A New Interpretation," *The Mississippi Valley Historical Review* 19, no. 2 (1932): 173–191; Don Rickey, "The British-Indian Attack on St. Louis, May 26, 1780," *Missouri Historical Review* 55, no. 1 (October 1, 1960): 35–42; A "mere plundering foray" comes from Theodore Roosevelt, *The Winning of the West* (New York, 1889–96), 2:179.
7 See DuVal, *Independence Lost*.

8 Lingering Spanish influence in the trans-Appalachian frontier continued to influence relations between the U.S. and Spain into the nineteenth century. Arthur Whitaker, *The Spanish-American Frontier, 1783–1795: The Westward Movement and the Spanish Retreat in the Mississippi Valley* (Lincoln: University of Nebraska Press, 1969); François Furstenberg, "The Significance of the Trans-Appalachian Frontier in Atlantic History," *The American Historical Review* 113, no. 3 (2008): 647–677; J. C. A. Stagg, *Borderlines in Borderlands: James Madison and the Spanish-American Frontier, 1776–1821* (New Haven: Yale University Press, 2009).

9 For Spain's acceptance of French Louisiana and the territory's role as a protective buffer, see David Weber, *The Spanish Frontier in North America* (New Haven: Yale University, 1992), 198–203; Paul Mapp, *The Elusive West and the Contest for Empire, 1713–1763* (Chapel Hill: University of North Carolina Press, 2011), 387–412.

10 Louis Houck, *The Spanish Regime in Missouri: A Collection of Papers and Documents*, 2 vols. (R. R. Donnelley & Sons Company, 1909), 1:166.

11 John Vattas to Haldimand, Michilimackinac, June 16, 1773, in *Michigan Pioneer and Historical Collections* [hereafter MPHC], 2nd ed., 40 vols. (Lansing, MI: Michigan Historical Commission, 1911), 19:302–304. See also Abraham Nasatir, "Ducharme's Invasion of Missouri, an Incident in the Anglo-Spanish Rivalry for the Indian Trade of Upper Louisiana, Part III," *Missouri Historical Review* 24, no. 3 (1930): 420–39.

12 Piernas to Unzaga, Ste. Genevieve, July 15, 1772 and Piernas to Unzaga, St. Louis, November 6, 1771, Archivo General de Indias, *Papeles de Cuba*, quoted in Nasatir, "The Anglo-Spanish Frontier in the Illinois Country during the American Revolution 1779–1783," *Journal of the Illinois State Historical Society* 21, no. 3 (October 1, 1928): 293.

13 After France transferred Louisiana to Spain, Spanish Indian policy in the Mississippi River Valley followed earlier French forms, which relied upon gift giving, formal councils, and well-established diplomatic rituals. See David Weber, *Bárbaros: Spaniards and Their Savages in the Age of Enlightenment* (New Haven: Yale University Press, 2005), 181–188. For French antecedents, see Robert Morrissey, *Empire by Collaboration: Indians, Colonists, and Governments in Colonial Illinois Country* (Philadelphia: University of Pennsylvania Press, 2015); Richard White, *The Middle Ground: Indians, Empires, and Republics in the Great Lakes Region, 1650–1815* (Cambridge: Cambridge University Press, 1991).

14 Report of Francisco Rui, May 2, 1769 in *Wisconsin Historical Collections* [hereafter WHC], 18:299–304.

15 Clark to de Leyba, July 13, 1778, letter reprinted in Nasatir, "The Anglo-Spanish Frontier in the Illinois Country during the American Revolution 1779–1783," *Journal of the Illinois State Historical Society* 21, no. 3 (October 1, 1928): 300.

16 See Lawrence Kinnaird, ed., "Documents: The Clark-Leyba Papers," *The American Historical Review* 41 (January 1, 1935): 92–112.

17 For British strategy on the Upper Mississippi and in the Great Lakes, see "Documents Relating to the Attack upon St. Louis," [reprinted from the Canadian Archives] *Missouri Historical Society Collections* 5 vols. 2:41–50.

18 Sinclair to Haldimand, May 29, 1780, *Missouri Historical Society Collections*, 2:44.

19 Rickey, "Attack on St. Louis," 39; see also Michael McDonnell, *Masters of Empire: Great Lakes Indians and the Making of America* (New York: Hill and Wang, 2015), 300–305.

20 Fernando de Leyba to Francisco Valle, St. Louis, May 9, 1780, in Abraham Nasatir, "St. Louis during the British Attack of 1780," in *New Spain and the Anglo-American West: Historical Contributions Presented to Herbert Eugene Bolton*, ed. Charles Hackett, 2 vols. (Los Angeles, 1932), 1:242; See also James Musick, *St. Louis as a Fortified Town: A Narrative and Critical Essay of the Period*

of Struggle for the Fur Trade of the Mississippi Valley and Its Influence upon St. Louis (St. Louis: Press of R.F. Miller, 1941).
21 Rickey, "Attack on St. Louis," 44.
22 For de Leyba's report on the battle, see de Leyba to the Governor, June 8, 1780, St. Louis, republished in Nasatir, "St. Louis during the British Attack of 1780," in *New Spain and the Anglo-American West*, 1:243–249. See also Quintero Saravia, *Gálvez*, 154–155.
55.
23 Sinclair to Haldimand, July 8, 1780, Michilimackinac, in "Documents Relating to the Attack upon St. Louis," [reprinted from the Canadian Archives] *Missouri Historical Society Collections* IV (1906): 48–50.
24 Picoté de Belestre to the Governor, July 10, 1780, St. Louis, republished in Nasatir, "St. Louis during the British Attack of 1780," in *New Spain and the Anglo-American West*, 1:259–261.
25 Rickey, "The British-Indian Attack," 35–42.
26 Harvey Carter, *The Life and Times of Little Turtle: First Sagamore of the Wabash* (Urbana: University of Illinois Press, 1987), 74–81.
27 DePeyster to Gen. Powell, January 8, 1781, in *MPHC*, 19:591–592. See also De Leyba to the Governor, June 20, 1780, St. Louis, republished in Nasatir, "St. Louis during the British Attack of 1780," in *New Spain and the Anglo-American West*, 1:253–254.
28 Susan Sleeper-Smith, "'Ignorant bigots and busy rebels': The American Revolution in the Western Great Lakes," in David Skaggs and Larry Nelson, eds., *The Sixty Years' War for the Great Lakes, 1754–1814* (East Lansing: Michigan State University Press, 2001), 145–165.
29 Cruzat to Gálvez, St. Louis, November 13, 1780, in Lawrence Kinnaird, ed., *Annual Report of the American Historical Association for the Year 1945: Spain in the Mississippi Valley, 1765–1794*, 4 vols., (Washington D.C.: Government Printing Office, 1949), 2:396–397.
30 Ibid, 397; see also Malliet to Cruzat, January 9, 1781, in ibid.
31 For the significance of Chevalier's role in the expedition, see Sleeper-Smith, in Skaggs and Nelson, *The Sixty Years' War*, 145–165.
32 Full report included in Cruzat to Miró, St. Louis, August 6, 1781, in Kinnaird, ed. *Spain in the Mississippi Valley*, 2:431–334.
33 Ibid., 432.
34 Eugene Pouré, "Spanish Act of Possession for the Valleys of the St. Joseph and Illinois Rivers," February 12, 1781, in Kinnaird, *Spain in the Mississippi Valley*, 2:418–419.
35 Acts of possession had a long precedent in the Great Lakes and elsewhere. For a wider study of comparative European practices in the Americas, see Patricia Seed, *Ceremonies of Possession in Europe's Conquest of the New World, 1492–1640* (Cambridge: Cambridge University Press, 1995).
36 "Indian Council," *MPHC*, 10:453–455.
37 Cruzat to Miró, St. Louis, August 6, 1781, in Kinnaird, ed. *Spain in the Mississippi Valley*, 2:433.
38 "Espagne, de Cadiz," *Mercure de Français*, March 13, 1782; "Espagne," *Journal politique de Bruxelles*, April 1782; "Spagna, Da Madrid," *Journal historique et littéraire*, April 15, 1782; *Notizie del Mondo*, December 1782.
39 Jay to Livingston, April 28, 1782, in Sparks, *Correspondence*, 8:76.
40 *Secret Journals of the Acts and Proceedings of Congress*, 4 vols. (Boston: Thomas Wait, 1820), 4:72.
41 For navigation of the Mississippi and other issues see Whitaker, *Spanish-American Frontier*; Eliga Gould, *Among the Powers of the Earth: The American Revolution*

    and the Making of a New World Empire (Cambridge, MA: Harvard University Press, 2012), 123–131; DuVal, *Independence Lost*, 262–269.
42 John Jones to John Hamtranck, Kaskaskia, October 29, 1789 in Clarence Alvord, ed. *Kaskaskia Records* (Springfield: 1909): 514–517.
43 Arthur St. Clair to the President, June 11, 1790 in William Henry Smith, *The St. Clair Papers: The Life and Public Services of Arthur St. Clair: Soldier of the Revolutionary War, President of the Continental Congress; and Governor of the North-Western Territory: With His Correspondence and Other Papers* (R. Clarke & Company, 1882), 174.
44 John Smith to Le Maistre, Detroit, October 20, 1790. *MPHC*, 24:108.

8 Spain and the American Revolution
A Pacific perspective

Emmanuelle Perez Tisserant

Writing a history of early Spanish and Mexican California in the 1870s, after it had been annexed by the United States (1848), ex-Mexican governor Juan Bautista Alvarado, born in California in 1809, offered his readers an anecdote about the first time the commandant of Monterey saw the flag of the new United States flying on a ship arriving in Monterey Bay.[1] Alvarado dates this encounter to 1817, a very late date even for this far-away Spanish Pacific province.[2] The whole narrative has to be read with care since it was written much later and after the annexation of California by the United States, a fact that might color the a posteriori reading of history. But, in spite of these caveats, this story is interesting in that it shows that the Californians, while acknowledging the strangeness of this new "player at the table," considered it within the world they were familiar with, not as something radically new, politically speaking, nor especially threatening.[3]

After an alert from the watch that a ship was approaching, the commander of the fort of Monterey, José María de Estudillo, tried to contact the ship's captain with the help of his horn. The latter expressed that he "did not know Spanish" but still answered that their flag was "*Americana*" while hoisting it up the mast. Estudillo, the commander, tried to find the flag in his flag book but since it dated from the "past century" he was not able to find the said flag even after searching again and again. Annoyed not to find it, he threw the book on the floor in anger and asked the captain to come to shore to report on his trip.[4]

On shore, the captain met the Spanish governor of California, Pablo Vicente de Sola, who investigated whether the captain and his crew were spies. The captain told him that he had a cargo of China goods and was willing to sell to anyone who might be interested. In the end, the governor let him go without authorizing the sale of his merchandise, since it was forbidden by Spanish trade laws.

His arrival had created excitement among the population of the small frontier town of Monterey (the capital of Spanish Alta California) and Alvarado describes their reactions: what first struck them was how the captain was clothed with a "swallow tail" suit. It might seem a detail, but as Alvarado again insists on the Monterey population reaction to the physical appearance and clothes of the representative of the new Mexican government in 1822, it should prompt us to take those comments relatively seriously. For those people, seeing new costumes, new flags, and even new haircuts was a powerful and visual proof of change. As Alvarado put it, "in 1822, it was not difficult to distinguish the nationality of the people who visited California because the Spanish were not clothed as the British or the Mexicans."[5] In the late 1810s, more and more new flags were appearing as new nations were proclaimed, and the Californians witnessed these changes on the increasing number of ships that came to the coast, challenging Spanish trade restrictions weakened by the crisis of the monarchy. In 1817, the date given by Alvarado for this visit, Americans (and their flags) had been coming to the coast for some time: around 1796 for Monterey, and as early as 1784 for the unsettled northern coast considered Northern California by the Spanish monarchy. But Alvarado has, I think, two reasons for mentioning this date. First, because it helps him set the context for the coming of the pirate Bouchard, disguised as an English explorer, in 1818, told right after: the people of Monterey and the Spanish authorities had to be careful about each ship coming in and who they pretended to be. Second, the awareness about the significance of the "Anglo-Americanos"[6] was brought to the fore during the revolutionary wars of the Spanish empire and particularly in 1818 with, adding to the crisis of Spain and its colonies, Andrew Jackson's campaign against the Floridas. However apocryphal, Alvarado's story points to the fact that the Anglo-Americans were not so much feared by the Spanish authorities for their revolutionary ideas but for their potential infringement of trade regulations, or worse, for their spying on the poor defenses of Spanish California for the sake of their government or for another foreign power. And finally, this episode about Captain Colorado highlights the main reason of the American presence on the Pacific coast of North America; that is, the development of American trade and commerce in the Pacific through new western routes.

Drawing from this anecdote, this chapter focuses on the relation between Spain and the American Revolution from a northern Pacific perspective, in particular from Alta California. Looked at from this standpoint, where the United States and Spain were not formally neighbors until 1819, allows for a slightly different narrative where the United States appears less as a new nation consolidating its borders and more as one more player in the European competition over the Pacific Northwest.

Indeed, whereas on the Eastern part of the continent the previous British colonies of the United States were trying to build a confederation and later a federation, the western part of northern America was under native sovereignty. In fact, as various historians have pointed out, 1776 was not only the year of the Declaration of Independence but also of the Spanish settlement of the Bay of San Francisco.[7] The last quarter of the eighteenth century saw not only the birth of this new nation but also the apogee of the Spanish empire, in particular on the Pacific coast of North America.

The western part of the continent was under native sovereignty, but the coast since the 1740s and even more so the 1770s had been the scene of European rivalry, with an increase in expeditions from Great Britain, France, Russia and Spain.[8] Russian explorers had crossed in 1741 the strait between Asia and America, and had started to collect furs and employ the native Aleuts on the Southern coast of today's Alaska. The Spanish monarchy considered the Pacific Northwest to belong to Alta California and started to worry about potential territorial encroachment, based on information and rumors of future Russian expansion more to the south.[9] Starting in the mid-eighteenth century, explorers from Great Britain and France mainly started to explore the region and attract more travelers. They were particularly interested in the possibility of finding a passage through the continent to China, a "Northwest passage." Such concerns were only increased after the Seven Years War (1754–1763). It was inspector (and later minister of the Indies) José de Gálvez' mission to design a better defense of New Spain, and he was instrumental not only in fortifying the northern frontier but in deciding to colonize Alta California.[10] The Spanish settlements of Alta California were founded in the 1770s (San Diego, 1769; Monterey 1770; San Francisco 1776) in the shape of forts (presidios), Franciscan missions and scattered *pueblos* in order to protect the heart of New Spain from foreign attacks and to confirm Spain's claim over the Pacific Coast of North America.[11] British explorer James Cook's voyages in the 1770s were pivotal in this Pacific history. The Spanish authorities were very much concerned, especially when they were conducted while Spain was at war against Great Britain. Indeed, during the last expedition in 1776–1779, the crew explored and described the places that were going to be central in the future Pacific trade—Hawai'i and the Pacific Northwest—at the same time that on the Atlantic side, Spain, Great Britain, France and the new United States were at war. For that reason, the governor of California was given strict orders not to let Cook enter the California ports. Although he never came to the coast effectively occupied by Spain, he did visit the northern coast that was considered by the Spanish monarchy to belong to Alta California.

Reciprocally, Great Britain tried to protect the secrets of Cook's expeditions' findings, but they were made public in the early 1780s in Europe as in the United States.[12] Indeed, the crew, in their published diaries or in person, described how they were able to sell otter furs bought cheaply in the spring of 1778 from the natives of the northern Pacific coast at a very interesting price in Canton. Because Cook was already very famous and because the trading nations with China were in dire need of a way to balance their trade, this came as very opportune news and it started a small rush to the Pacific Northwest from mostly British ships: several visited the Nootka area (on today's Vancouver Island) in 1785–1788. In Cook's crew was also an American, John Ledyard, who published his diary in 1783 and conceived his own plans for the future of the young nation's trade with Asia. This was crucial to the new nation because they were cut off from their previous trade within the British empire. The first trip by an American ship to China, which took place in 1784, was initially planned by this man. His plan was to use the potential of the Pacific furs by stopping in the Nootka area as he had done with Cook, but the financial backers of the trip decided that it was too risky and preferred a more traditional, easterly route to China. Hence, the entrance of the new nation in the China trade was not a "Pacific" one.

Instead of sea otters from Nootka, it would be a commodity grown in the United States, ginseng, that would be the cargo to be exchanged in China.[13] This trip was highly symbolic since this first Asian trip was made by a ship refitted from the American Revolution and backed by Robert Morris, who was a signator of the Declaration of Independence and had been a financial pillar to the American Revolution. It also marked the possibility for the Americans to buy their own tea from China, a fitting conclusion to a sequence started by the "Boston Tea Party." In 1789, a Spanish expedition sent to renew the monarchy's claim to the region found American and British ships in Nootka Bay, on today's Vancouver Island. One British captain claimed to have bought land from local inhabitants, in order to settle a trading post. The Spanish seized the ships and their crew.[14] This incident over Nootka almost started a new war between Spain and Great Britain (with France as an ally of Spain, before a reversal of alliances due to the French Revolution), re-awakening the threats of the American Revolution war and before that, the Seven Years War, to Spanish overseas possessions: but it was the first time that it concerned the Pacific. At Nootka, Americans had also been found by the Spanish, but because they seemed to respect Spanish sovereignty over the area, they were not arrested and they were simply ignored in this incident and on the eventual agreement of 1794, by which the Spanish monarchy abandoned its claims over the Pacific Northwest. This neglect of Americans compared to the British in the 1780s is also visible in Monterey, the capital of Alta California: the Spanish authorities, even in times of peace, were much more worried by the British and Russians than by this new nation, considered to be very distant and only a threat as far as the Eastern provinces were concerned.

In 1795, following the start of the war against France, a plan was adopted for the re-enforcement of defenses in Alta California. But generally Spanish authorities in California were more concerned by the British than by the French, even in times of war against the latter and alliance with the former (as in 1793–1797), because of their rivalry in the North American continent. As elsewhere in the Borderlands, this rivalry was expressed through diplomacy with indigenous people and societies, and in 1797 for example, the governor of California instructed the commanders of the forts to counter English "propaganda" by telling the Indians that "the English were enemies of religion, that they would destroy the churches, rape the women etc."[15] One may argue that this description fitted more the Revolutionary French than the English, but it was both a customary way to qualify Protestants from a Catholic perspective and an expression that the fear in California was not so much of Revolution (and independence) than conquest. Thirty years later, in 1827, the Franciscan missionaries would again warn against how Anglo-Americans were speaking to the natives in the interior of California in order to convince them to desert the missions under Mexican rule and join them instead.[16] For the missionaries then, the Anglo-Americans were seen as heirs of their British ancestors, but became at this later time, even more threatening for being located within North America and having exhibited their territorial ambitions.

The first encounters between the United States and California after the Revolution show general confusion about the status of the new nation. Even before the first American ship arrived in 1796, American citizens were present in crews of British ships visiting Alta California; one man even ended up being buried in Mission San Carlos near Monterey in 1791. In 1795, a Bostonian of Irish descent asked permission to settle in the province (he was not allowed to do so).[17] In the sources, there is no mention of the United States, only that this person was "*Bostonés de nación*." New England was where most of the people visiting California from the States were from, so "*bostonés*" became a common way of identifying people from the States. But it also shows that for the Spanish settlers and authorities of California at the time, the United States as a continental republic was not a distinct idea. An official document about the arrival of Captain William Shaler in 1802 mentions Thomas Jefferson as the "president of the colonies."[18] Often, in the sources, Americans are confused with the English, especially if they seem to pose a risk as in Shaler's visit.[19] Indeed, because Shaler and his crew were caught in the act of smuggling, they had to escape in a hurry and use their guns against the batteries in San Diego. In 1804, as one of the first merchant from the United States to trade and stay in Alta California, William Shaler wrote a description that he published in 1808 in the *American Register*.[20] There, he went beyond the usual description of the country and went so far as to criticize the government of the province and directly described the means to conquer it "easily" from Spain and keep it. He does not mention the United States explicitly to do it, but only a "great maritime power." Later readers of Shaler have made him the first to imply future annexation by the United States, which only proved right after the fact. What he did accounted more for lobbying: he was less a seer than a historical actor opening a possible direction that was indeed taken (and we remember more these than those who did not materialize). Shaler's biographer Roy F. Nichols suggests that Shaler might have been inspired by the recent acquisition of Louisiana by the United States in his words about the acquisition of California by a "great maritime power."[21] In any case, he was probably also inspired by George Vancouver's earlier description of Californian defenses.[22] Shaler was one of the people arguing for the new nation to become more interested in the Pacific and Pacific trade, one of those merchants who both by their actual trade and their writings would arouse interest in the potential of the Pacific Coast for the United States.[23] Some scholars have described those first merchants as a preview of what was going to come, the annexation of California, a so-called "Trojan horse," but the story was not written in advance.[24] As historian Duggan has shown, the California settler population, and especially those who were able to run contraband or receive gifts from the smugglers, benefited from this early forbidden trade (which does not mean that they started being "Americanized" for that reason),[25] which helped strengthen Spanish and Mexican California.

The clear change in perception came after the French invasion of Spain in 1808 and the first revolutionary movements in the Spanish empire from 1810, and even more so with the British-American war in 1812, when the United States seized Mobile to prevent it from falling into British hands. When before the missionaries had been quite silent about Anglo-Americans, like the Spanish officials had been in 1789 at Nootka, in 1813 they started warning that American ships were by then very familiar with the Spanish Pacific coast, where they had "intimate connections," in particular with people that were "engaged for independence from Spain." They even feared that American ships had left guns hidden on some beaches in preparation for an independent uprising. "Oh God! Anglo-Americans with the Hispano-Americans, beautiful union!"[26] exclaimed in 1813 the Franciscan father José Señan.

His nightmare was actually indeed taking place in other Borderlands to the East, although not as official United States diplomacy. The American Secretary of State did send some envoys to New Spain during the Mexican wars of independence, but not as an official support to the revolution. But individuals, in the name of the American Revolution and its ideals, and also to advance the United States' interests, were willing to do what they could: raise an army, gather intelligence, lobby their government to encourage Mexican independence. Those early filibusters did not meet success and were blamed by the government, but earned some support in the west were they were freer from the surveillance of federal officials and where relations with Spanish provinces were more ambiguous.[27] During that period also the Spanish authorities became quite weary of Joseph Napoleon's envoys to their colonies and often suspected Americans to be such envoys (not only in California but also elsewhere in their possessions).[28]

Hence, it was during this period of the 1810s that the potential of the American Revolution became fully understood, but concerning Alta California itself, it was more a fate similar to the *presidios* of the Gulf Coast that worried the Spanish friars. And, indeed, no insurgent uprising happened in Alta California during the wars of independence of Mexico. But Alta California suffered from the interruptions of supplies and communications by sea with the rest of New Spain in those years,[29] and was attacked in 1818 by Hippolyte Bouchard, a Frenchman who had put himself at the service of the Buenos Aires rebels and attacked loyalist positions in the Spanish Pacific.[30] By that year, Andrew Jackson had seized Pensacola and San Marcos de Appalachee in West Florida, and the news was known in California, at least by the Franciscan missionaries and the governor:

"The Americans have declared the war to us and they took Pensacola and Florida; the insurgents have blocked Panama. How much time before they come to California to destroy us?"[31] asked one of the friars.

Although Shaler had suggested it implicitly in his journal of 1804, there was no authorized plan or attempt to seize California ports from Spain during the Mexican troubles, contrary to what was happening on the Gulf Coast. Indeed, the situation in the Pacific stood in sharp contrast to the situation in the East, where the United States had a shared disputed border with Spain following the Louisiana Purchase, and where the American government feared a British attempt to profit from Spain's weaknesses in New Spain to gain control of territories or influence in the region and threaten their independence. This situation favored filibustering and concerned quite different societies. In California, the natives were a majority, and the settlers, although of mixed ancestry, were few and mostly from Northern Mexico.[32] In the East, earlier colonization from the Atlantic, proximity of Southern and Caribbean plantations, rivalry among European and Anglo-American powers for colonization and native support made the Gulf Coast a very complex place to understand loyalties, identities and strategies in the Age of Revolutions. Indeed, the Spanish provinces of Louisiana and both Floridas were engulfed in the Revolution, as recently retold by Kathleen DuVal.[33] Very early on the American Revolution had consequences on the Eastern Borderlands region, with historical actors focusing on access to the Mississippi and the Gulf Coast so that the people in the trans-Appalachian regions could export their goods. It led to mobilization and conflicts from those new communities and to antithetic but complementary projects of separatism and early filibustering. Moreover, when the wars of independence started in Mexico, contrary to Alta California, Texas, Louisiana and the Floridas were affected. As shown in other parts of this book, the American Revolution and the early period of the United States were a time of territorial fluidity in Eastern North America. The United States were not then as solid and victorious as may be thought given its later history. Those times were full of possibilities (and threats), including more independences or more territories allying with Spain. The American Revolution actually offered various options to North American communities: opting (back) for the British empire, as was considered in Vermont, forming yet another independent polity, joining the United States or even joining Spain.[34]

The situation started to get less fluid after 1810 in the East. As sensed by the governor and the Franciscans in California, the crisis of the Spanish empire caused by the French invasion of Spain and abdication of the Bourbon monarchs, marked a turning point.[35] Indeed, not only did it prompt the US government to seize Spanish ports on the Gulf Coast weakened by the Spanish crisis, but it also gave more meaning to the idea of America as the continent of freedom and opened possibilities, increasing considerably the potential of the ideas of self-government.[36] It was also, more pragmatically, the opportunity for the United States to negotiate in favorable terms about access to the Mississippi and their border with the Spanish empire, still in dispute after the Louisiana Purchase of 1803.[37] In dire straits, Spain agreed in 1819 to a boundary that held advantages for the United States both East and West: it gave the US the Floridas and access to the Mississippi and transmitted whatever rights Spain had on the Pacific Northwest north of the 42nd parallel. This definition of a US border west of the Rockies could then be used in negotiations with the British about the Pacific Northwest.[38]

When Mexico became independent in 1821, the new government worried about the loyalties of Alta California: they considered this territory as a part of their own jurisdiction but feared another power would take advantage of the situation to seize it. Lacking news from Monterey, the regency tried to gather intelligence from merchant ships or officers in cities or ports that were closer to the North and supposedly in contact with the far-away province: Guadalajara, San Blas, Mazatlan. The governor of Guadalajara was not able to give any specific news but warned of the danger that the province be seized by "the Russians, the British or the North Americans."[39] Although the North Americans are mentioned in the list, the Russians generally focused all the attention from the new government. They suspected that Spain could have preferred to give California to the Russians rather than letting it be part of independent Mexico, especially in the context of the European Holy Alliance.[40] One letter did convey the rumor of Americans disembarking in Alta California but in fact acquiring California would not be on the agenda of the US government and most Americans until much later. As for the Russians, they soon suspected that it was no longer in the power of Spain to give any right to any territory in North America.[41]

To conclude, from 1776 to 1783, the Spanish monarchy tried to consolidate its hold on North America by settling Alta California, sending ships to the Pacific Northwest and trying and connecting its northwestern possessions. This was less a response to the American Revolution than to fragilities demonstrated by the previous wars and increased foreign presence in the Pacific. The American Revolution was in itself also an evolution of the imperial situation of North America, partly emerging from the consequences of the Seven Years War. The new Union was a fragile, bold experiment, but one that had important consequences for the rest of the continent. Those consequences were varied, manifold and did not follow the same chronology. In California, as we saw, there was a delay in the perception of the newness of the United States and the consequences of the American Revolution for the Spanish monarchy and its colonial enterprise in North America. It was the conjunction of the War of 1812 and the crisis of the Spanish empire that really made the Californians enter into the world the Atlantic Revolutions created. In terms of political ideas, it would only be much later that a younger generation of Californians, after the independence of Mexico and after they would become convinced about the potential of republican and liberal politics that the American Revolution would become an inspiration (among others) for some in California.[42] As with the American Revolution, the Mexican independence process and federal and republican constitution had opened options of self-government and local independence,[43] a lesson that was not lost on the northern frontier.[44] Hence, the annexation of Alta California by the United States in 1848 cannot only be interpreted as a natural and logical consequence of this increased American presence in the Pacific. But as David Igler argues, they did play a role: "US commercial interests in the Pacific long predated and ultimately influenced its geopolitical and military interests of the mid nineteenth century."[45] In this way, the so-called "conquest of the west" was, as far as the far west and Pacific coast are concerned, also a conquest of the East. The Pacific trade of the infant United States and the burgeoning merchant communities active in it were crucial factors in the will to occupy Hawai'i, Oregon and California. But there was also a conjunction of other factors. At that moment, because of a lack of resources, the Mexican government was not able to gather the conditions of a proper security for Alta California against foreign attacks and raids from the interior, by groups of natives that had lived in the Franciscan missions before their secularization in the 1830s and American mountain men and adventurers who participated in a long-term traffic of cattle and stolen horses.[46] In the 1840s, immigration to Oregon often paired with immigration to the interior California almost making of the fort of Johann Sutter an American enclave.[47] On the American side, things had much changed, too, in terms of political culture and participation, integration of the trans-Appalachian West, slavery expansion and the subsequent tensions, and racialized nationalism.[48]

Notes

1 Alvarado, *History of California*, volume 1, pp. 125–131, manuscript held by the Bancroft Library (C-D 1).
2 The first American ship probably came around 1796.
3 William J. Barger, "New Players at the Table: How Americans Came to Dominate Early Trade in the North Pacific," *Southern California Quarterly* 90:3 (October 2008): 227–257.
4 Alvarado, *History*, 1, p. 194. A little later, Alvarado narrates how, at the arrival of the first Mexican ship, after the independence of Mexico the same Estudillo became so angry again to see that yet another flag was not in his book that he definitely threw it away.
5 Alvarado, *History*, 1, p. 195.
6 The Spanish Californians used several words for calling people from the United States, the most frequent being "Anglo-Americanos," "Americanos del Norte" or "Yankees."
7 Claudio Saunt, *West of the Revolution: An Uncommon History of 1776* (New York: W.W. Norton & Company, 2014); Anne Farrar Hyde, *Empires, Nations, and Families: A History of the North American West, 1800–1860* (Lincoln: University of Nebraska Press, 2011).
8 Katrina Gulliver, "Finding the Pacific World," *Journal of World History* 22: 1 (2011): 83–100.

9 David J. Weber, *The Spanish Frontier in North America* (New Haven: Yale University Press, 1992); Glynn Barratt, *Russia in Pacific Waters, 1715–1825: A Survey of the Origins of Russia's Naval Presence in the North and South Pacific* (Vancouver: University of British Columbia Press, 2011).
10 Luis Navarro Garcia, *Don Jose de Gálvez y la Comandancia General de las Provincias Internas del norte Nueva España* (Seville: G.E.H.A., 1964).
11 Weber, *The Spanish Frontier in North America*; Sylvia L. Hilton, *La Alta California española* (Madrid: Editorial MAPFRE, 1992).
12 Official publication was authorized after the end of the American Revolution war in 1784.
13 John Rogers Haddad, *America's First Adventure in China: Trade, Treaties, Opium, and Salvation* (Philadelphia: Temple University Press, 2014).
14 Warren L. Cook, *Flood Tide of Empire: Spain and the Pacific Northwest, 1543–1819* (New Haven: Yale University Press, 1973); James R. Gibson, *Otter Skins, Boston Ships, and China Goods: The Maritime Fur Trade of the Northwest Coast, 1785–1841* (Seattle: University of Washington Press, 1992); Annick Foucrier, "Rivalités européennes dans le Pacifique : l'affaire de Nootka Sound (1789–1790)," *Annales historiques de la Révolution française* 307:1 (1997): 17–30.
15 Provincial Records, 1, p. 182, Bancroft Library (hereafter BL).
16 Archives of the Archbishopric of San Francisco, 1935 (hereafter AASF).
17 "Mozo bostonés."
18 Provincial State Papers, 18, p. 244, BL (hereafter PSP).
19 PSP, 18, p. 265 José Velazquez calls the captain "el Inglés."
20 Shaler, *American Register*, p. 160.
21 Roy F. Nichols, "William Shaler: New England Apostle of Rational Liberty," *The New England Quarterly* 9:1 (1936): 74.
22 David Igler, "Diseased Goods: Global Exchanges in the Eastern Pacific Basin, 1770–1850," *The American Historical Review* 109: 3 (2004): 693–719.
23 David Igler, *The Great Ocean: Pacific Worlds from Captain Cook to the Gold Rush* (New York: Oxford University Press, 2013).
24 Doyce B. Nunis, "Alta California's Trojan Horse: Foreign Immigration", in *Contested Eden: California before the Gold Rush*, Ramón A. Gutiérrez and Richard J. Orsi, eds. (Berkeley: University of California Press, 1998), 299–330.
25 Marie Christine Duggan, "Market and Church on the Mexican Frontier: Alta California, 1769–1832." (Ph.D. dissertation, New School for Social Research, 2000).
26 AASF, 397, p. 262, Jose Señan to Governor Pablo Vicente de Sola, Mission San Buenaventura, March 18, 1813.
27 David E. Narrett, "Liberation and Conquest: John Hamilton Robinson and U.S. Adventurism toward Mexico, 1806–1819," *The Western Historical Quarterly* 40:1 (2009): 23–50.
28 PSP, 19, p. 282, 1810.
29 Because of native hostility, land communications had been cut in 1781.
30 Miguel Angel de Marco, *Corsarios argentinos* (Buenos Aires: Planeta, 2002).
31 AASF, 841, 911, 912, quote from 912. January 12, 1819 Fr. Luis Antonio Martinez to Governor Sola.
32 Ramón A. Gutiérrez and Richard J. Orsi, eds., *Contested Eden: California Before the Gold Rush* (Berkeley: University of California Press, 1998); Steven W. Hackel, ed., *Alta California: Peoples in Motion, Identities in Formation, 1769–1850* (Berkeley: University of California Press, 2010).
33 Kathleen DuVal, *Independence Lost: Lives on the Edge of the American Revolution* (New York: Random House, 2014).
34 James G. Cusick, *The Other War of 1812: The Patriot War and the American Invasion of Spanish East Florida* (Gainesville: University Press of Florida, 2003); Peter J. Kastor, *The Nation's Crucible: The Louisiana Purchase and the Creation of*

America (New Haven: Yale University Press, 2004); Kevin T. Barksdale, "The Spanish Conspiracy on the Trans-Appalachian Borderlands, 1786–1789," *Journal of Appalachian Studies* 13 (2007): 96–123; John Charles Anderson Stagg, *Borderlines in Borderlands: James Madison and the Spanish-American Frontier, 1776–1821* (New Haven: Yale University Press, 2009); Jason Farr, "A Glorious Failure: The State of Franklin and American Independence," *Tennessee Historical Quarterly* 70:4 (2011): 276–287. Jason Farr, review of *Review of American Emperor: Aaron Burr's Challenge to Jefferson's America*, by David O. Stewart, *Tennessee Historical Quarterly* 71:3 (2012): 259–260.

35 François-Xavier Guerra, *Modernidad e independencias: ensayos sobre las revoluciones hispánicas* (Madrid: Editorial MAPFRE, 1992); Virginia Guedea, "The Process of Mexican Independence," *American Historical Review* 105:1 (2000): 116–130; Manuel Chust Calero, "La revolución novohispana y la independencia de México," in *La patria no se hizo sola: las revoluciones de las independencias iberoamericanas*, eds. Manuel Chust Calero and Ivana Frasquet (Madrid: Sílex, 2012), 95–119.

36 Fitz, *Our Sister Republics*.

37 Piero Gleijeses, "The Limits of Sympathy: The United States and the Independence of Spanish America," *Journal of Latin American Studies* 24:3 (1992): 481–505.

38 Cook, *Flood Tide of Empire: Spain and the Pacific Northwest, 1543–1819*.

39 PI, 23, 14 and 18. Andrade to Iturbide, October 22, 1821.

40 PI, 23, 16, Andrade to the Regency, December 10, 1821.

41 Russell H. Bartley, *Imperial Russia and the Struggle for Latin American Independence, 1808–1828* (Austin: Institute of Latin American Studies, University of Texas at Austin, 1978), 140.

42 Douglas Monroy, *Thrown among Strangers: The Making of Mexican Culture in Frontier California* (Berkeley: University of California Press, 1990); Juan Gómez-Quiñones, *Roots of Chicano Politics, 1600–1940* (Albuquerque: University of New Mexico Press, 1994); Rosaura Sanchez, *Telling Identities: The Californio Testimonios* (Minneapolis: University of Minnesota Press, 1995); Michael J. González, *This Small City Will Be a Mexican Paradise: Exploring the Origins of Mexican Culture in Los Angeles, 1821–1846* (Albuquerque: University of New Mexico Press, 2005); Louise Pubols, *The Father of All: The De La Guerra Family, Power, and Patriarchy in Mexican California* (Berkeley: University of California Press and Huntington Library, 2009); Emmanuelle Perez, "The Evolution of Political Practices in Mexican Alta California and the Rise of the *Diputados*," *California History* 91:1 (2014): 72–73; Emmanuelle Perez Tisserant, "Nuestra California. Faire Californie entre deux constructions nationales et impériales (vers 1810–1850)." (PhD dissertation, EHESS, 2014).

43 Charles A. Hale, *Mexican Liberalism in the Age of Mora, 1821–1853* (New Haven: Yale University Press, 1968); D.A. Brading, *The Origins of Mexican Nationalism* (Cambridge: University of Cambridge, Centre of Latin American Studies, 1985); François-Xavier Guerra, *Modernidad e independencias: ensayos sobre las revoluciones hispánicas* (Madrid: Editorial MAPFRE, 1992); Peter F. Guardino, *The Time of Liberty: Popular Political Culture in Oaxaca, 1750–1850* (Durham: Duke University Press, 2005).

44 Andrés Tijerina, *Tejanos and Texas under the Mexican Flag, 1821–1836* (College Station: Texas A & M University Press, 1994); Timothy E. Anna, "Inventing Mexico: Provincehood and Nationhood after Independence," *Bulletin of Latin American Research* 15:1 (1996): 7–17; Andres Resendez, "Getting Cured and Getting Drunk: State versus Market in Texas and New Mexico, 1800–1850," *Journal of the Early Republic* 22:1 (2002): 77–103.

45 David Igler, "Diseased Goods", 707.

46 George Harwood Phillips, *Indians and Intruders in Central California, 1769–1849* (Norman: University of Oklahoma Press, 1993); Brian Delay has argued that such

raids on the northern regions of Mexico made them more vulnerable to the American conquest Brian DeLay, *War of a Thousand Deserts: Indian Raids and the U.S.-Mexican War* (New Haven: Yale University Press, 2008).
47 Albert L. Hurtado, "Empires, Frontiers, Filibusters, and Pioneers: The Transnational World of John Sutter," *Pacific Historical Review* 77:1 (2008): 19–47.
48 Reginald Horsman, *Race and Manifest Destiny: The Origins of American Racial Anglo-Saxonism* (Cambridge: Harvard University Press, 1981); Robert W. Johannsen, *To the Halls of the Montezumas: The Mexican War in the American Imagination* (New York: Oxford University Press, 1985); Mary P. Ryan, *Civic Wars: Democracy and Public Life in the American City during the Nineteenth Century* (Berkeley: University of California Press, 1997); Roger G. Kennedy, *Cotton and Conquest: How the Plantation System Acquired Texas* (Norman: University of Oklahoma Press, 2013); Fitz, *Our Sister Republics*.

9 Law in early modern diplomacy
The Jay–Floridablanca negotiations of 1780

Benjamin C. Lyons

Introduction

In April 1780, John Jay became the first accredited minister of the United States to set foot in Madrid. He had three assignments from Congress: to persuade his majesty, Carlos III, to 1) accede to the Franco-American alliance, 2) sign a treaty of commerce with the United States, and 3) grant the Americans a financial subsidy or loan. Jay achieved none of those objectives. He left Spain two years later, in May 1782, without treaty or agreement of any kind—and it is likely for this reason that scholars have shown little interest in his work. Yet the records of his negotiations, I will argue, are significant for the insight that they offer into the nature of diplomatic law in the revolutionary era.[1]

The term most often used to describe law in diplomacy during the early modern era is the "law of nations." Scholars generally approach this law via a series of treatises, published in northern Europe during the seventeenth and eighteenth centuries by philosophers such as Hugo Grotius (1583–1645), Samuel von Pufendorf (1632–1694), and Emerich de Vattel (1714–1767). Treatises of this kind were important to American revolutionaries, who leaned on them for insight into European legal norms, and historians often assume, consequently, that they must have governed the conduct of early modern diplomacy. In reality, European diplomats based their conduct on a separate set of norms—the "customary law of nations"—which they derived from precedent and common usage.[2]

Scholars have given scant attention to customary law to date—in part because it was unwritten and is hard to access, and in part because it was enforced in ways that runs counter to modern legal ideals.[3] The flaws were real; yet the customary law was not therefore insignificant. It constituted a sophisticated body of norms that governed matters ranging from war, to finance, to commerce and diplomacy. It required knowledge, skill, and experience to employ; and it played a particularly important role in the American Revolution—a contest that hinged on the Americans' claim to membership in the law-bound community of European states. Two facets of customary law were especially influential during Jay's tenure in Spain. Before examining their influence, however, some historical context is necessary.

The context for the Jay–Floridablanca negotiations

The American revolutionaries had been seeking political and financial support from Spain since at least February 1777, when their first agent, Arthur Lee, set out for Madrid. The Americans had reason to hope for a favorable response. Like most Spanish monarchs of that era, Carlos III harbored an abiding resentment of Great Britain for its earlier conquests of Spanish territory, the unequal treaties that it had foisted upon the Spanish crown, and British merchants' persistent illicit trade with Spain's American colonies. Since his accession to the throne in 1759, the king had in fact been preparing for a war that he hoped would destroy Britain's hegemony on the high seas and restore Spanish control over its empire and colonial markets.[4]

Yet the American Revolution was not the conflict that Carlos III or his ministers had in mind. As the ruler of an overseas empire, he was loathe to endorse a colonial rebellion. He also doubted the strength of the American cause—fearing that the rebels might reconcile with Britain and attack Spanish territory. Even if the Americans did prevail, the prospect of an independent state in the new world posed a greater threat to Spanish interests than Britain had to date. As a consequence, he rebuffed the Americans' initial overture in 1777—although he did promise to send covert material aid—and a year later, he rejected Louis XVI's similar request that he join the Franco-American alliance of February 1778. Not until April 1779 did Carlos III finally consent to enter the war, and he did so then as a reluctant ally of France—and not of the United States.[5]

For all of these reasons, Jay's mission had little chance of success. It might have ended quickly but for two new factors that gave the Spanish court a temporary interest, in 1780, in opening negotiations with the United States. The first had to do with Spain's military and strategic position. When Carlos III entered the war in 1779 he did so on condition that the French court agree to an immediate invasion of England, with the goal of bringing the war to a rapid end. The invasion failed and by December 1779 Spain faced a lengthy conflict with little prospect for gain. In that context, Carlos III allowed his prime minister, the Conde de Floridablanca, to open secret negotiations for peace with Great Britain. Jay's arrival in 1780, and the ostensible threat of a Spanish–American rapprochement, offered Floridablanca a useful means of pressuring the British to negotiate.[6]

The second factor had to do with a territorial dispute that arose between Spain and the United States at the start of the American Revolution. Since the conclusion of the Seven Years War in 1763, Spain had held title to all of the territory in North America west of the Mississippi River. The region was remote and difficult to defend, but it had been shielded from the threat of Anglo-American incursions by the British "Proclamation of 1763," in which George III barred American settlements west of the Appalachian Mountains. The American Revolution now threatened that detente. The Americans claimed title to the trans-Appalachian west, and with it navigation rights on the Mississippi River and into the Gulf of Mexico. It was imperative for Spain to curtail their ambitions. Yet the continental interior lay beyond the reach of Spain's military. The issue would have to be resolved through diplomacy, which was hindered by the fact that Spain did not have an accredited minister in Philadelphia. Jay's arrival in 1780 provided Carlos III with a chance to resolve this issue.[7]

Jay, as it turned out, was not authorized to cede ground vis-à-vis American claims to the western lands, and the negotiations might still have ended quickly but for a third factor that arose while Jay was en route to Europe. Just over six weeks after Jay's departure, Congress began to draw funds on his account in anticipation of his having received financial support from Spain. They did so by issuing what were known as "bills of exchange"—which functioned as currency in the Atlantic World until they reached the payee, who was required to redeem the bills for specie.[8]

Congress began issuing the bills in December 1779—in expectation that they would not reach Spain until several months after Jay had arrived. Jay's journey to Madrid, however, was delayed by technical mishaps at sea, such that the first bills arrived in May, just as his negotiations with Floridablanca were about to begin.[9] The bills put Jay in the position of a supplicant, needing to request specie from Spain in order to preserve the credit of the United States. Not surprisingly, Floridablanca seized on Jay's predicament as a means of extracting concessions vis-à-vis the Mississippi—thus setting the stage for a tense and protracted series of negotiations. As noted at the outset, Jay remained in Spain until May 1782. I will focus here on the first round of negotiations, which ran from June through September 1780, and which illustrate two aspects of customary law in diplomacy: the role of legal procedure in establish political legitimacy, and the role of honor as a mechanism for enforcing legal standards.

Legal procedure

As noted above, Carlos III could not conduct diplomatic negotiations with the United States prior to Jay's arrival, because he did not have an accredited representative in Philadelphia. He had not posted an emissary, in turn, because to do so would have been to recognize the statehood of the United States—a step that risked provoking the British and/or setting a bad example for his own colonies by endorsing a colonial rebellion. The issue was not limited to the establishment of foreign embassies. Any transaction carried out under the auspices of the "law of nations"—whether political, commercial, or financial in nature—conveyed at least some degree of political legitimacy. As a consequence, it was not even possible for Carlos III to conduct negotiations vis-à-vis an accredited American emissary in Europe, such as Benjamin Franklin, for even those negotiations required an exchange of credentials that carried with them a mark of political recognition.[10]

What made Jay's negotiations with Floridablanca possible was that the prime minister was not bound by the usual protocol. He had authority *ex officio*, or by virtue of his office, to speak on behalf of Carlos III. As a consequence, an exchange of credentials was not necessary and negotiations could commence without either party having to take a step contrary to its essential interests. Floridablanca did not have to publicly recognize the United States and Jay did not have to submit to procedures that would undermine the public dignity of the United States or its claim to statehood and independence. The situation was advantageous for Spain, yet it also gave Jay a degree of leverage in that Floridablanca now had an interest in keeping Jay in Madrid, as it was the only place where negotiations with the United States could conveniently take place.[11]

Honor

The second facet of customary law that came to the fore during the negotiations had to do with the concept of honor. Despite the gradual expansion of bureaucratic institutions over the preceding century, foreign affairs in Europe remained the exclusive prerogative of the sovereign. Sovereigns were by nature above the law, and yet their conduct in foreign affairs was not therefore altogether lawless. They were bound by their conscience and by a code of honor, which was tied to their public reputation.[12] Reputation in turn served as a guarantee for all public agreements between states. As such it was an asset that had to be preserved.[13] Of course, tensions invariably arose between a given king's interests and his honor or prior commitments, in which case it was incumbent on the king's ministers to preserve his interests while doing as little damage to his reputation as possible.

In the case of the Jay–Floridablanca negotiations, honor came to the fore in two ways. First, it was incumbent on Jay, as the representative of an inchoate political entity without a king, to establish the character of the United States in his public conduct. Secondly, and more importantly, the dispute that soon crystalized over the propriety of American conduct, in drawing on Jay's account without the prior authorization of Spain, was adjudicated in terms of honor. Success in that context hinged on accurate knowledge of normative standards of conduct, a precise estimation of the strength of one's position, and the ability to make a reasoned defense of that position.

The Jay–Floridablanca negotiations

When Jay arrived in the Spanish port city of Cádiz, in January 1780, he did not immediately proceed to Madrid, but sent a messenger to announce his arrival and ascertain how he would be received. Floridablanca responded in late February, welcoming Jay with the caveat that it was not yet "proper" for him to assume the "formal Character" of an accredited minister—though he could nevertheless be assured, "of the honest & sincere dispositions of [Carlos III] ... and [of] his desire that every difficulty whatever may be removed for [their] mutual felicity."[14] In his reply, Jay began to perform the public character of the United States, while also drawing attention to those attributes of Carlos III that had inspired the Americans' hopes.[15] "The Honor and Probity which have ever characterized the Conduct of Spain," he began, "together with the exalted Reputation which his Majesty has acquired by being an eminent Example of both, have enduced the People of the united States to repose the highest Confidence in ... his friendly Disposition towards them."[16] "Permit me to ... assure his Majesty," he continued, "that the People of the united States are convinced, that ... they can in no other way establish and perpetuate a national Character, honorable to themselves & their Posterity; than by an unshaken Adherence to the Rules, which Religion Morality and Treaties, may prescribe for their Conduct."[17] Jay then set out for Madrid, where he arrived in early April.

As formal negotiations were about to begin near the end of April, the first of Congress's bills arrived. They immediately left Jay with the difficult question of how to present the issue to the Spanish court. He determined to adopt a posture of confidence and to frame Congress's decision as an expression of their confidence in the king's generosity. "The drawing Bills," he wrote, "previous to notice of obtaining the Money to satisfy them, may at first view appear indelicate." He expressed hope, however, that the king's "Magnanimity" would "readily excuse it." "The Eyes of america," he went on, "are now drawn towards his Majesty ... and I flatter myself it will not be long before their hearts and affections will also be engaged by such marks of his majesty's Friendship, as his Wisdom & Liberality may prompt, and their occasions render expedient."[18]

As might be expected, Floridablanca seized on Jay's predicament as leverage with which to obtain concessions from the United States. At a conference on May 11 he affirmed the kindly dispositions of Carlos III, stating "repeatedly and in the strongest manner" that it was the king's intention to help the Americans, "whether formally connected with America by Treaty or not." Yet he also went on to recount the expenses that Spain had incurred in the course of the war, and the difficulties that they now faced in securing specie given that the treasure fleets had been suspended. He suggested that it would be in his power to advance £25,000—£40,000 by year's end. In the meantime, he promised on the basis of the king's personal credit to "take such measures as would satisfy the owners of [any bills that might be presented]."[19] Yet he emphasized that the Americans needed to offer some form of compensation in return—perhaps a number of "light Frigates, Cutters, or swift sailing Vessels of that Size, loaded with Tobacco or other Produce."[20]

As for the Americans' desire for a treaty with Spain, Floridablanca stated frankly that, "there was but one obstacle ... and this arose from the Pretensions of America to the navigation of the Mississippi." The issue, he continued, "was an Object that the King had so much at Heart, that he would never relinquish it." He nevertheless "hoped some middle way might be hit on ... to get over this Difficulty," and urged "Mr. Jay to turn his thoughts and attention to the Subject," while emphasizing "the King's favorable Disposition, his inviolable Regard to his Promises &c. &c."[21]

Floridablanca accomplished three practical objectives with his response. First, he performed his principal duty of protecting the king's public reputation. He also enticed Jay to remain in Spain for the next few months—by suggesting the possibility of future aid, though without making a formal commitment. Finally, he established the principle of compensation—the notion that the Americans had a moral or legal obligation to give something in exchange for Spanish aid. As Jay immediately noted, however, the United States was in no position to produce ships during time of war. It was true, he wrote on June 9, that "Timber, Iron, Masts, Shipwrights, Pitch Tar & Turpentine," were available, "but [they cannot] be procured without money." "[Congress's] necessities will not permit them to supply money to these purposes," Jay concluded, "and I should deceive your Excellency with delusive Expectations, were I to lead you to think otherwise."[22]

Floridablanca was of course aware of the Americans' financial predicament, and he likely made his suggestion in hopes that Jay would be compelled to offer rights to the Mississippi River as the only viable alternative. Jay rather turned the focus back to Carlos III's reputation, writing that: "The enlarged Ideas my Constituents entertain of the power, wealth, and resources of Spain are equal to those they have imbibed of the wisdom and probity of his Catholic Majesty"—leaning again on the king's magnanimity. He also pushed back at the notion that compensation was obligatory in such instances. "It is not uncommon," he wrote, "for ancient and oppulent Nations to find it necessary to borrow money in time of war." What more can "be expected from a young Nation brought forth by oppression, and rising amidst every species of Violence and Devastation." "I am ready," he reiterated, "to pledge [my constituents'] faith for repaying to his Majesty within a reasonable term after the war, and with a reasonable interest ... What more can I offer? What more can they do?"[23]

The two sides had now established their basic positions, and the core issue was as much moral and reputational as it was geopolitical and strategic. Congress was guilty of an impropriety in having drawn on Jay without permission. But was Spain justified in requiring compensation in exchange— and was the Mississippi a reasonable price for that aid?[24] Who had the better argument and who would back down first? At this juncture Jay upped the ante by informing Floridablanca that he had not yet asked Congress to stop drawing on his account. "I still flatter myself," he wrote to Floridablanca, "that some Expedients may be devised to surmount the present difficulties ... Influenced by this hope I shall delay transmitting any intelligence respecting this matter to Congress, till your Excellency shall be pleased to communicate his Majesty's further pleasure on the Subject."[25]

Floridablanca did not reply but rather allowed Jay's predicament to intensify. In late June he encouraged, "Mr. Jay not to be discouraged, for that with Time and Patience all would go well." Yet, for the first time, he declined to accept additional bills for payment.[26] When more bills arrived in the weeks that followed, Jay wrote again to request aid on July 11. Floridablanca responded that nothing could be done until a "certain person" had arrived in court. He gave the same reply on July 29, and again on August 12, stating now that he was "mortified" by the delays but could do nothing further. Thereafter, he ceased to respond altogether. When Jay attempted to visit the prime minister on August 26, he was told that Floridablanca was "indisposed."[27]

Matters finally came to a head in late August when Jay met with the French ambassador, the Comte Montmorin. Montmorin encouraged Jay to write again and "pray" for an audience with Floridablanca—remembering that the United States were "as yet only rising States, not firmly established or generally acknowledged &c." Jay refused. He had come to Spain, he said, to make "*Propositions* not *Supplications*." He considered America to be "Independent in *fact*" and could not "imagine Congress would agree to purchase from Spain the acknowledgment of [that] fact, at the Price she demanded for it." He intended "to abide Patiently the fate of the Bills, and should transmit to Congress an account of all matters relative to them." He would then write Floridablanca one more "Letter on the Subject of the Treaty, and if that should be treated with like neglect ... I should then consider my Business at an End."[28]

It is not clear whether Montmorin intervened on Jay's behalf, but in early September Floridablanca finally informed Jay's secretary that "the person" had arrived and that a meeting might be arranged shortly.[29] The person in question was Diego de Gardoqui, a merchant fluent in English and familiar with the American Revolution.[30] On September 3, Gardoqui called on Jay to review the state of the negotiations and reiterate Spain's demand that the Americans offer "Consideration" for a loan.[31] He returned that evening and "pointedly proposed" that Jay offer "the navigation of the Mississippi as a consideration for aids." When Jay objected that the River could not "come in question in a Treaty for a Loan of One hundred thousand pounds," Gardoqui asked Jay to meet him the next day at the house of Bernardo del Campo, Floridablanca's Secretary.

At this second meeting, the gloss of politeness was removed. Del Campo stressed the "Impropriety" of Congress having drawn bills on Jay without prior consent. He stated that Congress ought to have drawn on France, which was richer than Spain, and complained that Spain had been brought into the war as a consequence of the Americans' quarrel with Britain, but had "received no Advantage" for their efforts, and had heard of nothing but demands." Jay responded simply that if "he had been told plainly [in May] that no Money could be advanced, further drafts would soon have been prevented," but that "a contrary conduct" had been adopted (i.e. Floridablanca had encouraged Jay to remain in hopes of obtaining future aids) and "Expectations ... excited."[32]

When Jay persisted in that position, Floridablanca finally went on record as refusing additional assistance to the United States. On September 6, he authorized Gardoqui to accept bills valued at $1,110, while also delivering a *verbal* message that "the Exigencies of the State would not permit his Majesty to provide for the Payment of more of the Bills drawn upon [Jay] than had been already accepted."[33] When Jay asked for the message in writing, Floridablanca responded with an unsigned letter—dictated to Gardoqui, and thus not in Floridablanca's handwriting—in which he repeated the message while also averring that it was "not his majesty's intention to stop assisting the States whenever means can be found to do it," and stressing that the king "does not nor will change his Ideas, & will always retain those of humanity, friendship, & compassion that he had towards the Colonies." When Jay noted the absence of a signature, Gardoqui reluctantly penned his name.[34] Only at this point did Jay finally inform Congress that they should stop drawing bills on his name.[35]

In compelling Floridablanca to publicly deny funding to the United States, I argue that Jay won a tactical diplomatic victory—evidenced by Floridablanca's reluctance to put his decision on the record. The question is why did it matter, and what did Jay actually achieve? The victory did not yield funding for the United States, nor did it result in any dramatic change to the status quo. The French court ultimately agreed to cover the bills drawn on Jay to that point in the negotiations—such that the United States did not suffer a loss of financial credit. When additional bills arrived later that winter, Jay's negotiations with Floridablanca revived and would continue until May 1782.[36]

The incident nevertheless serves to highlight the importance of legal procedure and honor in the diplomacy of the revolutionary era. As noted above, states in the European system established their status as *states* every time they transacted business in accordance with the rules that the law of nations prescribed—i.e. through an exchange of credentials etc. At a deeper level, however, exchanges of that kind were but a superficial expression of confidence in the respective parties' character or good faith. In theory, states were still the possession of the sovereigns who presided over them, and whose individual character reflected that of the body politic as a whole.

In that context, diplomacy was not merely a contest over material or strategic interests. It was also a contest over reputation. Every formal statement that Jay and Floridablanca made in the course of their negotiations became part of the public record, and implicated the reputation of their respective sovereigns. Floridablanca's reluctance to publicly deny assistance to the United States demonstrates how important it was for Carlos III to retain a reputation as a magnanimous ruler. Yet reputation mattered all the more to Americans who—as Montmorin stressed in his conference with Jay—were not yet "firmly established or generally recognized." In the absence of formal acknowledgments of statehood, the Americans needed to prove their status through their conduct.

Law in early modern diplomacy   155

To succeed in this environment, it was not sufficient to slavishly follow the rules. One rather had to articulate a reasoned defense of one's policies and positions. A reasoned defense in turn required knowledge of the rules of conduct, and an accurate assessment of one's relative position. Congress was clearly guilty of an impropriety in drawing on Jay's account without permission. Had Floridablanca refused aid at the outset of the negotiations, the United States would have had no cause for complaint. He took a risk, however, in enticing Jay to remain in Madrid with deceptive promises of aid. Jay succeeded in this context by recognizing Floridablanca's ploy, and holding him to account in the face of intense pressure. In so doing, he pinned responsibility for the potential loss of American credit on Floridablanca, and defended the public reputation of the United States. He also drew our attention to the existence of customary laws that undergirded the conduct of diplomacy in the early modern era.

Notes

1 For Jay's instructions see "From the President of Congress," October 16, 1779 in Elizabeth Nuxoll, ed., *The Selected Papers of John Jay* (Charlottesville: University of Virginia Press, 2014) 1:716–717 (hereafter cited as *SPJJ*). Dated accounts of Jay's mission can be found in Rafael Sánchez Mantero, "La Mision de John Jay en España (1779–1782)," *Anuario de Estudios Americanos* 24 (1967): 1389–1431; Juan F. Yela Utrilla, *España Ante la Independencia de los Estados Unidos* (Madrid: Ediciones Istmo, 1988), 424–458; and Richard B. Morris, *Peacemakers: The Great Powers and American Independence* (New York: Harper & Row, 1965) 43–66 and 218–287.
2 One of the few historians to examine the influence of customary law is Paul Schroeder, *The Transformation of European Politics, 1763–1848* (Oxford: Clarendon Press, 1994)—though Schroeder's emphasis is on the early nineteenth century and he has relatively little to say about law in the revolutionary era. An oft-cited introduction to the concept of a law of nations is Arthur Nussbaum, *A Concise History of the Law of Nations* (New York: Macmillan, 1947). See also Benjamin C. Lyons, "John Jay and the Law of Nations in the Diplomacy of the American Revolution" (Ph.D. diss., Columbia University, 2017) for evidence that Americans relied on the treatises to compensate for their dearth of experience with professional diplomacy.
3 Randal Lesaffer, for example, writes that law in early modern diplomacy resulted in "political compromises" that made "no allowance for the dictates of justice," "Alberico Gentili's ius post bellum and Early Modern Peace Treaties," in *The Roman Foundations of the Law of Nations: Alberio Gentili and the Justice of Empire*, in Benedict Kingsbury and Benjamin Straumann, eds., (Oxford: Oxford University Press, 2010), 214.
4 For the context surrounding Spanish policy toward the American Revolution see Brian Hamnett, *The End of Iberian Rule on the American Continent, 1770–1830* (New York: Cambridge University Press, 2017); Allan J. Kuethe and Kenneth J. Andrien, *The Spanish Atlantic World in the Eighteenth Century: War and the Bourbon Reforms, 1713–1796* (New York: Cambridge University Press, 2014); and Stanley J. Stein and Barbara H. Stein, *Apogee of Empire: Spain and New Spain in the Age of Charles III, 1759–1789* (Baltimore: Johns Hopkins University Press, 2003).
5 For a summary of Spain's posture toward the American Revolution see Light Townsend Cummins, *Spanish Observers and the American Revolution: 1775–1783*

(Baton Rouge: Louisiana State University Press, 1991), 54–60. For early American efforts to engage the support of Spain see Richard Henry Lee, *Life of Arthur Lee, LL.D.* (Freeport, NY: Books for Libraries Press 1969 [1829]), 65–85. For the terms by which Spain agreed to enter the war as an ally of France see the Convention of Aranjuez in Samuel F. Bemis, *The American Secretaries of State and their Diplomacy* (New York: Alfred A. Knopf, 1927), 1:294–299.

6 For the failed invasion of England see A. Temple Patterson, *The Other Armada: The Franco-Spanish Attempt to Invade Britain in 1779* (Manchester: Manchester University Press, 1960). For Floridablanca's secret negotiations with England in 1780, see Samuel F. Bemis, *The Hussey-Cumberland Mission and American Independence: An Essay in the Diplomacy of the American Revolution* (Gloucester, MA: Peter Smith, 1968); and H. M. Scott, *British Foreign Policy in the Age of the American Revolution* (Oxford: Clarendon Press, 1990), 310–315. For Franco-Spanish relations during the American Revolution see Jonathan Dull, *The French Navy and American Independence: A Study of Arms and Diplomacy, 1774–1787* (Princeton: Princeton University Press, 1975); and Larrie D. Ferreiro, *Brothers at Arms: American Independence and the Men of France & Spain who Saved It* (New York: Alfred A. Knopf, 2016).

7 For the Mississippi Valley as a factor in Spanish diplomacy see Gonzalo Quintero Saravia, *Bernardo de Gálvez: Spanish Hero of the American Revolution* (Chapel Hill: University of North Carolina Press, 2018), 262–269; and Cummins, *Spanish Observers*, 158–160 and 165–166. See also reports from Juan de Miralles, Spain's unofficial "observer" in Philadelphia, along with related French correspondence in Mary Giunta, ed., *Emerging Nation: A Documentary History of the Foreign Relations of the United States under the Articles of Confederation* (Washington, DC: NHPRC, 1996), 1:1–25.

8 For Congress's decision to draw on Jay for up to £100,000 see "From the Committee of Foreign Affairs," December 11, 1778, in Nuxoll, *SPJJ*, 2:5. Congress issued the bills to avert a crisis caused by the depreciation of the Continental currency. On bills of exchange, see Jay's commentary in his letter to Floridablanca, of June 9, 1780, in Nuxoll, *SPJJ*, 2:147–148. For the currency crisis see E. James Ferguson, *The Power of the Purse: A History of American Public Finance, 1776–1790* (Chapel Hill: The University of North Carolina Press, 1961).

9 Jay's ship was dismasted off the coast of Newfoundland, and re-routed to the Caribbean—resulting in a delay of about two months. See Jay's report to Congress in Nuxoll, *SPJJ*, 1:733–743.

10 Over the sixteenth and seventeenth centuries, the principal sovereigns of Europe asserted exclusive jurisdiction over the conduct of diplomacy and foreign affairs such that transactions in those realms became a marker of statehood. There is a large literature on this subject, but for an introduction see Robert Jackson, *Sovereignty: Evolution of an Idea* (Cambridge: Polity Press, 2007). European states could and did conduct negotiations with non-state actors—such as Indian nations or kingdoms outside of the European legal system. Such negotiations, however, were subject to a different set of legal standards. Moreover, they were not a viable option in this case in that the United States was asserting membership in the *European* system of states.

11 See Jay's letter to the Conde de Aranda on September 10, 1782, in which Jay alludes to the fact that "his Excellency the Count de Florida Blanca…was *ex officio* authorized to confer with me." Nuxoll, *SPJJ*, 3:114.

12 Daniela Frigo, ed., *Politics and Diplomacy in Early Modern Italy: The Structure of Diplomatic Practice, 1450–1800* (New York: Cambridge University Press, 2000), writes that even in the eighteenth century, "the principles of 'distinction' and 'honour'… dominated relations among…European powers," 21.

13 See, for example, the French Foreign Minister's statement regarding Louis XVI that "Damage to his interests can be repaired; nothing would compensate him for the loss of his reputation." Vergennes to Montmorin, April 21, 1780, in Henri Doniol, ed., *Histoire de la participation de la France à l'éstablissement des États-Unis d'Amérique. Correspondance diplomatique et documents* (Paris: Imprimerie nationale, 1886–1892), 4:476.
14 To John Jay from Floridablanca, February 24, 1780, in Nuxoll, *SPJJ*, 2:41.
15 See also David M. Golove and Daniel J. Hulsebosch, "A Civilized Nation: The Early American Constitution, the Law of Nations, and the Pursuit of International Recognition," *New York University Law Review* 85 (October, 2010): 936, 943, for an argument that states acquired legitimacy through "performance" of law.
16 Jay to Floridablanca, March 6, 1780, in Nuxoll, *SPJJ*, 2:51.
17 Jay to Floridablanca, March 6, 1780, in Nuxoll, *SPJJ*, 2:51–52.
18 Jay to Floridablanca of April 29, 1780, in Nuxoll, *SPJJ*, 2:91.
19 "Notes on John Jay's Conference with Floridablanca," May 11, 1780, in Nuxoll, *SPJJ*, 2:105–106.
20 "Notes on John Jay's Conference with Floridablanca," May 11, 1780, in Nuxoll, *SPJJ*, 2:105–106. In early June, Floridablanca reiterated his position, stating that if the United States would supply Spain with "four good Frigates, and some other lighter Vessels," outfitted with Spanish materiel but manned with American sailors, and to be sailed under Spanish colors, the King would commit to paying the full £100,000 that Congress had requested in two years' time. Floridablanca to John Jay, June 7, 1780, in Nuxoll, *SPJJ*, 2:145.
21 "Notes on John Jay's Conference with Floridablanca," May 11, 1780, in Nuxoll, *SPJJ*, 2:107. Jay arrived in Madrid on April 4, but was consumed for several weeks in preparing a response to a lengthy questionnaire on American affairs that Floridablanca compelled him to fill out—likely as a means of delaying the negotiations, as he was then awaiting the arrival of the British agent, with whom he would be discussing a way out of the war.
22 Jay to Floridablanca, June 9, 1780 in Nuxoll, *SPJJ*, 2:148–149.
23 John Jay to Floridablanca, June 22, 1780 in Nuxoll, *SPJJ*, 2:165–167.
24 The £100,000 that Congress had voted to draw on Jay's account was roughly equivalent to four 70-gun ships of the line. See John Lynch, *Bourbon Spain: 1700–1808* (Oxford: Basil Blackwell, 1989), 314. By July 1780, however, Jay had received only $14,000 or £3,200 worth of bills. Meanwhile, Floridablanca was planning another invasion of England, with an approximate price tag of £1 million: Patterson, *Other Armada*, 228.
25 John Jay to Floridablanca, June 9, 1780 in Nuxoll, *SPJJ*, 2:151.
26 See Notes on John Jay's Conference with Floridablanca, July 5, 1780, in Nuxoll, *SPJJ*, 2:187–190.
27 See Jay's later description of these events in his letter to the President of Congress, November 6, 1780, in Nuxoll, *SPJJ*, 2:331.
28 Again, Jay to the President of Congress, Nov. 6, 1780, in Nuxoll, *SPJJ*, 2:332.
29 According to Bemis, *Hussey-Cumberland*, 80–97, Floridablanca's change of demeanor was linked to the ongoing negotiations with England, which came to a head at that point, and then ended without a resolution.
30 For more on Gardoqui see Mary Jo Kline's essay in this volume, which references Michael A. Otero, *The American Mission of Diego de Gardoqui, 1785–1789* (Ph.D. diss., University of California, Los Angeles, 1948); Natividad Rueda Soler, *La Compania de Comercio 'Gardoqui e Hijos': Sus Relaciones Politicas y Economicas con Norteamerica, 1770–1780* (Servicio Central de Publicaciones del Gobierno Vasco, 1992); and Alfonso Carlos Saiz Valdivielso, *Diego de Gardoqui: Esplendor y Penumbra* (Bilbao: Muelle de Uribitarte, 2014).

31 Jay replied, as before, that the United States stood ready to offer their good faith in exchange for principal to be repaid with interest. See "An Account of John Jay's conferences with Diego de Gardoqui and Bernardo del Campo, September 3 and 4, 1780," in Nuxoll, *SPJJ*, 2:232–233.
32 See again "Account of Conferences with Gardoqui and del Campo," in Nuxoll, *SPJJ*, 2:232–233. All of these statements were made off the record, by emissaries lacking the authority to speak on behalf of the king. As a consequence, they did not implicate the king's honor or undermine his professions of friendship.
33 The conference with Floridablanca was eventually postponed from September 5 to the 23rd.
34 Jay to Floridalbanca, September 14, 1780, in Nuxoll, *SPJJ*, 2:247; and from Diego de Gardoqui, September 15, 1780, in Nuxoll, *SPJJ*, 2:248.
35 To the President of Congress, September 16, 1780, in Nuxoll, *SPJJ*, 2:250
36 For French aid, see Franklin to Jay, October 2, 1780, in Nuxoll, *SPJJ*, 2:279–281. The dispute over rights to the Mississippi continued into the post-war era and was not fully resolved until the signing of Treaty of San Lorenzo in October 1795.

10 Sarah Livingston Jay (1756–1802)
A republican lady in Spain

Mary-Jo Kline

Sarah Jay's decision to accompany her husband John to Spain in October 1779 made her America's "first diplomatic spouse" while he served as the nation's first envoy in Madrid. Her thirty months in Spain should have ensured her, as well, of an honored place in the history of Spanish–American relations of the period. An educated woman and skilled writer, her letters for the period should create a brilliant legacy of word pictures of Spanish life and customs for her correspondents and later scholars. Logically too, the story of her life in Madrid should anticipate her later career as a popular public figure and diplomatic hostess in Paris and New York.

Sadly, these expectations were disappointed. While she remained a faithful correspondent with friends and family in America, her letters soon became almost entirely personal and domestic, seldom giving a sense of the Spanish world at large. They serve the interests of students of American "women's history" far better than those of scholars of diplomatic or international social history. If she is mentioned at all by historians of eighteenth century Spanish–American relations, it is as the vain, money-hungry, and domineering beauty portrayed in a 1785 memorandum from Diego de Gardoqui, Spain's postwar minister to the United States. Gardoqui was so convinced of her shallow, grasping nature, that he believed he could easily ply her with flattery and gifts so that she would persuade her devoted husband to accept Spain's terms in treaty negotiations.

The facts of Sarah Jay's earlier life make the sad outcome of her years in Spain seem all the more puzzling. Few American women could have seemed as surely destined for a brilliant and happy residence in the Spanish capital. The mere fact that Sarah spent nearly four and a half years in Europe is one of the most remarkable parts of the tale. Her husband was hardly the only American the Continental Congress sent abroad to seek aid from the Old World, but he was the only one to make the Atlantic voyage accompanied by his wife. Franklin, Adams, Deane, Lee –all left their families safely behind. The Jays left America together in October 1779 and returned together in June 1784, their time in Madrid followed by two years in Paris.

Her own family deserves part of the credit for her willingness to follow this novel and adventurous path. The Livingston heritage in New York mixed wealth, power, and radical politics. At her birth in August 1756, she was the fifth surviving child of William Livingston, the "American Whig," a lawyer-politician who opposed royal government in two royal colonies (his birthplace of New York and his adopted home, New Jersey) and led the State of New Jersey as governor through the Revolution. For the eight Livingston children who survived to adulthood, law and politics were equally the "family business." Another practical Livingston tradition meant giving girls the best education available to American women. Tutors ensured that Sarah and her four sisters learned to read critically and to write clear, lively English as well as to master French, mathematics, and the classics.[1]

The daughter of one patriot statesman, she became the wife of another. Not surprisingly, the beautiful Sally Livingston chose a husband as brilliant and increasingly "American" in outlook as her father, John Jay of New York. Just months after their wedding in 1774, Sarah's bridegroom and her father left their homes for the First Continental Congress in Philadelphia. Then came years in which Jay served in the various Congresses, Conventions, and Councils that governed patriot New York once war broke out. Their meeting places changed constantly as they fled enemy troops and raiders from British-held New York City, yet even after the birth of her son Peter Augustus in January 1776, Sarah made every effort to be at her husband's side. As she traveled from one small Hudson Valley town to another to be with him, the boy lived with Sarah's parents and unmarried siblings at Liberty Hall, the Livingston estate near modern Elizabeth, NJ. When John was returned to the Continental Congress in 1779 and was elected President, he rushed to rent a suitable house in Philadelphia so that Sally could be one of the few wartime "First Ladies" of the Continental Congress to join her husband. While there were plans to reunite parents and child, national events intervened.[2]

In September 1779, Jay was named the first U.S. minister plenipotentiary to Spain, and Sarah continued her established pattern of nomadic, quasi-public life to accommodate her husband's political career, sailing to Europe with him and leaving her young son behind in the care of his indulgent grandparents, aunts, and uncles. While duty may have played a part in the decision, the more basic explanation lay in the fact that the Jays liked being together. They were a notoriously happy married couple. As her brother remarked: "Mr. and Mrs. Jay can be lonely nowhere. They love each other too well."

When the Jays set sail for Europe in 1779, they were accompanied by Jay's official secretary, William Carmichael; Sarah's younger brother Brockholst; Jay's 12-year-old nephew, Peter Jay Munro; and Sarah's maid Abby, a slave who had been part of the Livingston family. They left behind two extended families, both in areas under constant threat of British raids and both expecting lengthy reports of the Jays' travels. In New Jersey, the Livingstons used maps in the family library to trace Sally's route in advance, and her brother William reminded her that, as devoted readers of Cervantes, they expected her to let them know "whether the ravishing Wit & Beauty of the

Ladies & the valorous Gallantry of the Men reign in them only" in the tales of Don Quixote.[3]

Sarah Jay was determined to oblige them with accounts of her life as a visitor and observer of the Bourbon kingdoms of France and Spain, beginning with her descriptions of the first leg of her voyage to Europe. A tropical storm nearly sank their ship, and Sarah admitted to her sister:

> It's true we have been in imminent dangers & to be very candid I did once think I never should have seen relations, friends, or Country more; but to confess the whole truth ... I determin'd with Cornelia to fall with decency, or rather with submission to acquiesce in the dispensations of Providence.[4]

They barely reached safety in Martinique, where Sarah rested and delighted in gorging on tropical fruits—and probably realized that she was pregnant with her second child. A 13-year-old slave boy, Benoit, was purchased there (with the understanding that he would be manumitted in half a dozen years), and in late December, this enlarged party set sail again on a French warship, landing in Cadiz on January 22, 1780. While Carmichael rode ahead to Madrid to investigate the reception they were likely to receive, the Jays remained in Cadiz nearly two months. Now in the second trimester of her pregnancy, Sarah gamely kept up her side of social obligations in the port: "tho' it was with difficulty I bore the fatigue of dressing, I return'd those visits I received."[5] In March, the party began the 300-mile overland journey to Madrid. An Irish serving woman joined them, and their two carriages were crowded with passengers and the supplies necessary for road travel in eighteenth century Spain – food, bedding, cooking utensils—in addition to baggage the Americans had brought across the Atlantic. Their first night on the road made them painfully aware that they'd neglected to purchase basic equipment needed to clean the filthy rooms of Spanish inns. "Was ever a broom deem'd part of travelling equipage before!" Sarah asked indignantly.

They detoured to the legendary city of Cordoba, and an Irish merchant took the Americans to see the great cathedral, which Sarah described breathlessly as "a vast & splendid Edifice." They trudged on, passing small wood crosses along the highway – memorials to victims of murder by bandits. Remembering her family's fondness for Quixote, Sarah wrote: "[W]hen we came to la Mancha we naturally recollected the exploits that had been there achieved by the renowned knight of the rueful countenance & looked but in vain for those large trees that sometimes afforded a safe retreat for the affrighted squire." Conscious of her responsibilities to her gentleman-farmer father in New Jersey, she closed with a practical analysis of Andalusian agriculture, paying tribute to the German settlers who had "made the barren wilderness to Smile."[6]

In Madrid, the Jays rented a pleasant house near the city wall. Sarah bragged that it had "the advantage of a fountain in the yard, a circumstance that few of the inhabitants can boast as they are supplied with all the water they use from publick fountains"[7] The house proved far more welcoming than Madrid at large. At first, all went well. Sarah's brother reported that a "master" had been hired to coach the household in Spanish, consoling themselves that the language should be easier to master than French.[8] In mid-May, Sarah wrote her mother that "I am pleased with Madrid, and expect that my satisfaction will be increased when I have acquired the language of the Country." Confined by advancing pregnancy, she had "made but five acquaintances among the ladies and the chief amusement I have hitherto taken has been in the riding way."[9]

Optimistic plans for a social life in Madrid evaporated when John Jay learned that the Spanish court refused to recognize his official rank as U.S. minister. He proudly declined any invitations to public events that did not include that honor. His vain pursuit of that recognition – and his constant search for funds for the American cause – meant that he had to follow the royal court as it moved among the king's favored country palaces, while Sarah's life in Madrid became one of odd isolation in a busy capital. In the first two months of her residence, "not a single Spanish lady" visited her, and protocol and pregnancy dictated that she could not visit them.[10] This proved the norm for the next two years, with the Jays' social life limited largely to the local French community of diplomats and merchants and visiting Americans. While her younger brother Brockholst was freer to roam the streets and observe life in Madrid, he had little good to say about what he saw there— "The Stupidity of their comedies is exceeded only by the Cruelty of their Bullfights – And when they attempt Tragedy, the whole is one continued scene of murder ..."[11]

The birth of her daughter Susan in mid-July and the baby's tragic death a few weeks later delayed any plans Sarah had for exploring Madrid as a private citizen. Only when winter came, and her husband returned from his obligatory visit to the court at San Ildefonso, did her spirits rally. Sarah became a tourist—for the first time in her life, visiting museums and being enchanted by the process. First, there was the Royal Armory at Alcazar. "I had no idea that the ancients were so well guarded from spears," she joked to her father while lamenting that "Poor Montezuma's wooden spear and painted Armor ... make but an humble appearance among those of the Europeans." Madrid's royal palace was "magnificent," as was its exhibition of "natural curiosities." King Charles III devoted so much time and money to improving his capital city that he was known as "el rey alcalde," the mayor-king, and Sarah praised his accomplishments lavishly: "beautiful walks, handsome fountains and excellent roads; the trees alone with which he has adorned the roads and walks would be to you sufficient proof of his taste."

As for the royal country palaces, she had to wait until May 1781 to see Aranjuez, the king's spring and summer residence, "[which] is generally thought to be the most beautiful."[12] She was not disappointed when she finally accompanied her husband to that grand new palace on the Tagus River south of Madrid. "Mrs. Jay is delighted with Aranjuez," Jay reported happily to Gardoqui, "It is without Exception the most charming Place I have ever seen."[13]

In the fall of 1781, when she accompanied her husband on his second pilgrimage to San Ildefonso, Sarah was even more impressed. Of the palace gardens she wrote:

> I can only say that they surpass description. I had often heard of them as being very magnificent, but still the Idea I had formed of them was inadequate as would be that of a person who should take his Idea of a first-rate ship of war from the view of a ferry-boat.

In the statuary, she saw

> [th]e whole heathen mythology & the metamorphoses of Ovid represented in an admirable manner by figures vastly larger than life; the fountains, Statues & marble urns are almost innumerable, & the water which forms the cascades, & that which is thrown up by the fountains (by some of them upwards of a hundred feet) is perfectly transparent.

Inside the palace, a carefully orchestrated guided tour of its "very valuable antiquities" failed to satisfy Sarah: "[I]n the lower apartments I think I sh[oul]d. Have remained immovable had not our conductor too frequently interrupted my attention by informing us there yet remained a vast deal to be seen ..."[14]

The need for such distractions increased as tensions developed within that pleasant house with a fountain where the Americans lived and worked. Even in Martinique in December 1779, John Jay and his secretary, William Carmichael, began to have differences. Six years Jay's senior, with earlier experience in the American diplomatic service, Carmichael chafed at his subservient role. In Madrid, Sarah's brother Brockholst fell under Carmichael's sway, and the pair drove Sarah to fury whenever they showed disrespect to her husband. For his part, John had to quell Sarah's outbursts as well as deal with the men who triggered them. By the summer of 1781, the household was divided into two armed camps.[15]

The year 1781 closed with several bright spots for Sarah Jay. Her brother Brockholst agreed to return to America, thus removing one cause of conflict. She was near the close of her third pregnancy, and news arrived that Cornwallis had surrendered to Washington at Yorktown. If the first two years of the Jay's residence in Spain had not been a brilliant success, there was hope that their public and private lives would improve shortly. In official terms, that hope lay in the possibility that Cornwallis's surrender might ease some of the constraints on their life in Madrid. Should Spain finally recognize American independence, their social horizons would broaden, and financial transactions would be eased. Meanwhile, the birth of a second daughter, Maria, in February 1782, brought new joy to the family, and the baby's Uncle Brockholst's departure for America was another cause for rejoicing. By the last week in April, Jay could report "Mrs. Jay's Time is much employed in nursing, and amusing herself with her little Girl. We are cheerful, and not unhappy, tho distant from our Friends."[16]

In a few days, the picture brightened even further. Jay received a letter from Franklin summoning him to Paris to join the other American commissioners named to negotiate peace with Britain. Jay acted quickly, asking his friend Montmorin, the French envoy, to determine whether Spain had any serious thoughts of recognizing America's independence and his position as her envoy. If not, he concluded, he would leave immediately for France.[17] Montmorin confirmed Jay's suspicions that there was no point in remaining in Madrid. Within two weeks, he and Sarah, their infant daughter, and their servants Ben and Abby were packed and on their way north to Paris.

Sarah's life in France was unquestionably happier than those twenty-seven months in Madrid. Jay and his colleagues scored a diplomatic triumph, negotiating a treaty that secured United States independence, with national boundaries stretching to the eastern banks of the Mississippi. Parisians welcomed the couple enthusiastically, and Sarah found herself in the midst of a social whirl that included trips to the opera (where she was mistaken for Marie Antoinette) and all of the city's notable landmarks. She welcomed another daughter, Ann, in 1783, and delighted in shopping – filling the orders of friends and relatives back in America.

Limited and isolated as her life in Madrid may have been, however, it had not been time wasted. Rather, it proved to be an invaluable tutorial for a woman destined to distinguish herself later in her home country, earning a place in the informal pantheon of "Founding Mothers." Maturity and sophistication came at a fast pace, living thousands of miles from home and family and learning to function in a strange society, struggling to master a new foreign language. Just as important, she used her days to learn about herself and the meaning of citizenship in that new republic far across the ocean. The realities of revolutionary America had already forced her to show patriotism in unexpected ways. Sarah Jay was not destined to live the private, "domestic" life her parents expected for her. The Livingston daughters were raised to think about public affairs, and their correspondence is filled with reports of government and war as well as family news and fashions, remedies for scurvy and gossip of the day—all topics their family deemed appropriate for members of their sex. Sarah's marriage to John Jay meant that she pursued these studies of public affairs more openly and no longer observed them from a purely private vantage point.

Thus, while seeing the wonders of Spain, it was no wonder that Sarah felt herself becoming more and more "American" with each month. Her family reinforced this pride with reports of the latest activities of American women patriots. On reading published descriptions of one women's fund-raising campaign for the relief of troops, Sarah admitted that she was "quite charmed" with the documents as well as with everything "truly American."[18] In raising their daughters with a taste for public affairs, the Livingstons may also have anticipated the concept later dubbed "republican motherhood," the conviction of America's revolutionary generation that the ideals of republicanism should be instilled in daughters as well as sons so that these girls could pass these values on to their own children, creating still another generation of patriots.[19] Residence on another continent did not excuse Sarah Jay from the responsibilities of motherhood any more than from those of patriotism, and her correspondence from Spain details just what she felt those obligations were.

Modern scholars marvel at the record of her long-distance guidance of the education of the 3½-year-old son she left behind in New Jersey in 1779. Few expressed as well as she what "republican motherhood" meant. Writing her sister from Madrid in the summer of 1781, she reflected on her choice of the fabric she had sent for a suit for her boy— cloth that was "a proper color & kind for a little republican to play about in & pursue those exercises which strengthen the Constitution & thereby enable him one day to serve his Country in those employments which require vigour of body as well as strength of mind." She admonished the boy's aunt to keep young Peter focused on "two great objects for his pursuit" that of pleasing God and making "himself useful to his fellow creatures, especially to his own Country, which after the Deity has the first right to his services not excepting his life itself. Perhaps," she admitted, "you'll think me premature in my advice, but really I'm of a different opinion, & think the human mind susceptible of great & good impressions at a very tender age ..."[20]

Both sides of their extended families were, of course, part of the campaign to give Sarah and John Jay's first-born son a proper, republican education. His Grandfather Livingston obliged the 5-year-old's request by buying him a copy of the *Continental Primer*, and bragged to his daughter that he'd written a note to his grandson "imitating printers types which he was able to read & understand."[21] Six months later, Peter could print his name at the foot of a letter dictated to his aunt and reported that he had not only finished the primer but also read through "Aisops Dull Ass" and "a very well-illustrated pretty book of Tales" while he awaited a shipment of books from another aunt who was visiting Philadelphia.[22] In the Hudson Valley, the Jays encouraged the boy's progress just as vigorously, and there was more than a little rivalry between the two clans in their determination to encourage Peter's progress in reading and writing.[23]

While appropriate educational materials were scarce in Spain, Sarah transmitted regular orders through visiting Americans on their way north. David Franks, for instance, was commissioned to buy a set of maps in Nantes similar to some Sarah remembered from her own girlhood so that "he [Peter] may learn Geography while he only thinks of amusement."[24] Later, in France, Sarah could indulge her purchases in juvenile literature in person. She subscribed to Berquin's monthly *L'Amie des Enfans* and suggested to her father that they translate into English

> those little volumes [in which] the excellence of virtue and the depravity of vice is contrasted by the examples of Children of amiable and unamiable characters in so natural and easy a manner as cannot fail to impress the tender and uncorrupted minds of children with proper dispositions.[25]

These efforts to raise a young patriot apparently worked, for Peter was bitterly disappointed when he was not given gunpowder to make explosive "squibs" to celebrate Cornwallis's surrender in October 1781. While Sarah approved her father's decision to keep gunpowder out of the hands of a 5½-year-old boy, she admitted: "I am glad to find that my little spark had kindled upon that occasion, & am pleas'd when I reflect that where he is, the sentiments of Liberty will be cherish'd in him by education …"[26]

That "little spark" was more than 8 years old before his mother could resume personal supervision of that education—it was June 1, 1784, before the Jays, their two young daughters, their nephew Peter Jay Munro, and Sarah's French maid set sail from Dover for New York City. After four and a half years, they were home – reunited with their son and ready to start a new adventure, one that kept Sarah in the public eye and returned her briefly to the story of "Spain and the American Revolution."

Congress had plans for John Jay other than a quiet retirement spent building the mansion whose plans he'd been drafting for months. Well before his arrival back home, he was elected Secretary for Foreign Affairs, a post left embarrassingly vacant for more than a year. After due consideration, Jay agreed to serve—once Congress agreed to a list of conditions that included an end to their restless moves and a permanent settlement—preferably in Manhattan, the Jays' preferred residence. In December 1784, Jay began to set up the New York office where he would work for the next four and a half years.

His position in the government took on a significance he could not have anticipated. Not only did he head the most important department under the Articles of Confederation, but he would also prove to be the only permanent member of the executive branch of that government until the installation of the new federal regime in 1789. Indeed, one historian describes Jay as "premier" of the United States for that era. This, in turn, made the Jays' grand stone mansion on Broadway the site of formal government receptions and weekly dinners and receptions for American worthies, visiting foreigners, and the diplomatic corps. Presiding over this, Sarah, without title or formal recognition, became the republic's unofficial "first lady," employing all that she had learned of European etiquette and customs as she entertained guests from Britain and the Continent in the style to which they were accustomed.[27] Remarkably, she displayed her knowledge of the proprieties of the Old World while proudly bearing her New World patriotism. On meeting her for the first time in 1788, Abigail Adams said: "mrs Jay has all the vivacity of a French woman blended with the modesty & Softness of an American Lady."[28]

Meanwhile, the Spanish government finally named its first official envoy to America, the same Diego de Gardoqui who had worked with Jay in Madrid. Gardoqui was commissioned in the fall of 1784, well before Jay accepted his government post, and the Basque merchant-diplomat sailed for America, unsure of whom he might be dealing with. As luck had it, Gardoqui's ship foundered, and vessel and passengers wintered in Havana. Once Gardoqui resumed his journey, he directed the ship to Philadelphia, unaware that the government had decamped to New York.

Otherwise, Gardoqui felt himself well prepared. He brought a plan of action approved by Floridablanca, the Spanish foreign minister, one that Gardoqui believed would enable him to bend both Jay and the Congress to the Spanish court's wishes. Success rested on the accuracy of Gardoqui's assessment of Jay as a man

> who is generally considered to possess talent and capacity enough to help conceal a natural weakness, [who] reveals himself consistently to be a very self-centered man, a passion his wife encourages, because, in addition to having a high opinion of herself and being rather vain, she likes to be catered to and even more to receive presents.

Gardoqui's portrait of Sarah Jay was no more flattering: "This woman, whom he loves blindly, dominates him and nothing is done without her consent, so that her opinion prevails, though her husband at first may disagree. From this," he concluded, "I infer that a little management in dealing with her and a few timely gifts will secure the friendship of both, because I have reason to believe that they are resolved to make a fortune." Further, he wrote, Jay

> is not the only one in his country with this weakness, for there are many poor men among the Congress, the governing body, and I believe a skillful professional who knows how to seize favorable opportunities, how to give dinners, and above all to entertain with good wine, may profit without appearing to manipulate them.[29]

In New York, Gardoqui lost no time putting his scheme into action. On the first of October 1785, his card and a "valuable Present" were delivered to the Jays' home. John was out of town, and Sarah waited for his return so that "so delicate an occasion" could be addressed. Three days later, the boxes were returned to Gardoqui, with a brief note from John explaining why the gifts could not be accepted: "several Considerations have weight with public Characters, that do not apply to private Individuals," while assuring Gardoqui that the "mark of Attention and the Friendship' & Regard it manifests" was duly appreciated.[30]

Gardoqui was not discouraged. Jay had asked his help in obtaining a permit to buy a horse in Spain and bring it to the United States. Gardoqui interpreted this as a broad hint and wrote Madrid that Jay would be delighted to receive the horse as a gift. A stallion was chosen and shipped on his way to New York, where Jay faced the awkward dilemma of deciding what to do with the animal. He told Gardoqui immediately that he could not accept such a gift without his government's permission, and he submitted an official query on the matter to Congress. At the same time, Jay wrote in confidence to Charles Thomson, secretary of Congress, suggesting that if there was any problem in his accepting the gift, "I would immediately press Mr Gardoqui to put the Horse to Death – the Length of the Passage would account for it and further Discussions be avoided." Luckily Congress approved Jay's acceptance of the animal, and bloodshed was avoided.[31]

There is no evidence whatever that Gardoqui's gift-giving campaign (both aborted and actual) had any effect on Spanish–American relations. For the remainder of his stay in New York, he and the Jays exchanged social invitations. Gardoqui's name appeared regularly in Sarah's detailed "invitation lists" for the period,[32] and the Spaniard fulfilled his promise of lavish entertainment for Congressmen and other officials.[33] Gardoqui's plan of attack may have improved Manhattan's social life, 1785–1789, but there was to be no progress in his broader diplomatic mission. Congress remained adamant in demanding American rights to Mississippi navigation, and Jay remained faithful to the instructions Congress gave him. There would be no treaties or even informal agreements.

Modern observers are left to puzzle over the question of how Diego de Gardoqui reached the conclusions he did about the Jays. Everything we know about the couple from their own writings and contemporary observations contradicts the concept of two were money-grubbing social climbers, with a husband so blinded by love for his domineering wife that he had no mind of his own. Don Diego was generally credited with good judgment as a merchant and diplomat,[34] but he had had limited opportunities to see and evaluate the couple in Spain, where their contacts were confined almost entirely to meetings in Jay's home office centered on Jay's desperate search for funds and Gardoqui's understandable caution in promising aid. Jay's refusal to participate in the social life normally open to a diplomat in Madrid further limited their contact. Gardoqui was ignorant of the Jay and Livingston families' secure social position and wealth in America – he saw only a couple in a strange land, isolated from their neighbors, focused on obtaining funds for themselves and their struggling nation.

None of this accounts for the venom and contempt in his evaluation of the Jays. Blame here likely falls on William Carmichael, Jay's embittered secretary, who was left behind to represent American interests in Spain for more than two decades. Carmichael was delighted to accept the social overtures of the Spanish court and was reputed to be Floridablanca's personal friend.[35] Gardoqui's remarks in 1784 are nearly identical to views Carmichael expressed in a letter of January 1783 when he wrote of Jay: "Nothing surprises me in the conduct of a man, who with great parts, is guided by female caprice, female resentment, and female avarice."[36]

By itself, the tale of Sarah Jay's experiences with the Spanish kingdom and its subjects may seem of only narrow significance. While the record of her years in Spain is a rich source for students of her own nation, it tells us little about the world in which she lived as an isolated visitor. Gardoqui's skewed picture of her can be dismissed as one of many examples of a man's underestimation of a pretty woman. Even if Sarah Livingston Jay's contributions to the course of purely American social and political history seem to outweigh her effect on the course of Spanish–American relations, her story serves a broader purpose. It reminds us that the pattern of misunderstandings, mistrust, and misperceptions that marked her experiences with Spain and its people also distorted relations between Spain and the United States at a national level. The two countries found each other useful, if unofficial, allies in the Revolution, but they had less success in forming a healthy peacetime partnership. There was no official pact of amity or commerce between the two to mark the end of the Revolution, and Jay and Gardoqui failed to achieve that goal during the Confederation. Not until 1795 did Pinckney's "Treaty of Friendship, Limits, and Navigation between Spain and the United States" attempt to initiate a cordial, neighborly relationship. The "Spanish" chapter in Sarah Jay's life, then, was part of a broader, even more trouble-ridden historical saga.

Notes

1. For Sarah Jay's family, see Milton M. Klein, *The American Whig: William Livingston of New York* (New York: Garland, 1993); and Cynthia A. Kierner, *Traders and Gentlefolk: The Livingstons of New York, 1675–1790* (Ithaca, NY: Cornell, 1992).
2. The standard source for his life and public career is Walter Stahr's *John Jay* (New York: Hambledon & London, 2006).
3. William Livingston, Jr., to Sarah Jay, October 16, 1779: Richard B. Morris, et al., eds., *John Jay: Unpublished Papers* (2 vols; New York: Harper & Row, 1975, 1980), 1:677. Hereafter cited as Morris, *Jay Papers*.
4. To Susan V.B. Livingston, August 28, 1780, Louise V. North, et al., eds., *Selected Letters of John Jay and Sarah Livingston Jay: Correspondence by or to the First Chief Justice of the United States and His Wife* (Jefferson, NC: McFarland, 2004), p. 88–90. Hereafter cited as North, *Selected Letters*.
5. To Catharine Livingston, May 18, 1781, *ibid.*, 105–106.
6. To Susan Livingston, August 28, 1780, *ibid.*, 89.
7. To her mother, May 13, 1780, *ibid.*, 79.
8. To William Livingston, May 5, 1780, Carl E. Prince, et al., eds., *The Papers of William Livingston* (5 vols., New Brunswick: Rutgers, 1978–1988), 3:374–375.
9. May 13, 1780, Morris, *Jay Papers*, 1:696.
10. North, *Selected Letters*, 80.
11. To William Livingston, Jr., September 4, 1780; Livingston Papers, Massachusetts Historical Society.
12. To William Livingston, March 14, 1781, North, *Selected Letters*, 101–102.

13 May 20, 1781, Elizabeth Miles Nuxoll, et al., eds., *The Selected Papers of John Jay* (5 vols. to date; Charlottesville: University of Virginia, 2010–2017), 3:448. Hereafter cited as Nuxoll, *Jay Papers*.
14 N.d. September 1781, North, *Selected Letters*, 115.
15 Sarah vividly described the drama in a letter of June 24, 1781, addressed to her father but sent to her sister for safekeeping, Nuxoll, *Jay Papers*, 2:479–485.
16 John Jay to Robert Morris, April 25, 1782, *ibid.*, 2:279
17 Letter of May 1, 1782, *ibid.*, 2:782.
18 Sarah to John Jay, September 22, North, *Selected Letters*, 93, and to Catharine Livingston, December 1, 1780, Jay Papers, Columbia University; Mary Beth Norton, *Liberty's Daughters: The Revolutionary Experience of American Women, 1750–1800* (Boston: Little, Brown, 1980), 178.
19 Modern usage of the term came with Linda Kerber's "The Republican Mother: Women and the Enlightenment. An American Perspective," *American Quarterly*, Vol. 28, No. 2 (Summer, 1976), 187–205, and her *Women of the Republic: Intellect and Ideology in Revolutionary America* (Chapel Hill: University of North Carolina, 1980).
20 To Catharine Livingston, July 22, 1781, North, *Selected Letters*, 113.
21 January 14, 1781, *ibid.*, 98.
22 Letter of July 18, 1781, Morris, *Jay Papers*, 2:194–95.
23 For a lively example of this rivalry, see Frederick Jay to John Jay, January 26, 1783, Jay Papers, Columbia University.
24 To Catharine Livingston, July 25, 1781, Nuxoll, *Jay Papers*, 3:525–28.
25 July 18, 1783, Morris, *Jay Papers*, 2: 611–612.
26 To her father-in-law, Peter Jay, April 29, 1782, North, *Selected Letters*, 118.
27 Abigail Adams Smith to Abigail Adams, September 7, 1788, L.H. Butterfield, et al., eds., *Adams Family Correspondence* (13 vols. to date, Cambridge: Harvard, 1963–2017), 8:293.
28 To John Adams, January 12, 1789, *ibid.*, 8:324.
29 The document's full text appears in Miguel Gómez Del Campillo, ed., *Relaciones Diplomáticas Entre España Y Los Estados Unidos Según Los Documentos Del Archivo Histórico Nacional* (2 vols., Madrid: Archivo Histórico Nacional, 1944–45), 1:xxxv. This translation is adapted from the literal one in Samuel Flagg Bemis, *Pinckney's Treaty: America's Advantage from Europe's Distress, 1783–1795* (rev. ed., New Haven: Yale, 1960), 62.
30 To Gardoqui, October 4, 1785, Nuxoll, *Jay Papers*, 4:195.
31 To Gardoqui, March 1, and to Thomson, March 3, 1786, *ibid.*, 4:304–305.
32 For samples of these invitation lists, see Nuxoll, *Jay Papers*, vol. 4: 195, 522, 534, 545, 555, 640, 648, 653, 714, 718.
33 Michael A. Otero, "The American Mission of Diego de Gardoqui, 1785–1789." (Ph.D. Dissertation, University of California, Los Angeles: 1948), 235 et seq.
34 There is no definitive modern biography of Gardoqui. We have only Otero's 70-year-old dissertation and shorter studies such as Natividad Rueda Soler, *La Compañia de comercio 'Gardoqui e Hijos': Sus relaciones políticas y económicas con norteamerica (1770–1780)* (Vitoria-Gasteiz: Goberno Vasco, 1992) and Saiz Valdivielso, *Diego de Gardoqui: Esplendor y Penumbra* ([Bilbao]: Muelle de Unbitarte, 2014).
35 Samuel G. Coe, *The Mission of William Carmichael to Spain* (Baltimore: Johns Hopkins, 1926), 53–54.
36 Nuxoll, *Jay Papers*, 4:242, n.4.

11 Securing the borderlands/seas in the American Revolution

Spanish–American cooperation and regional security against the British Empire

Ross Michael Nedervelt

On May 6, 1782, an agreement born of opportunity and mutual necessity between Spanish and American forces manifested in a campaign to invade the Bahamas and subdue the Bahamian and American loyalist privateers terrorizing the Straits of Florida and the neighboring Atlantic. Under the authority of Captain-General Juan Manuel de Cagigal of Spain and the privateer Commodore Alexander Gillon of South Carolina, the force of 57 ships and 2,000 soldiers laid siege to the hardscrabble and poorly defended Bahamian capital of Nassau on New Providence Island.[1] Francisco de Miranda undertook negotiations with the Bahamas' governor, Lieutenant Colonel John Maxwell, and demanded the archipelago surrender to Imperial Spain within twelve hours.[2] If the colony refused to capitulate, the American warships would begin bombarding Fort Nassau.[3] Following deliberations between Maxwell and Cagigal, the governor surrendered the Bahamas to Imperial Spain's authority on May 8, 1782.[4] Spanish and American patriot forces' operation to capture the Bahamas served an important strategic purpose beyond stifling hostile privateers, because it solved a regional problem with wider national and imperial security objectives for Spain and the United States.

The Spanish–American attack and occupation of the Bahamas emerged from Spain and the United States' desires to secure their frontier regions from British incursions and military attacks. In 1776, American patriot officials envisioned a new order in the western hemisphere, one devoid of Britain's presence on the North American continent, and secure from Britain's colonial and military presence that threatened the nascent United States with borderland conflicts.[5] For Imperial Spain, the outbreak of an imperial civil war between Britain and thirteen of its North American colonies heralded a promising opportunity for Imperial Spain to regain its territory lost to Britain in the Seven Years' War and Treaty of Paris of 1763. Spain viewed the rebellious thirteen colonies as neither hostile subjects of Great Britain nor friends of Spain, and considered the American patriots to be neutral and entitled to limited aid demanded by hospitality.[6] Following its entry into the war as France's ally, Spain independently pursued its own military campaigns against Britain. Cagigal and Gillon's campaign against the Bahamas represents an important instance of Spanish forces and the rebellious Americans working to suppress a mutual threat, and simultaneously achieve their own independent strategic aims. The Spanish–American invasion of the Bahamas put both Spain and the United States in a strategic position to push Britain out of the Floridas and the surrounding Straits of Florida border region, which would consequentially create a wider division between Britain's North American and Caribbean forces. Spanish and American forces' efforts put Spanish diplomats in a better position during peace negotiations to secure the Straits of Florida and southeastern American frontier against Britain after the American Revolution.

Historical scholarship on the cooperative efforts between American patriot forces and European colonial powers along the margins between the Caribbean and North America remain largely unexplored beyond naval and American loyalist histories. Rayford Logan, J. Franklin Jameson, and Lucille Horgan's works have illuminated the impact of American patriots using foreign Caribbean colonies as entrepôts to funnel European arms and supplies to Continental forces on the rebellious mainland.[7] While historians exploring the North American borderlands during the Revolution, such as Kathleen DuVal and Alan Taylor, have turned to examining localized relationships and power struggles in North American and Atlantic frontier regions, and the partisan efforts to convert disparate groups living throughout these regions to support the British or American side.[8] Eric Beerman and James A. Lewis, the scholars responsible for the principal English-language works on the Spanish–American assault on the Bahamas in 1782, focus their attention on the military campaign and Spanish occupation of the British colony, as well as elaborating on the critical role American patriots played in anti-privateering activities in the Straits of Florida region.[9] Historians of the Bahamas and American loyalist diaspora, such as Michael Craton, Gail Saunders, and Sandra Riley, regard the Spanish–American attack and the Spanish occupation as turning points, which preceded the loyalist campaign to retake the islands and establish new settlements of southern loyalist refugees that transformed colonial Bahamian society.[10] This chapter aims instead to expand the scope outwards to highlight the strategic political and military motivations that underscored the Spanish–American attack against the Bahamas, specifically securing the Straits of Florida for the United States and Spanish Empire against Great Britain during and after the American Revolution.

This chapter applies Atlantic and borderland/border-sea perspectives to the problems the Bahamas caused the revolutionary United States and Imperial Spain in the Straits of Florida region, which reveal a situation that was both of regional and international importance to the security of the United States and Spain. By approaching the Spanish–American invasion from a borderland standpoint, the Bahamas' privateering operations—let alone its mere presence as a British foothold straddling multiple trade routes between the Atlantic and Caribbean—made it a strategic threat to the nascent United States and Imperial Spain's security. Delegates to the

Continental Congress interpreted the Bahamas' hostility as evidence of the long-term threat the British Empire posed to the country's fragile sovereignty in a post-revolution world. In Madrid, King Carlos III saw the Bahamas as both a threat to Spain's trade to Cuba and Santo Domingo, as well as a serious complication to the empire's efforts to retake the Florida peninsula and capture Jamaica. By approaching the Spanish and American effort to capture the Bahamas from Atlantic, borderlands, and security perspectives, Imperial Spain and the Continental Congress' peace treaty negotiations with Britain in 1783 reveal the Bahamas' role as a means for both resorting Spain's control of the Florida peninsula, and providing the post-revolutionary United States with some measure of safety by preventing Britain from continuing to hold a neighboring southern border on the North American mainland.

The Bahamas' emerged as a threat to Imperial Spain and the United States as Bahamian and American loyalist privateers attempted to fill a void caused by British forces' activities in North America and the Caribbean. British military and naval strategies for engaging the Continental Army in North America and its French and Dutch allies in the eastern Caribbean created a rupture in Britain's military continuity in the western Atlantic. The allied Continental and French forces' defeat of Lord Cornwallis' army at Yorktown in October 1781 confined the British Army's major North American force to the Virginia tidewater. In the Caribbean, Admiral George Rodney and his Royal Navy squadron found the riches of Dutch St. Eustatius an inviting target for plunder and personal enrichment. Admiral Rodney's occupation of St. Eustatius and refusal to pursue further military operations in the Caribbean and Atlantic prevented support from reaching Lord Cornwallis.[11] Consequently, the approximately 1,592-mile gap between the British Army at Yorktown and naval reinforcements in the eastern Caribbean created an exploitable crack in Britain's military presence around the Bahamas and Straits of Florida. Inside this space, however, American loyalist and Bahamian privateers attempted to maintain the line of British authority, and launched campaigns of harassment and raiding against American patriot and Spanish merchant vessels.

British privateering in the region gained strength from American loyalists fleeing the revolutionary conflict in the Lower South, who turned to British-held East Florida and the Bahamas as zones of safety, and turned the Bahamas and East Florida into bases for launching retaliatory strikes against Continental forces and patriot commerce. American loyalist privateers driven by vengeance joined with Bahamian privateers pursuing income and supplies, and plunged the western Atlantic sea-lanes into a contest between privateer hunters and merchant prey. American loyalist and Bahamian privateers hauled 37 American vessels to Nassau's vice-admiralty court by June 30, 1780.[12] By April 1782, roving patrols captured and impounded 127 vessels in Bahamian courts, and their efforts inflicted great financial distress on merchants and mariners in Cuba, St. Domingue, and the rebellious mainland.[13] The privateers' actions increased the number of prisoners held on New Providence to a level that stressed local food and supply stocks as the colony proved unable to "keep or Victual them," and Governor Maxwell appealed for additional support from the Royal Navy to "keep the Privateersmen in Order."[14] Maxwell, in an effort to avoid stressing the island colony further, decided to implement a catch-impound-release strategy that stripped patriot ships of their cargoes and returned them to the nearest American port.[15] Consequently, this strategy turned the Bahamas' vice-admiralty court into a revolving door for Atlantic privateering.

The Bahamas' emergence as a hostile privateering base forced the Continental Congress to terminate its commercial relationship with the islands. Congress fixated on two principal transformations in the American patriot-Bahamian relationship: 1) the rise of a colonial military dictatorship under Maxwell's predecessor, Governor Montfort Browne; and, 2) the Bahamian privateers' frequent attacks against American vessels.[16] "Such privateers and armed vessels have," the delegates observed, "actually captured divers[e] vessels, the property of the citizens of these states, on the coast of South Carolina," and necessitated Congress's embargo exemption be "held void."[17] Congress's termination of its embargo exemption, a policy that had been in effect since 1775, isolated the few remaining patriot-sympathizers who had not emigrated to the patriot-held mainland, and turned the colony's populace into practical loyalists. Subsequently, the islanders relied on illicit trade and privateering as the primary means of acquiring income and provisions to sustain their families and communities between 1779 and 1782.

The Bahamians' firm embrace of Britain's authority and the war effort also demonstrated to the Congress the islands' threat to American domestic and regional security. James Madison, joined by James Duane of New York, made a joint motion before the chamber against the continuation of commerce with the Bahamians, and advocated for ceasing the commercial intercourse originally designed to import wartime stores from "virtuous individuals."[18] The on-going Bahamian-American trade gave rise to Madison and Duane's suspicions that "a clandestine trade and intercourse is carried on" with British forces and sympathizers, which "better enabled to support the burdens of the war, and prosecute the arts of seduction among the citizens of these States ... [and] give colour to their misrepresentations in Europe of a latent predilection in these States towards them."[19] Bahamians' circulation of rumors and false intelligence concerning Continental forces and their European allies imperiled Congress's hard-won trans-Atlantic political and military relationships, which were crucial to the United States' independence, as well as France and Spain's efforts to fracture Britain's hold on eastern North America and the Caribbean. Aware of this reality, Madison and Duane pointed to how misrepresentations did "not accord" with the current "friendship and convention alliances intimate connection subsisting" between the United States and France, and potential divisions only added to the "resources of the common enemy" in a protracted war.[20]

American representatives focused on mutual regional security against Britain in the Bahamas and the Floridas in their efforts to negotiate a formal military and commercial alliance with Imperial Spain. In letters to John Jay, the American ambassador to Spain, members of the Continental Congress asserted their willingness to assist Spain in its attempts to expel British forces from the border regions neighboring the rebellious American states and Spain's Caribbean and North American territories. Robert Morris, Jr., a Pennsylvania delegate on the Secret Committee of Trade and the Committee of Correspondence, urged Ambassador Jay to offer Continental forces' assistance to Spain for its plans concerning "the reduction of the Floridas, & Bahamas, & perhaps of Jamaica."[21] American military assistance for Spain's operations against Britain in the Gulf of Mexico and the western Caribbean, Morris asserted, would benefit Spain's commercial and maritime security because it would reduce and drive out British privateers and smugglers undermining Spain's commercial power that "is so much interrupted."[22] Morris and the Congress attempted to assuage any concerns Jay had about this effort to persuade Spain into an alliance by arguing that the United States' shared border with the Spanish Empire would pose no serious threat to either country's security.[23] American delegates optimistically believed that the "century to come most probably will be entirely turned to agriculture and commerce," and an allied or neutral Spanish port in East Florida would facilitate a mutually beneficial commercial relationship.[24]

Spain's imperial government also concluded that the Bahamians' privateering constituted a strategic threat to its Cuba and Santo Domingo trade. King Carlos III focused directly on the Bahamas as the first target in Spain's military plans to retake East Florida and secure the Straits of Florida for trans-Atlantic Spanish commerce.[25] The Governor of Louisiana, Bernardo de Gálvez, argued in a letter to his uncle José de Gálvez, a member of the Council of the Indies in Spain, that by controlling the Bahamas and suppressing British privateers, the movements of Spanish and French forces would be unconstrained, and able to launch a combined invasion of Jamaica from Guárico (Cap-Haïtien), St. Domingue.[26] Captain-General Cagigal concurred with Governor Gálvez. The captain-general contended that the Bahamas would also provide Spanish forces with an important strategic vantage point to monitor the movements of British naval vessels, as well as intercept hostile warships traveling through the Straits of Florida en route to attack Havana.[27]

Imperial officials initiated their own plans for an invasion of the Bahamas as part of a multipart offensive against British forces in the Caribbean. Bernardo de Gálvez amassed an invasion force in Havana throughout 1781 in preparation to launch an assault on the heart of the Bahamian and American loyalist privateering threat.[28] Gálvez appointed Cagigal to take command of the 45 Spanish transport ships and approximately 2,000 soldiers, which constituted the majority of the invasion's armed personnel and transport vessels.[29] Cagigal, however, lacked warships to protect the transport vessels because of their needed availability for a planned assault against Jamaica, and finding a suitable escort delayed the invasion force's departure.[30]

The Bahamian and American loyalist threat prompted a military venture between Spanish authorities in Cuba and American patriot military commanders to secure the region. Commodore Alexander Gillon's arrival at Havana on January 20, 1782 with revolutionary South Carolina's naval fleet offered Cagigal the naval support necessary to escort his troop transports to attack New Providence Island. The American fleet would provide a sufficient substitute for Spanish naval support, and Cagigal concluded that the Americans could be persuaded with a monetary incentive.[31] Cagigal negotiated with Gillon for his small twelve-ship fleet to escort the main invasion force, and offered a fixed-rate monetary compensation to Gillon of ten *pesos* and four *reales* per ton for each month the fleet was in Spain's service until eight days following the Bahamas' surrender.[32]

While Gillon negotiated with Spanish authorities in Havana to participate in a military operation against the Bahamas, he took advantage of Imperial Spain's open port to sell captured goods and resupply his fleet. Spain's decision to open its ports to American patriot merchants, privateers, and the Continental Navy for the duration of the American Revolution provided safe harbors to rest crews, load cargoes, and repair and provision ships.[33] With his fleet anchored at Havana, Gillon auctioned five captured British merchant vessels and sold their cargoes. Sales in Havana netted Gillon over $70,000 to replenish his fleet's provisions and supplies, make necessary repairs, and pay his crewmembers.[34] The Spanish–American operation also provided Gillon with the opportunity to recruit soldiers and sailors from Havana to replenish his fleet's depleted ranks of marines, which lost 20 to 25 percent of their strength between 1778 and 1782.[35] Consequently, Gillon and Cagigal reached an amicable, albeit unwritten, agreement, and the invasion force departed Havana on April 22, 1782.

Despite Cagigal and Gillon sharing a determination to advance their respective countries' security interests against Britain, the murky nature of their operation with respect to Spanish–American relations led to disagreements over each other's standing. Although they forged an agreement on the mission's objectives and compensation from Spanish authorities in Havana, they neglected to clarify their respective roles and relationship for when the attack commenced. When the armada arrived at New Providence, Cagigal took a hard stance that the invasion was a Spaniard-led operation with an auxiliary American escort.[36] Since Spanish soldiers constituted the majority of the landing force this was a justifiable argument; but Gillon contended that he and his forces were partners in an invasion against a common enemy, and deserved a place at the negotiating table when the Bahamian government surrendered.[37]

Cagigal and Gillon's differing perspectives were rooted in the misunderstanding of Spain's military and political stance towards the United States. Spanish officials, such as José de Gálvez and Diego José Navarro, emphasized that the Spanish Empire was to treat the United States as a neutral country, and not a direct ally despite having a common enemy in Great Britain and a mutual ally in France.[38] Cagigal viewed the relationship with Gillon and the American fleet as transactional in nature, meaning that the Americans supplied a service to the Spanish Empire by escorting the troop transports and received monetary compensation in exchange. Once the Spanish force reached New Providence, then Gillon's role in the mission ended and Cagigal's forces could proceed with capturing the Bahamian capital. Gillon, on the other hand, either mistakenly considered the United States and Spain to be allies because Britain was their mutual adversary, or regarded the operation against the Bahamas as a joint expedition because a greater financial reward could be gained for him and his men. An exclusive invasion by Spain's military meant that there would be no need to divide the Bahamian privateers' and merchants' vessels, as well as captured prizes anchored in the harbor, while a joint expedition would permit the American privateers to lay a claim to a portion of the prizes.[39]

With British forces' power diminished, the Bahamas' colonial government and inhabitants attempted to bolster their military strength to deter attacks from the rebellious Americans. Governor Maxwell spent the first year of his governorship assembling the largest armed force to defend the Bahamas since the American Revolution's outbreak with 247 British regulars, 338 militiamen, and 800 armed sailors spread across a dozen privateering vessels.[40] Even with the increased troop presence and armed privateers, Maxwell's efforts were undermined by three historical problems that plagued the colony for much of the eighteenth century: 1) the archipelago's perceived lack of importance to the British government; 2) its crumbling fortifications and dearth of revenue for repairs; and 3) the strategic difficulties associated with defending a small island against superior naval and army forces.[41] These problems proved the undoing of the Bahamas and its privateering force when confronted with Cagigal and Gillon's armada on May 6, 1782.

The Spanish–American force's overwhelming strength, combined with New Providence's defensive constraints, presented the Bahamian officials and inhabitants with one viable decision: surrender. The Bahamas' lack of profitable cash crops led the British government to neglect the archipelago's defensive infrastructure and troop garrison in favor of fortifying its profitable Caribbean sugar colonies. While Maxwell increased the Bahamas' military forces, on the day the Spanish–American armada arrived the troops present and fit for duty had decreased to 203 regulars and 132 militiamen.[42] Forts Nassau and Montagu, Nassau's primary defensive structures, were in states of severe disrepair after suffering two attacks and occupations by the Continental Navy in March 1776 and January 1778.[43] Both American assaults left Fort Nassau's walls breeched with large cracks and buttresses crumbling into the harbor.[44] On May 6, Maxwell sent a request to General Alexander Leslie for "three British frigates" to be dispatched immediately from

Charleston to the Bahamas, which the governor believed could rescue him and the islanders from their present situation.[45] Yet, if the British military had forces to spare for the Bahamas' immediate defense, they were days or weeks away from the Bahamian capital. The armada's position off New Providence's northern coast bottled the privateer fleet and available merchant vessels in Nassau harbor, which prevented the Bahamians from both launching an effective naval defense and receiving munitions and provisions necessary for surviving a siege.

Spanish and American forces' capture of the Bahamas hemmed in and isolated British East Florida. Hostile Spanish and American patriot-controlled territories surrounded the colony on nearly all sides, and left Britain's Sixtieth Royal American Regiment and local militia forces undermanned and with precarious supply links to British-held Savannah.[46] Bernardo de Gálvez's capture of West Florida and push up the Mississippi valley left East Florida as Spain's next target in the region, and with its possession of the Bahamas Spain would effectively secure the Straits of Florida under its authority.[47] Following the Bahamas' capture and the threat posed by Bahamian privateers diminished, Gillon and his fleet unleashed their own counteroffensive against British vessels in the Straits of Florida, and Spanish privateers and fishermen from Cuba trading with East Florida's Native Americans spread rumors of a coming Spanish attack to undermine local British support.[48]

By controlling the Bahamas, Spain procured a territory to exchange in the peace settlement negotiations between Britain and the United States and its allies. The Bahamas could be a part of a larger collection of captured British territories Spanish negotiators offered in exchange for Britain returning Gibraltar to Spain's authority. Yet, Spain would need to relinquish its control over West Florida if a deal to regain Gibraltar were to be successful, which Spain proved unwilling to do.[49] Instead, Spanish officials negotiated to return the Bahamas for control of East Florida, which would achieve one of Spain's wartime objectives and solidify its control over the Florida peninsula. British and Spanish negotiations over the preliminary and final treaty articles drew specific attention to the control of the Bahamas and East Florida in three of twelve articles, which detailed the return of authority and the time period for officials and civilians to leave East Florida and the Bahamas.[50]

The Bahamas' capture enabled Spain and the United States to achieve strategic victories by forcing Britain from the Floridas at the American Revolution's conclusion. In exchanging the Bahamas for the Floridas, Spain retained a degree of control over the Straits of Florida by denying Britain the continued possession of both the strait's Floridian and Bahamian sides, and secured safe harbors for Spanish merchants and warships traveling to and from Spain's Caribbean possessions. Delegates in the Continental Congress saw that the United States stood to benefit significantly from Spain's treaty negotiations and the Floridas return to Spanish rule, because it removed the threat posed by British troops and warships stationed along a porous southern U.S.–British Empire border.[51] Virginia delegate Arthur Lee professed it "unwise to prefer G[reat] B[ritain] to Spain as our neighbor," because doing such was analogous to "the viper which was ready to destroy the family of the man in whose bosom it had been restored to life."[52] Spain's control of the Floridas gave the United States a less hostile neighbor that might grant permission for American merchant ships to enter and leave the Mississippi, Alabama, and Apalachicola rivers safely.[53]

Spain's hold on the Bahamas proved to be short lived, however, as American loyalist forces and refugees were pushed from the Carolinas and Georgia into the Straits of Florida. On April 1, 1783, almost eleven months after Cagigal's capture of the Bahamas, a contingent of South Carolinian loyalist militiamen and privateers under the leadership of Colonel Andrew Deveaux launched an expedition to recapture the Bahamas, which arrived off New Providence on April 13.[54] Deveaux's invasion force initially baffled the Spanish commander and acting governor Don Antonio Claraco y Sanz, who received word a week earlier of Spain's preliminary peace treaty that returned the Bahamas to Britain.[55] On the morning of April 14, Deveaux landed a force of around 230 militiamen to challenge the 500 Spanish soldiers garrisoned around Nassau.[56] Claraco, believing that an engagement with Deveaux's men would prove futile and imprudent with the coming territorial exchange, surrendered to Deveaux on April 18.[57] After being held hostage by Deveaux for several weeks, Claraco and his forces departed for Cuba where he was charged with the unwarranted surrender of Nassau to an inferior force, and imprisoned in Havana and Madrid until his acquittal in 1791.[58]

Cagigal and Gillon's transactional agreement and military operation endeavored to secure the emergent United States' security from future British attacks out of the Floridas and the Bahamas, while safeguarding Imperial Spain's commercial trade in the northern Caribbean and attempting to release Spain's forces for a potential invasion of Jamaica. The military venture against the Bahamas succeeded in returning control of the Floridas to Spain, and preventing Britain from retaining a toehold to challenge the United States along its southern frontier. Yet, the long-term consequences of Cagigal and Gillon's agreement and operation against the Bahamas produced mixed results in the years following the American Revolution. Spain and the United States' hard-won gains vanished with Britain's military and socio-cultural entrenchment in the Bahamas during the late 1780s and 1790s, and Spain's declining control over its Florida territory in the early nineteenth century. Britain's concession of the Floridas in the Treaty of Paris of 1783 pushed new waves of virulent American loyalist refugees into the Bahamas, which transformed the islands and Straits of Florida into an Anglo-Spanish border-sea.

Spaniards' and American patriots' military efforts against the Bahamas in 1782 demonstrate the complicated relationship Spain and the United States had when confronted by a mutual British threat during the American

Revolution. By examining the Spanish and American invasion from borderland and security perspectives, Cagigal and Gillon's agreement illustrates how Spaniards and American patriots went around the lack of a formal alliance between their respective governments, and how that decision proved mutually beneficial to Spain and the United States' efforts to secure the Straits of Florida region from British threats. British privateering and naval presence required improvisation with available resources and military support, which challenged formal political and international relationships along the border regions separating European colonies in North America and the Caribbean. Authorities, such as Cagigal and Gillon, making strategic military and political decisions impacted Spain's plans to engage British forces in the Caribbean, and their transactional relationship challenged Spain's association with the United States as an imperial power not directly allied with the rebellious Americans. By focusing on individual and provincial agreements between Imperial Spain's colonies and the rebellious United States, a nuanced picture emerges of the Spanish–American relationship during the American Revolution.

Notes

1 John Maxwell to Lord George Germain, May 11, 1782, CO 23/25/61, The National Archives (TNA); Juan Manuel de Cagigal to John Maxwell, May 6, 1782, CO 23/25/62, TNA.
2 CO 23/25/62, TNA.
3 Ibid.
4 Articles of Capitulation, May 8, 1782, CO 23/25/57–59, TNA; John Maxwell to Lord George Germain, May 14, 1782, CO 23/25/55–56, TNA.
5 Benjamin Franklin, "Sketch of Propositions for a Peace," in *The Papers of Benjamin Franklin*, eds. William B. Willcox et al., vol. 22, *March 23, 1775 through October 27, 1776* (New Haven, CT: Yale University Press, 1982), 630–631; Continental Congress, "Monday, December 30, 1776," in *Journals of the Continental Congress, 1774–1789*, eds. Worthington Chauncey Ford et al., vol. 6, *October 9, 1776 – December 31, 1776* (Washington, D.C.: Government Printing Office, 1906), 1054–1058; "The Committee of Secret Correspondence to the American Commissioners," in *The Papers of Benjamin Franklin*, eds. William B. Willcox et al., vol. 23, *October 27, 1776 through April 30, 1777* (New Haven, CT: Yale University Press, 1983), 96–99; Continental Congress, "Treaty of Alliance, Eventual and Defensive," in *Journals of the Continental Congress, 1774–1789*, eds. Worthington Chauncey Ford et al., vol. 11, *May 2, 1778 – September 1, 1778* (Washington, D. C.: Government Printing Office, 1908), 448–453.
6 Diego José Navarro, Memorandum included in an official letter copy, Havana, June 27, 1779, Archivos General de Indias (AGI), Santo Domingo 2082.
7 Rayford W. Logan, "Saint Domingue: Entrepôt for Revolutionaries," in *The American Revolution in the West Indies*, ed. Charles W. Toth, National University Publications Series in American Studies (Port Washington, New York and London: Kennikat Press, 1975), 101–111; J. Franklin Jameson, "St. Eustatius in the American Revolution," in *The American Revolution in the West Indies*, ed. Charles W. Toth, 86–100; Lucille E. Horgan, *Forged in War: The Continental Congress and the Origin of Military Supply and Acquisition Policy*, Contributions in Military Studies 219 (Westport, CT and London: Greenwood Press, 2002), 7–11.

8 Kathleen DuVal, *Independence Lost: Lives on the Edge of the American Revolution* (New York: Random House, 2015); Alan Taylor, *The Divided Ground: Indians, Settlers, and the Northern Borderlands of the American Revolution* (New York: Alfred A. Knopf, 2006).
9 Eric Beerman, "The Last Battle of the American Revolution: Yorktown. No, the Bahamas! (The Spanish-American Expedition to Nassau in 1782)," *The Americas* 45, no. 1 (July, 1988): 79–95; James A. Lewis, *The Final Campaign of the American Revolution: Rise and Fall of the Spanish Bahamas* (Columbia: University of South Carolina Press, 1991); James A. Lewis, *Neptune's Militia: The Frigate* South Carolina *during the American Revolution* (Kent, OH and London: Kent State University Press, 1999).
10 Michael Craton, *A History of the Bahamas* (London: Collins, 1962); Michael Craton and Gail Saunders, *Islanders in the Stream: A History of the Bahamian People, Volume One: From Aboriginal Times to the End of Slavery* (Athens: University of Georgia Press, 1999); Sandra Riley, *Homeward Bound: A History of the Bahama Islands to 1850 with a Definitive Study of Abaco in the American Loyalist Plantation Period* (Miami: Island Research, 2000).
11 Andrew Jackson O'Shaughnessy, *An Empire Divided: The American Revolution and the British Caribbean* (Philadelphia: University of Pennsylvania Press, 2000), 230–232.
12 Craton, *A History of the Bahamas*, 157–158.
13 Craton, *A History of the Bahamas*, 158; John Maxwell to Lord George Germain, August 31, 1780, CO 23/25/7, TNA.
14 CO 23/25/7, TNA.
15 Craton, *A History of the Bahamas*, 158; CO 23/25/7, TNA.
16 Continental Congress, "Monday, March 29, 1779," in *Journals of the Continental Congress, 1774–1789*, eds. Worthington Chauncey Ford et al., vol. 13, *January 1, 1779 – April 22, 1779* (Washington, D.C.: Government Printing Office, 1909), 388.
17 Ibid., 388.
18 Continental Congress, "Friday, March 16, 1779," in *Journals of the Continental Congress, 1774–1789*, eds. Worthington Chauncey Ford et al., vol. 19, *January 1, 1781 – April 23, 1781* (Washington, D.C.: Government Printing Office, 1912), 270.
19 Ibid., 270.
20 Ibid., 270–271.
21 Robert Morris, Jr. to John Jay, July 4, 1781, 8, Historical Society of Pennsylvania, The Papers of John Jay digital collection, Columbia University Libraries. Reference URL: https://dlc.library.columbia.edu/jay/ldpd:10354.
22 Ibid., 9–10.
23 Ibid., 10–11.
24 Ibid.
25 Eric Beerman, "The Last Battle of the American Revolution," 83. Primary sources relevant to this are cited as: "Plan de Operaciones," González de Castejón to José de Solano, El Pardo, April 8, 1780, AGI, Santo Domingo 2086; José de Gálvez to Diego José Navarro, San Lorenzo del Escorial, October 18, 1780, AGI, Papeles Procedentes de Cuba 1290.
26 Bernardo de Gálvez to José de Gálvez, January 1, 1780, AGI, Indiferente General 1578; Lewis, *The Final Campaign of the American Revolution*, 34–35; Beerman, "The Last Battle of the American Revolution," 83.
27 Beerman, "The Last Battle of the American Revolution," 83.
28 Juan Ignacio de Urriza to Bernardo de Gálvez, List of the Fleet and the Form of the Fleets Sailing … against the Bahama Islands, April 29, 1782, AGI, Indiferente General 1579 in Domestic Letters of the Department of State, M40, reel 3, pp. 48–53, 68–69, National Archives of the United States.
29 Ibid.; Lewis, *The Final Campaign of the American Revolution*, 21, 115–116n7, 116n8.

30 José de Gálvez to Juan Manuel de Cagigal, January 20, 1782, AGI, Santo Domingo 2085; Beerman, "The Last Battle of the American Revolution," 84.
31 Lewis, *Neptune's Militia*, 60.
32 Juan Ignacio de Urriza to Bernardo de Gálvez, April 29, 1782, AGI, Indiferente General 1579; Beerman, "The Last Battle of the American Revolution," 85.
33 Juan Ignacio de Urriza to José de Gálvez, April 21, 1780, AGI, Santo Domingo 1657; José de Gálvez to the Intendente of Havana, to the Governor of Santo Domingo, to the Governor of Puerto Rico, to the Intendente of Caracas, to the Governor of Yucatan, to the Governor of Caracas, and to the Governor of Cuba, August 29, 1782, AGI, Santo Domingo 2188; Martín Navarro to Arturo O'Neill, June 27, 1782, AGI, Cuba 83; Luis de Unzuago to Bernardo de Gálvez, May 24, 1783, AGI, Indiferente General 1583; Diego José Navarro to José de Gálvez, October 23, 1778, AGI, Santo Domingo 1598 A and B.
34 Lewis, *Neptune's Militia*, 62–64.
35 Marquis de Vanmark to Juan Manuel de Cagigal, April 5, 1782, AGI, Indiferente General 1579; Marquis de Vanmark to Juan Manuel de Cagigal, May 24, 1782, AGI, Indiferente General 1579; Lewis, *Neptune's Militia*, 61.
36 Juan Manuel de Cagigal to Alexander Gillon, May 6, 1782, in Domestic Letters of the Department of State, M40, reel 3, pp. 54–60, National Archives of the United States.
37 Alexander Gillon to William Moultrie, June 28, 1786, in Domestic Letters of the Department of State, M40, reel 3, pp. 2–7, National Archives of the United States; Lewis, *Neptune's Militia*, 69.
38 Diego José Navarro, Memorandum included in an official letter copy, Havana, June 27, 1779, AGI, Santo Domingo 2082; Gonzalo M. Quintero Saravia, *Bernardo de Gálvez: Spanish Hero of the American Revolution* (Chapel Hill: University of North Carolina Press, 2018), 253–254.
39 Lewis, *Neptune's Militia*, 69.
40 John Maxwell, State of the Royal Garrison Battalion, April 29, 1782, British Headquarters Papers, reel M-355, document 4508; John Maxwell to Henry Clinton, April 15, 1782, British Headquarters Papers, reel M-354, document 4401; Craton and Saunders, *Islanders in the Stream*, 168–169.
41 A Narrative of the Transactions & on the Invasion of the Island of New Providence by the Rebels in 1776, June 15, 1779, CO 23/9/113, TNA; At a Council held this Day, March 3, 1776, CO 23/9/122r, TNA; Craton and Saunders, *Islanders in the Stream*, 164–168; O'Shaughnessy, *An Empire Divided*, 169–172.
42 John Maxwell, State of the Troops on the Island of New Providence, Fort Nassau, May 6, 1782, CO 23/25/67, TNA.
43 CO 23/9/112–113; *Good News for America: Salem, Tuesday, April 16, 1776*, 1, Massachusetts Historical Society; Craton and Saunders, *Islanders in the Stream*, 162, 166–168.
44 Craton and Saunders, *Islanders in the Stream*, 166–168.
45 CO 23/25/61, TNA; John Maxwell to Alexander Leslie, May 6, 1782, CO 23/25/65, TNA.
46 J. Leitch Wright, Jr., *Florida in the American Revolution* (Gainesville: University Presses of Florida, 1975), 83.
47 Ibid.
48 Beerman, "The Last Battle of the American Revolution," 91; Wright, Jr., *Florida in the American Revolution*, 83.
49 DuVal, *Independence Lost*, 236.
50 *The Definitive Treaty of Peace and Friendship, between His Britannick Majesty, and the King of Spain. Signed at Versailles, the 3d of September, 1783* (London: T. Harrison and S. Brooke, 1783), 1.
51 Continental Congress, "Wednesday, October 4, 1780," in *Journals of the Continental Congress, 1774–1789*, eds. Worthington Chauncey Ford et al., vol. 18,

Securing the borderlands/seas 183

September 7, 1780 – December 29, 1780 (Washington, D.C.: Government Printing Office, 1910), 901–902.
52 Continental Congress, "Saturday, 22 March," in *Journals of the Continental Congress, 1774–1789*, eds. Worthington Chauncey Ford et al., vol. 25, *September 1, 1783 – December 31, 1783* (Washington, D.C.: Government Printing Office, 1922), 939.
53 Continental Congress, "Wednesday, October 4, 1780," in *Journals of the Continental Congress, 1774–1789*, eds. Worthington Chauncey Ford et al., vol. 18, *September 7, 1780 – December 29, 1780*, 901–902; Continental Congress, "Tuesday, October 17, 1780," in *Journals of the Continental Congress, 1774–1789*, eds. Worthington Chauncey Ford et al., vol. 18, *September 7, 1780 – December 29, 1780*, 935–947.
54 Riley, *Homeward Bound*, 131–132; Testimony of Daniel Wheeler, May 21, 1783, CO 23/26/42–43, TNA.
55 Lewis, *The Final Campaign of the American Revolution*, 66.
56 CO 23/26/42–43, TNA; Andrew Deveaux, "Extract of a letter dated New Providence, April 25, 1783", *South-Carolina Weekly Gazette*, May 24, 1783, 4; "Articles entered upon between Don Antonio Claraco Sauz, Governor of the Bahama Islands, &c&c, and his Honour Andrew Deveaux, Colonel and Commander in Chief of the Expedition," *South-Carolina Weekly Gazette*, May 24, 1783, 4; Riley, *Homeward Bound*, 132–133.
57 Craton and Saunders, *Islanders in the Stream*, 170–171.
58 Ibid., 171.

12 Spain and the birth of the American Republic

Establishing lasting bonds of kinship in the Revolutionary Era

Gregg French

From his residence in Philadelphia on April 12, 1783, the unofficial Spanish representative to the United States, Francisco Rendón, wrote two letters. The first was addressed to the Captain General of Cuba, Luis de Unzaga, and the second was sent to the Minister of the Indies, José de Gálvez. In these reports, Rendón informed his superiors that news of the articles of peace that would bring an end to the American Revolutionary War had reached the United States. Rendón went on to state his concern that only a few Americans knew about the support that Spain provided to the United States throughout the conflict; this was because a formal alliance was never signed between the two nations, and that Spanish military supplies and economic aid was often provided through clandestine networks. Despite his efforts to convey to the American public that King Carlos III would be "a sincere and trustworthy friend and protector of the United States," Rendón was still concerned that a war would eventually occur between the United States and Spain in the borderlands between Georgia and the Spanish Floridas, as well as along the Mississippi River.[1]

Rendón's precarious position as the unofficial Spanish representative to the United States provides historians with a point of departure to explore how the informal transnational bonds that were created between American representatives and their Spanish counterparts during the Revolutionary Era played a vital role in shaping foreign relations between the two countries during the forthcoming century. Furthermore, Rendón's analysis of the political climate in the United States at the conclusion of the war and the lack of knowledge surrounding Spain's contribution to the conflict can begin to explain why historians have been influenced by American exceptionalism and the Black Legend narrative. Incorrectly believing that Spain and the United States had an adversarial relationship during the Revolutionary War has facilitated an oversimplified understanding of the past. This perspective has clouded how historians have approached the history of U.S.–Spanish relations and has only begun to change in the past two decades with the rise of both transnational and inter-imperial histories. Cultural approaches to these new fields of study have enabled scholars to explore how Spain influenced the creation of the American historical narrative throughout the nineteenth century, as well as the U.S. Empire's imperial identity in the decades surrounding the War of 1898.[2]

Understanding the nuanced relationships that existed between U.S. and Spanish representatives during the Revolutionary War is essential to comprehending the independence of the United States and the ethos that was used to justify the country's territorial expansion in the years following the conflict.[3] Additionally, in the minds of prominent eighteenth- and nineteenth-century Americans, Spanish assistance during the struggle created a Whig-based narrative that was predicated on the belief that Spain had played an essential role in transporting European civilization to the New World in 1492. By supporting the birth of the American republic during the Revolutionary War, Spain had once again assisted the United States, which was now positioned by influential Americans as not just an equal player on the world stage but as the vanguard of the east-to-west movement of civilization.[4] American and Spanish representatives would draw on this narrative throughout the long nineteenth century as the U.S. Empire expanded into once held Spanish territories.[5]

This work will explore the relationships that formed between prominent Americans and their Spanish peers during the late eighteenth century. These connections include: the creation of private trading companies in France and Spain; bonds between Spanish colonial governors and American representatives in the Mississippi Valley; Juan de Miralles's liaisons with influential Americans; and relationships that followed the end of the conflict, as diplomatic representatives from both countries drew on networks that had been established by their predecessors during the Revolutionary War. These individuals worked to peacefully resolve their nation's outstanding disputes along the border between Georgia and the Spanish Floridas, as well as over navigational rights on the Mississippi River.

While the development of these connections will serve as the focal point of the work, the events that began with the Battles of Lexington and Concord in 1775 and concluded with the signing of the Treaty of San Lorenzo in 1795 will provide the historical backdrop. During this time period and in the century that followed, the United States declared itself an independent nation, took part in an imperial conflict to overthrow British rule, and subsequently expanded its empire. Conversely, the Spanish Empire reached its geographic zenith in the 1780s and by the first decade of the nineteenth century was beginning to decline. Despite these diverging paths and the fact that the United States often inherited Spanish territorial possessions, agents of the American Empire were often cautious not to adversely affect the honor of Spain or her imperial representatives, whose predecessors had played an active role in the foundation of the American historical narrative and the country's imperial identity.

Establishing private trading companies

Members of the Spanish Court received news of the American Revolutionary War with both enthusiasm and sympathy.[6] Throughout the eighteenth century, the Spanish and British empires had been constantly at war with one another. Consequently, eminent Spaniards, such as the Ambassador to the French Court, the Count de Aranda; the Prime Minister, Jerónimo Grimaldi; and the Bilbaoan merchant, Diego de Gardoqui, sought to support the American cause in the hopes of weakening the British Empire and reacquiring former Spanish territories.

In the mid-1770s, Spain was unwilling to publicly support U.S. independence. This was primarily because Spanish representatives were uncomfortable with the precedent that they would be setting as an imperial power if they decided to support colonists as they attempted to overthrow their European overseers. In turn, Aranda and Grimaldi, with the assistance of their French and Spanish agents, Pierre-Augustin Caron de Beaumarchais and Diego de Gardoqui, set out to use private trading companies to secretly back the United States. The covert nature of this support perpetuated the belief that Spain only reluctantly joined the Revolutionary War in 1779 and refused to ally with the United States during the conflict. In reality, even before the signing of the Declaration of Independence, Beaumarchais had already met with Arthur Lee. During their encounter, Beaumarchais conveyed to the American representative that both France and Spain were willing to support the American colonists as they attempted to establish their independence.[7]

Following this initial meeting in February of 1776, Beaumarchais returned to France and began using his private enterprise, Roderigue Hortalez and Company, to establish an elaborate system that would enable the French and Spanish courts to support the Continental Army with funds and provisions to assist with their war of independence. Held together by personal relationships, this system enabled the two courts to claim neutrality in the conflict, while still meeting their desired objectives.[8]

As assistance increased throughout 1776, so did British intuitions that the French and Spanish courts were supporting the American colonists. Aranda responded by distancing himself from Beaumarchais in an attempt to maintain an appearance of Spanish neutrality. Furthermore, the Spanish Ambassador began arranging his own covert operation that would benefit Spanish merchants and would still enable the court in Madrid to provide aid to the United States. Aranda met with Benjamin Franklin, Silas Deane, and Arthur Lee in Paris on December 29, 1776. During the meeting, Aranda developed a particularly strong bond with Franklin and Lee. The positive outcomes of this initial engagement prompted Aranda to petition the Spanish Court to continue to covertly support the American cause.[9] However, late in 1776, Aranda had fallen out of favor with the Spanish Court and in turn, the details of how this support would reach the United States was left to Lee, Grimaldi, and Gardoqui.[10]

On March 4, 1777, a secret gathering occurred in Burgos, Spain between the three men. The former Spanish Prime Minister was dispatched to meet with Lee because he was familiar with the preexisting relationships between U.S. and Spanish representatives, while Gardoqui was sent to serve as the business representative of his family's company, the House of José Gardoqui and Sons, which had established a trading network with North American merchants during the pre-Revolutionary Era.[11] At the meeting, the informal agents developed a bond with one another that eventually enabled a significant increase in supplies to arrive in the United States from the Spanish Court, which was filtered through Gardoqui's private company and the Spanish colonial ports of Havana and New Orleans. An initial request for supplies and funds included orders for 80,000 blankets, 20,000 shoes, 100 tons of gunpowder, one brass cannon, as well as approximately 400,000 livres, which was provided by Spanish accounts in Holland.[12] Due to the fact that economic and military aid sent to the United States by the Spanish had to pass through so many clandestine networks, even Gardoqui was unable to accurately define which shipments were provided as gifts and which were given in the form of loans. This confusion, which was purposely designed by Lee, Grimaldi, and Gardoqui, has contributed to the lack of knowledge surrounding Spanish support for the American cause.

At least thirteen Spanish shipments left Spain and France between 1777 and 1778.[13] However, because Lee was unable to secure a formal alliance between the United States and the Spanish Court, both Franklin and the Continental Congress viewed his mission as a failure.[14] In reality, Lee's encounter with Grimaldi and Gardoqui facilitated two significant events that affected U.S.–Spanish relations throughout the remainder of the Revolutionary Era. First, because a formal alliance did not exist between the two nations, essential economic and military aid flowed from Spain to the Continental Army without raising the suspicions of British spies.[15] Second, Gardoqui's involvement in the meeting and his creation of a transatlantic network empowered him to increase his personal wealth and to form connections with influential Americans. Through these networks and friendships, Gardoqui became one of the foremost experts on U.S.–Spanish relations. Subsequently, he became the first official Spanish Chargé d'Affaires to the United States in May of 1785 and continued a productive relationship between Spanish representatives and their American contemporaries.

Forging transatlantic networks in the Mississippi Valley

The American merchant, Oliver Pollock, became the main go-between for American and Spanish forces in the Mississippi Valley following the Declaration of Independence. As a result of the relationships that Pollock formed between himself and Spanish colonial administrators in the region, he was able to secure a meeting between Captain George Gibson of the Continental Army and the Spanish Governor of Louisiana, Luis de Unzaga. The encounter occurred in August of 1776, at which time Gibson requested military provisions from the Spanish Governor.[16] This interaction marked the commencement of a series of informal relationships between agents of the American and Spanish governments in the Mississippi Valley, as well as the construction of a transatlantic network that enabled economic and military aid to flow from Bilbao to the United States, through the ports of Havana and New Orleans.[17]

Following the meeting between Gibson and Unzaga, the Spanish Governor made a unilateral decision to provide the American troops who accompanied Gibson with 100 quintals of gunpowder, Spanish ships to transport the supplies up the Mississippi River, and the right to spend the winter months at Arkansas Post in Spanish Louisiana. To reduce the suspicions of any British spies in New Orleans, Gibson was temporarily imprisoned. In October, he was released and was transported to Philadelphia on one of Pollock's ships, which sailed under the Spanish flag. The ship also contained additional gunpowder for the American cause and a letter from Pollock to Robert Morris. The letter began a formal correspondence between Pollock and the commerce committee of the Continental Congress, which eventually led to his appointment as an official commercial agent for the United States.[18]

On January 1, 1777, Luis de Unzaga was replaced by Bernardo de Gálvez. Following in his predecessor's footsteps, Gálvez developed a relationship with Pollock. From 1777 to 1779, the bond between Pollock and Gálvez continued to grow, as did the amount of aid from Spain that was entering North America at the port of New Orleans and was being transported up the Mississippi River on Spanish ships.[19] Gálvez also provided accommodations to American military personnel and ship captains, as well as loans to both Pollock and the future American representative in Spain, John Jay. This essential role played by Gálvez in support of the American cause increased his correspondences with other well-connected Americans. The intelligence and assistance exchanged between Gálvez and these Americans enabled Continental troops to weaken British positions in the interior of the continent and set the stage for Gálvez's military campaigns into the lower Mississippi Valley and West Florida, after Spain officially joined the conflict in June of 1779.[20]

Following Spain's declaration of war against the British Empire, little changed between U.S and Spanish representatives in the Mississippi Valley. This lack of alteration demonstrates that Spain's formal refusal to ally itself with the United States during the Revolutionary War mattered little to influential Americans and Spanish agents who were aware of the preexisting relationships between representatives of the two nations. Throughout the remainder of the war, Pollock and Gálvez continued to develop their partnership and to assist Spanish and American troops as they made war on British forces in the area.

The "Worthy Old Castilian" forms lasting bonds in America[21]

On May 14, 1778, news reached Edenton, North Carolina that Benjamin Franklin had concluded a treaty of alliance with the French Court. The following evening a banquet was held by the Municipal Council of Edenton to celebrate the pact. A member of the Continental Congress, Francis Lewis, served as the master of ceremonies for the event and seated to his right was the unofficial Spanish representative in the United States, Juan de Miralles.[22]

It may be odd for historians to learn that it was not a French or American representative that was seated in the prominent position to the right of the master of ceremonies during the banquet. This confusion may be compounded by the fact that Spain and the United States never agreed upon their own alliance during the conflict and engaged in a series of disputes throughout the following century. However, as this work demonstrates, the lack of a formal agreement between the two powers mattered little to American and Spanish agents who engaged with one another throughout the Revolutionary War.

Juan de Miralles was born in Petrer, Spain and spent the majority of his adult life as a merchant in the port of Havana, trading with British colonists in North America and the Caribbean Basin. When war broke out in 1775, Miralles became the obvious candidate to be sent to North America to serve as an unofficial agent of the Spanish Court. He entered Charleston, North Carolina on January 9, 1778 and was warmly welcomed by the Governor of South Carolina, John Rutledge. Following his arrival, Miralles immediately integrated himself into the influential social circles that existed in the city. These contacts allowed him to send information back to both Cuba and Spain about British troop movements, and to report on the positive disposition that several prominent Americans had towards Spain's involvement in the conflict.[23]

By March, Miralles secured himself a position as the royal commissioner to the Continental Congress of the United States and arranged to travel to Philadelphia with the elected delegate, John Mathews.[24] Throughout his journey, Miralles was received as an official foreign diplomat by a series of noteworthy Americans including the Governor of North Carolina, Abner Nash; Governor Patrick Henry of Virginia; and the aforementioned Francis Lewis.[25] Upon arriving in Philadelphia in late June, Miralles continued his relationship with Robert Morris. The two had known each other since 1762 and were responsible for the transportation of supplies on five ships between Philadelphia and Havana. Morris's connections in the city enabled Miralles to develop a relationship with the President of the Continental Congress, Henry Laurens, who affectionately referred to Miralles as a "worthy Old Castilian."[26] While in the city, Miralles also established a reputation as a superb host and gift giver.[27] Both of these skills enabled the Spanish agent to further integrate himself into American social life and to increase his interactions with powerful political representatives. However, all of these engagements would fail to compare to the friendship that developed between Miralles and General George Washington following their introduction on December 23, 1778.

During their initial encounter, Washington greeted Miralles with "the greatest distinction" and expressed his "great love and supreme veneration" for the Spanish King.[28] In the days following their initial meeting, the two dignitaries frequently visited each other and on December 31 Miralles hosted a dinner party in Washington's honor.[29] After Washington's relocation to Middlebrook, New Jersey, the two men continued their correspondence and began to exchange gifts with one another. When Miralles visited the General at his headquarters in May of 1779, Washington honored the Spanish representative by assigning Spanish passwords for entrance into the camp and allowing Miralles to ride in the third position in a military parade, behind only Washington and his field assistant.[30] During these engagements, the bond between these two men continued to grow as did the frequency in which they petitioned their own governments to support the other against their common enemy.

The Spanish declaration of war against the British Empire in June of 1779 did little to change the preexisting relationships that existed between Miralles and prominent American figures. In March of 1780, Miralles reported that he and the French Minister were planning to visit General Washington at Morristown, New Jersey.[31] The two men set out from Philadelphia on April 17 and arrived at Washington's camp two days later. During the trip, Miralles was struck with a terrible ailment and arrived at the camp quite ill. Despite Washington's attempts to aid his ailing friend, Spain's unofficial diplomatic representative to the United States succumbed to his illness on April 28, 1780 and died at the age of 65.[32]

The General was noticeably shaken by his friend's death. Unfamiliar with Catholic funeral rites, he immediately ordered two military officers to consult Miralles's personal secretary, Francisco Rendón, on all of the decisions regarding the ceremony. Washington also sent out funeral invitations to officers under his immediate command. Finally, on April 29, a distinguished group of American military generals, members of Congress, and foreign dignitaries met at a Presbyterian burying ground in Morristown, New Jersey to honor the life of Juan de Miralles, whom Washington later referred to as a man who was "universally esteemed" throughout the United States.[33]

Revolutionary Era lineages and the resolution of border disputes

Following Juan de Miralles's death, Francisco Rendón assumed the position as the unofficial Spanish representative to the United States.[34] In Philadelphia, Rendón developed relationships between himself and influential Americans who had previously been in contact with Miralles. While in Philadelphia during the winter of 1781–1782, General Washington lived with Rendón, at which time the two began exchanging information about the movement of troops and supplies.[35] Rendón also befriended the U.S. Secretary of the Department of Foreign Affairs, Robert R. Livingston, who he stated was a "brilliant man devoted to the interests of his country and those of Spain."[36] Rendón sustained a close relationship with these two men, as well as Robert Morris, in an attempt to continue to be informed of military actions, to stimulate trade between the United States and Spain, and to maintain a peaceful political relationship between the two nations in the years following the conflict.[37]

As talks between the belligerent powers occurred in Paris throughout 1782 and 1783, Rendón and his network of contacts remained informed of the negotiations. Both sides feared that individuals living in the contested regions along the borders between Georgia and the Spanish Floridas, as well as along the Mississippi River, might draw the two nations into a conflict. When writing to José de Gálvez, Rendón also alluded to the fact that the Americans who were aware of Spain's contribution during the Revolutionary War were "filled with due gratitude and were well disposed" to Spain and King Carlos III. However, Rendón understood that these individuals were in the minority and did not possess the same beliefs as those who were unaware of Spain's assistance during the conflict.[38]

The final terms of the agreements that brought the American Revolutionary War to an end were signed in January and September of 1783. In these treaties, the British Empire recognized the sovereignty of the United States, and both East and West Florida were returned to the Spanish Empire; however, Britain, Spain, and the United States never came to an agreement on where the border would exist between Georgia and the Spanish Floridas. Additionally, in the Treaty of Paris, Britain and the United States agreed that citizens from both countries would be given navigational rights on the Mississippi River, a claim that Spain refused to recognize.[39] This misunderstanding occurred because Britain signed separate peace agreements with the United States and Spain. This confusion would continue to adversely affect U.S.–Spanish relations for the foreseeable future.

In May of 1785, Diego de Gardoqui arrived in the United States as the Chargé d'Affaires of the Spanish Government.[40] The Bilbaoan merchant was a wise choice for the position because of the integral role that he played in supporting the United States during the Revolutionary War and the friendships that he formed with influential Americans during the conflict. The Spanish Court sent Gardoqui to the United States with instructions to establish a treaty that would resolve the outstanding border issues between the two countries.[41] However, upon arriving in the United States, Gardoqui quickly realized that a sectional conflict was developing in the young nation and despite being warmly welcomed by eastern elites, it was going to be difficult to establish a treaty that would satisfy congressional representatives whose constituents desired access to the Mississippi River.[42]

Throughout the winter of 1785–1786, Gardoqui and Jay, who had initially developed a relationship in Madrid while Jay was stationed in the city as the unofficial American representative to the Spanish Court, began negotiations in the hopes of resolving the issues between the two nations, specifically, regarding navigational rights on the Mississippi

River.[43] Jay had become the U.S. Secretary of Foreign Affairs a year earlier and was willing to ignore western interests in exchange for a commercial agreement with Spain.[44] After several meetings, Gardoqui and Jay came to a preliminary agreement in February of 1786. In the treaty, Jay conceded American claims to the Mississippi River and in exchange, the Spanish Empire would open its ports to American merchants. Jay presented the treaty to Congress on August 3, 1786. Representatives of western and southern states perceived Spanish control of the Mississippi River as an economic and territorial limitation on their rights as American citizens. In turn, the Jay–Gardoqui Treaty of 1786 did not receive the necessary votes to pass, and the land claims and water rights issues that existed between the two nations continued to be unresolved in the postwar era.[45]

In the years following the failed Jay–Gardoqui Treaty, Americans continued to move throughout the continent. As they did, they increasingly came into contact with Spain's colonial inhabitants in Louisiana and the Floridas. As tempers flared in the borderlands, Gardoqui was replaced by his two secretaries, José Igancio de Viar and José de Jaudenes. Both men continued to engage with influential Americans in New York and Philadelphia, building diplomatic networks in each city, which had initially been established by Miralles during the Revolutionary War.[46] The continuation of these networks provided representatives of the U.S. and Spanish governments with an opportunity to avoid a formal military engagement between the two nations. However, both sides knew that the boundary issues needed to be resolved before a military conflict became inevitable.

After the signing of the Jay Treaty in November of 1794, the Spanish Prime Minister, Manuel Godoy, feared that Britain and the United States would form a military alliance and challenge Spain's imperial possessions in North America. Compounding these fears was the fact that Spain was in the process of leaving their brief alliance with the British Empire, which they eventually did following the signing of the Peace of Basel in July of 1795.[47] The new U.S. Minister to the Spanish Court, Thomas Pinckney, arrived in Madrid in the midst of this chaotic period in June of 1795.[48] Without the assistance of a translator, Godoy and Pinckney met on several occasions throughout the summer months of 1795 and by October they had reached a settlement.[49]

In the agreement, known formally as the Treaty of Friendship, Limits, and Navigation, or more colloquially as either the Treaty of San Lorenzo or Pinckney's Treaty, Spain submitted to all of the United States' demands. These requests included that the border between the state of Georgia and the Spanish Floridas be re-established at its pre-1763 boundary and that the citizens of the United States be given navigational rights on the Mississippi River. In exchange, Godoy requested from Pinckney that "There shall be a firm and inviolable peace and sincere friendship between his Catholic Majesty, his successors, and subjects, and the United States and their citizens, without exception of persons or places."[50] This sincere friendship was established during the early years of the Revolutionary War and continued to influence U.S.–Spanish relations throughout the long nineteenth century.

Conclusion: remembering U.S.–Spanish relations during the Revolutionary Era

In the decades following the signing of the Treaty of San Lorenzo in 1795, citizens of the United States continued to build the American transcontinental empire and the country began to present itself as a formidable player on the world stage. Conversely, after reaching its territorial highpoint at the conclusion of the American Revolutionary War, Spain was invaded by the French in 1808, leading to a sequence of events that caused the Spanish American Wars of Independence and the eventual destruction of the majority of the Spanish Empire. Despite these diverging paths, prominent Americans continued to maintain transatlantic bonds of friendship with Spanish representatives. These Americans also cared deeply for the country that supported Christopher Columbus's "discovery" of the New World and contributed to the United States during its war of independence.

For example, the fondness and affection that influential Americans had for Spain and the country's imperial legacy was put on display at a public dinner that was held at Boston's Exchange Coffeehouse on January 24, 1809. The event was hosted by the citizens of the city to show their solidarity with the Spanish patriots who were challenging Napoleon's rule over Spain and to reinforce the transatlantic bond that existed between the two nations. During the celebration, toasts were given to the Spanish people and the country's government for supporting the independence of the United States. Songs were also sung, which reinforced the gratitude that Americans had for Spain's "discovery" of the New World. Absent from the event was any hint of the Black Legend narrative or any disparaging comments regarding the lack of a formal alliance between the two countries during the Revolutionary War. Instead, Spain was presented as a "sleeping lion," which those in attendance hoped would awaken and return to its powerful position on the world stage.[51]

This dinner was not an isolated event in the history of U.S.–Spanish relations during the long nineteenth century. However, formal French support during the American Revolutionary War, the existence of the Black Legend narrative, and the War of 1898 have overshadowed the bonds of kinship that existed between Spanish and American representatives, both during the Revolutionary Era and in the century that followed. Often hidden from public view, these relationships enabled American citizens to establish their country's independence and their own empire in North America, the Caribbean, and the Pacific. Although this expansion often occurred in territories that were once held by the Spanish Empire, well-informed American representatives continued to draw on Whig-based narratives and were conscious to honor the Spanish past throughout the United States and the American Empire.

Notes

1. Rendón to Unzaga, April 12, 1783, Manuscript Reading Room at the Library of Congress (LOC), The Papers of Aileen Moore Topping (PAMT), Box 2, Folder 3; Rendón to Jose de Gálvez, April 12, 1783, LOC, PAMT, Box 2, Folder 3; Gene Allen Smith and Sylvia L. Hilton (editors), *Nexus of Empire: Negotiating Loyalty and Identity in the Revolutionary Borderlands, 1760s-1820s* (Gainesville, FL: University Press of Florida, 2010).
2. Thomas E. Chávez, *Spain and the Independence of the United States: An Intrinsic Gift* (Albuquerque, NM: University of New Mexico Press, 2002); Richard L. Kagan, "The Spanish *Craze* in the United States: Cultural Entitlement and the Appropriation of Spain's Cultural Patrimony, ca. 1890–ca.1930," *Revista Complutense de Historia de América* 36 (2010), 37–58; Christopher Schmidt-Nowara, "Spanish Origins of the American Empire: Hispanism, History, and Commemoration, 1898–1915," *International History Review* 30, no. 1 (March 2008), 32–51; Paul A. Kramer, "Historias Transimperiales: Raíces Españolas del Estado Colonial Estadounidense en Filipinas," in *Filipinas, Un País Entre Dos Imperios*, edited by María Dolores Elizalde y Josep M. Delgado (Barcelona, Spain: Edicions Bellaterra, 2011), 125–144.
3. Antonia Sagredo, "Personal Connections between Spaniards and Americans in the Revolutionary Era: Pioneers in Spanish-American Diplomacy," in *Legacy: Spain and the United States in the Age of Independence, 1763–1848*, edited by Dru Dowdy, Raquel Mesa, and Jordi Penas (Washington, D.C.: Smithsonian Institution, 2007), 44–63.
4. Richard L. Kagan (editor), *Spain in America: The Origins of Hispanism in the United States* (Urbana, IL: University of Illinois Press, 2002); Elise Bartosik-Vélez, *The Legacy of Christopher Columbus in the Americas: New Nations and a Transatlantic Discourse of Empire* (Nashville, TN: Vanderbilt University Press, 2014); Valerie I.J. Flint, *The Imaginative Landscape of Christopher Columbus* (Princeton, NJ: Princeton University Press, 1992).
5. Antonio Feros, "'Spain and America: All Is One': Historiography of the Conquest and Colonization of the Americas and National Mythology in Spain c. 1892 – c. 1992," in *Interpreting Spanish Colonialism: Empires, Nations, and Legends*, edited by Christopher Schmidt-Nowara and John M. Nieto-Phillips (Albuquerque, NM: University of New Mexico Press, 2005), 109–134; Iván Jakšić, *The Hispanic World and American Intellectual Life, 1820–1880* (New York: Palgrave Macmillan, 2007).
6. Buchanan Parker Thomson, *Spain: Forgotten Ally of the American Revolution* (North Quincy, MA: The Christopher Publishing House, 1976), 17.
7. Louis W. Potts, *Arthur Lee: A Virtuous Revolutionary* (Baton Rouge, LA: Louisiana State University Press, 1981), 152–153.
8. Beaumarchais to the Committee of Secret Correspondence, August 18, 1776, in *The Diplomatic Correspondence of the American Revolution, Volume I*, edited by Jared Sparks (Boston, MA: N. Hale, Gray, and Bowen, 1829), 35–39.
9. Sagredo, 48–49; Franklin to the Committee of Secret Correspondence, January 4, 1777, *Volume III*, 9–10.
10. Anthony McFarlane, "The American Revolution and the Spanish Monarchy," in *Europe's American Revolution*, edited by Simon P. Newman (New York: Palgrave Macmillan, 2006), 31–32.
11. Reyes Calderón Cuadrado, *Empresarios Españoles en el Proceso de Independencia Norteamericana: La Casa Gardoqui e Hijos de Bilbao* (Madrid: Instituto de Investigaciones Económicas y Sociales, 2004); Lee to the Committee of Secret Correspondence, March 18, 1777, *Volume II*, 47–53.
12. Thomson, 54–56.
13. Potts, 207.

14 Lee to the President of Congress, May 31, 1779, *Volume II*, 246.
15 Thomson, 51–52.
16 James Alton James, "Oliver Pollock: Financier of the American Revolution in the West," *Studies: An Irish Quarterly Review* 18, no. 72 (1929), 634–635; Kathleen DuVal, *Independence Lost: Lives on the Edge of the American Revolution* (New York: Random House, 2015), 42.
17 James Alton James, *Oliver Pollock: The Life and Times of an Unknown Patriot* (New York: Appleton-Century, 1937).
18 J. Barton Starr, *Tories, Dons, and Rebels: The American Revolution in British West Florida* (Gainesville, FL: The University Press of Florida, 1976), 63; Light Townsend Cummins, *Spanish Observers and the American Revolution, 1775–1783* (Baton Rouge, LA: Louisiana State University Press, 1991), 51; James, 639.
19 Gonzalo M. Quintero Saravia, *Bernardo de Gálvez: Spanish Hero of the American Revolution* (Chapel Hill, NC: The University of North Carolina Press, 2018), 97 and 139–142.
20 John Walton Caughey, *Bernardo de Gálvez in Louisiana, 1776–1783* (Gretna, LA: Pelican Publishing Company, 1972); Light Townsend Cummins, "The Gálvez Family and Spanish Participation in the Independence of the United States of America," *Revista Complutense de Historia de América* 32, (2006), 187.
21 Henry Laurens to John Laurens, July 26, 1778, in *Letters of Delegates to Congress, 1774–1789 – Volume 10*, edited by Paul H. Smith (Washington, D.C.: Library of Congress, 1983), 356.
22 Miralles to Navarro, May 13, 1778, LOC, PAMT, Box 1, Folder 1; Miralles to Navarro, May 16, 1778, LOC, PAMT, Box 1, Folder 1.
23 Miralles to José de Gálvez, February 13, 1778, LOC, PAMT, Box 1, Folder 1.
24 Miralles to Navarro, March 16, 1778, LOC, PAMT, Box 1, Folder 1.
25 Miralles to José de Gálvez, June 6, 1778, LOC, PAMT, Box 1, Folder 1; Miralles to Navarro, May 13, 1778, LOC, PAMT, Box 1, Folder 1; David J. Weber, *The Spanish Frontier in North America* (New Haven, CT: Yale University Press, 1992), 267.
26 Miralles to José de Gálvez, August 20, 1778, LOC, PAMT, Box 1, Folder 1; Helen Matzke McCadden, "Juan de Miralles and the American Revolution," *The Americas* 29, no. 3 (1973), 361; Herminio Portell Vilá, *Juan de Miralles, Un Habanero Amigo de Jorge Washington* (Havana: Sociedad Colombista Panamericana, 1947), 9–13.
27 Laurens to Laurens, July 26, 1778, in *Letters*, 356.
28 Miralles to José de Gálvez, December 28, 1778, LOC, PAMT, Box 1, Folder 1.
29 Miralles to Navarro, February 15, 1779, LOC, PAMT, Box 1, Folder 2.
30 Miralles to Navarro, May 4, 1779, LOC, PAMT, Box 1, Folder 2.
31 Miralles to José de Gálvez, March 14, 1780, LOC, PAMT, Box 1, Folder 4.
32 Rendón to Navarro, May 5, 1780, LOC, PAMT Box 1, Folder 4; Washington to Anne-César, Chevalier de La Luzerne, April 26, 1780, *Founders Online*, National Archives.
33 Rendón to Navarro, May 5, 1780, LOC, PAMT, Box 1, Folder 4; Washington to Navarro, April 30, 1780, *Founders Online*, National Archives.
34 Rendón to Navarro, August 23, 1780, LOC, PAMT, Box 1, Folder 5.
35 Rendón to José de Gálvez, December 10, 1781, LOC, PAMT, Box 2, Folder 1; Rendón to José de Gálvez, December 15, 1781, LOC, PAMT, Box 2, Folder 1.
36 Rendón to José de Gálvez, April 20, 1782, LOC, PAMT, Box 2, Folder 1.
37 Rendón, Memorial on the Commerce of the United States of America, August 31, 1783, LOC, PAMT, Box 2, Folder 3.
38 Rendón to Jose de Gálvez, April 12, 1783, LOC, PAMT, Box 2, Folder 3; Rendón to José de Gálvez, February 12, 1785, LOC, PAMT, Box 2, Folder 4.

39 French Ensor Chadwick, *The Relations of the United States and Spain* (New York: Russell and Russell Publishing, 1968), 29.
40 Rendón to Jose de Gálvez, June 28, 1785, LOC, PAMT, Box 2, Folder 5.
41 Arthur Preston Whitaker, *The Spanish-American Frontier: 1783–1795* (Boston, MA: Houghton Mifflin Company, 1927), 64–73.
42 Thomson, 114–115; Washington to Carmichael, June 10, 1785, in *The Papers of George Washington – Confederation Series – Volume 3*, edited by W.W. Abbot (Charlottesville, VA: University Press of Virginia, 1994), 47–48; Chadwick, 32.
43 Jay to Gardoqui, September 5, 1780, LOC, Papers of John Jay, Box 1, Folder: Letterbook, 1779–1782 (Part 2).
44 Samuel Flagg Bemis, *Pinckney's Treaty: America's Advantage from Europe's Distress, 1783–1800* (New Haven, CT: Yale University Press, 1960), 82; Arthur Preston Whitaker, *The Mississippi Question, 1795–1803* (Gloucester, MA: P. Smith, 1962), 23.
45 *Secret Journals of the Acts and Proceedings of Congress – Volume IV* (Boston, MA: Thomas B. Wait, 1821), 44–63.
46 Enrique Fernández, "Spain's Contribution to the Independence of the United States," *Revista/Review Interamericana* X, no. 3 (Fall 1980), 303.
47 Raymond A. Young, "Pinckney's Treaty: A New Perspective," *The Hispanic American Historical Review* 43, no. 4 (1963), 527–528.
48 Bemis, 245.
49 Young, 530–531.
50 "Treaty of Friendship, Limits, and Navigation, signed at San Lorenzo el Real October 27, 1795," in *Treaties and Other International Acts of the United States of America – Volume 2, Documents 1–40: 1776–1818*, edited by Hunter Miller (Washington, D.C.: Government Printing Office, 1931), 318–346.
51 Robert Treat Paine, "Spain: An Account of the Public Festival Given by the Citizens of Boston - January 24, 1809" (Boston, MA: Printed by Russell and Cutler, 1809).

13 A new guardian

The values of the American Revolution in post-Revolutionary Spanish Louisiana settlements

Eric Becerra

On November 30, 1789, fourteen Americans swore an oath of loyalty to Spain.[1] These men had come to the newly established settlement of New Madrid to take up the Spanish offer of free land and unrestricted trade on the Mississippi River and at the port of New Orleans. Notably, the settlers were not required to learn Spanish or convert to Catholicism; all that the oath mandated was their loyalty to His Spanish Majesty and a promise to defend the colony in the event of an invasion.[2]

The settlers at New Madrid represented a new colonial strategy for the Spanish Empire, inspired by a longstanding struggle to develop Louisiana. When France ceded Louisiana to Spain in the Treaty of Paris in 1763, most Europeans considered the colony to be underdeveloped. On colonial maps, the immense colony stretched north from New Orleans to Canada and west from the Mississippi River to Spanish New Mexico, though of course much of "Louisiana" was in reality the territory of dozens of sovereign Indian nations. To help develop the colony, Louisiana Governor Bernardo Gálvez allowed refugees of the American Revolution to settle in Louisiana, even allowing them to practice Protestantism, although the only public religion could be Catholicism.[3] Whereas for the previous 400 years the Spanish Empire allowed only Catholic settlers, Spanish officials in Louisiana now allowed Protestants to immigrate.[4]

In 1787, the new Governor of Louisiana, Esteban Miró, and the Spanish Intendant, the officer who oversaw the treasury and economic policy, Martin Navarro, wrote to the Minister of the Indies recommending a continuation of the policy implemented by Gálvez.[5] While Louisiana remained unprofitable, the colony was a key buffer state protecting the silver mines of Mexico, with lands fertile enough to potentially generate cash and food crops for the rest of the empire. Navarro realized the colony could become profitable by increasing the population to sustain trade.[6] Now, Miró and Navarro saw the best way to entice settlers was by offering free land, freedom from religious coercion, and exemption from import duties in exchange for an oath of allegiance.[7]

Historians have argued that these Spanish settlements were destined to fail; but, in fact, Americans showed much interest in the intrigues.[8] The eventual expansion of the United States should not mask the fact that, during this period, some borderlands settlers were willing to swear allegiance to a new foreign power in exchange for a chance to gain land, access to the Mississippi River, and freedom from taxation. American settlers who occupied the contested spaces known as borderlands found themselves on the peripheries of their nation, largely outside its influence and protection, and often infringing upon the borders of Native nations.[9] In such turbulent regions, where different powers challenged one another for resources and people, individuals shaped their identities to whatever national disguise provided the best opportunities.[10] Most settlers emigrated to Spanish settlements in the pursuit of self-sufficiency. Spanish officials were fully aware of the settlers' materialistic pursuits and used Spanish resources to entice Anglo settlers. Spaniards imagined that once the new subjects established homesteads they would become invested in their new home. More importantly, the settlers' children would only know loyalty to Spain.[11]

This chapter explores the history of two towns, Natchez and New Madrid, from 1785 to 1790, to explore Spain's new policy. As one of the oldest colonial towns in the region and one of the first settlements to experience Spain's change in immigration policy, Natchez offers an opportunity to understand both Spanish officials' motivations in encouraging Anglo settlement in Louisiana and Americans' reactions to this offer. In contrast to Natchez, New Madrid was the brainchild of an American speculator, and he worked with Spanish officials to establish the new settlement to entice American settlers. This chapter not only seeks to answer why and how the Spanish recruited settlers and speculators but also why Americans might choose to become Spanish subjects so shortly after achieving independence.

Louisiana appealed to white Americans in the aftermath of the War for Independence because Spanish officials' recruitment strategy tapped into the Revolutionary value of liberty, the essential promise of the American Revolution. Liberty in the late eighteenth-century borderlands was tied to various types of freedoms such as land ownership, access to markets, security, judicial rights, protection of property, religious freedom, and local control over taxation, all of which were promised by the Spanish.[12] Yet, in the earliest years of the American republic, the United States was an unstable confederacy, incapable of fulfilling the Revolution's promises. Spanish officials recognized the weakness of the fledgling American government and aimed to entice the American settlers, in the process acting as a new guardian of liberty.

Spanish overtures were viable because self-sufficiency was key to Americans' liberty. In the new republic, liberty required land and property; self-sufficiency guaranteed that a man was free from dependency and coercion, meaning no one could influence his decisions.[13] While Revolutionary patriots fought for political principles, governmental overreach was not the main concern for borderlands settlers who did not meet the property qualifications to vote. Instead, many Americans were concerned about their ability to remain self-sufficient in order to protect their personal freedoms, and they did not trust the weak and unstable United States to defend them.

Spanish Louisiana was a tempting choice for American settlers. George Washington himself voiced concern that if the Atlantic and western states did not maintain an economic connection between them, "the ties of consanguinity ... will soon be no bond" and the settlers would seek out "commercial connexions ... with the Spaniards."[14] In contrast to the fragile Continental dollar, the Spanish used a stable currency, backed by a powerful government. Moreover, Spain provided a market for foodstuffs as many of the empire's other colonies focused on cash crops and the extraction of precious minerals at the expense of agriculture. Indeed, prosperity in the trans-Appalachian West especially depended on Mississippi River trading networks, to which the Spanish had sole access via the port of New Orleans. King Carlos III's Chief Minister, José Moñino y Redondo, Conde de Floridablanca, believed that providing immigrant Americans "their liberty"[15] meant "furnishing them with an outlet through New Orleans for their produce and an opportunity in that City to provide themselves with what they need from other countries."[16] Despite U.S. claims to free navigation at the end of the American Revolution, Spain controlled the river, which continued to be its great leverage in the competition for the Mississippi Valley borderlands.[17] When negotiating the Jay–Gardoqui Treaty in 1786, John Jay secured access to Atlantic port trade agreements, but Spain was unwilling to cede rights to the Mississippi.[18] Although southern states with land interests in the west blocked the treaty, the negotiations earned the ire of western settlers.[19]

Most important among Spain's assets was land. In the early stages of the Revolution, colonists felt that settlement restrictions installed by the Proclamation Line of 1763 were a threat to their liberty, as they were trapped east of the Appalachians and forced to pay taxes to the oppressive British government.[20] This, in part, launched a revolution. In Spanish Louisiana, however, there were no settlements for 500 leagues north of New Orleans, meaning settlers had access to plenty of land.[21] Moreover, the land Miró offered the potential immigrants was free and, even after settling, the immigrants did not need to pay land taxes.[22]

Borderland settlers were among the most disconnected from the nation, often believing that those on the Atlantic coast held little regard for their interests, and were therefore enticed by Spanish officials' immigration policies.[23] The *New York Morning Post and Daily Advertiser* told its readers that in "Kentucky ... many of the principal people of that district, are warmly in favor of a separation from the union."[24] A contributor to borderland *Kentucky Gazette* newspaper similarly warned that "the moment [American leaders] attempt to give up the trade of the Mississippi, the western Country ... will be lost" to foreign entities who could provide them access to the Mississippi.[25]

Another of Spain's greatest inducements was the security it could offer its subjects. Security was the basis for the social contract: with property rights serving as the foundation to Americans ideas of liberty, a threat to property rights became a threat to liberty itself.[26] After the Revolutionary War, land-hungry settlers poured over the Appalachians, staking a claim to Indian country and coming into conflict with the region's original inhabitants. As violence broke out, the United States had no standing army and remained in financial and political disarray from its revolution, meaning it could not protect its western settlers.[27] Indeed, James Robertson, one of the founders of Nashville, named North Carolina's territory around the Cumberland River the District of Miró, after Governor Miró to gain Spain's support and protection against raids by the Creeks and the Cherokees. In his eyes, this action was necessary as "[the] United States afford us no protection."[28]

In the Mississippi borderlands, the Spanish provided security by maintaining friendly relations with various Native nations, who used the Spanish as much as the Spanish used them. Miró, while often frustrated, wisely chose not to engage in a direct conflict and instead armed the Native "nations most faithful to us."[29] The alliances proved a powerful inducement for settlers. In 1789, James White, a leader of North Carolina's western settlements negotiated with Miró about joining the Spanish in exchange for protection against Indian raids for Cumberland settlers. Miró promptly sent a letter to the Creek Chief Alexander McGillivray, who stopped the attacks in the district.[30]

To convince American settlers to switch their loyalty to Spain, new Spanish settlements needed to embody the ideals of the American Revolution by providing liberty in the form of land, security, and markets, without impeding that liberty with religious obligations or taxation. The experiment began in the Lower Mississippi Basin. Natchez offered English-speaking settlers a chance to attain their personal liberty through financial success. On this experimental ground, Spain altered its immigration policy to continue developing the region, first by recruiting French colonists and former British loyalists, and later American immigrants.

Natchez and its surrounding areas held a diverse set of colonists. After the Seven Years War, Great Britain acquired the colony from France and allowed Anglo immigrants to populate the town.[31] However, the Spanish reconquered these settlements during the American Revolution. While British loyalists rebelled in 1781 and briefly retook Natchez to aid Britain, Spanish forces held it at the war's end.[32] By the latter half of the century, Natchez was home to settlers from all three empires.

Louisiana's diverse settlers nevertheless fit relatively well into the Spanish Empire. After dealing with a French uprising in 1768, Spain managed to gain French Louisianans' loyalty by emphasizing their shared economic interests, religion, and hatred of the British.[33] In contrast to the French, the Spanish viewed Anglo settlers with both caution and optimism. Although Miró incorporated them into the colony, he had no plans to create a religiously diverse society. Miró instead aimed to gradually convert Louisiana's Anglo settlers and sponsored Catholic parishes to proselytize to them, assigning two parishes to Natchez.[34] By 1785, Spanish officials proceeded to allow non-Catholic Christians to stay and to immigrate, setting the precedent for other Anglo settlers as well.

American interest in Natchez heightened in the 1780s as European and American diplomats failed to create a clear border following the American Revolution.[35] The Treaty of Paris had a secret provision that extended American territory to the 31st parallel, but, the treaty signed with Spain had no clear northern border. Thus, both Spain and the United States felt the right to claim the lands between the Mississippi River and the Appalachian Mountains and north of the 31st parallel, which included Natchez. A group of Americans first tested their claim in 1785. During the spring of that year, a small party of Georgians arrived in Natchez and demanded that the Spanish surrender the settlement, according to the terms of the Treaty of Paris. The Spanish refused and Miró ordered the party's leader, Thomas Green, sent to New Orleans.[36] A second party of Georgians arrived a few months later, but they were expelled by the Spanish and soon after attempted unsuccessfully to hide among the Choctaws and the Chickasaws.[37] Unfortunately for the Georgians, the Creek Chief Alexander McGillivray ordered one of them killed, and the rest returned to U.S. territory.[38]

The Americans' challenge to Spanish sovereignty paradoxically helped consolidate Spain's control over the district. Land-hungry Americans received a clear message that they could not count on Anglo settlers in Natchez to support an American takeover. While Green attempted to take the district, a group of Anglo settlers in Natchez signed a petition stating Georgian control would only bring "ruin and destruction."[39] As Natchez resident John Gordon wrote, "I shall prefer the Spanish government to the American, for the taxes give me the headache."[40] In an ironic turn of events just after the Revolution, it was former British colonists who rejected American rule for fear of taxes.

Commander Francisco de Bouligny, the son of a Frenchman who immigrated to Spain, was living proof that immigrants could serve their adopted empire loyally.[41] When considering how to "maintain the tranquility" of the population, Bouligny trusted immigrants enough to create a militia composed of recent American settlers who would elect their own commanders.[42] Despite the risks of arming the former Americans, Bouligny was "inclined to think that they are not capable of forming a rebellion" against their new government.[43] As he explained, Americans were "full of gratitude for the benefits they have received from the [Spanish] Government."[44] Bouligny observed that Americans prioritized opportunities for land and trade, and that their allegiance depended on their individual well-being.

Natchez served as an example of how Spain could entice former subjects of other empires and even citizens of the United States. Although most of the Anglo settlers in Natchez were former British subjects rather than Americans, the settlement proved a relatively successful testing ground for allowing

Protestant colonists. From 1787 to 1789, 293 Americans settled in the district.[45] With their help, trade boomed. In 1789, Natchez planters, most of whom were Anglo inhabitants, produced 1,402,725 pounds of tobacco.[46]

Though the immigration of Americans into Natchez was a positive step in developing Louisiana, it was still insufficient for Spain's ultimate goals. While American immigrants buttressed existing settlements, to create a successful colony, Spain would need to create new settlements altogether. Spanish and American speculators co-sponsored new settlements based on what they believed liberty meant to American settlers. One of these settlements, New Madrid, was the brainchild of Minister Gardoqui and Colonel George Morgan, a veteran of the American Revolution and former agent of Indian affairs. Yet, while the Spanish emphasized liberty in terms of owning land and being financially independent, Morgan later stressed that for Americans, "Our love of Liberty Civil and religious is our ruling Passion."[47] These differing interpretations of liberty ultimately led to conflict and impeded New Madrid's growth as both sides felt uncompromising towards their respective interpretations.

Like many other Revolutionary officers, Morgan hoped to benefit financially from the nation's independence and the subsequent opening of western lands after the removal of the Proclamation Line of 1763, submitting proposals to Congress for 2 million acres of land in the Northwest Territory.[48] However, by 1788, Morgan had not received his lands. After the war, Virginia ceded its claims to the Northwest Territory to Congress, which thereafter sold the lands to pay for its war debts. Deprived of his venture, Morgan formed the New Jersey Land Society to purchase western land.[49] In the meantime, however, Morgan received a more promising offer from the Spanish Minister Diego de Gardoqui to help establish a settlement in Louisiana.

In response, Morgan promptly dropped out of the New Jersey Land Society and wrote numerous detailed proposals to Gardoqui.[50] Morgan assured Gardoqui that under his supervision, the settlement would develop into one with 100,000 souls within ten years.[51] In return for his efforts, Morgan requested command of the town, a salary, and a land grant of a thousand acres for himself, his wife, and his children.[52] Over the next year, Morgan and Gardoqui planned the settlement that would become New Madrid.

Gardoqui also embraced the opportunity. He wrote to the Spanish Chief Minister that Morgan's project "seems to me to be of prime importance, and the talents of that person encourage me to reiterate my recommendation of him."[53] Citing reports from "confidential communications," Gardoqui wrote that the inhabitants of Kentucky grew "exasperated by the first reports that Congress [was] discussing surrender of the navigation of the River for 25 years, and they [had] openly asserted that if this [was] done they will seek aid from another Power as an Independent State."[54] Gardoqui quickly approved Morgan's proposals and wrote him a passport to find suitable lands for the settlement.[55]

Without waiting for the Spanish Crown's final approval, Morgan took the initiative to advertise the settlement, taking care to emphasize how the Spanish could provide personal liberty to settlers. In a handbill, he promised his recruits "320 Acres of land, at one eight of a Dollar per Acre."[56] New Madrid's initial settlers, recruited personally by Morgan, wrote letters printed in eastern newspapers claiming "there is not an acre of [New Madrid] uncultivable, or even indifferent land, within a thousand square miles."[57] For potential tradesmen, Morgan guaranteed free navigation of the Mississippi as well as permission to trade with New Orleans and other Spanish colonies.[58]

Morgan assured his recruits that Spain would safeguard important values of the Revolution, claims he made without the official consent of the Spanish Crown. Although Morgan required new settlers to pay an initial land payment, they were to pay no taxes thereafter, an essential inducement in attracting a population that had just fought a war in opposition to tyrannous taxes.[59] Furthermore, while Morgan was to command New Madrid under the authority of His Majesty, he stressed that "the trial by jury & liberty of regulating their own interior police, must stand also foremost as a charter right inherent to this new Province."[60] For Americans, trial by jury held a special importance. Among the most hated features of the Stamp and Townshend Acts, which precipitated the Revolution, was the denial of a trial by jury.

Notably, Morgan also promised potential settlers that the Spanish "will meet with Encouragement" any Christian "of every Denomination."[61] With this policy, Morgan tapped into another key aspect of liberty: the freedom to practice one's own religion. While Spain already promised private toleration of Protestants, Morgan took the unapproved additional step of promising public toleration for all types of Christians.

Morgan, with Gardoqui's approval, created a set of instructions for the construction of New Madrid that highlighted religious toleration, access to land, free trade, and peaceful coexistence.[62] He began by stating how the colonists were going to gain access to land and how the city was going to be designed and settled. His statement that the first 600 settlers would receive free land, after only paying a dollar for a patent, highlights the urgency to settle the town quickly. The main street of New Madrid was named King Street while the lots adjacent to King Street were designated for a Roman Catholic school and church.[63] Notably, the emphasis on royalty and Catholicism contrasted sharply with the Anglo Protestants immigrating from a republic with no official religion. However, Morgan also designed New Madrid with different church districts, embedding Christian tolerance into the town.

Morgan also took considerable efforts to demonstrate how settlers would avoid clashing with local Native Americans. In a 1789 speech to a collection of Delawares, Shawnees, and Cherokees at New Madrid, he assured the assembled that "you shall have all the liberty to hunt and kill all the Game in the Country" and that although Morgan and the settlers would hunt in the surrounding area, he "will not allow any white men to hunt herefor [sic] the sake of skins of furs."[64] In return, Morgan requested that the Indians respect white men's property.[65] By outlawing commercial hunting, Morgan intended to keep Indians and settlers from competing for resources. The slight limitation to commercial liberty was a necessary tradeoff. After all, security was a fundamental element of liberty.

Spanish alliances with Native peoples were mutually beneficial. Not only did the Spanish maintain peace with the Indians, they drew much of their economic strength in the area from their alliances with Native nations. The Shawnees, Delaware, and Cherokees all traded with New Madrid.[66] The Spanish highly valued this trade and assigned additional trading agents to live with the Chickasaws, the Choctaws, and the Creeks, and by 1793, an estimated 2,000 Indians "received their Supplies at New Madrid."[67] Native Americans also made this trade relationship a priority. After the Revolutionary War, when the British withdrew from the southeast, many Native American groups that had allied with the British, such as the Creeks, made new alliances with the Spanish. Although the Spanish fought on the side of the Americans during the Revolution, gaining access to European goods, especially guns and ammunition, and an ally against American expansion, was paramount for Native peoples.

Gardoqui agreed with Morgan's proposal, and their plan successfully attracted settlers. Morgan himself recruited about "39 households," who each received "at least 160 English acres."[68] By 1788, the first immigrants arrived and began clearing land.[69] The settlement seemed promising for the Spanish, though troubling for U.S. officials. In a letter to the governor of Virginia, Beverly Randolph, Virginia politician, John Dawson wrote that because of New Madrid, "a door will be open'd through which the United States will [lose] many thousands of her best citizens."[70] Morgan's plan, he claimed, was "far superior to that of Congress" and that "sacred assurances of freedom in religious matters, a free navigation of the Mississippi to New Orleans, clear of all duties and taxes, besides being entitled to all of the King of Spain's rich dominions are inducements sufficient to draw the attention of the industrious and enterprising."[71] Just as opportunities had pulled settlers west, the enticements of Louisiana threatened to pull them farther west still.

Unfortunately for Morgan, his actions disturbed Governor Miró because they were implemented without the consent of the Spanish Crown. Specifically, Miró viewed Morgan's efforts as an attempt to establish "a Republic within its own domains" and therefore "highly detrimental to the welfare and service of Spain."[72] As such, Miró sought to rein in Gardoqui's and Morgan's vision. Instead, Miró listened to the American general James Wilkinson, who also approached the Spanish with a plan to create new settlements along the Mississippi.[73] According to Wilkinson's proposal, the Spanish needed to close off the Mississippi, which would encourage western settlers to break off from the United States and negotiate separate agreements with the Spanish.[74]

To Miró, the number of civic freedoms that helped define Morgan's and the Americans' version of liberty did not fit into the array of liberties that the Spanish were willing to offer. Miró wrote to Morgan, telling the Colonel that he had "exceeded" himself in selling the land and promising so many civic freedoms.[75] Although Miró had no plans of persecuting Protestants, he asserted that "Catholicism [would] be the only public religion."[76] Miró would then offer free land to Americans in order to entice them to become Spanish subjects and gradually convert Anglo settlers through the use of English-speaking Irish Catholic priests.[77] He believed that providing free land to settlers would earn their loyalty.[78] Although bothered that Morgan had taken such liberties in designing New Madrid, Miró nevertheless honored Morgan's previous promises to the settlers and allowed them to keep their land grants.

Yet, Miró's intervention had denied Morgan his idealistic, and profitable, community. While the Colonel kept in contact with Gardoqui for some time, once Morgan inherited his brother's sizable fortune, he left Louisiana and returned to Pennsylvania.[79] When Morgan inherited property, he no longer needed the Spanish to obtain his own personal liberty or fortune. By the end of 1789, Morgan had completely abandoned New Madrid.[80]

Morgan's departure ultimately compromised Spain's ability to promise liberty to Americans, affecting the settlement's growth. As Morgan's replacement, Spanish Commander Pedro Foucher reported to Miró, the only new immigrants to arrive by April 1790 were a few deserters from Virginia, in contrast to the wealthy planters who settled Natchez.[81] No longer guaranteed their version of liberty, most of those whom Morgan brought to New Madrid left the settlement and returned back to the United States by May of 1790.[82]

The new Spanish immigration policy used at Natchez and New Madrid ultimately had mixed results. The steady stream of immigration contributed to the population growth of the Natchez District from 1,600 in 1784 to 5,381 in 1796.[83] In contrast, it is difficult to determine how many non-Catholic settlers took up the Spanish offer in New Madrid. While the Spanish register of 1791 counts 220 settlers at New Madrid, there were also numerous deserters from the Continental army who joined the settlement but do not appear on the Spanish records.[84] Notably, many of those who swore oaths to Spain in 1789 did not appear in the register taken in 1791.[85]

Although New Madrid increased in population, it failed to grow into the spectacular success Spanish officials had imagined only a few years prior. The greatest reason for this disappointment was that, despite the rhetoric, New Madrid did not succeed in offering the vision of liberty settlers wanted. When Spanish officials used liberty to attract immigrants to Natchez, they limited liberty to encompass security, financial independence, and private religious toleration. In contrast, when Morgan planned New Madrid, he targeted Americans and promised settlers too much in terms of civil liberties and public religious toleration, promises that were subsequently repealed by Miró.

Even Morgan's economic promises remained unfulfilled. While Natchez had successfully attracted settlers due to its rich resources, as surveyor Andrew Ellicott noted, New Madrid and its surrounding areas suffered from poor quality soil that was often flooded.[86] Other towns avoided this pitfall; Natchez, for example, was established on higher land and New Orleans used a system of levees. Another reason for New Madrid's failure was that since the settlement could not live up to its promised potential, its settlers left for more profitable parts of Louisiana like New Orleans.[87]

Still, many of the immigrants who settled permanently remained Spanish subjects even after Spain eventually deprioritized Louisiana. As Napoleon took power in the late eighteenth century, the Spanish shifted their attention to Europe and signed away sole access to the Mississippi to the United States in the 1795 Treaty of San Lorenzo. When Spain agreed to the terms of the treaty, the empire no longer provided the land, security, and trade the inhabitants required. Ultimately, settlers in the borderlands were not particularly loyal to the United States or the Spanish. They were loyal to liberty itself, prioritizing landed liberty over national identity. By the time the United States reabsorbed the settlers who left, it had grown into a nation that could fulfill its promises of providing new lands and trade opportunities. Thus, the settlers happily joined the government that could once again provide them liberty.

Although the United States eventually took over the settlements, the fact that Spain, in the eyes of many borderland Americans, had once challenged the United States as a provider of liberty gives pause to the traditional historiography of American success. In the late eighteenth century, the developing nation was particularly vulnerable and not necessarily destined for expansion. Spain's potential to become the new guardian of liberty and the viability of Spanish settlements like Natchez and New Madrid spoke to the vulnerability of the United States following the Revolution.

Notes

1. "Some Persons who took the Oath of Allegiance at New Madrid from 1789 to 1796," *The Spanish Regime in Missouri*, ed. and trans. Louis Houck (Chicago: Donnelley & Sons, 1909), 334.
2. Ibid.
3. Gonzalo M. Quintero Saravia, *Bernardo de Gálvez: Spanish Hero of the American Revolution* (Chapel Hill: The University of North Carolina Press, 2018), 117–119.
4. Richard Arena, "Land Settlement Policies and Practices in Spanish Louisiana," in *The Spanish in the Mississippi Valley 1762–1804* (Chicago: University of Illinois Press, 1974), 57.
5. Miró and Navarro to the Minster of the Indies, September 25, 1787, "Papers from the Spanish Archives Relating to Tennessee and the Old Southwest," trans. and ed. D.C. and Roberta Corbitt, *East Tennessee Historical Society's Publications* 12 (Knoxville: The East Tennessee Historical Society, 1944): 105–107.
6. Navarro, Political Reflections on the Present Condition of the Province of Louisiana New Orleans, ca. 1785, *Louisiana under the Rule of Spain France, and the*

United States, 1785–1807: Social, Economic, and Political Conditions of the Territory Represented in the Louisiana Purchase (Cleveland, Ohio: The Arthur H. Clark Company, 1911), 1: 238.
7 Caroline Maude Burson, *The Stewardship of Don Esteban Miró, 1781–1792: A Study of Louisiana Based Largely on the Documents in New Orleans* (New Orleans: American Printing Company, 1940), 129.
8 A.P. Whitaker, *The Spanish American Frontier 1783–1795* (Gloucester, MA: Peter Smith, 1962); Jeremy Adelman and Stephen Aron, "From Borderlands to Borders: Empires, Nation-States, and the Peoples in between in North American History," *American Historical Review* 104 (1999), 826.
9 In this chapter, borderland generalizations will refer to the borderlands of the North American Southeast. Juliana Barr, "Geographies of Power: Mapping Indian Borders in the 'Borderlands' of the Early Southwest," *William and Mary Quarterly* 68 (2011), 8.
10 Andrés Reséndez, *Changing National Identities at the Frontier: Texas and New Mexico, 1800–1850* (New York: Cambridge University Press, 2004), 2.
11 Esteban Miró and Martin Navarro to the Minster of the Indies, September 25, 1787, "Papers from the Spanish Archives Relating to Tennessee and the Old Southwest," trans. and ed. D.C. and Roberta Corbitt, *East Tennessee Historical Society's Publications* 12 (Knoxville: The East Tennessee Historical Society, 1944): 105–107.
12 See Bernard Bailyn, *The Ideological Origins of the American Revolution* (Cambridge: The Belknap Press of Harvard University Press, 2017).
13 J. W. Cooke, "Jefferson on Liberty," *Journal of the History of Ideas* 34 (1973), 573.
14 George Washington to Henry Lee, June 18, 1786, *The Writings of George Washington*, ed. Worthington C. Ford (New York and London: G.P. Putnam's Sons, 1893), 41.
15 José Moñino y Redondo, conde de Floridablanca to Diego de Gardoqui, May 24, 1788, "Papers from the Spanish Archives Relating to Tennessee and the Old Southwest," 16: 95.
16 Ibid., 95–96.
17 Gálvez, "Navigation of the Mississippi Not Free," *The Spanish Regime in Missouri*, 237.
18 John Jay to Jefferson, January 9, 1786, *The Correspondence and Public Papers of John Jay*, ed. Henry P. Johnston (New York: G.P. Putnam's Sons, 1891), 2: 178–9.
19 Narrett, *Adventurism and Empire: The Struggle for Mastery in the Louisiana-Florida Borderlands, 1762–1803* (Chapel Hill: University of North Carolina Press, 2015), 128.
20 Alan Taylor, *The Civil War of 1812: American Citizens, British Subjects, Irish Rebels, & Indian Allies* (New York: Vintage Boks, 2010), 16.
21 A Description of Louisiana, December 12, 1785, *Spain in the Mississippi Valley, 1765–1794*, ed. and trans. Lawrence Kinnaird (Washington DC: Government Printing Office, 1946), 1: 160.
22 Miró and Navarro to the Minister of the Indies, 107.
23 Kevin T. Barksdale, *The Lost State of Franklin: America's First Secession* (Lexington, KY: The University of Kentucky Press, 2009), 18.
24 *Morning Post and Daily Advertiser* February 17, 1789, enclosed in Gardoqui to Floridablanca, March 4, 1789, "Papers from the Spanish Archives Relating to Tennessee and the Old Southwest," 19: 92.
25 *Kentucky Gazette*, November 22, 1788.
26 John Locke, *Two Treatises of Government* (London: Printed for Thomas Tegg; 1823), 159.
27 Kathleen DuVal, *Independence Lost: Lives on the Edge of the American Revolution* (New York: Random House, 2015), 333.

28 James Robertson to Miró, September 2, 1789, *Spain in the Mississippi Valley*, 279.
29 Miró to Cruzat, May 15, 1787, *Spain in the Mississippi Valley*, 201.
30 Miró to Smith, April 27, 1780, *Spain in the Mississippi Valley*, 272.
31 Din, *Populating the Barrera*, 41.
32 DuVal, *Independence Lost*, 110.
33 Ibid., 37; 139.
34 Din, *Populating the Barrera*, 41.
35 DuVal, *Independence Lost*, 234.
36 Narrett, *Adventurism and Empire*, 121–122.
37 Alexander McGillivray to Vincente Manuel de Zespedes, October 6, 1787, *McGillivray of the Creeks*, ed. John Walton Caughey (Norman: University of Oklahoma Press, 1938), 162.
38 McGillivray to O'Neill, July 25, 1787, *McGillivray of the Creeks*, 159.
39 Ellis, Gaillard, and Banks to the Citizens of Natchez, June 1785, "Papers Relating to Bourbon County, Georgia, 1785–1786," *American Historical Review Volume XV October 1909 to July 1910* (London: The Macmillan Company, 1910), 77.
40 John Gordon to George Profit, June 25, 1785, "Papers relating to Bourbon County, Georgia, 1785–1786," 96.
41 Gilbert Din, *Francisco Bouligny: A Bourbon Soldier in Spanish Louisiana* (Baton Rouge: Louisiana State University Press, 1993), 3.
42 Bouligny to Miró, August 22, 1785, Folder 107, Louisiana Papers, Bancroft Library.
43 Ibid.
44 Ibid.
45 Census, *Spanish Regime in Missouri*. The math is corroborated by Gilbert Din in *Populating the Barrera*, 76.
46 Grand Pré, March 2, 1790, *Spain in the Mississippi Valley*, 305–311.
47 Morgan to Gardoqui, February 24, 1791, quoted in Savelle, *George Morgan: Colony Builder* (New York: Columbia University Press, 1932), 200.
48 Ibid., 200.
49 Proposals of George Morgan and Associates, May 15, 1788, *Kaskaskia Records, 1778–1790*, ed. Clarence Walworth (Springfield, IL: Trustees of the Illinois State Historical Library, 1909), 471.
50 John W. Reps, "New Madrid on the Mississippi," *Journal of the Society of Architectural Historians* 18 (1959), 21.
51 Houck, *The Spanish Regime in Missouri*, 299.
52 Reps, "New Madrid on the Mississippi," 21.
53 Gardoqui to Floridablanca, October 24, 1788, "Papers from the Spanish Archives Relating to Tennessee and the Old Southwest," 18: 135.
54 Gardoqui to Floridablanca, October 28, 1786, "Papers from the Spanish Archives Relating to Tennessee and the Old Southwest," 16: 87.
55 Gardoqui to Floridablanca, October 24, 1786, "Papers from the Spanish Archives Relating to Tennessee and the Old Southwest," 18: 133–137.
56 George Morgan, Morgan's handbill, quoted in Max Savelle, *George Morgan*, 207.
57 Letter to Messrs. Bedford and Turnbull from settlers at New Madrid, April 14, 1788, quoted in Reps, "New Madrid on the Mississippi," 22.
58 Morgan, Morgan's handbill, quoted in Savelle, *George Morgan*, 207.
59 Morgan to Gardoqui, August 20, 1789, *Spanish Regime in Missouri*, 295.
60 Morgan to Gardoqui, April 1789, *Spanish Regime in Missouri*, 306.
61 George Morgan, Morgan's handbill, quoted in Max Savelle, 207.
62 Morgan to Gardoqui, Directions, *Spanish Regime in Missouri*, 302–305.
63 Ibid., 304–305.
64 The Speech of Colonel Morgan to the Deleware, Shawnese and Cherokee at his First Meeting them at New Madrid, April 1789, Papers of the Morgan Family,

1768–1938, MSS #367, Historical Society of Western Pennsylvania, Detre Library & Archives, Heinz History Center.
65 Ibid.
66 Thomas Mitchell to Alexander Hamilton, August 27, 1793, *The Papers of Alexander Hamilton*, ed. Harold C. Syrett and Jabe E. Cooke (New York, Columbia University Press, 1996), 15: 292.
67 Ibid.
68 "List of the persons who have subscribed to Colonel George Morgan their acceptance of the plots of land, which he has promised to allot them in his projected settlement of New Madrid," Pontalba Papers, Temple Bodley Collection, Filson Historical Society, Louisville, KY.
69 Savelle, *George Morgan*, 214.
70 John Dawson to Beverly Randolph, January 29, 1789, *Calendar of Virginia State Papers and Other Manuscripts, from January 1, 1785 to July 2, 1789 Preserved in the Capitol at Richmond*, ed. William P. Palmer, 4 (Richmond: R.U. Derr, Superintendent of Public Printing, 1884), 554–555.
71 Ibid.
72 Miró to Morgan, May 23, 1789, Pontalba Papers.
73 Savelle, *George Morgan*, 215.
74 Ibid.
75 Miró to Morgan, May 23, 1789, Pontalba Papers.
76 Savelle, *George Morgan*, 215.
77 Miró to Morgan, May 23, 1789, Pontalba Papers.
78 Miró to Don Antonio Valdes, May 20, 1789, *Spanish Regime in Missouri*, 277.
79 Savelle, *George Morgan*, 227.
80 Ibid.
81 Foucher to Miró, April 10, 1790, *Spain in the Mississippi Valley*, 3, 305.
82 Savelle, "Founding of New Madrid," *Mississippi Historical Review* 19, no. 1 (1932), 55.
83 Din, *Populating the Barrera*, 76.
84 New Settlers of New Madrid, *Spanish Regime in Missouri*, 327. Thomas Mitchell to Alexander Hamilton, August 27, 1793, *The Papers of Alexander Hamilton*, 15, 292.
85 Foucher to Miró, April 30, 1791, *Spanish Regime in Missouri*, 328–329.
86 Andrew Ellicott, entry for February 3, 1797, *Surveying the Early Republic: The Journal of Andrew Ellicott U.S. Boundary Commissioner in the Old Southwest 1796–1800* (Baton Rouge, Louisiana State University Press, 2016), 48.
87 Foucher to Miró, April 30, 1791, *Spanish Regime in Missouri*, 328–329.

14 Spanish America and US constitutionalism in the Age of Revolution

Eduardo Posada-Carbó

I

This chapter examines the impact of US constitutionalism in Spanish America, with specific attention to New Granada (Colombia today) during the early independence period. By doing so, it aims to revise the current historiographical trend that has tended to focus its attention on the Cádiz constitution of 1812 as the most important early constitutional development in Spanish America, neglecting or simply denying not only the 'influence' of the US but also ignoring altogether the significant constitutional movement that took place in the region, in processes that were running either independently from or in confrontation with the Cádiz Cortes. While I consider the national US constitution, I am particularly interested in exploring the extent to which the Spanish American founders were familiar with the early state constitutions, 'often overlooked documents [that] occupy a critical position in the development of American constitutionalism'.[1]

Four constitutional texts were adopted in New Granada before the Cádiz Cortes approved the 1812 constitution; three more were published before the latter crossed the Atlantic. Indeed, between 1811 and 1815, the provinces of New Granada adopted at least ten constitutions. In addition, Venezuela issued four constitutions in 1811–1812, three preceding the Cádiz constitution.[2] It is surprising how little attention this first wave of constitutionalism in Spanish America has received from modern historiography, with the exception of some scholars who study New Granada and Venezuela.[3] George Athan Billias, a constitutional historian of the United States, has looked at the impact of US constitutionalism in the first decades of independence but, while acknowledging the Venezuelan experience, seems to ignore the New Granadan texts.[4] Political scientists, who have been paying increasing attention to the subject, have also by and large overlooked the early constitutional history of the region.[5] In contrast, the literature on the Cádiz constitution has flourished in recent decades.[6] There are of course good and important reasons for the latter case – a development to be welcomed, no doubt. However, any examination of the origins of Spanish American constitutionalism that leaves aside the early experiences of New Granada (and Venezuela) is at a minimum incomplete. Indeed, their study seems essential to appreciate the wider dialogue involved in the constitutional movement of the period. Although the focus here will be on the connections with the US, the chapter in the end raises questions about our approaches to the field.

I have looked at the impact of the US constitution in New Granada in a previous essay,[7] where I examined its translation into Spanish by Miguel de Pombo in 1811, a publication aimed at serving the federal cause as the independent movement unfolded. This publication, which also included the US Declaration of Independence and the Federal Act, was preceded by a lengthy prologue written by Pombo himself. If the aim of that exercise was to study whether or not 'translations ever instigated a crisis or shaped the way in which it developed', it also served the purpose of illustrating the constitutional trajectory of New Granada, a trajectory that does not seem to have been especially aligned with the Cádiz process. In that essay, I took issue with those who have argued that the independence of the United States had little influence on the emancipation of Spanish America.[8] In the end, however, I was left with more questions than answers, particularly about the federal question – at the centre of the debate in New Granada during its first republican experiment between 1811 and 1815.

The federal question was at the core of the origins of Spanish American constitutionalism. Those who declared in favour of federalism were soon accused of copying US institutions. 'Intoxicated by the appealing idea of federation ... and seduced by the example of the United States of North America', José Manuel Restrepo lamented in his *Historia de la revolución*, 'the provinces stopped thinking about sending deputies to Santafé, or about preserving the centralization of government'.[9] An influential participant in this process, Restrepo observed that most deputies who did attend the meeting convened in Santafé to discuss the Acta de Federación, adopted in 1811, also subscribed to the US model, following the 1776 Articles of Confederation.[10] Modern scholars that have looked at the influences of the US in this process have discussed whether or not the founders of New Granada paid more attention to the latter than to the US constitution.[11] However, Restrepo acknowledged other sources of inspiration that have passed generally unnoticed by the historiography: the various constitutions adopted by the different states of the US.[12]

The first sixteen states of the US adopted eighteen constitutions between 1776 and 1798.[13] To what extent were these constitutions known to the founders of New Granada? In their constitutional endeavours, were the latter just imitating the US provincial constitutions and, if so, which among them was the most influential? This chapter is an attempt to address these and other related questions. At first glance, the task at hand would seem impossible since the evidence is so fragmentary. However, we do have the full texts of the constitutions. Through close readings of these documents, we should be able to identify similarities and contrasts among them, even if we are not able to ascertain with precision the extent to which the constitution makers in

New Granada and Venezuela were inspired or not by the state constitutions in the US. In the following pages, I can only offer an outline of what I think should be developed into a wider, ambitious research project. Before doing so, let me review the evidence we so far have on those early US constitutions and their possible influence in Spanish America.

II

Key individual figures were certainly familiar with the provincial constitutions of the US, even before independence. When Francisco de Miranda visited the country in 1783–1784, he discussed the Massachusetts constitution with Samuel Adams, and that of New Hampshire with that state's president, Nathaniel Folsom.[14] A French edition of a compilation of the constitutions was published in Philadelphia in 1778 – one copy found its way to Antonio Nariño's library in Bogotá, confiscated by the Spanish authorities when he was prosecuted for sedition in 1794.[15] During the independence period, perhaps the greatest disseminator of the US revolutionary ideas was the Venezuelan Manuel García de Sena. In 1811, he translated into Spanish selected passages of Paine's *Common Sense* and *Dissertation of the First Principles of Government*, in a volume that also included the state constitutions of Massachusetts, Connecticut, New Jersey, Pennsylvania and Virginia.[16] Passages of these texts were 'cited in the Venezuelan Congress and reprinted in the *Gazeta de Caracas*'.[17] As Simmons has noted, García de Sena's books 'circulated widely in Spanish America', beyond Venezuela and New Granada.[18] In particular, the 1780 constitution of Massachusetts seemed to have been consulted by the Uruguayan José Gervasio Artigas when producing the project for the 1813 *Constitución oriental* and by the authors of the Apatzingan constitution of 1814.[19]

That the state constitutions of the US were well known in New Granada can also be inferred by reading at least two of the most prominent leaders of the independent movement: Miguel de Pombo and Camilo Torres, both described by Restrepo as 'enthusiast and servile adorers of the institutions of the United States of North America'.[20] Pombo's lengthy prologue to his translation of the US constitution offers plenty of evidence of his close acquaintance with US history, including the conditions of the various states – his is a fairly well-known document, commented upon by several historians. Here I want to draw our attention to a perhaps lesser-known text, a letter by Camilo Torres, written on 29 May 1810, in answer to his uncle, Ignacio Tenorio, who was proposing a scheme of government to save the colonies for Ferdinand VII.[21] Note the date of the document: almost two months before the declaration of independence in Santafé (20 July 1810), which Torres helped to write. For Torres, it was time to come to terms with the fact that Spain was in ruins, conquered by the Napoleonic forces. The question for the Americans therefore was 'what measures do we have to take to sustain our independence and freedom?' He rejected his uncle's suggestions for a government elected by all the provinces in America to rule on behalf of Ferdinand.

To start with, so argued Torres, convening elections for the whole region posed insurmountable barriers – as the election for the Junta Central in 1809 had shown. In addition, each province would aspire to be the centre of such new 'Reino', creating new ties of dependency: 'we would be *colonos de colonos*, and this would be the worst of our ills'.[22] Torres went further. Since America was already independent – the Spanish monarchy having been dissolved, the links with the metropolis broken – 'Why do you like that our juntas, our congresses, and the wise government that we elect be made on behalf of an elf or a ghost?' There was no need to cover the newly acquired freedom with the name of a king. Sovereignty had been resumed by the 'mass of the nation', and nations had the 'right' to change of government and 'to reform the Constitution, as long as from those reforms and changes happiness is achieved'. Torres also rejected his uncle's suggestion to form centralised governments. He favoured instead governments in each 'Reino o provincia', therefore approaching the form of government of the North Americans – an argument that Torres backed up citing Richard Price, a Welsh philosopher who supported the US independence and wrote several pamphlets about US constitutionalism that circulated widely in England, France and the US.[23] 'Any *reino* ... or province in America that, given its size, wealth and population, considers itself capable of forming ... an independent state', Torres concluded, 'can and must do so.' That was, he added, 'what the States of Vermont, Kentucky and Tennessee in North America have done'. The road ahead was to imitate 'the conduct of the North Americans, let's follow the steps of that philosophical people and we will be as happy as them. Let us thus work to form a similar Government and, if possible, equal in all respects to those republicans.'[24]

Finally, we can count on José Manuel Restrepo's testimonies, mentioned above. He was directly involved in some of the key events during the first wave of constitutionalism: Restrepo contributed to the writing of three constitutions: those of the United Provinces in 1811, and those of Antioquia in 1811 and 1815.[25] He soon abandoned the federalist cause in favour of a centralist republic. Over a decade later, in 1827, in his *Historia de la revolución*, as already observed, Restrepo claimed that all his fellow constitutionalists were doing was copying the respective documents produced in the various states of the US: 'Hallucinated as the political novices of New Granada were by the rapid growth of the United States', he pointed out, 'they had adopted without much consideration their constitutions, too liberal for people educated under the Inquisition ... Some provinces were ruled, with light alterations, by the fundamental laws of Pennsylvania, others by those of Virginia; here those of Massachusetts, there those of Maryland.'[26]

So what do these pieces of evidence tell us? We know for sure that at least the earlier constitutional texts of Massachusetts, Connecticut, Pennsylvania, New Jersey and Virginia were translated into Spanish, published and circulated in Hispanic America. Some Spanish Americans had earlier access to these texts in their French editions that had circulated in the

1790s. These were not any individuals. These were key figures, closely involved in the constitutional movement of the period: indeed Torres and Pombo were co-authors of some of the constitutions in New Granada. For the purposes of this chapter, the role of these constitution makers is what matters most. This does not mean that the wider, social impact of US constitutionalism should not be of interest. Let me just make a few observations on the latter.

Firstly, these texts reached more than a handful of people. Henry Marie Brackenbridge, an American official who visited South America in 1817, believed that de Sena's book had been 'read by nearly all who can read [in Buenos Aires] and have produced a most extravagant admiration of the United States'.[27] Secondly, the contents of these texts reached a wider audience, indirectly, as they were echoed by newspapers, which flourished after 1808. Thirdly, we should avoid the temptation of assuming that the print word only had consequences in literate societies – illiteracy is no impediment to the circulation of ideas. None the less, let me insist that what concerns us here is the role of those individuals who sat in the constituent assemblies that gathered in the provinces of New Granada between 1811 and 1815, and the sources of inspiration in the process of constitution-making. Again we know for sure that the example of the US experience was cited in some of the discussions of the constituent assemblies,[28] and there is plenty of evidence to show that the articles of the confederation, the US constitution and the declaration of independence were used in the public debate that surrounded the constitutional processes in the first republics, in both New Granada and Venezuela. What is less clear is the extent to which the constitution makers resorted to the early state constitutions of the US, even less clear if they just copied those constitutions, as claimed by the likes of Restrepo.

We do have at our disposal, however, the constitutional texts that were produced at the time. A brief exercise, comparing some of the first US state constitutions with some of the state constitutions in New Granada, soon reveals that while there were some similarities there were also important distinctions. Since the clearest piece of contemporary evidence at our disposal is García de Sena's volume, it seems valid to limit the comparative analysis to the US texts he included: the constitutions of Massachusetts (1780), Connecticut (n.d.), New Jersey (1776), Pennsylvania (1790) and Virginia (1776). Rather than offering a comprehensive examination, bringing together all the constitutions adopted in New Granada during the years 1811–1815, my purpose here is to illustrate some of the similarities and distinctions by looking at some key aspects of their respective constitutional designs.

There were significant parallels in some of the basic principles that informed all these constitutions, north and south. All adopted the republic – the earlier constitution of Cundinamarca of 1811 had exceptionally gone for a constitutional monarchy, though in spirit this was a republican text, as it required Ferdinand to come and live in Santafé, and it abolished the hereditary principle. All adopted the division of powers into three branches: the legislative, the executive and the judiciary.²⁹ Exceptionally in the US, the Pennsylvania constitution of 1776, influenced by radical 'democrats', favoured a unicameral assembly,³⁰ but this was abandoned in the 1790 constitution and subsequently all states adopted two cameras for the legislature. The exception in New Granada was the Antioquia constitution of 1815 – but the rule there was bicameralism as well. Some similarities cannot be generalised, since the provincial constitutions in both the US and New Granada also differed from each other. For example, all the states' constitutions in New Granada adopted a separate chapter with a declaration of rights, as did those of Massachusetts and Pennsylvania– but the constitutions of New Jersey, Virginia and Connecticut included in García de Sena's volume did not.³¹ It is important to note that most of these features set these early American constitutional experiences far apart from the Cádiz constitution, whose text adopted a parliamentary monarchy, a single chamber for the legislature, kept the hereditary principle alive and did not include a separate chapter for rights.

Being similar does not mean that they replicated each other. In fact, as already suggested, there were variations among the US provincial constitutions. They differed in their formal presentation, from the short text of that of New Jersey to the more elaborate structure of that of Massachusetts, clearly organised around demarcated sections with subheadings and enumerated articles. In this respect, the constitutions of New Granada resembled the latter. It is true that the 1812 constitution of Cartagena and the 1815 constitution of Mariquita copied almost verbatim the 'preamble' of the Massachusetts's text. When declaring against the hereditary principle, the 1811 constitution of Tunja seems to have drawn, almost word for word, from the Massachusetts's document as well. Nonetheless, Restrepo's accusation against New Granadan constitutionalists – that all they did was to copy the various US constitutions – should be subject to further scrutiny. The 'translations' often came with important additions, as Clément Thibaud has observed. The article against the hereditary principle in the Tunja constitution, noted above, included further critical sentences which, according to Thibaud, did not constitute any 'textual borrowing, nor a translation, but an original elaboration of the New Granadan constituents'.³² A closer examination may reveal some important distinctions. In the paragraphs that follow, I propose to look into three selected areas: the organisation of the executive; slavery and race; and religion.

It has been commonly asserted that Latin America transplanted from the US the presidential system following independence, though in an 'exaggerated form' – indeed to some 'a caricature of the North American model'.³³ While some of the New Granadan constitutions used the word 'president' (others opted for 'governors'), it does not seem that the executives carried more power than the legislatures. Indeed a glance at some of the constitutions immediately raises questions about the existence of a 'presidential system' in these early constitutional experiments. Consider the

1812 constitution of Cundinamarca, which instituted a plural executive, formed by a president and two 'consejeros ... con voto deliberativo' – any decision required the approval of all three. They were to be elected in staggered fashion, so the executive was subject to renovation each year, with no re-election. Title V of the constitution listed in details all the functions and limitations of the post. The latter abounded, be it when calling the army at times of war,[34] or when deciding about taxation. Indeed, the legislature not only had the exclusive power over taxation but also of 'legislating in all matters conducive to the happiness of the republic'.[35] The creation of any public post, including those in the army, and decisions about salaries of public employees, was the exclusive prerogative of the legislature as well. The 1812 constitution of Antioquia similarly adopted a plural executive – a president plus two 'consejeros' as well, elected after nominations from the legislature.[36] Most states in the US also 'provided their governors with executive councils', in arrangements that resembled plural executives. However, a glance at the various texts clearly suggests significant differences from state to state and from province to province, both in the US and New Granada, which are worth exploring further. It would seem that in some US cases the constitutional design allowed for a stronger executive than in New Granada: the governor of Pennsylvania, for example, elected for three years, could stand for consecutive re-election twice, therefore with the possibility of staying in office for up to nine years, while the power of the Cundinamarca president was limited to a single year.

While important distinctions can be observed around the central issues of slavery and race, they do not always trace a clear dividing line between north and south. Common to all, none of the constitutions acknowledge the contradiction in adhering to the principle of equality while maintaining the institution of slavery. Some provinces did show earlier inclinations against it. In New Granada, a notable expression in favour of abolition came from the Socorro's *Cabildo* (City Council), which in 1809 instructed its deputy to request the Junta Suprema Central to abolish in 'perpetuity' the 'trade of blacks', a 'degradation of human nature' and to take the necessary steps to free the slaves.[37] Yet this did not translate into constitutional provisions in the province once it proclaimed its independence. The story was different in Cartagena, with its large free black population, actively involved in the independence movement.[38] Its 1812 constitution devoted a few articles to the subject. While it did not abolish the institution, it did abolish the 'importation of slaves into the state', instructed the legislature to establish a manumission fund, and to give legal protection to slaves against the arbitrariness and cruel behaviour of slave holders.[39] Similar measures were introduced by the Mariquita constitution in 1815 – in addition, this text adopted the freedom of womb.[40] Some states in the US also outlawed the importation of slaves; the constitution of the territory of Vermont went further by abolishing slavery altogether in 1777. The point to be taken from this brief account is not to highlight any clear distinction between the US and New Granada but rather to note that, when it came to slavery, each state or province was setting up its own constitutional provisions, very likely determined by its own individual circumstances.

The constitutional treatment of the indigenous people, however, differed sharply between the US and New Granada. None of the US state constitutions included in de Sena's volume mentioned the Indians: indeed, they seem to have been considered neither citizens nor nationals.[41] In contrast, the 1812 constitution of Cundinamarca explicitly stated that, 'Indians enjoy all the rights of citizens, and have voice and vote in all elections, as the rest [of the people] in this republic'. Not all constitutions in New Granada were as explicit as the Cundinamarca text, but there were no exclusions of citizens based on race. In 1815, the Mariquita constitution lamented that 'the portion of citizens that until now have been referred to as Indians' had not managed to enjoy the protection of the law, and urged the authorities to 'deploy all possible means to attract [these] natural citizens ... and make them to understand the intimate union they share with the rest of citizens ... and] the rights they enjoy by the mere fact of being men equal to all'.[42]

Where it is perhaps possible to discern more clearly the work of constitutional makers in New Granada, independently from whatever they read in the US state constitutions, is on the issues related to religion. Here the difference with the US constitutions was not so much about the separation of state and church. The Massachusetts constitution guaranteed the exercise of one's religion in private, but the text explicitly favoured Protestants, and instructed the legislature to provide for the support of Protestant teachers. Legal protection was limited to 'all Christian sects'. Moreover, to be elected governor it was a condition to 'profess the Christian religion'. This was one of the objections to the Massachusetts constitutions that Miranda raised when he met Samuel Adams during his visit to Boston in 1784.[43] Miranda's more liberal approach to the subject, however, was far from been shared in Venezuela or New Granada, where the Catholic religion was proclaimed, as in Cartagena, 'the only truthful and the Religion of the state'. The real difference was on the specific type of religion generally supported by one or the other.

Of course, the latter was no mean difference. Nor were the other distinctions identified here, be it the design of the executive power or the constitutional treatment of race. These are all fundamental and indeed defining aspects of political systems and nation-states. A closer look at all these constitutions may reveal other significant differences. The form of government, for example, was not defined in equal terms. In New Granada, most constitutions tend to follow the words used by the Cundinamarca constitution of 1812, where the state was identified with 'a republic, whose government is popular representative'. The expression 'popular representative' seems absent from the Massachusetts text. The 'people' were of course present but its constitution defined its form of government just as a 'free, sovereign and independent state, with the name of the republic of Massachusetts'. Not all rights were equally adopted by all constitutions. The 'right to bear arms' (Art. XIII, Pennsylvania), for example, is absent in the Cundinamarca constitution. In turn, whole chapters devoted to the Juicio de Residencia, an interesting legacy from Spanish imperial rule, are absent from the US constitutions.

III

This chapter has explored the possible impact of US constitutionalism in Spanish America, with a focus on the first republics in New Granada. It has looked in particular at the assertion, made by some contemporaries and replicated by scholars in the scant historiography on the subject, that all the New Granadan constitutions did, during the period 1811–1815, was to copy the US provincial constitutions. In doing so, this exercise had two further wider aims: to rescue a wealth of constitutional texts from historical oblivion, and to revise the prevailing notion that Spanish American constitutionalism during the early decades of independence was almost exclusively dominated by the strictures of the Cádiz constitution of 1812.

By the time the Cádiz text landed on the shores of South America, some ten constitutions had already been published in New Granada and Venezuela. Without denying the connections with Cádiz, a charter that was as much American as Spanish, this chapter has shown that Spanish American constitutionalism was also in close dialogue with the US experience from its inception. US constitutional texts were known among intellectual circles of the late colonial period, and their circulation expanded following Spanish America independence as they were translated and published in newspapers and books. Manuel de Sena's *La independencia de la Costa Firme* (1811) stands out since it included five of the US state constitutions: those of Massachusetts, Pennsylvania, Connecticut, New Jersey and Virginia. This book and its diffusion serve to show that constitutional drafters had at their disposal Spanish versions of some US constitutional texts. It also allows us to pursue a selective comparative analysis, as the one proposed here.

The conclusions drawn from this chapter are as tentative and modest as the exercise developed in the previous pages. The drafters of constitutions in New Granada did copy some texts from US state constitutions – parts of the preamble of the Massachusetts constitution, as illustrated above, were replicated in those of Cartagena and Mariquita. A more comprehensive and systematic examination may be able to trace more replicas. However, some of the articles that were copied included new passages of local vintage. And in at least the three areas examined here – the executive, slavery and race, and religion – it is possible to identify distinct provisions, some indeed original. This was still an era of constitutional experimentation when there were 'no well established theoretical models' to follow.[44] As in the US, constitutional makers in New Granada were also grappling with a reality that made 'political life ... a struggle by trial and error in pursuit of few essentials', including achieving independence and imagining a republic. To this aim, the US offered some new institutions that they were ready to adapt as they suited their needs and local circumstances.

No other aspect of US constitutionalism was perhaps more attractive to New Granadans than federalism.[45] In distinguishing the US from the French experiences, Willi Paul Adams noted that, in the former, 'the struggle for independence was carried on by a large number of already organized and nearly autonomous political entities: the towns, counties, colonial assemblies, and provincial congresses', and that 'a federal compromise was the result, rather than a monolith that placed all the sovereignty in the central government, as was to be the case in France'.[46] Similarly the independence movement in New Granada was carried on mostly by municipalities but, in contrast to the US, there were no previous provincial congresses – towns in fact gained political autonomy (and claimed sovereignty) as the authority of Spanish monarchy collapsed following the Napoleon usurpation of the Crown. To those building the postcolonial order, the US provincial constitutions offered 'models' that seemed highly appealing. Perhaps it should not be surprising that leading figures like Torres suggested that the path to follow was to 'imitate' the US. Yet we should not take his expression at face value. As this chapter has demonstrated, the first constitutions of New Granada were not mere copies of the US state constitutions. These were certainly read, used and followed in the various provinces. But constitution-making entailed much more: as in any process of adaptation, the outcome should be appreciated on its own terms. In addition, other 'influences' (not under examination here) were also at play.

While this chapter opened by addressing the question of the possible impact of US constitutionalism in New Granada, this exercise ends by suggesting a cautionary tale. The history of constitutionalism in Spanish America may do well in moving away from the 'diffusionist' approach that tends to dominate research in the field. In such an approach, Isidro Vanegas has warned, 'the people who produced the 'constitutions become mere notaries (escribanos)', while the societies from which these texts emerge disappear: these constitutions 'can be best understood if they are studied as coherent documents in themselves rather than a sum of influences'.[47] There is thus much to be learned from the constitutions of the first republics in Spanish America.

Notes

1 Donald S. Lutz, *The Origins of American Constitutionalism* (Baton Rouge: Louisiana State University Press, 1988), 96.
2 For a list of the constitutional texts issued in Latin America from 1811 to 1819, see Victor Uribe-Urán, 'Derecho y cultura legal en la "era de las revoluciones" en México, Colombia y Brasil, 1750–1850. La génesis de lo público y lo privado', in María Teresa Calderón and Clément Thibaud, eds., *Las revoluciones en el mundo Atlántico* (Bogotá: Taurus, 2006), 283. A longer list of constitutional texts in New

Granada (up to fourteen between 1810 and 1815) is given by Isidro Vanegas in his book *El constitucionalismo fundacional* (Bogotá: Plural 2012), 42–43.

3 Among the exceptions: Anthony McFarlane, 'Building Political Order: The "First Republic" in New Granada, 1810–1815', in Eduardo Posada-Carbó, ed., *In Search of a New Order: Essays on the Politics and Society in Nineteenth-Century Latin America* (London: Institute of Latin American Studies 1988), 8–33; Uribe-Urán, 'Derecho y cultura legal', and 'Insurgentes de Provincia: Tunja, Nueva Granada y el constitucionalismo en el mundo hispánico en la década de 1810', *Historia y Memoria*, (Tunja) July–December 2012), 17–48; Daniel Gutiérrez Ardila, *Un nuevo reino. Geografía política, pactismo y diplomacia durante el interregno en Nueva Granada, 1808–1816* (Bogotá: Universidad Externado, 2010); Clément Thibaud, 'La coyuntura de 1810 en tierra firme: confederaciones, constituciones, repúblicas', *Historia y Política* (Madrid: July–December 2010), vol. 24, 23–45; Vanegas, *El constitucionalismo fundacional*; Allan R. Brewer-Carías, *Orígenes del constitucionalismo moderno en Hispanoamérica* (Caracas: Editorial Jurídica Venezolana, 2014); Jorge Giraldo, ed., *Procesos políticos antioqueños durante la revolución neogranadina* (Medellín: Eafit, 2013); J.L. Soberanes Fernandez, ed., *El primer constitucionalismo iberoamericano* (Madrid: Marcial Pons, 1992). Tellingly, one of the most comprehensive modern study of Colombian federalism registers some of the early constitutions but there is no attempt to examine them; Robert Louis Gilmore, *El federalismo en Colombia, 1810–1858* (Bogotá: Universidad Externado, 1995), vol. 1, chapter 1.

4 George Billias, *American Constitutionalism Heard Round the World, 1776–1989: A Global Perspective* (New York and London: New York University Press, 2011), chapter 4.

5 See, for example, Roberto Gargarella's work, who only gives marginal attention to the constitutions of the 1810s: *Los fundamentos legales de la desigualdad. El constitucionalismo en América, 1776–1860* (Madrid: Siglo XXI, 2005), and *Latin American Constitutionalism, 1810–2010* (Oxford: Oxford University Press, 2013). In his study 'Diffusion and the Constitutionalization of Europe', Zachary Elkins seems to ignore the New Granadan constitutions examined here as well as the US state constitutions; *Comparative Political Studies*, 43:8/9 (2012), 969–999.

6 The literature is vast. For a recent example, see Scott Eastman and Natalia Sobrevilla Perea, *The Rise of Constitutional Government in the Iberian Atlantic World: The Impact of the Cádiz Constitution of 1812* (Tuscaloosa: The University of Alabama Press, 2015). See also Marta Lorente and José Maria Portillo, eds., *El momento gaditano. La constitución en el orbe hispánico, 1808–1826* (Madrid: Congreso de Diputados, 2011); and Manuel Chust, *La tribuna revolucionaria. La constitución de 1812 en ambos hemisferios* (Cádiz: Museo de las Cortes de España, 2014). In his most recent book, Brian Hamnett devotes a whole chapter to Cádiz, while the early constitutionalism in New Granada and Venezuela barely receives a couple of pages; *The End of Iberian Rule on the American Continent, 1770–1830* (Cambridge: Cambridge University Press, 2017), 141–144, and 176–208. For a useful historiographical account on Cádiz in New Granada, see Victor Uribe-Urán, 'La constitución de Cádiz en la Nueva Granada. Teoría y realidad, 1812–1821', in Heraclio Bonilla, ed., *La constitución de 1812 en Hispanoamérica y España* (Bogotá: Universidad Nacional de Colombia, 2012), 275–280.

7 'Translating the US Constitution for the Federal Cause in New Granada at the Time of Independence', in David Hook and Graciela Iglesias-Rogers, eds., *Translations in Times of Disruption: An Interdisciplinary Study in Transnational Contexts* (London: Palgrave, 2017), 119–145.

8 Jaime E. Rodríguez O., 'Sobre la supuesta influencia de la independencia de los Estados Unidos en las independencias hispanoamericanas', *Revista de Indias*, LXX:250 (2010), 691–714. A recent reassessment of the global significance of the

American Revolution, that includes a well-informed chapter on Spanish America, can be found in Jonathan Israel, *The Expanding Blaze: How the American Revolution Ignited the World, 1775–1848* (Princeton and Oxford: Princeton University Press), 1–24, and especially chapter 16, 423–455. See also his *Democratic Enlightenment: Philosophy, Revolution and Human Rights, 1750–1790* (Oxford: Oxford University Press, 2011), 522–534.

9 My own translation, as subsequently in the chapter. José Manuel Restrepo, *Historia de la revolución de la República de Colombia en la América Meridional* (Bogotá: Biblioteca Popular de Cultura Colombiana, 1942, first published in 1827), vol. 1, 117.
10 Ibid., 164.
11 See, for example, McFarlane, 'Building Political Order: The First Republic in New Granada, 1810–1815', 21.
12 Restrepo, *Historia de la revolución*, vol. 2, 149. For exceptions, see Thibaud, 'La coyuntura de 1810', and Uribe-Urán, 'Insurgentes de Provincia'. Both identified some similarities and differences between the constitutions of Tunja (1811) and Massachusetts (1780). For a perceptive overall assessment that acknowledges the impact of US state constitutions in the early constitutional debates of New Granada, see Israel, *The Expanding Blaze*, 446.
13 Lutz, *The Origins*, 97.
14 Francisco de Miranda, *Diario de viaje a Estados Unidos, 1783–1784* (Santiago: Dirección de Bibliotecas, Archivos y Museos, 1998), 152, 168.
15 *Recueil des loix constitutives des colonies angloises conféderées sous la dénomination d'Etats-Unis de L'América septentrionales* (Philadelphia, 1778), cited in Vanegas, *El constitucionalismo fundacional*, 97. For a good summary of French translations of North American 'revolutionary papers' published before 1800, see M. E. Simmons, *US Political Ideas in Spanish America before 1830: A Bibliographical Study* (Bloomington: Indiana University Press, 1977), 15–22. 'Five collected editions of the United States state constitutions appear to have been published in France between 1776 and 1786; in England and Scotland, at least six bound editions appeared in 1782 and 1783 alone', in Linda Colley, 'Empires of Writing: Britain, America and Constitutions, 1776–1848', *Law and History Review*, 32:2 (2014), 248.
16 *La independencia de la Costa Firme justificada por Thomas Paine treinta años ha. Extracto de sus obras, traducido del inglés al español por D. Manuel García de Sena* (Caracas: Instituto Panamericano de Geografía e Historia, 1948, originally published in Philadelphia, 1811).
17 Billias, *American Consitutionalism*, 115.
18 Simmons, *US Political Ideas in Spanish America*, 36. See also Gutiérrez Ardila, *Un nuevo reino*, 100–101.
19 Billias, *American Constitutionalism*, 123, 129.
20 Restrepo, *Historia de la revolución*, vol. 2, 72–73. Restrepo on Torres: 'Eran sus defectos, escasos conocimientos del mundo y de los hombres, y esa veneración, que se acercaba a la idolatría, por las instituciones de los Estados Unidos del Norte-América, que juzgaba podían adoptar nuestros pueblo sin variación alguna', ibid., vol. 2, 44.
21 Torres to Tenorio, Santafé, 29 May 1810; the full text is in 'Los tres Torres. La familia Torres', *Boletín de Historia y Antiguedades* (Bogotá, 1905), vol. 28, 260–271.
22 Ibid., 264.
23 Ibid., 265. See Carl B. Cone, 'Richard Price and the Constitution of the United States', *The American Historical Review*, 53:4 (July 1948), 735. On the significance of Price, see the various references in Israel, *The Expanding Blaze*, 3, 6, 9, 19.
24 Torres to Tenorio, in 'Los tres Torres', 270.
25 Sergio Mejía, *La revolución en letras. La historia de la revolución de Colombia de José Manuel Restrepo, 1781–1863* (Bogotá and Medellín: Universidad de los Andes, 2007), 73.

26 Restrepo, *Historia de la revolución*, vol. 2, 149. For a similar observation by a contemporary, see 'Oficio del Supremo Poder Executivo de Antioquia al de la Unión', *Gazeta Ministerial de Cundinamarca*, Bogotá, 26 May 1814. Restrepo's criticisms were echoed by later constitutionalists, who attributed the failure of the first republics to the fact that they were imitating foreign institutions; José María Samper, *Derecho público interno de Colombia* (Bogotá: Bublioteca Popular, 1951; first published in 1886), I, 122.

27 H.M. Brackenbridge, *Voyage to South America Performed by order of the American Government in the Years 1817 and 1818 in the Frigate Congress* (London: T. and J. Allam, 1820), vol. 2, 142. When William Duane visited Colombia in 1822–1823, he came across a 'secular clergyman' in a rural town in 'the bossom of the Andes' who talked 'with [...] mastery of the North American revolutions, the constitution of England [...] and those of the United States'; Duane, *A Visit to Colombia in the Years 1822 and 1823* (Philadelphia: Thomas H. Palmer, 1826), 419.

28 Gutiérrez Ardila, ed., *Las asambleas constituyentes*, 163.

29 Not all the earlier constitutions in the US demarcated the separations of powers with the clarity of later documents. New Jersey, for example, 'did not include the Judiciary among [the three branches of power]'. The separation and the balance of power in South Carolina and New Hampshire were also 'rather incomplete'; Willi Paul Adams, *The First American Constitutions: Republican Ideology and the Making of the State Constitutions in the Revolutionary Era* (Lanham: Rowman & Littlefield, 2001; first published in 1973), 264–265.

30 Robert F. Williams, 'The Influences of Pennsylvania's 1776 Constitution on American Constitutionalism During the Founding Decade', *The Pennsylvania Magazine of History and Biography*, 112:1 (January, 1988), 30–31; *The Constitution of the Commonwealth of Pennsylvania as Established by the General Convention ...* (Philadelphia: John Dunlap, 1776), 10. The 1790 Pennsylvania constitution stated that the legislative power resided in a General Assembly, formed by a Senate and a House of Representatives.

31 They also drew from the 'French declaration of 1789 or from the French constitutions of 1793 and 1795'. See McFarlane, 'Building Political Order', 27.

32 Thibaud, 'La coyuntura de 1810 en Tierra Firme', 26.

33 Billias, *American Constitutionalism*, 108. For another recent assertion, though with variation of emphasis and from a different perspective, see José Antonio Cheibub, Zachary Elkins and Tom Ginsburg, 'Latin American Presidentialism in Comparative and Historical Perspective', *Texas Law Review*, 89:7 (2011). For the latter, 'Latin American constitutions are uniquely inclined to empower presidents to decree law, initiate legislative proposals, and exert powers in emergency conditions', ibid., 3. Cheibub et al. seem to ignore the constitutions under examination in this chapter. See also Karl Loewenstein, 'The Presidency outside the United States: A Study in Comparative Political Institutions', *Journal of Politics*, 11:3 (1949), 452–453.

34 While the executive in Cundinamarca was entitled to convene the armed forces at times of war, and to provide leadership, neither the President nor his 'consejeros' could command the troops. All the constitutions in the US 'made the governor or the president of the executive council commander-in-chief of the military [...]. Once military forces were mobilized [...] the governor was given supreme command over them'; Adams, *The First American Constitutions*, 272.

35 'Constitución de la república de Cundinamarca', in Manuel A. Pombo and José Joaquín Guerra, eds., *Constituciones de Colombia* (Bogotá: Biblioteca Popular de la Cultura Colombiana, 1951), 19.

36 'Constitución de Antioquia de 1812', in Pombo and Guerra, eds, *Constituciones de Colombia*, 324. This measure seems to have been adopted from the 1812 Cundinamarca constitution. See Daniel Gutiérrez Ardila, ed., *Las asambleas*

constituyentes de la independencia. Actas de Cundinamarca y Antioquia, 1811–1812 (Bogotá: Universidad del Externado, 2010), 277. According to Carlos Restrepo Piedrahita, the plural executive drew inspiration from the French constitutions; see his 'Las primeras constituciones políticas de Colombia y Venezuela', in Fernandez, ed., *El primer constitucionalismo*, 115.

37 Angel Rafael Almarza Villalobos and Armando Martínez Garnica, eds., *Instrucciones para los diputados del Nuevo Reino de Granada y Venezuela ante la Junta Central de España y las Indias* (Bucaramanga: Universidad Industrial de Santander), 133.

38 Marixa Lasso, *Myths of Harmony: Race and Republicanism during the Age of Revolution. Colombia, 1795–1831* (Pittsburgh: University of Pittsburgh Press, 2007), 78.

39 'Constitución política del Estado de Cartagena de Indias expedida el 14 de junio de 1812', in *Documentos para la historia de la provincia de Cartagena de Indias hoy Estado Soberano de Bolívar en la Unión Colombiana* (Bogotá: Imprenta de Medardo Rivas,1883), 540–541. For a critical note, undervaluing the significance of those provisions, see Aline Helg, *Liberty and Equality in Caribbean Colombia, 1770–1835* (Chapel Hill and London: The University of North Carolina Press, 2004), 140.

40 'Constitución o forma de Gobierno del estado de Mariquita' (1815), in Pombo and Guerra, *Constituciones de Colombia*, vol. 2, 332.

41 'The legal status of Indians, especially in regard to citizenship and the right to vote, would remain shrouded in confusion and conflict for many years' throughout the nineteenth century; see Daniel McCool et al., *Native Vote: American Indians, the Voting Rights Act and the Right to Vote* (Cambridge: Cambridge University Press, 2007), 2.

42 'Constitución o forma de gobierno del Estado de Mariquita', in Pombo and Guerra, eds, *Constituciones de Colombia*, 331.

43 Miranda, *Diario de viaje*, 152. He raised a similar criticism about the constitution of New Hampshire during his conversation with the president of that state; ibid, 168.

44 See José Antonio Aguilar, *En pos de la quimera. Reflexiones sobre el experimento constitutional atlántico* (Mexico: Fondo de Cultura Económica, 2000), 22.

45 Very few topics attracted more attention in the public debate during the early period of independence than federalism, a debate that was full of references to the experience of the United States. See, for example, *El Argos Americano*, Cartagena, 24 September and 10, 24 December 1810; the 'Cartas políticas' (1811) by Joaquín Camacho, in Armando Martínez et al., eds, *José Joaquín Camacho. Biografía y documentos de su pensamiento y acción política en la revolución de independencia* (Tunja: Academia Boyacense de Historia), 300–301, 328; *Argos de la Nueva Granada*, Tunja, 2 December 1813; *Gazeta Ministerial de Cundinamarca*, 26 March 1812; 25 November 1813; 13 January and 10 February 1814. My thanks for these references to Luis Gabriel Galán. See also McFarlane, 'Building Political Order'; and Posada-Carbó, 'Translating the US Constitution for the Federal Cause', 137–138.

46 Adams, *The First American Constitutions*, 5.

47 Vanegas, *El constitucionalismo fundacional*, 162–163. For a recent rejection of the 'diffusionist model' when studying the history of democracy, see Joanna Innes and Mark Philp, eds., *Re-Imagining Democracy in the Age of Revolutions: America, France, Britain and Ireland, 1750–1850* (Oxford: Oxford University Press, 2013), 7. On a note of caution when looking at the impact of foreign ideas, see Gabriel Paquette, *Enlightenment, Governance, and Reform in Spain and its Empire, 1759–1808* (Basingstoke: Palgrave, 2008), 4–5, 152.

Bibliography

Abarca, Ramon E. "Bourbon 'Revanche' against England: The Balance of Power, 1763–1770." PhD diss., Notre Dame: University of Notre Dame, 1965.
Abarca, Ramon E. "Classical Diplomacy and Bourbon 'Revanche' Strategy, 1763–1770." *Review of Politics* 32 (1970): 313–337.
Abbey, Kathryn. "Efforts of Spain to Maintain Sources of Information in the British Colonies Before 1779." *Mississippi Valley Historical Review* 15, no. 1 (1928): 56–68.
Abbot, W.W., ed. *The Papers of George Washington*. Confederation Series. Charlottesville, VA: University Press of Virginia, 1994.
Abol-Brasón y Álvarez-Tamargo, Manuel de. "El conde de Floridablanca y la política de su época." In *José Moñino y Redondo, conde de Floridablanca (1728–1808): Estudios en el bicentenario de su muerte*, edited by Jesús Menéndez Peláez, 55–178. Gijón: Fundación Foro Jovellanos del Principado de Asturias, 2009.
Acosta Rodríguez, Antonio. *La población de Luisiana Española (1763–1803)*. Madrid: Ministerio de Asuntos Exteriores, 1979.
Adams Papers. https://founders.archives.gov/?q=Project%3A%22Adams%20Papers%22&s=1511211111&r=1 (accessed February 1, 2018).
Adams, Willi Paul. *The First American Constitutions: Republican Ideology and the Making of the State Constitutions in the Revolutionary Era*. Lanham: Rowman & Littlefield, 2001 [1st ed. 1973].
Adelman, Jeremy, and Stephen Aron. "From Borderlands to Borders: Empires, Nation-States, and the Peoples in between in North American History." *The American Historical Review* 104, no. 3 (1999): 814–841.
Adkins, Lesley, and Roy Adkins. *Gibraltar: The Greatest Siege in British History*. London: Little, Brown, 2017.
Aguilar, José Antonio. *En pos de la quimera. Reflexiones sobre el experimento constitutional atlántico*. Mexico: Fondo de Cultura Económica, 2000.
Aguilar, José Antonio, and Rafael Rojas, eds. *El republicanismo en Hispanoamérica: Ensayos de historia intelectual y política*. México D.F.: Fondo de Cultura Económica, 2002.
Alcaide Yebra, José Antonio. *La toma de Menorca (1782)*. Pozuelo de Alarcón: La Espada y la Pluma, 2004.
Alden, Dauril. *Royal Government in Colonial Brazil*. Berkeley: University of California Press, 1968.
Almarza Villalobos, Angel Rafael, and Armando Martínez Garnica, eds. *Instrucciones para los diputados del Nuevo Reino de Granada y Venezuela andte la Junta Central de España y las Indias*. Bucaramanga: Universidad Industrial de Santander, 2008.

Alonso Baquer, Miguel. "Los ministros de Carlos IV frente a la revolución francesa." *Revista de Historia Militar* 14, no. 29 (1970): 79–99.
Alsina Torrente, Juan. *Una guerra romántica 1778–1783. España, Francia e Inglaterra en la mar: Trasfondo naval de la independencia de Estados Unidos*. Madrid: Ministerio de Defensa, Instituto de Historia y Cultura Naval, 2006.
Alvarez Bonilla, Enrique. "Los tres Torres. La familia Torres." *Boletín de Historia y Antiguedades* 27 (1905): 260–271.
Alvord, Clarence. "The Conquest of St. Joseph, Michigan, by the Spaniards in 1781." *Missouri Historical Review* 2 (1908): 195–210.
Alvord, Clarence, ed. *Kaskaskia Records*. Springfield: The Trustees of the Illinois State Historical Library, 1909.
Anna, Timothy E. "Inventing Mexico: Provincehood and Nationhood after Independence." *Bulletin of Latin American Research* 15, no. 1 (1996): 7–17.
Ardash Bonialian, Mariano. *El Pacífico Hispanoamericano: Política y Comercio Asiático en el Imperio Español (1680–1784): La Centralidad de lo Marginal*. Mexico DF: El Colegio de México, 2012.
Arena, Richard. "Land Settlement Policies and Practices in Spanish Louisiana." In *Spanish in the Mississippi Valley 1762–1804*, edited by John Francis McDermott, 51–60. Urbana: University of Illinois Press, 1974.
Armillas Vicente, José Antonio. "El nacimiento de una gran nación. Contribución española a la independencia de los Estados Unidos de América del Norte." *Cuadernos de investigación: Geografía e Historia* 3, nos. 1–2 (1977): 91–98.
Armillas Vicente, José Antonio. "Nuevas consideraciones sobre la deuda de guerra de los Estados Unidos con España." In *Actas del Congreso de Historia de los Estados Unidos, La Rábida, 5 a 9 de julio de 1976*, 51–63. Madrid: Ministerio de Educación y Ciencia, 1978.
Armillas Vicente, José Antonio. "Ayuda secreta y deuda oculta: España y la independencia de los Estados Unidos." In *Norteamérica a finales del siglo XVIII: España y los Estados Unidos*, edited by Eduardo Garrigues, Emma Sánchez Montañés, Sylvia L. Hilton, Almudena Hernández Ruigómez, and Isabel García-Montón, 171–196. Madrid: Fundación Consejo España–Estados Unidos and Editorial Marcial Pons, 2008.
Armitage, David. *The Declaration of Independence: A Global History*. Cambridge, MA and London: Harvard University Press, 2007.
Armitage, David. "Three Concepts of Atlantic History." In *The British Atlantic World, 1500–1800*, edited by David Armitage and Michael J. Braddick, 13–32. New York: Palgrave Macmillan, 2009.
Armitage, David. "Declarations of Independence, 1776–2012." In Armitage, *Foundations of Modern International Thought*, 215–232. Cambridge: Cambridge University Press, 2013.
Armitage, David, and Sanjay Subrahmanyam, eds. *The Age of Revolutions in Global Context, c. 1760–1840*. New York: Palgrave Macmillan, 2010.
Armytage, Frances. *The Free Port System in the British West Indies: A Study in Commercial Policy, 1766–1822*. London: Longmans, Green, & Co., 1953.
Astigarraga, Jésus, ed. *The Spanish Enlightenment Revisited*. Oxford: Voltaire Foundation, 2015.
Aulard, A. "La dette Américaine envers la France." *Revue de Paris* 10 (1925): 319–338.
Ávila, Antonio. "Pensamiento republicano hasta 1823." In *El republicanismo en Hispanoamérica: Ensayos de historia intelectual y política*, edited by José Antonio

Aguilar and Rafael Rojas, 313–350. México D.F.: Fondo de Cultura Económica, 2002.
Avilés Fernández, Miguel. *Carlos III y el fin del antiguo régimen*. Madrid: EDAF, 1982.
Babcock, Matthew. *Apache Adaptation to Hispanic Rule*. Cambridge: Cambridge University Press, 2016.
Bails, Benito. *Arismética [sic] para negociantes*. Madrid: Viuda de Ibarra, 1790.
Bailyn, Bernard. *The Ideological Origins of the American Revolution*. Cambridge, MA: The Belknap Press of Harvard University Press, 2017.
Bannon, John Francis. *The Spanish Borderlands Frontier, 1513–1821*. New York: Rinehart and Winston, 1970.
Barger, William J. "New Players at the Table: How Americans Came to Dominate Early Trade in the North Pacific." *Southern California Quarterly* 90, no. 3 (2008): 227–257.
Barksdale, Kevin T. "The Spanish Conspiracy on the Trans-Appalachian Borderlands, 1786–1789." *Journal of Appalachian Studies* 13, no. 1/2 (2007): 96–123.
Barksdale, Kevin T. *The Lost State of Franklin: America's First Secession*. Lexington: The University of Kentucky Press, 2009.
Barr, Juliana. *Peace Came in the Form of a Woman: Indians and Spaniards in the Texas Borderlands*. Chapel Hill: University of North Carolina Press, 2007.
Barr, Juliana. "Geographies of Power: Mapping Indian Borders in the 'Borderlands' of the Early Southwest." *William and Mary Quarterly* 68 (2011): 5–46.
Barratt, Glynn. *Russia in Pacific Waters, 1715–1825: A Survey of the Origins of Russia's Naval Presence in the North and South Pacific*. Vancouver and London: University of British Columbia Press, 2011.
Bartley, Russell H. *Imperial Russia and the Struggle for Latin American Independence, 1808–1828*. Austin: Institute of Latin American Studies, University of Texas at Austin, 1978.
Bartosik-Vélez, Elise. *The Legacy of Christopher Columbus in the Americas: New Nations and a Transatlantic Discourse of Empire*. Nashville, TN: Vanderbilt University Press, 2014.
Batista González, Juan. "Significación político-estratégica de la ruta juniperiana." *Revista de Historia Militar* 59 (1985): 73–106.
Baylin, Bernard. *Atlantic History: Concept and Contours*. Cambridge, MA and London: Harvard University Press, 2005.
Becker, Jerónimo. *España e Inglaterra, sus relaciones políticas desde las paces de Utrecht*. Madrid: Ambrosio Pérez y cía., 1906.
Beerman, Eric. "The Last Battle of the American Revolution: Yorktown. No, the Bahamas! (The Spanish-American Expedition to Nassau in 1782)." *The Americas* 45, no. 1 (1988): 79–95.
Beerman, Eric. *España y la independencia de Estados Unidos*. Madrid: MAPFRE, 1992.
Beerman, Eric. "Governor Bernardo de Galvez's New Orleans Belle: Felicitas de St. Maxent." *Revista Española de Estudios Norteamericanos* 7 (1994): 39–44.
Beerman, Eric, and Gilbert C. Din, trans. "Victory on the Mississippi, 1779." In *The Louisiana Purchase Bicentennial Series in Louisiana History, Vol. 2: The Spanish Presence in Louisiana, 1763–1803*, edited by Gilbert C. Din, 192–202. Lafayette: Center for Louisiana Studies, University of Southwestern Louisiana, 1996.
Bemis, Samuel F. *The American Secretaries of State and their Diplomacy*, vol. 1. New York: Alfred A. Knopf, 1927.

Bemis, Samuel F. *Pinckney's Treaty: America's Advantage from Europe's Distress, 1783–1800*. New Haven, CT: Yale University Press, 1960 [1st ed. Baltimore: The Johns Hopkins Press, 1926].

Bemis, Samuel F. *The Diplomacy of the American Revolution*. Bloomington: Indiana University Press, 1957 [1st ed. New York and London: D. Appleton & Century Company, Inc., 1935].

Bemis, Samuel F. *The Hussey-Cumberland Mission and American Independence: An Essay in the Diplomacy of the American Revolution*. Gloucester, MA: Peter Smith, 1968 [1st ed. Princeton: Princeton University Press, 1931].

Bentham, Jeremy. "Letter to the Spanish Nation on a Proposed House of Lords." In *Three Tracts Relative to Spanish and Portuguese Affairs with a Continual Eye on English Ones*. London, 1821.

Berquist Soule, Emily. "Early Anti-Slavery Sentiment in the Spanish Atlantic World, 1765–1817." *Slavery & Abolition* 31, no. 2 (2010): 181–205.

Berquist Soule, Emily. "From Africa to the Ocean Sea: Atlantic Slavery in the Origins of the Spanish Empire." *Atlantic Studies: Global Currents* 15, no. 1 (2018): 16–39.

Billias, George Athan. *American Constitutionalism Heard Round the World, 1776–1989: A Global Perspective*. New York andLondon: New York University Press, 2011.

Black, Jeremy. *The Collapse of the Anglo-French Alliance, 1727–1731*. New York: St. Martin's Press, 1997.

Blanco Núñez, José María. *La Armada Española en la Primera Mitad del Siglo XVIII*. Madrid: IZAR Construcciones Navales, 2001.

Blanco Núñez, José María. *La Armada Española en la Segunda Mitad del Siglo XVIII*. Madrid: IZAR Construcciones Navales, 2004.

Blasco Ibáñez, Vicente. *Queen Calafia*. London: Thornton Butterworth, 1925 [1st Spanish ed.: La reina Calafia. Valencia: Prometeo, 1923; 1st American ed.: New York: E.P. Dutton & Company, 1924].

Bolton, Herbert Eugene. "Defensive Spanish Expansion and the Significance of the Borderlands." In *The Trans-Mississippi West*, edited by James F. Willard and Colin B. Goodykoontz, 1–42. Boulder: University of Colorado, 1930.

Bolton, Herbert Eugene. "The Epic of Greater America." *American Historical Review* 38 (1933): 448–474.

Bolton, Herbert Eugene. "The Epic of Greater America." In *Wider Horizons of American History*, edited by Eugene H. Bolton, 1–54. New York: D. Appleton-Century Company Inc., 1939.

Bolton, Herbert Eugene, and Thomas Maitland Marshall. *The Colonization of North America, 1492–1783*. New York: The Macmillan Company, 1920.

Borucki, Alex. "The Slave Trade to the Río de la Plata: Trans-Imperial Networks and Atlantic Warfare." *Colonial Latin American Review* 20, no. 1 (2011): 81–107.

Borucki, Alex. *From Shipmates to Soldiers: Emerging Black Identities in the Río de la Plata*. Albuquerque: University of New Mexico Press, 2015.

Borucki, Alex. "Across Imperial Boundaries: Black Social Networks across the Iberian South Atlantic, 1760–1810." *Atlantic Studies: Global Currents* 14, no. 1 (2017): 11–36.

Borucki, Alex, and Gregory O'Malley. "Patterns in the Intercolonial Slave Trade across the Americas before the Nineteenth Century." *Revista Tempo* 23, no. 2 (2017): 315–338.

Borucki, Alex, and Gregory O'Malley, eds. *Final Passages: The Intra-American Slave Trade Database*, forthcoming.

Borucki, Alex, David Eltis, and David Wheat. "Atlantic History and the Slave Trade to Spanish America." *American Historical Review* 120, no. 2 (2015): 433–461.

Brackenbridge, Henry Marie. *Voyage to South America Performed by order of the American Government in the Years 1817 and 1818 in the Frigate Congress.* London: T. and J. Allam, 1820.

Brading, D.A. *Miners and Merchants in Bourbon Mexico 1763–1810.* Cambridge: Cambridge University Press, 1971.

Brading, D A. *The Origins of Mexican Nationalism.* Cambridge: University of Cambridge, Centre of Latin American Studies, 1985.

Brading, D A. *The First America: The Spanish Monarchy, Creole Patriots, and the Liberal State.* Cambridge: Cambridge University Press, 1991.

Breña, Roberto. *El primer liberalismo español y los procesos de emancipación de América 1808–1824: Una revisión historiográfica del liberalismo hispánico.* México D.F.: Colegio de México, 2006.

Breña, Roberto. *El imperio de las circunstancias: Las independencias hispanoamericanas y la revolución liberal española.* México: El Colegio de México and Marcial Pons, 2013.

Breña, Roberto. "The Emancipation Process in New Spain and the Cádiz Constitution: New Historiographical Paths Regarding the Revoluciones Hispánicas." In *The Rise of Constitutional Government in the Iberian Atlantic World: The Impact of the Cádiz Constitution of 1812*, edited by Scott Eastman and Natalia Sobrevilla Perea, 42–62. Tuscaloosa: University of Alabama Press, 2015.

Brewer-Carías, Allan R. *Orígenes del constitucionalismo moderno en Hispanoamérica.* Caracas: Editorial Jurídica Venezolana, 2014.

Brooks, James F. *Captives and Cousins: Slavery, Kinship, and Community in the Southwest Borderlands.* Chapel Hill: University of North Carolina Press, 2002.

Brown, Carolyn A. and Paul E. Lovejoy. "The Bight of Biafra and Slavery." In *Repercussions of the Atlantic Slave Trade: The Interior of the Bight of Biafra and the African Diaspora*, edited by Carolyn A. Brown and Paul E. Lovejoy, 1–16. Trenton: Africa World Press, 2011.

Brown, Jonathan. "Foreword. The Image of Spain in the United States." In *Spain in America: The Origins of Hispanism in the United States*, edited by Richard Kagan, ix–xi. Urbana and Chicago: University of Illinois Press, 2002.

Burnard, Trevor, and John Garrigus. *The Plantation Machine: Atlantic Capitalism in French Saint-Domingue and British Jamaica.* Philadelphia: University of Pennsylvania Press, 2016.

Burson, Caroline Maude. *The Stewardship of Don Esteban Miró 1781–1792: A Study of Louisiana Based Largely on the Document in New Orleans.* New Orleans: American Printing Company, 1940.

Butterfield, L.H., et al., eds. *Adams Family Correspondence.* 13 vols. to date. Cambridge, MA: Harvard University Press, 1963–2017.

Calderón Cuadrado, Reyes. "Alianzas comerciales hispano-norteamericanas en la financiación del proceso de independencia de los Estados Unidos de América: La Casa Gardoqui e hijos." In *Norteamérica a finales del siglo XVIII: España y los Estados Unidos*, edited by Isabel García-Montón, Eduardo Garrigues, Almudena Hernández Ruigómez, Sylvia L. Hilton, and Emma Sánchez Montañés, 197–218. Madrid: Fundación Consejo España–Estados Unidos and Editorial Marcial Pons, 2008.

Calderón Quijano, José Antonio. "El banco de San Carlos y las comunidades de indios de Nueva España." *Anuario de Estudios Americanos* 19 (1962): 1–144.

Calderón Quijano, José Antonio, ed. *Los virreyes de Nueva España en el reinado de Carlos III.* Vol.2: Seville: Escuela de Estudios Hispanoamericanos, 1968.

Campomanes, Pedro Rodríguez de. *Reflexiones sobre el comercio Español a Indias (1762)*, edited by Vicente Llombart Rosa. Madrid: Alisal, 1988.
Canga Argüelles, José. *Diccionario de Hacienda para el uso de los encargados de la suprema drección [sic] de ella.* Londres: Imprenta Española de M. Calero, 1827.
Cantillo, Alejando del, ed. *Tratados, convenios y declaraciones de paz y de comercio que han hecho con las potencias estranjeras los monarcas españoles de la Casa de Borbón.* Madrid: Imprenta de Alegría y Charlain, 1843.
Cantús, Dolores García. *Fernando Poo: Una Aventura Colonial Española.* Barcelona: Ceiba, 2006.
Cañizares-Esguerra, Jorge. *How to Write the History of the New World: Histories, Epistemologies, and Identities in the Eighteenth-Century Atlantic World.* Stanford: Stanford University Press, 2001.
Cañizares-Esguerra, Jorge, ed. *Entangled Empires: The Anglo-Iberian Atlantic, 1500–1830.* Philadelphia: University of Pennsylvania Press, 2018.
Carter, Harvey. *The Life and Times of Little Turtle: First Sagamore of the Wabash.* Urbana: University of Illinois Press, 1987.
Casas, Bartholomew [sic] de las. *An Account of the First Voyages and Discoveries Made by the Spaniards in America. Containing the Most Exact Relation Hitherto Publish'd of Their Unparallel'd Cruelties on the Indians, in the Destruction of Above Forty Millions of People. With the Propositions Offer'd to the King of Spain to Prevent the Further Ruin of the West-Indies.* London: J. Darby for D. Brown ... J. Harris ... and Andr. Bell, 1699.
Casaus [sic] Casas, Bartolomé de las. *Tears of the Indians: Being an Historical and True Account of the Cruel Massacres and Slaughters of Above Twenty Millions of Innocent People; Committed by the Spaniards in the Islands of Hispaniola, Cuba, Jamaica, &c. As also, in the Continent of Mexico, Peru, & other Places of the West-Indies, To the Total Destruction of Those Countries. Written in Spanish by Casaus, an Eye-witness of those things.* London: J. C. for Nath. Brook, 1656.
Caughey, John Walton. *Bernardo de Gálvez in Louisiana, 1776–1783.* Berkeley: University of California Press, 1934; reprint, Los Angeles: Pelican, Gretna, 1998.
Caughey, John Walton, ed. *McGillivray of the Creeks.* Norman: University of Oklahoma Press, 1938.
Cencillo de Pineda, Manuel. *El Brigadier Conde de Argelejo y su Expedición Militar a Fernando Poo en 1778.* Madrid: Instituto de Estudios Africanos, 1948.
Céspedes del Castillo, Guillermo. *América Hispánica (1492–1808).* Barcelona: Lábor, 1985.
Chadwick, French Ensor. *The Relations of the United States and Spain: Diplomacy.* New York: Russell & Russell Publishing, 1968.
Charters, Erica. *Disease, War and the Imperial State: The Welfare of the British Armed Forces during the Seven Years' War.* Chicago andLondon: University of Chicago Press, 2014.
Chartrand, René, and Patrice Courcelle. *Gibraltar 1779–83: The Great Siege.* London: Osprey, 2008.
Chávez, Thomas E. *Spain and the Independence of the United States: An Intrinsic Gift.* Albuquerque: University of New Mexico Press, 2002.
Chávez, Thomas E. "Spanish Policy and Strategy." In *Strategy in the American War of Independence: A Global Approach*, edited by Donald Stoker, Kenneth J. Hagan, and Michael T. McMaster, 163–175. New York: Routledge, 2010.
Cheibub, José Antonio, Zachary Elkins, and Tom Ginsburg. "Latin American Presidentialism in Comparative and Historical Perspective." *Texas Law Review* 89 (2011): 1–33.

Chevalier, Louis Édouard. *Histoire de la marine française pendant la guerre de l'indépendance américaine.* Paris: Hachette, 1877.

Chiaramonte, José Carlos. *La Ilustración en el Río de la Plata: Cultura eclesiástica y cultura laica durante el Virreinato.* Buenos Aires: Punto Sur, 1989.

Chiaramonte, José Carlos. *Nation and State in Latin America*, trans. Ian Barnett. New Brunswick andLondon: Transaction Publishers, 2012.

Chust Calero, Manuel, and Ivana Frasquet. *La patria no se hizo sola: las revoluciones de las independencias iberoamericanas.* Madrid: Sílex, 2012.

Chust, Manuel. *La tribuna revolucionaria. La constitución de 1812 en ambos hemisferios.* Cádiz: Museo de las Cortes de España, 2014.

Coatsworth, John. "Economic and Institutional Trajectories in Nineteenth-Century Latin America." In *Latin America and the World Economy since 1800*, edited by John Coatsworth and Alan M. Taylor, 23–54. Cambridge, MA: Harvard University Press, 1998.

Coe, Samuel Gwynn. *The Mission of William Carmichael to Spain.* Baltimore: Johns Hopkins University Press, 1928.

Coker, William S. *The Siege of Pensacola 1781 in Maps, with Data on Troop Strength, Military Units, Ships, Casualties and Related Statistics.* Pensacola: Perdido Bay Press, 1981.

Coker, William S., and Robert R. Rea, eds. *Anglo-Spanish Confrontation on the Gulf Coast during the American Revolution: Gálvez Celebration, Commemorating the Siege of Pensacola.* Pensacola: Gulf Coast History and Humanities Conference, 1982.

Collections of the State Historical Society of Wisconsin. 20 vols. Madison: Madison State Printer, 1888–1931.

Colley, Linda. *Captives: Britain, Empire, and the World, 1600–1850.* New York: Anchor Books, 2002.

Colley, Linda. "Empires of Writing: Britain, America and Constitutions, 1776–1848." *Law and History Review* 32, no. 2 (2014): 237–266.

Collier, Simon. *Ideas and Politics of Chilean Independence, 1808–1833.* Cambridge: Cambridge University Press, 1967.

Cone, Carl B. "Richard Price and the Constitution of the United States." *The American Historical Review* 53, no. 4 (1948): 726–747.

Conn, Stetson. *Gibraltar in British Diplomacy in the Eighteenth Century.* New Haven: Yale University Press, 1942.

Conrotte, Manuel. *La intervención de España en la independencia de la América del Norte.* Madrid: Victoriano Suárez, 1920.

The Constitution of the Commonwealth of Pennsylvania as Established by the General Convention. Philadelphia: John Dunlap, 1776.

Cook, Warren L. *Flood Tide of Empire: Spain and the Pacific Northwest, 1543–1819.* New Haven: Yale University Press, 1973.

Cooke, J.W. "Jefferson on Liberty." *Journal of the History of Ideas* 34, no. 4 (1973): 563–576.

Cooke, Jabe E., and Harold C. Syrett, eds. *The Papers of Alexander Hamilton*, vol. 15. New York: Columbia University Press, 1996.

Corbitt, Duvon C., ed., and Roberta D. Corbitt, trans. "Papers from the Spanish Archives Relating to Tennessee and the Old Southwest, 1783–1800." *The East Tennessee Historical Society's Publications* 9–50 (1937–1978).

Coughlin, Magdalen. "Boston Smugglers on the Coast (1797–1821): An Insight into the American Acquisition of California." *California Historical Society Quarterly* 46, no. 2 (1967): 99–120.

Crackel, Theodore J., et al., eds. *The Papers of George Washington Digital Edition.* Revolutionary War Series. Charlottesville: University of Virginia Press, Rotunda, 2007. https://rotunda.upress.virginia.edu/founders/GEWN.html (accessed February 1, 2018).
Craton, Michael. *A History of the Bahamas.* London: Collins, 1962.
Craton, Michael, and Gail Saunders. *Islanders in the Stream: A History of the Bahamian People, Vol. 1: From Aboriginal Times to the End of Slavery.* Athens: University of Georgia Press, 1999.
Cuadrado, Reyes Calderón. *Empresarios Españoles en el Proceso de Independencia Norteamericana: La Casa Gardoqui e Hijos de Bilbao.* Madrid: Instituto de Investigaciones Económicas y Sociales, 2004.
Cumberland, Richard. *Anecdotes of eminent painters in Spain, during the sixteenth and seventeenth centuries; with cursory remarks upon the present state of arts in that kingdom.* London: J. Walter, 1782.
Cumberland, Richard. *Memoirs of Richard Cumberland*, edited by Henry Flanders. New York: B. Blom, 1969 [1st ed. London: Lackington, Allen, 1806].
Cummins, Light Townsend. *Spanish Observers and the American Revolution: 1775–1783.* Baton Rouge: Louisiana State University Press, 1991.
Cummins, Light Townsend. "The Gálvez Family and Spanish Participation in the Independence of the United States of America." *Revista Complutense de Historia de América* 32 (2006): 179–196.
Cusick, James G. *The Other War of 1812: The Patriot War and the American Invasion of Spanish East Florida.* Gainesville: University Press of Florida, 2003.
Daly, Gavin. *The British Soldier in the Peninsular War: Encounters with Spain and Portugal 1808–1814.* London: Palgrave Macmillan, 2013.
Das, Sudipta. *De Broglie's Armada: A Plan for the Invasion of England, 1765–1777.* Lanham, MD: University Press of America, 2009.
Deacon, Philip. "Resisting Absolutism: Spanish Intellectual Freedom and its Enemies before 1812." In *1812 Echoes: The Cádiz Constitution in Hispanic History, Culture and Politics*, edited by Stephen G.H. Roberts and Adam Sharman, 34–49. Newcastle upon Tyne: Cambridge Scholars Publishing, 2013.
The Definitive Treaty of Peace and Friendship, between His Britannick Majesty, and the King of Spain. Signed at Versailles, the 3d of September, 1783. London: T. Harrison and S. Brooke, 1783.
DeLay, Brian. *War of a Thousand Deserts: Indian Raids and the U.S.-Mexican War.* New Haven and Dallas: Yale University Press, published in association with the William P. Clements Center for Southwest Studies, Southern Methodist University, 2008.
Delpar, Helen. *Looking South: The Evolution of Latin Americanist Scholarship in the United States, 1850–1975.* Tuscaloosa: University of Alabama Press, 2008.
Deverell, William Francis, and David Igler. *A Companion to California History.* Chichester, UK and Malden, MA: Wiley-Blackwell, 2008.
Din, Gilbert C. *Francisco Bouligny: A Bourbon Soldier in Spanish Louisiana.* Baton Rouge: Louisiana State University Press, 1993.
Din, Gilbert C., ed. *The Louisiana Purchase Bicentennial Series in Louisiana History, Vol. 2: The Spanish Presence in Louisiana, 1763–1803.* Lafayette: Center for Louisiana Studies, University of Southwestern Louisiana, 1996.
Din, Gilbert C. *Populating the Barrera: Spanish Immigration Efforts in Colonial Louisiana.* Lafayette: University of Louisiana at Lafayette Press, 2014.
Dircks, Richard J. *Richard Cumberland.* Boston: Twayne Publishers, 1976.

Documentos para la historia de la provincia de Cartagena de Indias hoy Estado Soberano de Bolívar en la Unión Colombiana. Bogotá: Imprenta de Medardo Rivas, 1883.

Donézar, Javier. "De las naciones-patrias a la 'nación-patria.' Del Antiguo al Nuevo Régimen." In *La monarquía de las naciones: Patria, nación y naturaleza en la monarquía de España*, edited by Bernardo García García and José Antonio Álvarez-Ossorio Alvariño, 93–120. Madrid: Fundación Carlos de Amberes, 2004.

Doniol, Henri. *Histoire de la participation de la France à l'établissement des États-Unis d'Amérique*. 6 vols. Paris: Imprimerie National, 1886–1890.

Duane, William. *A Visit to Colombia in the years 1822 and 1823*. Philadelphia: Thomas H. Palmer, 1826.

Duggan, Marie Christine. "Market and Church on the Mexican Frontier: Alta California, 1769–1832." PhD diss., New York: New School for Social Research, 2000.

Dull, Jonathan R. *The French Navy and American Independence: A Study of Arms and Diplomacy, 1774–1787*. Princeton: Princeton University Press, 1975.

Dull, Jonathan R. *A Diplomatic History of the American Revolution*. New Haven: Yale University Press, 1985.

Dull, Jonathan R. *The French Navy and the Seven Years' War*. Lincoln, NE: University of Lincoln Press, 2005.

DuVal, Kathleen. *The Native Ground: Indians and Colonists in the Heart of the Continent*. Philadelphia: University of Pennsylvania Press, 2006.

DuVal, Kathleen. *Independence Lost: Lives on the Edge of the American Revolution*. New York: Random House. 2015.

Dziennik, Matthew P. "The Miskitu, Military Labour, and the San Juan Expedition of 1780." *The Historical Journal* 61 (2018): 155–179.

Eastman, Scott. "The Sacred Mantle of the Constitution of 1812." In *The Rise of Constitutional Government in the Iberian Atlantic World: The Impact of the Cádiz Constitution of 1812*, edited by Scott Eastman and Natalia Sobrevilla Perea, 1–18. Tuscaloosa: University of Alabama Press, 2015.

Eastman, Scott, and Natalia Sobrevilla Perea, eds. *The Rise of Constitutional Government in the Iberian Atlantic World: The Impact of the Constitution of 1812*. Tuscaloosa: University of Alabama Press, 2015.

Echeverri, Marcela. *Indian and Slave Royalists in the Age of Revolution: Reform, Revolution, and Royalism in the Northern Andes, 1780–1825*. Cambridge: Cambridge University Press, 2016.

Ehrman, John. *The British Government and Commercial Negotiations with Europe 1783–1793*. Cambridge: Cambridge University Press, 1962.

Elkins, Zachary. "Diffusion and the Constitutionalization of Europe." *Comparative Political Studies* 43, no. 8/9 (2012): 969–999.

Ellicott, Andrew. *Surveying the Early Republic: The Journal of Andrew Ellicott U.S. Boundary Commissioner in the Old Southwest 1796–1800*, edited by Robert Bush. Baton Rouge: Louisiana State University Press, 2016.

Elliott, John H. *Empires of the Atlantic World: Britain and Spain in America, 1492–1830*. New Haven and London: Yale University Press, 2006.

Elliott, John H. "Britain and Spain in America: Colonists and Colonized." In *Spain, Europe & the Wider World, 1500–1800*, edited by John H. Elliot, 149–172. New Haven and London: Yale University Press, 2009.

Escudero, José Antonio. *Los orígenes del Consejo de Ministros en España: La Junta Suprema de Estado*, vol. 1. Madrid: Editorial Nacional, 1979.

Escudero López, José Antonio. *El supuesto memorial del Conde de Aranda sobre la independencia de América.* México D.F.: UNAM, 2014.
Farías, Luis M. *La América de Aranda.* México D.F.: Fondo de Cultura Económica, 2003.
Fehrenbacher, Don E. *The Slaveholding Republic: An Account of the United States Government's Relation to Slavery.* New York: Oxford University Press, 2001.
Ferguson, E. James. *The Power of the Purse: A History of American Public Finance, 1776–1790.* Chapel Hill: The University of North Carolina Press, 1961.
Ferlan, Luis. "Notas sobre la expedición del Conde de Argelejo y la presencia Española en el Golfo de Guinea (1778–1783)." In *VI Simposio de Historia Marítima y Naval Iberoamericana*, 19–23. Lima, Peru, November, 2001.
Fernández Sebastián, Javier. "Tolerance and Freedom of Expression in the Hispanic World between Enlightenment and Liberalism." *Past & Present* 211 (2001): 159–166.
Fernández, Enrique. "Spain's Contribution to the Independence of the United States." *Revista/Review Interamericana* 10, no. 3 (1980): 290–306.
Feros, Antonio. "'Spain and America: All Is One': Historiography of the Conquest and Colonization of the Americas and National Mythology in Spain c. 1892 – c. 1992." In *Interpreting Spanish Colonialism: Empires, Nations, and Legends*, edited by Christopher Schmidt-Nowara and John M. Nieto-Phillips, 109–134. Albuquerque: University of New Mexico Press, 2005.
Ferreiro, Larrie D. *Ships and Science: The Birth of Naval Architecture in the Scientific Revolution, 1600–1800.* Cambridge: MIT Press, 2007.
Ferreiro, Larrie D. *Measure of the Earth: The Enlightenment Expedition that Reshaped Our World.* New York: Basic Books, 2011.
Ferreiro, Larrie D. *Brothers at Arms: American Independence and the Men of France and Spain Who Saved It.* New York: Alfred A. Knopf, 2016.
Finestrad, Joaquín de. *El vasallo instruido en el estado del Nuevo Reino de Granada y en sus respectivas obligaciones*, transcription and introduction by Margarita González. Bogotá: Universidad Nacional de Colombia, 2001.
Fisher, John R. *Economic Aspects of Spanish Imperialism in America, 1492–1810.* Liverpool: Liverpool University Press, 2005.
Fitz, Caitlin. *Our Sister Republics: The United States in an Age of American Revolutions.* New York: W.W. Norton, 2016.
Fitzpatrick, John C., ed. *The Writings of George Washington from the Original Manuscript Sources, 1745–1799.* Washington, D.C.: Government Printing Office, 1931–1944.
Flint, Valeria I.J. *The Imaginative Landscape of Christopher Columbus.* Princeton: Princeton University Press, 1992.
Floyd, Troy S. *The Anglo-Spanish Struggle for Mosquitia.* Albuquerque: University of New Mexico Press, 1967.
Ford, Worthington Chauncey, ed. *The Writings of George Washington.* New York: G. P. Putnam's Sons, 1893.
Ford, Worthington Chauncey, ed. *Journals of the Continental Congress, 1774–89.* 34 vols. Washington, D.C.: Government Printing Office, 1904–1937.
Fortescue, J.W. *The Correspondence of King George the Third from 1760 to December 1783, Printed from the Original Papers in the Royal Archives at Windsor Castle, Arranged and Edited by the Hon. Sir John Fortescue.* London: Macmillan & Co. Ltd., 1927–1928.
Foucrier, Annick. "Rivalités européennes dans le Pacifique : l'affaire de Nootka Sound (1789–1790)." *Annales historiques de la Révolution française* 307, no. 1 (1997): 17–30.
French, David. *The British Way in Warfare, 1688–2000.* London and Boston: Unwin Hyman, 1990.

Frigo, Daniela, ed. *Politics and Diplomacy in Early Modern Italy: The Structure of Diplomatic Practice, 1450–1800*. New York: Cambridge University Press, 2000.
Fuente, Alejandro de la. "Slave Law and Claims-Making in Cuba: The Tannenbaum Debate Revisited." *Law and History Review* 22, no. 2 (2004): 339–369.
Furstenberg, François. "The Significance of the Trans-Appalachian Frontier in Atlantic History." *The American Historical Review* 113, no. 3 (2008): 647–677.
Gallardo Fernández, Francisco. *Origen, progresos y estado de las rentas de la corona de España: su gobierno y administracion*. Madrid: Imprenta Real, 1808.
Gally, Natacha. "Écrire le contraste au-delà des typologies: l'apport de l'histoire croisée à la comparaison internationale." *Revue Internationale de Politique Comparée* 1, no. 19 (2012): 19–38.
Gálvez, Bernardo de. "Diario que yo, d. Bernardo de Gálvez, brigadier de los Reales Ejércitos, gobernador de la provincia de la Luisiana, y encargado por S.M. de la expedición contra Panzacola y Mobila, formé de los acontecimientos que ocurren en ella." In *Mercurio Histórico Político, que contiene el estado presente de la Europa, lo sucedido en todas las Cortes, los intereses de los Príncipes, y generalmente todo lo mas curioso*, 198–226. Madrid: June, 1780.
Gálvez, Bernardo de. *Diario de las operaciones contra la plaza de Panzacola 1781*, edited by José Porrúa Turanzas. Madrid: José Porrúa Turanzas, 1959.
Gálvez, José de. "Discurso y reflexiones de un vasallo sobre la decadencia de nuestras Indias españolas." In *La política americana de José de Gálvez: según su "Discurso y Reflexiones de un Vasallo"*, edited by Luis Navarro García, 123–163. Málaga: Algazara, 1998.
García Cantús, Dolores. *Fernando Poo: Una Aventura Colonial Española*. Barcelona: Ceiba, 2006.
García Melero, Luis Ángel. *La independencia de los Estados Unidos de Norteamérica a través de la prensa española ("Gaceta de Madrid" y "Mercurio Histórico y Político"). Los precedentes (1763–1776)*. Madrid: Ministerio de Asuntos Exteriores, 1977.
García-Montón, Isabel, Eduardo Garrigues, Almudena Hernández Ruigómez, Sylvia L. Hilton, and Emma Sánchez Montañés, eds. *Norteamérica a finales del siglo XVIII: España y los Estados Unidos*. Madrid: Fundación Consejo España–Estados Unidos and Editorial Marcial Pons, 2008.
Gargarella, Roberto. *Los fundamentos legales de la desigualdad. El constitucionalismo en América, 1776–1860*. Madrid: Siglo XXI, 2005.
Gargarella, Roberto. *Latin American Constitutionalism, 1810–2010*. Oxford: Oxford University Press, 2013.
Gibson, Charles. *The Black Legend: Anti-Spanish Attitudes in the Old World and the New*. New York: Knopf, 1971.
Gibson, James R. *Otter Skins, Boston Ships, and China Goods: The Maritime Fur Trade of the Northwest Coast, 1785–1841*. Seattle: University of Washington Press, 1992.
Gil Munilla, Octavio. *Participación de España en la génesis histórica de los Estados Unidos*. Madrid: Publicaciones Españolas, 1952 [English trans. *Spain's Share in the History of the United States of America*. Madrid: Publicaciones Españolas, 1952].
Giraldo, Jorge, ed. *Procesos políticos antioqueños durante la revolución neogranadina*. Medellín: Eafit, 2013.
Giunta, Mary, ed. *Emerging Nation: A Documentary History of the Foreign Relations of the United States under the Articles of Confederation*, vol. 1. Washington, DC: NHPRC, 1996.
Gleijeses, Piero. "The Limits of Sympathy: The United States and the Independence of Spanish America." *Journal of Latin American Studies* 24, no. 3 (1992): 481–505.

Glete, Jan. *Navies and Nations: Warships, Navies and State Building in Europe and America 1500–1860*, 2 vols. Stockholm: Academitryck AB Edsbruk, 1993.

Golove, David M., and Daniel J. Hulsebosch. "A Civilized Nation: The Early American Constitution, the Law of Nations, and the Pursuit of International Recognition." *New York University Law Review* 85 (2010): 932–1066.

Gómez Del Campillo, Miguel, ed. *Relaciones Diplomáticas entre España y los Estados Unidos según los Documentos Del Archivo Histórico Nacional*, 2 vols. Madrid: Archivo Histórico Nacional, 1944–1945.

Gómez Hoyos, Rafael. *La revolución granadina de 1810: Ideario de una generación y de una época, 1781–1821*, vol.1. Bogotá: Temis, 1962.

Gómez-Quiñones, Juan. *Roots of Chicano Politics, 1600–1940*. Albuquerque: University of New Mexico Press, 1994.

González, Michael J. *This Small City Will Be a Mexican Paradise: Exploring the Origins of Mexican Culture in Los Angeles, 1821–1846*. Albuquerque: University of New Mexico Press, 2005.

Gonzalez-Silen, Olga. "Holding an Empire Together: The Spanish Resistance and Caracas in the Early Years of the War against Napoleon." PhD diss., Cambridge, MA: Harvard University, 2014.

Good News for America: Salem, Tuesday, April 16, 1776. Salem, MA: n.p., 1776.

Gould, Eliga H. "Entangled Histories, Entangled Worlds: The English-Speaking Atlantic as a Spanish Periphery." *American Historical Review* 112, no. 3 (2007): 764–786.

Gould, Eliga H. *Among the Powers of the Earth: The American Revolution and the Making of a New World Empire*. Cambridge, MA: Harvard University Press, 2012.

Guardino, Peter F. *The Time of Liberty: Popular Political Culture in Oaxaca, 1750–1850*. Durham: Duke University Press, 2005.

Guasti, Niccolò. *Lotta politica e riforme all'inizio del regno di Carlo III. Campomanes e léspulsione dei gesuiti dalla monarchia spagnola (1759–1768)*. Firenze: Alinea, 2006.

Guedea, Virginia. "The Process of Mexican Independence." *American Historical Review* 105, no. 1 (2000): 116–130.

Guerra, François-Xavier. *Modernidad e independencias: ensayos sobre las revoluciones hispánicas*. Madrid and México D.F.: MAPFRE - Fondo de Cultura Económica, 1992.

Guerra, François-Xavier. *Modernidad e independencias*. Madrid: MAPFRE, 1992.

Guerra, François-Xavier. "Lógicas y ritmos de las revoluciones hispánicas." In *Las revoluciones hispánicas: Independencias americanas y el liberalismo español*, edited by François-Xavier Guerra, 13–46, Madrid: Editorial Complutense, 1995.

Guillén Villafuerte, José Javier. "Guerras imperiales,donativos patrióticos y pueblos de indios en Chiapas, 1780–1814." *Fronteras de la Historia* 23, no. 128/1 (2018): 128–161.

Gulliver, Katrina. "Finding the Pacific World." *Journal of World History* 22, no. 1 (2011): 83–100.

Gutiérrez, Ramón A. *When Jesus Came, the Corn Mothers Went Away: Marriage, Sexuality, and Power in New Mexico, 1500–1846*. Stanford: Stanford University Press, 1991.

Gutiérrez, Ramón A., and Richard J. Orsi. *Contested Eden: California Before the Gold Rush*. California History Sesquicentennial Series. Berkeley and London: University of California Press, 1998.

Gutiérrez Ardila, Daniel, ed. *Las asambleas constituyentes de la independencia: Actas de Cundinamarca y Antioquia (1811–1812)*. Bogotá: Universidad Externado, 2010.

Gutiérrez Ardila, Daniel. *Un Nuevo Reino: Geografía política, pactismo y diplomacia durante el interregno en Nueva Granada (1808–1816)*. Bogotá: Universidad Externado, 2010.

Gutiérrez-Steinkamp, Martha. *Spain: The Forgotten Alliance. Independence of the United States*. North Charleston, SC: Create Space Publishing, 2013.

Hackel, Steven W. *Children of Coyote, Missionaries of Saint Francis: Indian-Spanish Relations in Colonial California, 1769–1850*. Chapel Hill: University of North Carolina Press, 2005.

Hackel, Steven W., ed. *Alta California: Peoples in Motion, Identities in Formation, 1769–1850*. Berkeley, CA: Published for Huntington-USC Institute on California and the West by University of California Press, Berkeley, California, and Huntington Library, San Marino, California, 2010.

Hackett, Charles, ed. *New Spain and the Anglo-American West: Historical Contributions Presented to Herbert Eugene Bolton*. Los Angeles: private printing, 1932.

Haddad, John R. *America's First Adventure in China: Trade, Treaties, Opium, and Salvation*. Philadelphia: Temple University Press, 2013.

Hale, Charles A. *Mexican Liberalism in the Age of Mora, 1821–1853*. New Haven: Yale University Press, 1968.

Hämäläinen, Pekka. *The Comanche Empire*. New Haven: Yale University Press, 2008.

Hamilton, Earl J. *El florecimiento del capitalismo y otros ensayos de historia económica*. Madrid: Revista de Occidente, 1948.

Hamilton, Peter. *Colonial Mobile: An Historical Study, Largely from Original Sources, of the Alabama-Tombigbee Basin from the Discovery of Mobile Bay in 1519 until the Demolition of Fort Charlotte in 1821*. New York: Houghton Mifflin, 1897.

Hamnett, Brian. "The Medieval Roots of Spanish Constitutionalism." In *The Rise of Constitutional Government in the Iberian Atlantic World: The Impact of the Constitution of 1812*, edited by Scott Eastman and Natalia Sobrevilla Perea, 19–41. Tuscaloosa: University of Alabama Press, 2015.

Hamnett, Brian. *The End of Iberian Rule on the American Continent, 1770–1830*. New York: Cambridge University Press, 2017.

Hamnett, Brian. *The Enlightenment in Iberia and Ibero-America*. Cardiff: University of Wales Press, 2017.

Hanke, Lewis. "Conquest and the Cross." *American Heritage* 14, no. 2 (1963): 4–19 and 107–111.

Hargreaves-Mawdsley, W.N. *Eighteenth-Century Spain, 1700–1788: A Political, Diplomatic, and Institutional History*. Totowa, NJ: Rowman & Littlefield, 1979.

Hay, Daisy. "Liberals, Liberales and *The Liberal*: A Reassessment." *European Romantic Review* 19, no. 4 (2008): 307–320.

Hayes, Carlton Joseph Huntley. *Los Estados Unidos y España: Una interpretación*. Madrid: Ediciones y Publicaciones Españolas, 1952.

Helg, Aline. *Liberty and Equality in Caribbean Colombia, 1770–1835*. Chapel Hill: The University of North Carolina Press, 2004.

Hernández de Alba, Guillermo. *El proceso de Nariño a la luz de documentos inéditos*. Bogotá: Editorial ABC, 1958.

Hernández Franco, Juan. *La gestión política y el pensamiento reformista del Conde de Floridablanca*. Murcia: Universidad de Murcia, 1984.

Hernández Franco, Juan. *Aspectos de la política exterior de España en la época de Floridablanca*. Murcia: Real Academia Alfonso X El Sabio, 1992.
Hernández Sánchez-Barba, Mario, ed. *1776: Bicentenario de la independencia norteamericana*. Madrid: Universidad Complutense de Madrid, 1977.
Hernández Sánchez-Barba, Mario. "El bicentenario de 1776: América y la estrategia de seguridad atlántica y el Reformismo español." *Revista de la Universidad Complutense* 26, no. 107 (1977): 9–48.
Hernández Sánchez-Barba, Mario. "El americanismo del conde de Floridablanca." *Anales de Historia Contemporánea* 8 (1991): 45–57.
Herr, Richard. *The Eighteenth Century Revolution in Spain*. Princeton: Princeton University Press, 1958.
Herzog, Tamar. "Los americanos frente a la Monarquía: El criollismo y la naturaleza española." In *La monarquía de las naciones: Patria, nación y naturaleza en la monarquía de España*, edited by Bernardo García García and José Antonio Álvarez-Ossorio Alvariño, 77–92. Madrid: Fundación Carlos de Amberes, 2004.
Hilton, Sylvia L. "El Americanismo en España, 1982–1983." *Revista de Indias* XLIII, no. 172 (1983): 847–914.
Hilton, Sylvia L. "El Americanismo en España, 1983–1984." *Revista de Indias* XLIV, no. 174 (1984): 573–680.
Hilton, Sylvia L. "El Americanismo en España: Bibliografía, 1984–1985." *Revista de Indias* XLV, no. 176 (1985): 589–640.
Hilton, Sylvia L. "El Americanismo en España: Bibliografía, 1985–1986." *Revista de Indias* XLVI, no. 178 (1986): 655–732.
Hilton, Sylvia L. "El Americanismo en España: Bibliografía, 1986–1987." *Revista de Indias* XLVII, no. 181 (1987): 913–1016.
Hilton, Sylvia L. "El Americanismo en España: Bibliografía, 1987–1988." *Revista de Indias* XLVIII, no. 184 (1988): 845–943.
Hilton, Sylvia L. "El Americanismo en España: Bibliografía, 1988–1989." *Revista de Indias* XLIX, no. 186 (1989): 463–530.
Hilton, Sylvia L. "Las relaciones anglo-españolas en Norteamérica durante el reinado de Carlos III: revisión historiográfica." In *Coloquio Internacional: Carlos III y su siglo, Actas*, 839–882. Madrid: Universidad Complutense, Departamento de Historia Moderna, 1990.
Hilton, Sylvia L. *La Alta California española*. Madrid: MAPFRE, 1992.
Hilton, Sylvia L. "American Studies in Spain: Recent Trends." *American Studies International* XXXII, no. 1 (1994): 41–69.
Hilton, Sylvia L. "Spanish Colonies in North America: Recent Historical Scholarship from Spain." *American Studies International* XXXII, no. 1 (1994): 70–95.
Hilton, Sylvia L. "España y Norteamérica, 1763–1821." In *Legado: España y los Estados Unidos en la era de la Independencia, 1763–1848*, 31–43. Madrid: Sociedad Estatal para la Acción Cultural Exterior, 2007.
Hilton, Sylvia L., and Amancio Labandeira. "El Americanismo en España, 1989–1990." *Revista de Indias* L, no. 190 (1990): 893–1022.
Hilton, Sylvia L., and Amancio Labandeira. "El Americanismo en España, 1990–1991." *Revista de Indias* LI, no. 193 (1991): 661–776.
Hilton, Sylvia L., and Amancio Labandeira. "El Americanismo en España, 1991–1992." *Revista de Indias* LIII, no. 197 (1993): 133–409.

Hilton, Sylvia L., and Matilde Paredes Manzanero. *American Studies Bibliography Published in Spain, 1994–1996*. Madrid: SAAS/Spanish Association for American Studies, Fulbright Commission, United States Information Service, 1996.

Hoffman, Ronald, and Peter J. Albert, eds. *Diplomacy and Revolution: The Franco-American Alliance of 1778*. Charlottesville: University Press of Virginia, 1981.

Holmes, Jack D.L. *Honor and Fidelity: The Louisiana Infantry Regiment and the Louisiana Militia Companies, 1766–1821*. Birmingham: n.p., 1965.

Holmes, Jack D.L. "Bernardo de Gálvez: Spain's 'Man of the Hour' during the American Revolution." In *Cardinales de Dos Independencias. (Noreste de México—Sureste de los Estados Unidos)*, edited by Francisco de Solano and Beatriz Ruiz Caytán, 16–174. México D.F.: Fomento Cultural Banamex, 1978.

Hore, Peter. *Nelson's Band of Brothers: Lives and Memorials*. Barnsley: Seaforth Publishing, 2015.

Horgan, Lucille E. *Forged in War: The Continental Congress and the Origin of Military Supply and Acquisition Policy*. Contributions in Military Studies 219. Westport, CT and London: Greenwood Press, 2002.

Horrible Atrocities of Spaniards in Cuba. An Historical and True Account of the Cruel Massacre and Slaughter of 20,000,000 of People in the West Indies by the Spaniards. New York: J. Boller, 1898.

Horsman, Reginald. *Race and Manifest Destiny: The Origins of American Racial Anglo-Saxonism*. Cambridge, MA: Harvard University Press, 1981.

Houck, Louis. *The Spanish Regime in Missouri: A Collection of Papers and Documents*, 2 vols. R. R. Donnelley & Sons Company, 1909.

Howarth, David. *The Invention of Spain: Cultural Relations between Britain and Spain, 1770–1870*. Manchester: Manchester University Press, 2007.

Hurtado, Albert L. "Empires, Frontiers, Filibusters, and Pioneers: The Transnational World of John Sutter." *Pacific Historical Review* 77, no. 1 (2008): 19–47.

Hyde, Anne Farrar. *Empires, Nations, and Families: A History of the North American West, 1800–1860*. Lincoln: University of Nebraska Press, 2011.

Igler, David. "Diseased Goods: Global Exchanges in the Eastern Pacific Basin, 1770–1850." *The American Historical Review* 109, no. 3 (2004), 693–719.

Igler, David. *The Great Ocean: Pacific Worlds from Captain Cook to the Gold Rush*. Oxford andNew York: Oxford University Press, 2013.

Irving, Washington. *A History of the Life and Voyages of Christopher Columbus*. New York: G. & C. Carvill, 1828.

Irving, Washington. *Chronicle of the Conquest of Granada*. Philadelphia: Carey, Lea & Carey, 1829.

Irving, Washington. *Voyages and Discoveries of the Companions of Columbus*. Philadelphia: Carey and Lea, 1831.

Irving, Washington. *The Alhambra, a Series of Tales and Sketches of the Moors and Spaniards* [later titled *Tales of the Alhambra*]. Philadelphia: Carey & Lea, 1832.

Israel, Jonathan I. *Democratic Enlightenment: Philosophy, Revolution, and Human Rights, 1750–1790*. Oxford: Oxford University Press, 2012.

Israel, Jonathan I. *The Expanding Blaze: How the American Revolution Ignited the World, 1775–1848*. Princeton and Oxford: Princeton University Press, 2017.

Jackson, Gabriel. "Concerning the Spanish Civil War and American Culture." In *El nuevo horizonte España / Estados Unidos. El legado de 1848 y 1898 frente al nuevo milenio*, edited by C. Flys, Carmen Junquera, and Juan Emerio Cruz Cabrera, 21–48. Alcalá de Henares: Instituto Universitario de Estudios Norteamericanos-Universidad de Alcalá, 2001.

Jackson, Robert. *Sovereignty: Evolution of an Idea*. Cambridge: Polity Press, 2007.
Jaksic, Iván. *The Hispanic World and American Intellectual Life 1820–1880*. New York: Palgrave Macmillan, 2007.
James, James Alton. "Oliver Pollock: Financier of the American Revolution in the West." *Studies: An Irish Quarterly Review* 18, no. 72 (1929): 634–635
James, James Alton. *Oliver Pollock: The Life and Times of an Unknown Patriot*. New York: Appleton- Century, 1937.
Jameson, J. Franklin. "St. Eustatius in the American Revolution." In *The American Revolution in the West Indies*, edited by Charles W. Toth, 86–100. New York and London: Kennikat Press, 1975.
Jay, John. *The Making of a Revolutionary: Unpublished Papers, 1745–1780*, vol. 1, edited by Richard B. Morris. New York: Harper & Row, 1975.
Jay, John. *The Winning of the Peace: Unpublished Papers, 1780–1784*, vol. 2, edited by Richard B. Morris. New York: Harper & Row, 1980.
Johannsen, Robert W. *To the Halls of the Montezumas: The Mexican War in the American Imagination*. New York and Oxford: Oxford University Press, 1985.
Johnston, Henry P., ed. *The Correspondence and Public Papers of John Jay, vol. 2: 1782–1793*. New York: G.P. Putnam's Sons, 1891.
Journals of the Continental Congress, 1774–1789. 34 vols. Edited by Worthington C. Ford et al. Washington, D.C.: Government Printing Office, 1904–1937.
Juderías, Julián. *La leyenda negra: Estudios acerca del concepto de España en el extranjero*. Madrid: Tip. de la Revista de Archivos, Bibliotecas y Museos, 1914.
Kagan, Richard, ed. *Spain in America: The Origins of Hispanism in the United States*. Urbana and Chicago: University of Illinois Press, 2002.
Kagan, Richard. "From Noah to Moses: The Genesis of Historical Scholarship on Spain in the United States." In *Spain in America: The Origins of Hispanism in the United States*, edited by Richard Kagan, 21–47. Urbana and Chicago: University of Illinois Press, 2002.
Kagan, Richard. "Introduction." In *Spain in America: The Origins of Hispanism in the United States*, 1–20. Urbana and Chicago: University of Illinois Press, 2002.
Kagan, Richard. "The Spanish Craze in the United States: Cultural Entitlement and the Appropriation of Spain's Cultural Patrimony, ca. 1890 – ca. 1930." *Revista Complutense de Historia de América* 36 (2010): 37–58.
Kastor, Peter J. *The Nation's Crucible: The Louisiana Purchase and the Creation of America*. New Haven: Yale University Press, 2004.
Kennedy, Roger G. *Cotton and Conquest: How the Plantation System Acquired Texas*. Norman: University of Oklahoma Press, 2013.
Kerber, Linda K. "The Republican Mother: Women and the Enlightenment – An American Perspective." *American Quarterly* 28, no. 2 (1976): 187–205.
Kerber, Linda K. *Women of the Republic: Intellect and Ideology in Revolutionary America*. Chapel Hill: University of North Carolina, 1980.
Kierner, Cynthia A. *Traders and Gentlefolk: The Livingstons of New York, 1675–1790*. Ithaca, NY: Cornell, 1992.
King, James Ferguson. "Evolution of the Free Slave Trade Principle in Spanish Colonial Administration." *The Hispanic American Historical Review* 22, no. 1 (1942): 34–56.
Kinnaird, Lawrence. "The Spanish Expedition against Fort St. Joseph in 1781: A New Interpretation." *The Mississippi Valley Historical Review* 19, no. 2 (1932): 173–191.
Kinnaird, Lawrence, ed. "Documents: The Clark-Leyba Papers." *The American Historical Review* 41 (1935): 92–112.

Kinnaird, Lawrence. *Spain in the Mississippi Valley, 1765–1794.* 3 vols. Washington: U. S. Government Printing Office, 1946–1949.

Kinnaird, Lawrence, ed. *Annual Report of the American Historical Association for the Year 1945: Spain in the Mississippi Valley, 1765–1794.* 4 vols. Washington D.C.: Government Printing Office, 1949.

Klein, Milton M. *The American Whig: William Livingston of New York.* New York: Garland, 1993

Klooster, Wim. *Revolutions in the Atlantic World.* New York: New York University Press, 2009.

Kocka, Jürgen. "Comparison and Beyond." *History and Theory* 42 (2003): 39–44.

Kramer, Paul A. "Historias Transimperiales: Raíces Españolas del Estado Colonial Estadounidense en Filipinas." In *Filipinas, Un País Entre Dos Imperios,* edited by María Dolores Elizalde and Josep M. Delgado, 125–144. Barcelona: Bellaterra Ediciones, 2011.

Kraselsky, Javier. "Las Juntas de comercio y el Consulado de Buenos Aires y sus relaciones con la Corona: Los préstamos y donativos a fines del siglo XVIII y principios del XIX." In *Cambio institucional y fiscalidad: Mundo hispánico, 1760–1850,* edited by Michel Bertrand and Zakarías Moutoukías, 329–345. Madrid: Casa de Velázquez, 2018.

Kuethe, Allan. *Cuba, 1753–1815: Crown, Military, and Society.* Knoxville: University of Tennessee Press, 1986.

Kuethe, Allan. and Kenneth J. Andrien. *The Spanish Atlantic World in the Eighteenth Century: War and the Bourbon Reforms, 1713–1796.* Cambridge: Cambridge University Press. 2014.

Landers, Jane. "Spanish Sanctuary: Fugitives in Florida, 1687–1790." *The Florida Historical Quarterly* 62, no. 3 (1984): 296–313.

Landers, Jane. "Gracia Real de Santa Teresa de Mose: A Free Black Town in Spanish Colonial Florida." *American Historical Review* 95 (1990): 9–30.

Landers, Jane. *Black Society in Spanish Florida.* Urbana: University of Illinois Press, 1999.

Landers, Jane. *Atlantic Creoles in the Age of Revolutions.* Cambridge, MA: Harvard University Press, 2010.

Lasso, Marixa. *Myths of Harmony. Race and Republicanism during the Age of Revolution. Colombia, 1795–1831.* Pittsburgh: University of Pittsburgh Press, 2007.

Leavelle, Tracy. "Geographies of Encounter: Religion and Contested Spaces in Colonial North America." *American Quarterly* 56, no. 4 (2004): 913–943.

Lee, Richard Henry. *Life of Arthur Lee, LL.D,* 2 vols. Freeport, NY: Books for Libraries Press 1969 [1829].

Lesaffer, Randal. "Alberico Gentili's ius post bellum and Early Modern Peace Treaties." In *The Roman Foundations of the Law of Nations: Alberico Gentili and the Justice of Empire,* edited by Benedict Kingsbury and Benjamin Straumann, 210–240. Oxford: Oxford University Press, 2010.

Lewis, James A. "Las Damas de la Havana, el Precursor, and Francisco de Saavedra: A Note on Spanish Participation in the Battle of Yorktown." *The Americas* 37, no. 1 (1980): 83–99

Lewis, James A. *The Final Campaign of the American Revolution: Rise and Fall of the Spanish Bahamas.* Columbia: University of South Carolina Press, 1991.

Lewis, James A. *Neptune's Militia: The Frigate South Carolina during the American Revolution.* Kent, OH and London: Kent State University Press, 1999.

Liss, Peggy K. *Atlantic Empires: The Network of Trade and Revolution, 1713–1826*. Baltimore: Johns Hopkins University Press, 1983.
Locke, John. *Two Treatises of Government*. London: Thomas Tegg, 1823.
Loewenstein, Karl. "The Presidency outside the United States: A Study in Comparative Political Institutions." *Journal of Politics* 11, no. 3 (1949): 447–496.
Logan, Rayford W. "Saint Domingue: Entrepôt for Revolutionaries." In *The American Revolution in the West Indies*, edited by Charles W. Toth, 101–111. National University Publications Series in American Studies. Port Washington, NY and London: Kennikat Press, 1975.
Longfellow, Henry Wadsworth. *The Spanish Student: A Play, in Three Acts*. Cambridge: J. Owen, 1843.
Longfellow, Henry Wadsworth. "The Spanish Jew's Tale; The Legend of Rabbi Ben Levi" (poem). In *Tale of a Wayside Inn*. Boston: Ticknor and Fields, 1863a.
Longfellow, Henry Wadsworth. "The Spanish Jew's Second Tale; Scanderbeg" (poem). In *Tale of a Wayside Inn*. Boston: Ticknor and Fields, 1863b.
Longfellow, Henry Wadsworth. "The Spanish Jew's Tale; Azrael" (poem). In *Tale of a Wayside Inn*. Boston: Ticknor and Fields, 1863c.
Longfellow, Henry Wadsworth. *Tale of a Wayside Inn*. Boston: Ticknor and Fields, 1863d.
López Cantos, Ángel. *Don Francisco de Saavedra, segundo intendente de Caracas*. Seville: Escuela de Estudios Hispano-Americanos, 1978.
López-Cordón Cortezo, María Victoria. "Secretarios y secretarías en la edad moderna: De las manos del príncipe a relojeros de la monarquía." *Studia historica. Historia moderna* 15 (1996): 107–131.
Lorente, Marta and José María Portillo, eds. *El momento gaditano. La constitución en el orbe hispánico, 1808–1826*. Madrid: Congreso de Diputados, 2011.
Lucena-Giraldo, Manuel. *Laboratorio tropical. La expedición de límites al Orinoco, 1754–1761*. Caracas: Monte Ávila-CSIC, 1993.
Lucena-Giraldo, Manuel, ed. *Premoniciones de la independencia. Las reflexiones de José de Ábalos y el Conde de Aranda sobre la situación de la América española a finales del siglo xviii*. Madrid: Mapfre, 2003.
Lutz, Donald S. *The Origins of American Constitutionalism*. Baton Rouge: Louisiana State University Press, 1988.
Lynch, John, "British Policy and Spanish America, 1783–1808." *Journal of Latin American Studies* 1, no. 1 (1969): 1–30.
Lynch, John. *Bourbon Spain: 1700–1808*. Oxford: Basil Blackwell, 1989.
Lynch, John. *La España del siglo XVIII*. 4th ed. Barcelona: Crítica, 2009.
Lyons, Benjamin C. "John Jay and the Law of Nations in the Diplomacy of the American Revolution." PhD diss., New York: Columbia University, 2017.
Maltby, William S. *The Black Legend in England: The Development of Anti-Spanish Sentiment, 1558–1660*. Durham, NC: Duke University Press, 1971.
Manfredi Cano, Domingo. *Españoles en el Atlántico norte*. Madrid: Publicaciones Españolas, 1955.
Manrique, Jorge. *Coplas de don Joge [sic Jorge] Manrique*, trans. Henry Wadsworth Longfellow. Boston: Allen and Ticknor, 1833.
Mapp, Paul W. "Interpretive Implications of a Continental Approach." Paper presented at the 2009 The William and Mary Quarterly-EMSI workshop, 3, 2009.
Mapp, Paul. *The Elusive West and the Contest for Empire, 1713–1763*. Chapel Hill: University of North Carolina Press, 2011.
Marco, Miguel Angel de. *Corsarios argentinos*. Buenos Aires: Planeta, 2002.

Marfil García, Mariano. *Relaciones entre España y la Gran Bretaña desde las paces de Utrecht hasta nuestros días*. Madrid: Est. tipográfico de los hijos de R. Álvarez, 1907.

Marichal, Carlos. "Las guerras imperiales y los préstamos novohispanos, 1781–1804." *Historia Mexicana* 39, no. 4 (1990): 881–907.

Marichal, Carlos. *Bankruptcy of Empire: Mexican Silver and the Wars between Spain, Britain, and France*. Cambridge: Cambridge University Press, 2007.

Marques, Leonardo. *The United States and the Transatlantic Slave Trade to the Americas, 1776–1867*. New Haven: Yale University Press, 2016.

Martínez Garnica, Armando, Daniel Gutiérrez Ardila, and Isidro Vanegas, eds. *José Joaquín Camacho, Biografía y documentos de su pensamiento y acción política en la Revolución de Independencia*. Tunja: Academia Boyacense de Historia, 2010.

Max, Stanley. "A Re-Evaluation of the Spanish Raid on Fort St. Joseph, Michigan, in 1781." *The Great Lakes Review* 11, no. 1 (1985): 12–22.

McCadden, Helen Matzke. "Juan de Miralles and the American Revolution." *The Americas* 29, no. 3 (1973): 359–375.

McCool, Daniel, Susan M. Olson, and Jennifer L. Robinson. *Native Vote: American Indians, the Voting Rights Act and the Right to Vote*. Cambridge: Cambridge University Press, 2007.

McDermott, John Francis, ed. *The Spanish in the Mississippi Valley 1762–1804*. Urbana: University of Illinois Press, 1974.

McDonnell, Michael. *Masters of Empire: Great Lakes Indians and the Making of America*. New York: Hill and Wang, 2015.

McFarlane, Anthony. "'The Rebellion of the Barrios': Urban Insurrection in Bourbon Quito." *Hispanic American Historical Review* 69, no. 2 (1989): 283–330.

McFarlane, Anthony. *Colombia before Independence: Economy, Society and Politics under Bourbon Rule*. Cambridge: Cambridge University Press, 1993.

McFarlane, Anthony. "Rebellions in Late Colonial Spanish America: A Comparative Perspective." *Bulletin of Latin American Research* 14, no. 3 (1995): 313–339.

McFarlane, Anthony. "Building Political Order: The First Republic in New Granada, 1810–1815." In *In Search of a New Order: Essays on the Politics and Society of Nineteenth-Century Latin America*, edited by Eduardo Posada-Carbó, 8–33. London: Institute of Latin American Studies, 1998.

McFarlane, Anthony. "Science and Sedition in Spanish America: New Granada in the Age of Revolution, 1776–1810." In *Enlightenment and Emancipation*, edited by Susan Manning and Peter France, 97–117. Lewisburg: Bucknell University Press, 2006.

McFarlane, Anthony. "The American Revolution and the Spanish Monarchy." In *Europe's American Revolution*, edited by Simon P. Newman, 26–50. London: Palgrave Macmillan, 2006.

McFarlane, Anthony. *War and Independence in Spanish America*. New York: Routledge, 2014.

Medina Encina, Purificación, ed. *Documentos relativos a la independencia de Norteamérica existentes en archivos españoles, vol. 1, Archivo General de Indias Sección de Gobierno (años 1752–1822)*. Madrid: Ministerio de Asuntos Exteriores, 1977.

Medina Rojas, F. de Borja. *José de Ezpeleta, Gobernador de La Mobila, 1780–1781*. Sevilla: Escuela de Estudios Hispano-Americanos, Consejo Superior de Investigaciones Científicas and Excma. Diputación Foral de Navarra, 1980.

Mejía, Sergio. *La revolución en letras. La historia de la revolución de Colombia de José Manuel Restrepo, 1781–1863*. Bogotá and Medellín: Universidad de los Andes, 2007.

Melaffe, Rolando. *Negro Slavery in Latin America*. Berkeley: University of California Press, 1975.
Merino, José Patricio. *Las cuentas de la Administración central española, 1750–1820*. Madrid: Instituto de Estudios Fiscales 1987.
Michigan Pioneer and Historical Collections. 40 vols. Lansing, MI: Michigan Historical Commission, 1886–1912.
Miranda, Francisco de. *Diario de viaje a Estados Unidos, 1783–1784*. Santiago: Dirección de Bibliotecas, Archivos y Museos, 1998.
Missouri Historical Society Collections. 5 vols. St. Louis: The Missouri Historical Society, 1900–1931.
Monroy, Douglas. *Thrown among Strangers: The Making of Mexican Culture in Frontier California*. Berkeley: University of California Press, 1990.
Morales Padrón, Francisco. *Participación de España en la independencia política de los Estados Unidos*. Madrid: Publicaciones Españolas, 1952a.
Morales Padrón, Francisco. *Spanish Help in American Independence*. Madrid: Publicaciones Españolas, 1952b.
Morales Padrón, Francisco. *Conquistadores españoles en Estados Unidos*. Madrid: Publicaciones Españolas, 1955a.
Morales Padrón, Francisco. *Pedro de Alvarado*. Madrid: Publicaciones Españolas, 1955b.
Moreno Alonso, Manuel. *La Forja del Liberalismo en España: Los Amigos Españoles de Lord Holland, 1793–1840*. Madrid: Congreso de los Diputados, 1997.
Morgan, Philip D., and Jack P. Greene. "Introduction: The Present State of Atlantic History." In *Atlantic History: A Critical Appraisal*, edited by Jack P. Greene and Philip D. Morgan, 3–34. New York: Oxford University Press, 2009.
Morris, Richard B. *Peacemakers: The Great Powers and American Independence*. New York: Harper & Row, 1965.
Morris, Richard B., et al., eds. *John Jay: Unpublished Papers*. New York: Harper & Row, 1975 and 1980.
Morrissey, Robert. *Empire by Collaboration: Indians, Colonists, and Governments in Colonial Illinois Country*. Philadelphia: University of Pennsylvania Press, 2015.
Musick, James. *St. Louis as a Fortified Town: A Narrative and Critical Essay of the Period of Struggle for the Fur Trade of the Mississippi Valley and Its Influence upon St. Louis*. St. Louis: Press of R.F. Miller, 1941.
Narrett, David E. "Liberation and Conquest: John Hamilton Robinson and U.S. Adventurism toward Mexico, 1806–1819." *The Western Historical Quarterly* 40, no. 1 (2009): 23–50.
Narrett, David. *Adventurism and Empire: The Struggle for Mastery in the Louisiana-Florida Borderlands, 1762–1803*. Chapel Hill: University of North Carolina Press, 2015.
Nasatir, Abraham. "The Anglo-Spanish Frontier in the Illinois Country during the American Revolution 1779–1783." *Journal of the Illinois State Historical Society* 21, no. 3 (1928): 291–358.
Nasatir, Abraham. "Ducharme's Invasion of Missouri, an Incident in the Anglo-Spanish Rivalry for the Indian Trade of Upper Louisiana, Part III." *Missouri Historical Review* 24, no. 3 (1930): 420–439.
Nassaney, Michael, et al. "*Fort St. Joseph 2017 Annual Report*." Kalamazoo, MI: January 2018.
National Archives. Founders Online: Correspondence and Other Writings of Six Major Shapers of the United States. https://founders.archives.gov (accessed February 1, 2018).

Navarro García, Luis. *Don Jose de Gálvez y la Comandancia General de las Provincias Internas del norte Nueva España*. Sevilla: G.E.H.A., 1964.

Nichols, Roy F. "William Shaler: New England Apostle of Rational Liberty." *The New England Quarterly* 9, no. 1 (1936): 71–96.

Niles History Center website. www.nilesmi.org/departments_and_divisions/niles_history_center/index.php/visit/fort-st-joseph-museum (accessed February 1, 2018).

Noizet de Saint-Paul, Gaspard. *Traité complet de fortification*. Paris: Barrois l'aîné, 1792. [Spanish translation: *Elementos de fortificación escritos en francés por Noizet Saint-Paul, coronel de ingenieros y traducidos al castellano para el uso de los caballeros cadetes del regimiento real de zapadores-minadores-pontoneros*. Madrid: Imprenta Real, 1818].

North, Louise V., et al., eds. *Selected Letters of John Jay and Sarah Livingston Jay: Correspondence by or to the First Chief Justice of the United States and His Wife*. Jefferson, NC: McFarland, 2004.

Norton, Mary Beth. *Liberty's Daughters: The Revolutionary Experience of American Women, 1750–1800*. Boston: Little, Brown, 1980.

Noya, Javier, Beatriz Rodríguez, and Antonia María Ruiz Jiménez. *La imagen de España en Estados Unidos, Documento de Trabajo no. 44 (2008)*. Madrid: Real Instituto Elcano, 2008.

Nunemaker, J. Horace. "Louisiana Anticipates Spain's Recognition of the Independence of the United States." *Louisiana Historical Quarterly* 26 (1943): 755–769.

Nussbaum, Arthur. *A Concise History of the Law of Nations*. New York: Macmillan, 1947.

Nuxoll, Elizabeth Miles, et al., eds. *The Selected Papers of John Jay*. Charlottesville: University of Virginia, 2010–2017.

O'Malley, Gregory. *Final Passages: The Intercolonial Slave Trade of British America, 1619–1807*. Chapel Hill: University of North Carolina Press, 2014.

O'Shaughnessy, Andrew Jackson. *An Empire Divided: The American Revolution and the British Caribbean*. Philadelphia: University of Pennsylvania Press, 2000.

Ortiz, Sergio Elías, ed. *Escritos de dos economistas coloniales*. Bogotá: Banco de la República, 1965.

Otero, Michael A. "The American Mission of Diego de Gardoqui, 1785–1789." PhD diss., Los Angeles: University of California, 1948.

Pagden, Anthony. *Spanish Imperialism and the Political Imagination*. New Haven and London: Yale University Press, 1990.

Pagden, Anthony. *Lords of All the World: Ideologies of Empire in Spain, Britain and France, c.1500–c.1800*. New Haven andLondon: Yale University Press, 1995.

Paine, Robert Treat. "*Spain: An Account of the Public Festival Given by the Citizens of Boston ... – January 24, 1809*." Boston, MA: Printed by Russel and Cutler, 1809.

Paine, Thomas. *La independencia de la Costa Firme justificada por Thomas Paine treinta años ha. Extracto de sus obras, traducido del inglés al español por D. Manuel García de Sena*. Caracas: Instituto Panamericano de Geografía e Historia, 1948 [first published in Philadelphia 1811].

Palmer, Robert R. *The Age of Democratic Revolution: A Political History of Europe and America, 1760–1800*. Princeton: Princeton University Press, 1959 and 1964.

Palmer, William. *Calendar of Virginia State Papers and Other Manuscripts from January 1, 1785 to July 2, 1789 Preserved in the Capitol at Richmond*, vol. 4. Richmond: R.U. Derr, Superintendent of Public Printing, 1884.

Panero, Daniel. *La campaña de Gibraltar 1779–1783*. Madrid: Almena, 2008.

"Papers relating to Bourbon County, Georgia, 1785–1786." *American Historical Review Volume XV, October 1909 to July 1910*. London: The Macmillan Company, 1910.

Paquette, Gabriel B. "Enlightened Narratives and Imperial Rivalry in Bourbon Spain: The Case of Almodóvar's *Historia Política de los Establecimientos Ultramarinos de las Naciones Europeas* (1784–1790)." *The Eighteenth Century* 48, no. 1 (2007): 61–80.

Paquette, Gabriel B. *Enlightenment, Governance and Reform in Spain and its Empire, 1759–1808*. New York: Palgrave Macmillan, 2008.

Paquette, Gabriel B. "The Dissolution of the Spanish Atlantic Monarchy." *Historical Journal* 52, no. 1 (2009): 175–212.

Paquette, Gabriel B. *Imperial Portugal in the Age of Atlantic Revolutions: The Luso-Brazilian World, c. 1770–1850*. Cambridge: Cambridge University Press, 2013.

Patterson, A. Temple. *The Other Armada: The Franco-Spanish Attempt to Invade Britain in 1779*. Manchester: Manchester University Press, 1960.

Pearce, Adrian J. *British Trade with Spanish America, 1763–1808*. Liverpool: Liverpool University Press, 2007.

Perez Tisserant, Emmanuelle. "Nuestra California. Faire Californie entre deux constructions nationales et impériales (vers 1810–1850)." PhD diss., Paris: École des Hautes Études en Sciences Sociales, 2014.

Perez Tisserant, Emmanuelle. "The Evolution of Political Practices in Mexican Alta California and the Rise of the Diputados." *California History* 91, no. 1 (2014): 72–73.

Perkins, Bradford. "Bemis Regit! A Diplomatic History of the American Revolution (Review)." *Reviews in American History* 14, no. 2 (1986): 195–199.

Phelan, John L. *The People and the King: The Comunero Revolution in Colombia, 1781*. Madison: University of Wisconsin Press, 1978.

Phillips, George Harwood. *Indians and Intruders in Central California, 1769–1849*. Norman: University of Oklahoma Press, 1993.

Pombo, José Ignacio de. *Comercio y contrabando en Cartagena*. Bogotá: Universidad Nacional de Colombia, 1986.

Pombo, Manuel A., and José Joaquín Guerra, eds. *Constituciones de Colombia*. Bogotá: Biblioteca Popular de la Cultura Colombiana, 1951.

Portillo Valdés, José M. *Crisis Atlántica: Autonomía e independencia en la crisis de la monarquía española*. Madrid: Marcial Pons, 2006.

Posada-Carbó, Eduardo, ed. *In Search of a New Order: Essays on the Politics and Society of Nineteenth-Century Latin America*. London: Institute of Latin American Studies, 1998.

Posada-Carbó, Eduardo. "Translating the US Constitution for the Federal Cause in New Granada at the Time of Independence." In *Translations in Times of Disruption: An Interdisciplinary Study in Transnational Contexts*, edited by David Hook and Graciela Iglesias-Rogers, 119–145. London: Palgrave, 2017.

Potts, Louis W. *Arthur Lee: A Virtuous Revolutionary*. Baton Rouge: Louisiana State University Press, 1981.

Powell, Philip Wayne. *Tree of Hate: Propaganda and Prejudices Affecting United States Relations with the Hispanic World*. New York: Basic Books, 1971.

Prado, Fabricio. *Edge of Empire: Atlantic Networks and Revolution in Bourbon Río de la Plata*. Berkeley: University of California Press, 2015.

Prado, Fabricio. "Inter-American Networks." *Colonial Latin American Review*, forthcoming.

Prescott, William Hickling. *History of the Reign of Ferdinand and Isabella, the Catholic*. Boston: American Stationers' Company, 1838.

Prescott, William Hickling. *History of the Conquest of Mexico.* Chicago: Hooper, Clarke, & Co., 1843.
Prescott, William Hickling. *History of the Conquest of Peru, with a Preliminary View of the Civilization of the Incas.* New York: Harper and Brothers, 1847.
Prescott, William Hickling. *History of the Reign of Philip the Second, King of Spain.* Boston: Phillips, Sampson & Co., 1858–1859.
Priestley, H.I. *José de Gálvez, Visitor-General of New Spain (1765–1771).* Berkeley: University of California Press, 1916.
Prince, Carl E., et al., eds. *The Papers of William Livingston.* New Brunswick: Rutgers, 1978–1988.
Pubols, Louise. *The Father of All: The De La Guerra Family, Power, and Patriarchy in Mexican California.* Berkeley: University of California Press and Huntington Library, 2009.
Quintero Saravia, Gonzalo M. *Bernardo de Gálvez: Spanish Hero of the American Revolution.* Chapel Hill: The University of North Carolina Press, 2018.
Real Academia Española. *Diccionario de la lengua castellana.* Madrid: Joaquín Ibarra, 1780.
Reeve, John. "British Naval Strategy: War on a Global Scale." In *Strategy in the American War of Independence: A Global Approach*, edited by Donald Stoker, Kenneth J. Hagan, and Michael T. McMaster, 73–99. New York: Routledge, 2010.
Renaut, Francis P. *Le Pacte de Famille et l'Amérique: La politique coloniale franco-espagnole de 1760 à 1792.* Paris: Leroux, 1922.
Reparaz, Carmen de. *I Alone: Bernardo de Gálvez and the Taking of Pensacola in 1781: A Spanish Contribution to the Independence of the United States* (trans. from the Spanish). Madrid: Ediciones de Cultura Hispánica, 1993.
Reps, John W. "New Madrid on the Mississippi." *Journal of the Society of Architectural Historians* 18, no. 1 (1959): 21–26.
Reséndez, Andrés. "National Identity on a Shifting Border: Texas and New Mexico in the Age of Transition, 1821–1848." *The Journal of American History* 86, no. 2 (1999): 668–688.
Reséndez, Andrés. "Getting Cured and Getting Drunk: State versus Market in Texas and New Mexico, 1800–1850." *Journal of the Early Republic* 22, no. 1 (2002): 77–103.
Reséndez, Andrés. *Changing National Identities at the Frontier: Texas and New Mexico, 1800–1850.* New York: Cambridge University Press, 2004.
Restrepo, José Manuel. *Historia de la revolución de la República de Colombia en la América Meridional.* Bogotá: Biblioteca Popular de Cultura Colombiana, 1942 [1st ed. 1827].
Restrepo Piedrahita, Carlos. "Las primeras constituciones políticas de Colombia y Venezuela." In *El primer constitucionalismo iberoamericano*, edited by José Luis Soberanes Fernández, 75–146. Madrid: Marcial Pons, 1992.
Ribes-Iborra, Vicente. "La era Miralles: El momento de los agentes secretos." In *Norteamérica a finales del siglo XVIII: España y los Estados Unidos*, edited by Isabel García-Montón, Eduardo Garrigues, Almudena Hernández Ruigómez, Sylvia L. Hilton, and Emma Sánchez Montañés, 143–169. Madrid: Fundación Consejo España–Estados Unidos and Editorial Marcial Pons, 2008.
Rickey, Don. "The British-Indian Attack on St. Louis, May 26, 1780." *Missouri Historical Review* 55, no. 1 (1960): 35–42.
Riley, Sandra. *Homeward Bound: A History of the Bahama Islands to 1850 with a Definitive Study of Abaco in the American Loyalist Plantation Period.* Miami: Island Research, 2000.

Rives, George L. "Spain and the United States in 1795." *American Historical Review* 4, no. 1 (1898): 62–79.
Roberts, Stephen G.H., and Adam Sharman, eds. *1812 Echoes: The Cádiz Constitution in Hispanic History, Culture and Politics*. Newcastle upon Tyne: Cambridge Scholars Publishing, 2013.
Robertson, James A. "Spanish Correspondence Concerning the American Revolution." *Hispanic American Historical Review* 1, no. 3 (1918): 299–316.
Robertson, James A., and Paul Alliot, ed., *Louisiana Under the Rule of Spain France, and the United States, 1785–1807: Social, Economic, and Political Conditions of the Territory Represented in the Louisiana Purchase*, vol. 1. Cleveland, OH: The Arthur H. Clark Company, 1911.
Roca Barea, María Elvira. *Imperiofobia y leyenda negra: Roma, Rusia, Estados Unidos y el Imperio español*. Madrid: Siruela, 2016.
Rodríguez, Mario. *La revolución americana de 1776 y el mundo hispánico: Ensayos y documentos*, Madrid: Technos, 1976.
Rodríguez Casado, Vicente. "Política exterior de Carlos III en torno al problema indiano." *Revista de Indias* 5 (1944): 227–266.
Rodríguez González, Agustín Ramón. *Trafalgar y el conflicto naval Anglo-Español del siglo XVIII*. Madrid: Actas Editorial, 2005.
Rodríguez O., Jaime E. *The Independence of Spanish America*. Cambridge: Cambridge University Press, 1998.
Rodríguez O., Jaime E. "Sobre la supuesta influencia de la independencia de los Estados Unidos en las independencias hispanoamericanas." *Revista de Indias* LXX, no. 250 (2010): 691–714.
Roosevelt, Theodore. *The Winning of the West*. New York: G.P. Putnam's Sons & The Knickerbocker Press, 1889–1896.
Rueda Soler, Natividad. *La compañía de comercio "Gardoqui e hijos", sus relaciones políticas y económicas con Norteamerica 1770–1780*. Vitoria-Gasteiz: Servicio central de publicaciones del Gobierno vasco-Eusko Jaurlaritzaren argitalpen zerbitzu nagusia, 1992.
Ruigómez de Hernández, María Pilar. *El gobierno español del despotismo ilustrado ante la independencia de los Estados Unidos de América: una nueva estructura de la política internacional (1773–1783)*. Madrid: Ministerio de Asuntos Exteriores, 1978.
Rush, N. Orwin. *Spain's Final Triumph over Great Britain in the Gulf of Mexico: The Battle of Pensacola, March 9 to May 8, 1781*. Tallahassee: Florida State University, 1966.
Ryan, Mary P. *Civic Wars Democracy and Public Life in the American City during the Nineteenth Century*. Berkeley: University of California Press, 1997.
Saavedra, Francisco de. *The Journal of Don Francisco Saavedra de Sangronis, 1780–1783*, edited by Francisco Morales Padrón, trans. Aileen Moore Topping. Gainesville: University of Florida Press, 1989.
Saavedra, Francisco de. *Los Decenios (Autobiografía de un sevillano de la Ilustración)*, edited by Francisco Morales Padrón. Sevilla: Servicio de Publicaciones del Excmo. Ayuntamiento de Sevilla, 1995.
Saavedra, Francisco de. *Diario de don Francisco de Saavedra*, edited by Francisco Morales Padrón. Sevilla: Universidad de Sevilla - Consejo Superior de Investigaciones Científicas, 2004.
Sagredo, Antonio. "Personal Connections between Spaniards and Americans in the Revolutionary Era: Pioneers in Spanish-American Diplomacy." In *Legacy: Spain and the United States in the Age of Independence, 1763–1848*, edited by Dru Dowdy,

Raquel Mesa, and Jordi Penas, 44–63. Washington, D.C.: Smithsonian Institution, 2007.

Saiz Valdivielso, Alfonso Carlos. *Diego de Gardoqui: Esplendor y Penumbra.* Bilbao: Muelle de Uribitarte, 2014.

San Francisco, Alejandro. "Independencia: Un concepto político y social en revolución, 1770–1870." In *Independencia: Iberconceptos II, tomo 4: Diccionario político y social del mundo iberoamericano*, edited by Javier Fernández Sebastián, 15–32. Madrid: Universidad del País Vasco, 2014.

Sánchez, Rosaura. *Telling Identities: The Californio Testimonios.* Minneapolis: University of Minnesota Press, 1995.

Sánchez Carrión, José María. *De Constructores a Ingenieros de Marina: Salto tecnológico y profesional impulsado por Francisco Gautier.* Madrid: Fondo Editorial de Ingeniería Naval, 2013.

Sánchez-Fabrés Mirat, Elena. *Situación histórica de las Floridas en la segunda mitad del siglo XVIII (1783–1819). Los problemas de una región de frontera.* Madrid: Ministerio de Asuntos Exteriores, 1977.

Sánchez Mantero, Rafael. "La Mision de John Jay en España (1779–1782)." *Anuario de Estudios Americanos* 24 (1967): 1389–1431.

Sánchez Valverde, Antonio. *Idea del Valor de la Isla Española.* Trujillo, Dominican Republic: Editora Montalvo, 1947.

Santoyo, Julio-César. *Arthur Lee: historia de una embajada secreta.* Vitoria: Obra Cultural de la Caja de Ahorros Municipal, 1977.

Sanz y Díaz, José. *Fray Junípero Serra (Evangelista y fundador de la Alta California).* Madrid: Publicaciones españolas, 1953.

Sarrailh, Jean. *La España ilustrada en la segunda mitad del siglo XVIII.* México D.F.: Fondo de Cultura Económica, 1957.

Saunt, Claudio. *West of the Revolution: An Uncommon History of 1776.* New York: W. W. Norton, 2014.

Savelle, Max. "The Founding of New Madrid." *Mississippi Historical Review* 19, no. 1 (1932): 30–56.

Savelle, Max. *George Morgan: Colony Builder.* New York: Columbia University Press, 1932.

Schmidt-Nowara, Christopher. "Spanish Origins of the American Empire: Hispanism, History, and Commemoration, 1898–1915." *International History Review* 30, no. 1 (2008): 32–51.

Schneider, Elena. "African Slavery and Spanish Empire: Imperial Imaginings and Bourbon Reform in Eighteenth-century Cuba and Beyond." *Journal of Early American History* 5, no. 1 (2015): 3–29.

Schroeder, Paul. *The Transformation of European Politics, 1763–1848.* Oxford: Clarendon Press, 1994.

Scott, H.M. "The Importance of Bourbon Naval Reconstruction to the Strategy of Choiseul after the Seven Years' War." *The International History Review* 1, no. 1 (1979): 17–35.

Scott, H.M. *British Foreign Policy in the Age of the American Revolution.* Oxford: Oxford University Press, 1990.

Secret Journals of the Acts and Proceedings of Congress. Boston: Thomas Wait, 1820.

Seed, Patricia. *Ceremonies of Possession in Europe's Conquest of the New World, 1492–1640.* Cambridge: Cambridge University Press, 1995.

Serulnikov, Sergio. *Revolution in the Andes in the Age of Tupac Amaru.* Durham: Duke University Press, 2013.

Shafer, R.J. *The Economic Societies in the Spanish World (1763–1821)*. Syracuse: Syracuse University Press, 1958.
Silva, Renán. *Los ilustrados de Nueva Granada, 1760–1808: Genealogía de una comunidad de interpretación*. Medellín: Banco de la República, 2002.
Silverblatt, Irene. "The Black Legend and Global Conspiracies: Spain, the Inquisition, and the Emerging Modern World." In *Rereading the Black Legend: The Discourses of Religious and Racial Difference in the Renaissance Empires*, edited by Margaret R. Greer, Walter D. Mignolo, and Maureen Quilligan, 99–116. Chicago: University of Chicago Press, 2007.
Simmons, Merle E. *US Political Ideas in Spanish America before 1830: A Bibliographical Study*. Bloomington: Indiana University Press, 1977.
Simmons, Merle E. *La revolución norteamericana en la independencia de Hispanoamérica*. Madrid: Mapfre, 1992.
Simms, Brendan. *Three Victories and a Defeat: The Rise and Fall of the First British Empire, 1714–1783*. New York: Basic Books, 2007.
Simon, Joshua. *The Ideology of Creole Revolution: Imperialism and Independence in American and Latin American Political Thought*. Cambridge: Cambridge University Press, 2017.
Skaggs, David, and Larry Nelson, eds. *The Sixty Years' War for the Great Lakes, 1754–1814*. East Lansing: Michigan State University Press, 2001.
Smith, Gene Allen and Sylvia L. Hilton eds. *Nexus of Empire: Negotiating Loyalty and Identity in the Revolutionary Borderlands, 1760s-1820s*. Gainesville, FL: University Press of Florida, 2010.
Smith, Paul H., ed. *Letters of Delegates to Congress, 1774–1789*. Washington, D.C.: Library of Congress, 1976–2000.
Smith, William Henry, ed. *The St. Clair Papers: The Life and Public Services of Arthur St. Clair: Soldier of the Revolutionary War, President of the Continental Congress; and Governor of the North-Western Territory: With His Correspondence and Other Papers*. Cincinnati: R. Clarke & Company, 1882.
Soberanes Fernández, José Luis. ed. *El primer constitucionalismo iberoamericano*. Madrid: Marcial Pons, 1992.
Sobrevilla Perea, Natalia. "Loyalism and Liberalism in Peru." In *The Rise of Constitutional Government*, edited by Scott Eastman and Natalia Sobrevilla Perea, 111–132. Tuscaloosa: The University of Alabama Press, 2015.
Sparks, Jared, ed. *The Diplomatic Correspondence of the American Revolution*. Boston: N. Hale, Gray, and Bowen, 1829.
Stagg, J.C.A. *Borderlines in Borderlands: James Madison and the Spanish-American Frontier, 1776–1821*. New Haven: Yale University Press, 2009.
Stahr, Walter. *John Jay*. New York: Hambledon, 2006
Starr, Joseph Barton. *Tories, Dons, and Rebels: The American Revolution in British West Florida*. Gainesville: University Presses of Florida, 1976.
Stein, Stanley J., and Barbara H. Stein. *Apogee of Empire: Spain and New Spain in the Age of Charles III, 1759–1789*. Baltimore: Johns Hopkins University Press, 2003.
Sundiata, Ibrahim K. *From Slaving to Neoslavery: The Bight of Biafra and Fernando Po in the Era of Abolition, 1827–1930*. Madison: University of Wisconsin Press, 1995.
Sweet, James H. "The Iberian Roots of American Racist Thought." *William and Mary Quarterly* 3, no. 54 (1997): 143–166.
Tannenbaum, Frank. *Slave and Citizen: The Negro in the Americas*. New York: A. A. Knopf, 1946.

Tavarez, Fidel J. "Viscardo's Global Political Economy and the First Cry for Spanish American Independence, 1767–1798." *Journal of Latin American Studies* 48 (2015): 537–564.

Taylor, Alan. *The Divided Ground: Indians, Settlers, and the Northern Borderlands of the American Revolution*. New York: Alfred A. Knopf, 2006.

Taylor, Alan. *The Civil War of 1812: American Citizens, British Subjects, Irish Rebels, & Indian Allies*. New York: Vintage Books, 2010.

Taylor, Alan. *American Revolutions: A Continental History, 1750–1804*. New York: W. W. Norton & Co., 2016.

Tedde de Lorca, Pedro. "La Real Hacienda de Carlos III y la guerra de independencia de los Estados Unidos." In *Norteamérica a finales del siglo XVIII: España y los Estados Unidos*, edited by Isabel García-Montón, Eduardo Garrigues, Almudena Hernández Ruigómez, Sylvia L. Hilton, and Emma Sánchez Montañés, 221–224. Madrid: Fundación Consejo España–Estados Unidos and Editorial Marcial Pons, 2008.

Teggart, Frederick. "The Capture of St. Joseph, Michigan, by the Spaniards in 1781." *Missouri Historical Review* 5, no. 4 (1911): 214–228.

Teijeiro de la Rosa, Juan Miguel. "La financiación de la guerra en el siglo XVIII." *Revista de Historia Militar* 51 (2007): 97–118.

TePaske, John J. "The Fugitive Slave: Intercolonial Rivalry and Spanish Slave Policy, 1687–1764." In *Eighteenth-Century Florida and Its Borderlands*, edited by Samuel Proctor, 2–12. Gainesville, FL: University Presses of Florida, 1975.

Ternavasio, Marcela. "The Impact of Hispanic Constitutionalism in the Río de la Plata." In *The Rise of Constitutional Government*, edited by Scott Eastman and Natalia Sobrevilla Perea, 133–149. Tuscaloosa: The University of Alabama Press, 2015.

Terrón Ponce, José Luis. *El gran ataque a Gibraltar de 1782*. Madrid: Ministerio de Defensa, 2000.

Terrón Ponce, José Luis. *La reconquista de Menorca por el duque de Crillón (1781–1782): aspectos militares y políticos*. Mahón: Museo Militar San Felipe, 1981.

Thibaud, Clément. "La coyuntura de 1810 en tierra firme: confederaciones, constituciones, repúblicas." *Historia y Política* 24 (2010): 23–45.

Thibaud, Clément. *Libérer le Nouveau Monde: La fondation des premières républiques hispaniques (Colombia y Venezuela 1780–1820)*. Bécherel: Les Perséides, 2017.

Thomas, Alfred B. "The Gálvez Campaigns, 1779–1780." In *Siege! Spain and Britain: Battle of Pensacola, March 9–May 8, 1781*, edited by Virginia Parks, 39–44. Pensacola: Pensacola Historical Society, 1981.

Thomson, Buchanan Parker. *Spain: Forgotten Ally of the American Revolution*. North Quincy, MA: The Christopher Publishing House, 1976.

Ticknor, George. *Syllabus of a Course of Lectures on the History and Criticism of Spanish Literature*. Cambridge: Hilliard and Metcalf, 1823.

Ticknor, George. *History of Spanish Literature*. New York: Harper and brothers, 1849.

Tierney. Dominic. *FDR and the Spanish Civil War: Neutrality and Commitment in the Struggle that Divided America*. Durham: Duke University Press, 2007.

Tijerina, Andrés. *Tejanos and Texas under the Mexican Flag, 1821–1836*. College Station, TX: Texas A & M University Press, 1994.

Tornero Tinajero, Pablo. *Relaciones de Dependencia entre Florida y los Estados Unidos (1783–1820)*. Madrid: Ministerio de Asuntos Exteriores, 1979.

Tornquist, Karl Gustaf. *The Naval Campaigns of Count de Grasse during the American Revolution, 1781–1783*. Philadelphia: Swedish Colonial Society, 1942.

Torres Sánchez, Rafael. "Crecimiento y expansión económica en el siglo XVIII." In *Historia económica de España*, edited by Agustín González Enciso and Juan Manuel Matés Blanco, 135–158. Barcelona: Ariel, 2006.
Torres Sánchez, Rafael. *El precio de la guerra: El estado fiscal-militar de Carlos III (1779–1783)*. Madrid: Marcial Pons, 2013.
"Treaty of Friendship, Limits, and Navigation, signed at San Lorenzo el Real October 27, 1795." In *Treaties and Other International Acts of the United States of America, Vol. 2: Documents 1–40: 1776–1818*, edited by Hunter Miller, 318–346. Washington, D.C.: Government Printing Office, 1931.
Uribe-Urán, Victor. "The Birth of a Public Sphere in Latin American during the Age of Revolution." *Comparative Studies in History and Society* 42, no. 2 (2000): 437–448.
Uribe-Urán, Victor. "Derecho y cultura legal en la 'era de las revoluciones' en México, Colombia y Brasil, 1750–1850. La génesis de lo público y lo privado." In *Las revoluciones en el mundo Atlántico*, edited by María Teresa Calderón and Clément Thibaud, 251–297. Bogotá: Taurus, 2006.
Uribe-Urán, Victor. "Insurgentes de Provincia: Tunja, Nueva Granada y el constitucionalismo en el mundo hispánico en la década de 1810." *Historia y Memoria* 5 (2012): 17–48.
Uribe-Urán, Victor. "La constitución de Cádiz en la Nueva Granada. Teoría y realidad, 1812–1821." In *La constitución de 1812 en Hispanoamérica y España*, edited by Heraclio Bonilla, 275–280, Bogotá: Universidad Nacional de Colombia, 2012.
Urtasún, Valentín. *Historia Diplomática de América, Primera Parte. La Emancipación de las colonias Británicas y la Alianza Francesa*. Pamplona: Higinio Coronas, 1920–1924.
Usner, Daniel H. *Indians, Settlers & Slaves in a Frontier Exchange Economy: The Lower Mississippi Valley before 1783*. Chapel Hill: University of North Carolina Press, 1992.
Usner, Daniel H. "Borderlands." In *A Companion to Colonial America*, edited by Daniel Vickers, 408–424. Malden: Blackwell, 2006.
Vaca de Osma, José Antonio. *Intervención de España en la Guerra de Independencia de los Estados Unidos*. Madrid: Aldus, S.A., 1952.
Valdez-Bubnov, Ivan. *Poder naval y modernización del Estado: política de construcción naval española, siglos XVI–XVIII*. Madrid: Iberoamericana, 2011.
Valle Pavón, Guillermina del. "Respaldo financiero de Nueva España para la guerra contra Gran Bretaña 1779–1783. La intermediación financiera del Consulado de México." In *Guerra y fiscalidad en la Iberoamérica colonial (Siglos XVII– XIX)*, edited by Ernest Sánchez Santiró and Ángelo Alves Carrara, 143–166. México D. F.: Instituto de Investigaciones Dr. José María Luis Mora, 2012.
Vanegas, Isidro. *El constitucionalismo fundacional*. Bogotá: Plural, 2012.
Varela Suances, Joaquín. "Los modelos constitucionales en las Cortes de Cádiz." In *Las revoluciones hispánicas: Independencias americanas y el liberalismo español*, edited by François-Xavier Guerra, 243–268. Madrid: Universidad Complutense, 1995.
Varela Tortajada, Javier. "Nación, patria y patriotismo en los orígenes del nacionalismo español." *Studia historica: Historia contemporánea* 12 (1994): 31–43.
Vargas, Pedro Fermín de. *Pensamientos políticos*. Bogotá: Universidad Nacional de Colombia, 1968.
Vázquez de Acuña, Isidoro. *Historial de la Casa de Gálvez y sus alianzas*. Madrid: Villena Artes Gráficas, 1974.
Vergé-Franceschi, Michel. "Marine et Révolution, les officiers de 1789 et leur devenir." *Histoire, économie et société* 9, no. 2 (1990): 259–286.

Vidal, Cécile. "Pour une histoire globale du monde atlantique ou des histoires connectées dans et au-delà du monde atlantique?" *Annales. Histoire, Sciences Sociales* 67, no. 2 (2012): 391–413.

Vilá, Herminio Portell. *Juan de Miralles, Un Habanero Amigo de Jorge Washington*. Havana: Sociedad Colombista Panamericana, 1947.

Villacañas Berlanga, José Luis, ed. *El siglo de Floridablanca (1728–1808): La España de las reformas*. Murcia: Universidad de Murcia, 2009.

Villiers, Patrick. "La tentative franco-espagnole de débarquement en Angleterre de 1779." *Revue du Nord, Le Transmanche et les Liaisons Maritimes XVIIIe-XXe Siècle* Hors-série 9 (1995): 13–29.

Villiers, Patrick. "Sartine et la préparation de la flotte de guerre française 1775–1778: refontes ou constructions neuves?" In *Les Marines de la Guerre d'Indépendance Américaine, 1763–1783: I. L'instrument naval*, edited by Olivier Chaline, Philippe Bonnichon and Charles-Philippe de Vergennes, 65–75. Paris: PUPS, Presses de l'Université Paris-Sorbonne, 2013.

Viscardo Guzmán, Juan Pablo. *Obra Completa*. Lima: Congreso de la República del Perú, 1998.

Voltes Bou, Pedro. "La tentativa de mediación de España en la guerra de independencia de los Estados Unidos." *Revista de Indias* 27 (1967): 313–334.

Voyages: The Atlantic Slave Trade Database. www.slavevoyages.org (February 1, 2018).

Walker, Charles. *The Tupac Amaru Rebellion*. Cambridge, MA: Harvard University Press, 2014.

Walworth, Clarence. *Kaskaskia Records, 1778–1790*. Springfield, IL: Trustees of the Illinois State Historical Library, 1909.

Ward, Christopher. *The War of the Revolution*. New York: Skyhorse, 2011.

Wasserman, Fabio. "El concepto de nación y las transformaciones del orden político en Iberoamérica, 1750–1850." In *Diccionario político y social del mundo iberoamericano: La era de las revoluciones, 1750–1850. (Iberconceptos-I)*, edited by Javier Fernández Sebastián, vol. 1, 851–869. Madrid: Fundación Carolina, Sociedad Estatal de Conmemoraciones Culturales, and Centro de Estudios Políticos y Constitucionales, 2009.

Weber, David J. *The Spanish Frontier in North America*. New Haven: Yale University Press, 1992.

Weber, David J. *Bárbaros: Spaniards and their Savages in the Age of Enlightenment*. New Haven: Yale University Press, 2005.

Werner, Michael and Bénédicte Zimmermann. "Beyond Comparison: Histoire Croisée and the Challenge of Reflexivity." *History and Theory* 45 (2006): 30–50.

Wharton, Francis, ed. *Revolutionary Diplomatic Correspondence of the United States*. Washington D.C.: Government Printing Office, 1889.

Wheat, David. *Atlantic Africa and the Spanish Caribbean, 1570–1640*. Chapel Hill: University of North Carolina Press, 2016.

Whitaker, Arthur Preston. *The Spanish-American Frontier: 1783–1795. The Westward Movement and the Spanish Retreat in the Mississippi Valley*. Boston, MA: Houghton Mifflin Company, 1927.

Whitaker, Arthur Preston. *The Mississippi Question, 1795–1803*. Gloucester, MA: P. Smith, 1962.

White, Richard. *The Middle Ground: Indians, Empires, and Republics in the Great Lakes Region, 1650–1815*. Cambridge: Cambridge University Press, 1991.

Willcox, William B., et al., eds. *The Papers of Benjamin Franklin*. New Haven: Yale University Press, 1959–2017.

Williams, Robert F. "The Influences of Pennsylvania's 1776 Constitution on American Constitutionalism during the Founding Decade." *The Pennsylvania Magazine of History and Biography* 112, no. 1 (1988): 25–48.

Wright, James Leitch, Jr. *Florida in the American Revolution*. Gainesville: University Presses of Florida, 1975.

Yela Utrilla, Juan F. *España ante la independencia de los Estados Unidos*. Lérida: Academia Mariana, 1925.

Young, Raymond A. "Pinckney's Treaty: A New Perspective." *The Hispanic American Historical Review* 43, no 4 (1963): 526–535.

Zavala, Silvio. "A General View of the Colonial History of the New World." *American Historical Review* 66, no. 4 (1961): 913–929.

Zepeda Cortés, María Bárbara. "Empire, Reform, and Corruption: José de Gálvez and Political Culture in the Spanish World, 1765–1787." PhD diss., La Jolla: UC San Diego, 2013.

Index

References to illustrations are in **bold**.

Ábalos, José de 97; proposal for self-governing kingdoms 43–4
Acta de Federación (1811) 211
Adams, Abigail 167
Adams, John 2, 20
Adams, Samuel 212, 217
Adams, Willi Paul 219
Álava, Ignacio María 75
Alcaçovas, Treaty of (1479) 103
Alta California: American annexation (1848) 143; Mexican claim on 142; Spanish settlement 137, 139, 140
Alvarado, Juan Bautista 135, 136
American Revolution: and borderlands 172, 201; and end of Ancien Régime 30; official reactions 42–5; a Pacific view 135–43; and the slave trade 104–9; and Spain: historiography 3–7; Spanish American reactions 45–7; and Spanish American rebellions 39–42, 46; Spanish economic aid 11–12; and Spanish global interests 7–11, 100; and Spanish golden age 30; and the Spanish monarchy 38–9; and "the Age of Revolutions" 30; *see also* American War of Independence
American settlers, in Spanish Louisiana 199
American War of Independence: causes 67; clash of empires 92; historiography 5–6; intelligence gathering 188; naval forces 15; peace treaties 26; Spanish mediation 10–11, 96; Spanish navy in 92
The Americas (c.1775) map **3**
Anglo-French Alliance 62
Anglo-Luso Methuen Treaty (1703) 107

Annobón 111, 116; potential slave trade entrepôt 116; Spanish acquisition 109, 110, 112
Aranda, Conde de 44, 79, 97, 186
Aranjuez, Treaty (1779) 14–15, 81
Areche, José Antonio, Gen 106
Arequipa (Peru), rebellion 39
Argelejo, Felipe de, Conde 110–11
Articles of Confederation (1776) 211
Artigas, José Gervasio 212
Asedo, Francisco 75
Atlas de la América Septentrional 96
Austrian Succession, War of (1740–48) 63

Bahamas: and borderlands 172–3; privateers/corsairs 171, 172, 173–4, 175, 177, 178, 179; Spanish-American attack on 171–2, 177–8
Bailén, Battle of (1808) 98
Baquíjano y Carrillo, José de 49
Basel, Peace of (1795) 192
Baton Rouge, Spanish capture of 19, 82
Beaumarchais, Pierre-Augustin Caron de 186
Bemis, Samuel Flagg 4
Bentham, Jeremy, on Spain 29–30
bicameralism, Spanish America 56
Bight of Biafra, slave trade 107, 109, 110–16
Billias, George Athan 210
Black Legend, anti-Spanish narrative 4, 30n7, 91, 129, 184, 193
Bogotá, Santafe de 93
Bolton, Herbert Eugene 4
borderlands 140; America-Spain 142, 201; and the American Revolution

172, 201; and the Bahamas 172–3; California 138; Eastern 141; entangled 122; Georgia/Spanish Floridas 192; Great Lakes and Mississipi River 131; Mississippi Valley 199, 200; Natchez town 201; settlers 199; Spanish 6; Spanish-Portuguese 107; *see also* boundaries
Borucki, Alex 108
Bouligny, Francisco de, Cmndr 201
boundaries: *Dissertacion historica y geographica sobre el meridiano de demarcación* 94; Spain-Portugal 94–5, 107; *see also* borderlands
Bourbon armada: failure (in invasion of Britain 64, 65, 66, 67–70, 74–5), (in Napoleonic Wars 74–5), (in Seven Years' War 64); formation 62; intelligence gathering 70; Pensacola battle 70; rebuilding of 65–6; success (in American War of Independence 66–74, 76), (at Battle of Toulon/Cap Sicié 63); *see also* Spanish navy
Bourbon Family Compacts (1733–92) 10, 62, 63, 66, 67; end of 74
Bourbon reforms (1713–96) 92; culmination of 98; impact 8–9; purpose 87fn1; Spanish American resistance to 93
Bourchard, Hippolyte 140
Brackenbridge, Henry Marie 214
Brading, David 9
British Sea Ports Act (1766) 103
British-American War (1812) 140
British-Austrian Alliance (1731) 62
Buenos Aires 110; British attack on 51; Centralism 55
Bunker Hill, Battle of (1776) 77

Caballero y Góngora, Antonio, Archbishop 93
Cádiz Company 107
Cádiz, Constitution of (1812) 29, 52, 210; and Catholicism 53; Centralism 56; elements 53, 215; influence 53–4, 218; and New Spain 53; unified monarchy principle 53
Cagigal, Juan Manuel de, Capt-Gen 171, 175–6, 176, 177, 180
California: borderlands 138; ethnic population 141; *see also* Alta California
Campbell, Archibald, Governor of Jamaica 25
Campbell, John, Gen 20

Cape St Vincent, Battle of (1797) 74
Cape Spartel, Battle of (1782) 16, 73, 74, 75
Cape Trafalgar, Battle of (1805) 75; ships present 75
Carlos III, King of Spain 10, 17, 27, 64, 79, 92, 108; accession 39; animosity to Great Britain 148; and Enlightenment ideas 47
Carmen ship 114
Carmichael, William, John Jay's secretary 160, 161, 163, 168–9
Carrera, José Miguel 54
Cartagena: constitution 215; slave trade 216
cartography: importance of 96–7; *Maritime Atlas of Spain, 1783–1788* 97
Catholicism 205; and Cádiz, Constitution (1812) 53; *see also* Protestantism
Caughey, John Walton 4, 80
Centralism: Buenos Aires 55; Cádiz Constitution (1812) 56; and Federalism 55, 56; Restrepo on 211; Spanish navy 62; Torres on 213
Céspedes del Castillo, Guillermo 10
Cevallos, Pedro Antonio 108
Charles III *see* Carlos III
Cherokees 203, 204
Chesapeake Bay, Battle of (1781) 23, 71
Chevalier, Louison 127
Chicksaws 17, 27
Chile, republicanism 54
Choctaws 17, 27
Choiseul, Etienne-François de 64, 65
Churruca, Cosme Damián 75, 97
Clark, George Rogers 12, 124
Colonia, Spanish conquest of 108
Columbus, Christopher 193
Comuneros revolt 39, 40–1, 43–4, 48, 93; and the Enlightenment 49
Concord, Battle of (1775) 185
Connecticut, constitution 214
Continental Congresses 1, 24, 26, 105, 160
Cook, James, voyages 137
Córdova, Capt-Gen 68, 69, 71, 72, 73
Córdova y Córdova, Luis de, Admrl 96
Cossío y Cossío, Pedro Antonio de 81–2, 85
Creeks 17, 27
Creole intellectuals 48–9
Crillon, Duc de 71
Cruzat, Francisco, Lt-Gov 126, 127, 129, 130

Index

Cuba 78, 104; slave trade 106; US-Spanish tensions 29
Cumberland, Richard 1
Cundinamarca: constitution (1811) 214, 216; and Native Americans 217
customary law of nations 147, 155; honor 151, 154; legal procedure 149–50, 154; reputation 151, 154; *see also* law of nations

Deane, Silas 186
Delawares 203, 204
Depeyster, Arendt Schuyler 125, 127, 128–9, 129
Duane, James 174
DuVal, Kathleen 141, 172

Elliott, George Augustus 96
Enlightenment 28, 40, 46; and Carlos III 47; and Comuneros rebellion 49; Moderate vs Radical 48; in Spanish America 47–8
"Entangled History" concept 7
Escaño, Antonio de 75
Escobedo, Jorge de 93
Estudillo, José María de 135

Falkland/Malvinas Islands, political crisis 66
Federal Constitution, US (1787) 53, 55
Federalism: and Centralism 55, 56; New Granada 219; Spanish America 56; US Constitution 53, 54, 55
Felipe V, King of Spain 62
Fernando Pó 111; map **101**; potential slave trade entrepot 114, 116; Spanish acquisition 109, 110, 112, 113
Fernando VII, King of Spain 52, 56, 212
Fidalgo, Joaquín Francisco 97
Finestrad, Joaquín 49, 60n41
Flórez, Viceroy of New Granada 39, 40
Florida, Straits 172, 175, 178
Floridablanca, Conde de (José Moñino) 10, 11, 39, 67, 77, 199; *see also* Jay-Floridablanca negotiations (1980)
Folsom, Nathaniel 212
Foronda, Valentin de 51–2
Fort St. Joseph, Spanish capture of 122–3, 126, 127–8, 129, 130–1
Franco, Francisco, Gen 4
Franco-American alliance (1778) 148
Franklin, Benjamin 2, 164, 186, 187, 188
French Constitution (1791) 53

French Revolution 74; and Spanish America 50–1
French-Spanish armada *see* Bourbon armada
Fulbright Scholarships Program, Spain 5

galofobia 92
Gálvez, Bernardo de, Lt-Col 7, 12, 16, 20, 27, 70–1, 77, 78, 175; American connections 188; victories in America 18–19, 21
Gálvez, José de 39, 40, 43; American Revolution, war preparations 78–9, 80–1, 86–7, 106; family prestige 86; Minister of the Indies 184
Gálvez, Matías de, Capt-Gen of Guatemala 25, 77, 78, 83
Gardoqui, Diego de 153, 159, 186, 202; envoy to America 167, 191; on John Jay 167
Gardoqui, José 75
Gautier, Jean-François, shipbuilder 65, 68
Geodesic Mission to the Equator (1735–44) 62
George III, King of Great Britain and Ireland 8, 17, 18
Gibraltar 14, 15, 29; British capture of 72; negotiations over 17–18; siege (1779–83) 96; Spanish campaign to regain 16, 72–3, 177
Gibson, George, Capt 187
Gillon, Alexander, Cdre 24, 171, 176, 177, 180
ginseng trade 138
Godoy, Manuel 192
Gould, Eliga H. 27; "Spanish Periphery" concept 7
Grasse, Comte de, Admrl 71, 84–5
Graves, Thomas, Sir, RAdmrl 23
Gravier, Charles, Comte de Vergennes 66
Gravina, Federico, Capt-Gen 75
Great Britain, Spain, slave trade cooperation 100
Great Lakes, Spanish presence 122–3
Green, Thomas 201
Grimaldi, Jerónimo 64, 65, 66, 186
Grotius, Hugo 147
Guatemala 78
Guichen, Comte de, Lt-Gen 71

Haitian Revolution 93

Havana 176; British capture of 9, 64, 78, 93, 104; recapture by Spain 104; slave trade 116
Hemingway, Ernest 4
Hispanics (Latinos), status in US census 5
HMS *Victory* 68
Horrible Atrocities of Spaniards in Cuba 4
Howe, Richard, Admrl 73
Huntington, Archer Milton, New York Hispanic Society 4

Iberian Peninsula, French invasion (1808) 9
Igler, David 143
Ildefonso, Treaty (1777) 109
Illinois, Spanish 124
immigration policies, Spain 143, 198–205
Inca revival 41
independence, Vattel on 45
Indians *see* Native Americans
intelligence gathering: American War of Independence 188; Bourbon armada 70; by French in England 65; in colonial wars 51; and Mexican wars of independence 140, 142; and siege of Gibraltar 72
Irving, Washington 4

Jackson, Andrew 140
Jackson, Gabriel 4
Jaksic, Ivan 29
Jamaica 23–4, 76
Jaudenes, José de 192
Jay, John 1–2, 129; diplomacy in Spain 147, 148, 149, 150–5, 164, 175; Secretary for Foreign Affairs 166
Jay, Sarah Livingston: domestic conflicts 163; education of family 165–6; family 159–60; in France 164; letters 159, 161; in Madrid 162; opinion of Aranjuez 162–3; "republican motherhood" 165; travels 160–2
Jay-Floridablanca negotiations (1980) 147, 150, 151
Jay–Gardoqui Treaty (1786), failure 192, 199
Jefferson, Thomas 27–8, 28, 105, 139
Juan, Jorge & Antonio de Ulloa, *Dissertacion historica y geographica sobre el meridiano de demarcación* 95

Kagan, Richard L. 4
Kickapoos 124

law of nations: treatises 147, 149; Vattel on 45; *see also* customary law of nations
Ledyard, John 137–8
Lee, Arthur 148, 186, 187
Lewis, Francis 189
Lewis, James 85
Lexington, Battle of (1775) 185
liberty, contested term 202
Livingston, Robert R. 190
Longfellow, Henry Wadsworth 4
Lorenzo, Treaty (1795) *see* Pinckney Treaty
Louis XV, King of France 62, 64
Louis XVI, King of France 30, 66
Louisiana: ceded to Spain by France 197; Protestants in 197, 200; religious toleration 198, 200–1; sale to French 74; size 197; *see also* Spanish Louisiana
Louisiana Purchase (1803) 141, 142
Leyva, Fernando de, Capt 20

Madison, James 174
Madrid, Treaty (1750) 95
Malvinas Islands *see* Falkland/Malvinas Islands
Manila 9, 93
Mariquita: constitution 215; slave trade 216
Maritime Atlas of Spain, 1783–1788 97
Maritz, Jean, artillery engineer 65–6
Marshall Plan, Spanish exclusion from 4
Mascoutens 124
Massachusetts: constitution (1780) 212; religion in constitution 217; religious toleration 217
Mathews, Thomas, Admrl 63
Mayorga, Martin de, Viceroy 81, 82
Mazzaredo, José de, Admrl 97
Menorca, Spanish recovery of 16–17, 38, 71–2, 96
Mesquaki people 126
Mexico: independence 142; *see also* New Spain
Miamis 124, 126
Miralles, Juan de 185; George Washington, friendship 189–90
Miranda, Francisco de 51, 212, 217
Miró, Esteban, Governor of Louisiana 197, 199, 200, 204, 205

Mississipi River: navigation rights 26, 122, 148–9, 151–2, 153, 168, 185, 191–2 (American 192), (Spanish control of 199)
Mobile, Spanish capture of 82
Moctezuma, Gerónimo Girón 19–20
Monterey 135, 138
Montmorin, Comte de 81, 153, 164
Moreno, Mariano 54
Morgan, George, Col 202–3; and Native Americans 203–4; religious tolerance 203
Morris, Richard 15
Morris, Robert 138, 175, 188, 189, 191
Munive, Gaspar de 94
Murray, James, Lt-Gen 71, 72

Nariño, Antonio 50; personal library 48
Natchez town/district 198; border issues 201; growth 205; Protestants in 201–2; religious toleration 200, 205; settlers 200; tobacco production 202
Native Americans: citizens in Spanish America 53, 55; and Cundinamarca 217; and George Morgan 203–4; Spanish policies towards 27–8, 132n13; trade with New Madrid 204; *see also* individual groups, Chicksaws, Choctaws, Creeks, Shawnees etc
Native-American communities, and Spain 6
naval forces, American War of Independence 15
Navarro, Diego José, Governor of Cuba 15–16, 19
Navarro, Juan José, Capt-Gen 63
Nelson, Horatio, V-Admrl 25, 75
New Granada 51, 52, 54, 55; Antioquia constitution 215; constitutions 210, 215, 218; federalism 219; slave trade 216; United Provinces of 55–6; US Constitution 211
New Jersey, constitution (1776) 214
New Madrid 197, 202–3; failure to grow 205–6; religious toleration 203; settlers 204; trade with Native Americans 204
New Spain 9, 78, 86; and Cádiz Constitution 53; constitutional monarchy 54; wealth 82, 83, 84, 85; *see also* Mexico
New York Hispanic Society 4
Nile, Battle of (1798) 74
Nootka Bay (Vancouver Island) 138

Odawas people 124
Ojibwas people 124
O'Malley, Gregory 102
Orinoco expeditions 94–5, 95; Solano y Bote 95
O'Shaughnessy, Andrew 25

Paine, Tom: *Common Sense* 40, 212; *Dissertation of the First Principles of Government* 212
Paquette, Gabriel 100
Paris, Treaty (1783) 26, 85, 179, 191
Peace of Paris (1763) 9, 64, 81
Pearce, Adrian 102
Peninsular War 29, 93
Pennsylvania Constitution (1776/1790) 40, 214, 215; 'right to bear arms' 218
Pensacola: American seizure of 140–1; siege 22–3, 71, 84, 96; Spanish attack on 21–2, 70
Peru 54; rebellions 39, 40, 41, 46; slave trade 106
Piankeshaws 124
Pinckney, Thomas 192
Pinckney Treaty (Treaty of San Lorenzo) (1795) 26–7, 169, 185, 192, 206
pirates *see* privateers/corsairs
Poinsett, Joel 54
Pollock, Oliver 12, 187, 188
Pombo, Ignacio de 52
Pombo, Miguel de 211, 212
Potawotomis people 124
Pouré, Eugenio, Capt 122, 127, 128, 129
Prescott, William Hickling, Prescott's Paradigm 4
Price, Richard 213
privateers/corsairs: against British trade 96; Bahamas 171, 172, 173–4, 175, 177, 178, 179
Proclamation Line (1763) 199, 202
property rights 199–200
Protestantism: in Louisiana 197, 200; in Natchez town 201–2; *see also* Catholicism
Pufendorf, Samuel von 147

Raynal, Guillaume Thomas, *Histoire Philosophique* 44–5, 49
Real Armada 92, 95; formation 62
Recueil de Loix Constitutives des États-Unis de l'Amérique 49
regalismo concept 47, 48
Reign of Terror (France) 74

religion: in Massachusetts constitution 217; and radical Enlightenment 48; *see also* religious toleration
religious toleration: Louisiana 198, 200–1; Massachusetts 217; Natchez town/district 200, 205; New Madrid 203
Rendón, Francisco 184, 190
Restrepo, José Manuel: on Centralism 211; *Historia de la Revolución* 211, 213
revolts *see* Comuneros revolt; Tupac Amaru revolt
Río de la Plata 52, 54, 107; slave trade 108
Robertson, James 200
Rodney, George, Sir, Admrl 24, 85, 96
Rodríguez de Campomanes, Pedro, *Reflexiones sobre el comercio Español a Indias* 104–5
Rodríguez, Manuel del Socorro 49–50
Roosevelt, Franklin D. 4
Royal Havana Company 107

Saavedra, Francisco de 22–3, 39–40, 43, 49; free trade law 82; royal award 84; Spanish crown agent 82–5
St. Clair, Arthur, Gov 130
St. Joseph *see* Fort St. Joseph
St. Louis, defense of 125, 127, 129
Saintes, Battle of the (1782) 24
San Francisco Bay, Spanish settlement 136
San Martín, José de 56, 98; map of Caribbean coast and islands 96–7
San Ramón ship 22
Santa Engracia ship 113
Santiago ship 113, 114
Santo Domingo 84, 106
Saratoga, Battle of (1777) 14
Sauk people 126
Sena, García de 212; *La independencia de la Costa Firme* 218
Seven Years' War (1756–1763) 9, 78, 104, 137; failure of Bourbon armada in 64; Spanish goals 96
Shaler, William, Capt 139, 141
Shawnees 203, 204
Simmons, Merle E. 212
Simms, Brendan 8
Sinclair, Patrick 125
slave trade: and the American Revolution 104–9; Atlantic 100; Bight of Biafra 107, 109, 110–16; Cartagena 216; contraband 102–3, 104, 109; Cuba 106; Havana 116; intra-American 102; Mariquita 216; New Granada 216; Peru 106; Río de la Plata 108; South Seas Company 102; Vermont 216; West African Coast, map **101**; *see also* Spanish slave trade
smuggling 9, 12, 98, 102, 103, 104, 139, 140, 175
Sola, Pablo Vicente de 135
Solano y Bote, José 71, 91, 281; and *Atlas de la América Septentrional* 96; Capt-Gen of Santo Domingo 95; Governor of Venezuela 95; Orinoco River expeditions 95; siege of Pensacola 96
Soledad ship 113
South America, United Provinces of 55
South Seas Company, slave trade 102
Spain: African expansion *see under* Annobón, Fernando Pó; Agreement on Defense Cooperation (US) 5; America, commerce regulation 27; American interest in 4; and the American Revolution (benefits 38), (covert support 186), (disbenefits 38), (finance provision 81–2, 85), (global interests 7–11), (gunpowder supply 188), (historiography 3–7), (networks 187–8, 192), (New World "discovery" 193), (a Pacific view 135–43), (trade 187); Bentham on 29–30; Constitution of Cádiz (1812) 29, 52, 53–4; economic aid to American Revolution 11–12; European Economic Community (1986) 5; France: alliance 10, 12, 14–15 (Napolenonic invasion 1, 92, 97, 140, 193); Fulbright Scholarships Program 5; Great Britain, trade 29; immigration policies 143, 198–205; imperial reforms *see* Bourbon reforms; Latin American dimension 5; Mutual Defense Assistance Agreement (US) 5; Native American policies in America 27–8, 132n13; and Native-American communities 6; NATO membership (1982) 5; Portugal, boundaries 94–5; war with Britain (1779–1783) 14–18, 39, 125, 188, 190 (cost 13–14, **13**)
Spanish America: bicameralism 56; Enlightenment in 47–8; federalism 56, 211; and the French Revolution 50–1; Native Americans as citizens 53; proto-republics 55–6; turbulence in

51–2; and US constitutionalism 210–19
Spanish American rebellions: and the American Revolution 39–42; and the French invasion of Spain 193
Spanish Armada 69, 74, 96, 97
Spanish Atlantic 97
Spanish Borderlands 6
Spanish Civil War, Non-Intervention Agreement 4
Spanish empire: rebellions 26; size 7; zenith 185
Spanish global interests, and the American Revolution 7–11
Spanish Inquisition, abolition 53
Spanish Louisiana 11, 18, 78, 91; American settlers 199
Spanish mediation, American War of Independence 10–11, 96
Spanish monarchy, and the American Revolution 38–9
Spanish navy 23; in American War of Independence 92; in battle of Cape St Vincent 74; Centralism 62; see also Spanish Armada
"Spanish Periphery" 7
Spanish slave trade 28; British cooperation 100, 103–4; demand for slaves 103
Spanish Succession, War of (1710–14) 62, 100
Spanish-American independence movement 28–9
Spanish-American War (1898) 4, 29
spies: British 12, 187, 188; Spanish 68, 78, 86, 87n6, 135

Taylor, Alan 172
Thibaud, Clément 94, 215
Ticknor, George 4
tobacco production, Natchez town/district 202
Tofiño, Vicente, *Maritime Atlas of Spain, 1783–1788* 96
Tordesillas, Treaty (1494) 107
Torres, Camillo 219; on Centralism 213; on government of Spanish colonies 212–13
Toulon: Battle of (1744) 95; British blockade (1743) 63

Trafalgar *see* Cape Trafalgar
Tucumán, Congress (1816) 55
Tunja, constitution 215
Tupac Amaru revolt 39, 41–2, 43, 93

Unzaga, Luis de, Capt-Gen 97, 184, 187
US Constitution: federalism 53, 54, 55; New Granada 211
US constitutions (1776–98) 211, 215
US constitutionalism: presidential system 215–16; social impact 214; and Spanish America 210–19
US Declaration of Independence (1776) 211
US-Spanish Agreements (1953) 5
Utrecht, Treaty of (1713) 16

Valdés, Antonio 97
Vanegas, Isidro 219
Vargas, Pedro Fermin, *diálogo entre Lord North y un filósofo* 45
Vattel, Emerich de 147; on independence 45; *The Law of Nations* 45
Venezuela 51, 54, 55; constitutions 210
Vergennes, Comte de 67
Vermont, slave trade 216
Versailles, Treaty of (1783) 38, 73
Viar, José Ignacio de 192
Ville de Paris ship 68
Villeneuve, Pierre Charles Silvestre de, V-Admrl 74
Viscardo y Guzmán, Juan Pablo 45–6; *Lettre aux espagnols-americaines* 46; *Projet pour rendre l'Amérique espagnole indépendante* 46

War of American Independence *see* American Independence War
War of Jenkins' Ear (*La Guerra del Asiento*) (1739–48) 63, 103
Washington, George, Gen 23, 67, 199; Miralles, friendship 189–90
Weas 124
Wilkinson, James, Gen 204
Worms, Treaty of (1743) 63

Yorktown, Battle of (1781) 173

Zéspedes, Vincente Manuel de 28

Contributor biographies

Eric Becerra is a Ph.D. candidate at the University of North Carolina, Chapel Hill.

Emily Berquist Soule is Professor of History at California State University, Long Beach. She is the author of *The Bishop's Utopia: Imagining Improvement in Colonial Peru*.

Larrie D. Ferreiro teaches at George Mason University. His book *Brothers at Arms: American Independence and the Men of France and Spain Who Saved It* was a 2017 Pulitzer Prize Finalist for History.

Gregg French teaches at Saint Mary's University in Halifax, Nova Scotia.

Mary-Jo Kline is the author of studies on Alexander Hamilton and Gouverneur Morris as well as *A Guide to Documentary Editing*.

Manuel Lucena-Giraldo is a research scientist at the Spanish Council for Scientific Research (CSIC), an adjunct professor in IE University, and a member of the European Academy.

Benjamin C. Lyons recently completed his Ph.D. at Columbia University.

Anthony McFarlane is Professor Emeritus of History at Warwick University and author, most recently, of *War and Independence in Spanish America*.

Ross Michael Nedervelt is a post-doctoral fellow at Florida International University.

John William Nelson is a Ph.D. candidate at the University of Notre Dame.

Gabriel Paquette is Professor of History and International Studies at the University of Oregon. He was Sons of the American Revolution Visiting Professor at King's College London in 2017–2018.

Emmanuelle Perez Tisserant is Assistant Professor of History at the University of Toulouse Jean Jaurès.

Eduardo Posada-Carbó is Professor of the History and Politics of Latin America at the University of Oxford, where he is also William Golding Senior Research Fellow at Brasenose College.

Gonzalo M. Quintero Saravia, a senior Spanish diplomat, is author of *Bernardo de Gálvez: Spanish Hero of the American Revolution*, which recently won the Society for Military History's Best Book Prize.

María Bárbara Zepeda Cortés is Assistant Professor of History at Lehigh University.

The Revolutionary Age

The Habsburg Monarchy and the American Revolution
Jonathan Singerton

Navigating Neutrality: Early American Governance in the Turbulent Atlantic
Sandra Moats

Ireland and America: Empire, Revolution, and Sovereignty
Patrick Griffin and Francis D. Cogliano, editors

www.ingramcontent.com/pod-product-compliance
Lightning Source LLC
Chambersburg PA
CBHW031803220426

43662CB00007B/514